White Vic

WITHDRAWN

From fears of "amalgamation" used to fan anti-abolitionist flames in nineteenth-century New York, to a white female highway patrol officer's "fear of a Mandingo sexual encounter" that was said to have led to the beating and arrest of black motorist Rodney King, conceptualizations of race and gender have fuelled fears about crime in the USA, past and present.

White Victims, Black Villains traces how race and gender have combined in news media narratives about crime and violence in US culture. The book argues that the criminalization of African Americans in US culture has been most consistently and effectively legitimized by news media deeply invested in protecting and maintaining white supremacy.

An illuminating and often shocking text, *White Victims, Black Villains* should be read by anyone interested in race and politics.

Carol A. Stabile is Associate Professor in the Department of Mass Communication at the University of Wisconsin, Milwaukee. She is the author of *Feminism and the Technological Fix* (1994), editor of *Turning the Century: Essays in Media and Cultural Studies* (2000), and co-editor of *Prime Time Animation: Television Animation and American Culture* (2003).

White Victims, Black Villains

Gender, race, and crime news in US culture

Carol Stabile

LIS - LIBRARY

Date	Fund
21/4/09	Ł

Order No.

2002 98 x

University of Chester

Routledge
Taylor & Francis Group

NEW YORK AND LONDON

First published 2006
by Routledge
270 Madison Avenue, New York, NY 10016

Simultaneously published in the UK
by Routledge
2 Park Square, Milton Park, Abingdon, Oxon, OX14 4RN

Routledge is an imprint of the Taylor & Francis Group, an informa business

© 2006 Carol A. Stabile

Typeset in Baskerville by The Running Head Limited, Cambridge
Printed and bound in Great Britain by Antony Rowe Ltd,
Chippenham, Wiltshire

All rights reserved. No part of this book may be reprinted
or reproduced or utilized in any form or by any electronic,
mechanical, or other means, now known or hereafter
invented, including photocopying and recording, or in any
information storage or retrieval system, without permission in
writing from the publishers.

British Library Cataloguing in Publication Data
A catalogue record for this book is available from the British Library

Library of Congress Cataloging in Publication Data
Stabile, Carol A.
White victims, black villains: gender, race, and crime news in US
culture/Carol A. Stabile.
p. cm.
Includes bibliographical references and index.
1. Crime and the press—United States—History. 2. African Americans—Press coverage—History. 3. Women—Press coverage—United
States—History. I. Title.
PN4888.C8583 2006
070.4' 493640973—dc22   2006000659

ISBN 10: 0–415–37481–2 (hbk)
ISBN 10: 0–415–37492–8 (pbk)
ISBN 13: 978–0–415–374811 (hbk)
ISBN 13: 978–0–415–374927 (pbk)

For Mrak and Tony

Contents

Illustrations

Acknowledgments

Nourishment, as any feminist worth her salt knows, comes in many different shapes and requires a wide array of physical, emotional, and intellectual labors. Much of this book was worked out while I was cooking and my first debt of gratitude is to the hungry intellectual community of which I was a part in Pittsburgh, Pennsylvania. Many of its members were my culinary guinea pigs and gustatory and political fellow travelers during the process of conceptualizing and writing this book. Thanks to the people who made that kitchen what it was. Allen Larson, David Leone, and Courtney Maloney stayed until the bittersweet end. Carrie Rentschler and Jonathan Sterne (two better colleagues and friends I will never know), Dan McGee and Gretchen Soderlund (Gretchen valiantly commented on multiple drafts of this book) were there from the beginning. Lisa Brush, Danae Clark, Alice Crawford and Geoff and Marcus Langdale, Kelly Happe, Maria Magro and Mark Douglas, Thomas Kane, Andrew Adam Newman, Dawn Schmitz and Holly Middleton, Lisa Schwartz, Michael Stabile III, Elayne Tobin, and Jennifer Wood brought songs, puns, covered dishes, and general hilarity to the table. Thanks to the Buffy Group (and *Buffy* itself) for bawdy Tuesday evening breaks! I am thankful as well to all those wonderful student-friends who stopped by: Michael Aronson, Tara Beichner, Alison Bodenhemier, Erin Deasy, Aimee-Marie Dorsten, Heather Fisher, Zack Furness, Jennifer Ghilani, Andrew Haley, Mark Harrison, David Haskell (whose assistance with the onerous task of reading microfilmed newspapers can never be repaid), Deepa Kumar, Matthew Reichek, and Michelle Rodino. All our lives may have been richer for the brownies and the carrot cakes, but mine in particular was the richer for the lessons you taught me at that kitchen counter.

I am thankful to the many women (and a few wonderful men) who helped me care for my son during the writing of this project: David Leone, Kelly Happe, Elayne Tobin, the workers at the University Child Development Center, especially Shalese Bennett, Ammie Hammala, Virginia Flournoy, Maureen Reilly, and Olivia Shay, Sarah Smarts, Aimee-Marie Dorsten, Maria Magro, Courtney Maloney, Lindsay Unger, and, of course, Mark Unger. Without such wonderful assistance, and the security that came with knowing that Tony was well tended, writing this book would have been impossible.

Dozens of people have left their intellectual fingerprints on this work and I very much hope that they will think the result worthwhile. The graduate students in my Cultural Studies Seminar (1997), Producing the News Seminar (1998), Consumerism Seminar (2002), and Feminist Theory Seminars (2003 and 2004) helped me sort through some of the ideas that became this book. Thom Baggerman and Heather Fisher convinced me to teach a directed study on television history that proved extraordinarily helpful.

During the course of several reading groups we organized, Lisa Frank and Csaba Toth influenced my thinking about crime, violence, and culture in significant ways. I am thankful for having been the beneficiary of their keen intellectual and political vision. My good friend Thomas Kane generously shared his research skills throughout—he and Mary E. Taintor helped me locate archival materials in New York City in record time, when I had no time to spare. Carrie Rentschler's work on crime victims has had a great influence on my own work and I am lucky to have been able to work closely with her. Kathleen Blee was an amazing mentor and friend in some trying circumstances. Jane Feuer is a true friend and was a staunch supporter during my time in Pittsburgh. I will always be grateful to Robin Means-Coleman for her support, not to mention her formidable intellectual vision. Lisa Brush, Nancy Glazener, Katie Hogan, and Carol Mason participated in various incarnations of a feminist reading group that provided important feedback on this project. I am especially thankful to Katie for taking the time to read through the first half of the book, and to Lisa for sharing her incredible theoretical and analytic clarity with me. Gil Rodman graciously read through several chapters of the manuscript shortly before it was completed, giving me a dose of encouragement when I needed it the most. I had the good fortune to have Ron and Mary Zboray listen to an early version of Chapter 2 and I hope they will agree that their comments made it a better piece of writing. I am additionally fortunate to have worked with some wonderful women at Routledge: Rebecca Barden, Aileen Irwin, and Natalie Foster, as well as Fran Brown, Carole Drummond and Geraldine Martin who oversaw the final stages of this project. I am honoured to have Teenie Harris' work on the cover of this book.

Over the course of a decade, numerous underpaid librarians at the University of Pittsburgh's Hillman Library cheerfully helped me locate sources and materials. Rachel Rodriguez found a document I had been looking for over a period of weeks in a matter of minutes. The folks at interlibrary loan were truly awesome, especially Jonah McAllister Erickson and Vicki Redclay. I am also grateful to the Vanderbilt Television News Archives. Without its collection and the archivists who maintain it, research on television news would be difficult if not impossible. In New York City, archivists at the New-York Historical Society assisted me in getting access to some popular criminal literature from the nineteenth century. And I owe a special thank you to Leonora A. Gidlund, director of the City of New York's Municipal Archives for her assistance in locating material on the anti-draft riots. Peter Osborne of the Minisink Historical Society helped me find some materials on the lynching that occurred in Port Jervis, New York, in 1892 and Jesse Legon of the Associated Press patiently helped me with an image for the book's conclusion.

The Unit for Criticism and Interpretive Theory and the Institute of Communication Research at the University of Illinois provided concrete support for this project in its embryonic stage in the shape of a postdoctoral fellowship and employment and introduced me to a community that remains my intellectual mainstay. The Women's Studies Program at the University of Pittsburgh gave me refuge and the company of some remarkable women whose good humor and chutzpah got me through some rough patches. The Marxist Literary Group's Summer Institute has always been a source of much-needed political solace and intellectual stimulation—I am particularly grateful to Rich Daniels, Fred Pfeil, Modhumita Roy, Matthew Ruben, Paul Smith, and Michael Sprinker. The folks at Conjunctures (Montreal 2005) gave me excellent feedback on chapter 2. My new colleagues in Journalism and Mass Communication at the University of Wisconsin-Milwaukee uncomplainingly gave me the time and space to finish this manuscript in fall 2005, even though it certainly meant more work for them. I hope they know how much I appreciated the gift of time. I am further indebted to an NEH Summer Stipend, two University of Pittsburgh Summer Stipends, and a Gilder Lehrman Institute for American History Fellowship, the last of which let me complete much of the research for this book.

Charles "Teenie" Harris' photograph (c. 1949) of a Republican campaign billboard on the cover of this book was reproduced with the permission of the Carnegie Museum of Art in Pittsburgh, Pennsylvania. The illustrations of Helen Jewett's life from George Wilkes' *The Lives of Helen Jewett and Richard P. Robinson* (1849) were reproduced with the permission of New-York Historical Society. A version of chapter 1 appeared in *Journalism* 6(4), November 2005 and is reprinted here with the permission of Sage Publications.

I wish that my mother, Mary Louise Stabile, had lived to see the publication of this book, since she always encouraged me to stand up for what I believed in, even when my beliefs conflicted with her own. My nephew, Michael Stabile III, sweetly retyped drafts of the first three chapters after my laptop crashed and his humor and good-natured cynicism have saved me from myself on more than one occasion. I am likewise fortunate to have shared the company of Allen Larson and David Leone, who were always (and I mean always) there when I needed them and who will forever remain this girl's best friends.

There are two other people who have made the writing of this project richer and more deeply important. Tony Unger was born in the midst of this project and it is my greatest hope that he will someday live in a world in which girls and boys of all races and classes will have access to the opportunities and privileges that he does. Tony has been mainly impatient with the writing of this book and I am grateful to him for ceding the computer to me long enough to finish it. Last but never least, there isn't a spreadsheet capable of calculating the balance of my debt to Mrak, heart of the heartless world, whose kindness, word-processing genius, and deep and abiding love of strong women (thank you, Florence and Mimi) have made everything possible. As a totally insufficient recompense for the many gifts, delights, and frustrations the two of them have shared with me, this book is dedicated to them, the two great loves of my life.

Introduction

> While white perception of black criminality is readily evoked, white awareness of black anger or anguish has been not only historically avoided but, on the deepest psychic levels, guarded against. Existentially, the concept of black people as vulnerable human beings who sustain pain and love and hatreds and fears and joy and sorrows and degradations and triumphs is not yet permitted in the national consciousness. Hence the constant need of the dominant society, in age after age, to reinforce linguistic and ritualistic symbols that deny black humanity. Historically, white terror is the sustaining principle of the system. Whether overtly applied or covertly threatened, not only has this basic device of subjugation never been nationally rejected, it has, on the contrary, always been sanctioned.
>
> (Gresham 1989: 120)

On 25 May 1997, Sherrice Iverson, a 7-year-old African American girl, was followed into the women's bathroom in a casino arcade by an 18-year-old white man named Jeremy Strohmeyer. Strohmeyer proceeded to rape and strangle the child, interrupted once by his friend David Cash who told him to stop, but who then immediately exited the restroom.[1] While the killing of JonBenet Ramsay just a year before had generated massive amounts of media attention, as had the murders of Polly Klaas, Megan Kanka, and Samantha Runnion, and the kidnapping of Elizabeth Smart, Sherrice Iverson never became a household name or the impetus for a legislative campaign.[2] Nor were Strohmeyer or Cash the subjects of endless debate about a potentially violent and psychotic white culture.[3]

This book grew out of a keen sense of the disparity between how white victims are treated in mainstream US news and the overall dismissal of black victims. Murder is a terrible act of violence and it makes no sense to engage in what historian Peter Novick (2000) describes as "Victimization Olympics," that pit victim against victim in an effort to compare and compete over degrees of savagery and barbarity. Still, the contrast between the quality and quantity of coverage of white victims of all genders and ages and that accorded to black victims is stunning in its consistency and historical continuity. As this book makes clear, representations of victims of crime have effects beyond mere publicity. Crime news, and cultural information about rates of crime and the identity of

criminals and victims, has served as the pretext for a range of ideological production and reproduction, as well as the justification for both punishment and
reparation. The behaviors of individuals, institutions, policy-makers, police, and
politicians, that is, take news about crime as their rationale for action and legitimation for various practices and behaviors that might otherwise seem ill-advised
or blatantly unjust. Representations of crime and criminals may be representations, but these have all too real material consequences.

Victims, in US culture, provide one of the most emotional and effective
representational modes for mobilizing sympathy, for producing outrage about
social injustice, and for political action, by both institutions and social movements.[4] To deny victim status to certain groups, or to ignore the victimization
that occurs to them, is at once to further marginalize the needs of particular communities, as well as their specific hopes and fears, and to construct
threats to the social order based on socially constructed assessments, to borrow
a phrase from Herman and Chomsky (1988), of worthy and unworthy victims.
From the era of slavery until the contemporary era, with precision and regularity, the ranks of worthy victims have long excluded African Americans, whose
anger and anguish, as Gresham puts it, have traditionally been denied in favor
of the production of white fear.

As I read newspapers from the nineteenth century, listened to radio programs from the 1930s, and watched television coverage of crime over a 30-year
period, a different picture emerged of the complex and contradictory nature
of the extraordinarily acquisitive and violent white society that flourished in
the USA, in which fictions of white terror have consistently displaced the material realities of white terrorism.[5] In a society founded in a violent revolution,
which expanded through a ceaseless series of Indian removals, border skirmishes, imperial adventures, and labor conflict, not to mention the foundational
violence of the institution of slavery, US society, historically and constitution-
ally speaking, is premised on the right of citizens to be violent. Historian Roger
Lane reminds us that the USA has long had the highest homicide rates of any
industrialized, or industrializing, country:

> during the 1920s the American homicide rate was 8.4 per 100,000, more
> than 10 times Japan's 0.8, 5 times the 1.6 for Ontario, nearly 17 times the
> 0.5 for England and Wales, and 47 times the Swiss 0.18. Only the provinces
> of southern Italy had higher rates than the overall U.S. average, but even
> there the 22.0 for Sicily was topped by 30.0 for the state of Florida.
>
> (1997: 229)

Of course, I do not believe that the media cause violence; nor do I believe
that many people's everyday lives, particularly those in economically devas-
tated neighborhoods, are not scarred by violence perpetrated by individuals
as well as the state. Violence and crime are, however, different issues and need
to be understood as such. Where violence refers to behaviors that are injuri-
ous to others, and is used throughout this book to describe behaviors that, like

lynching, harmed African Americans, crime is best defined as behavior deemed offensive to (and by) the state and therefore subject to punishment.

Not all crimes are violent and, as we will see in chapters 4 and 5, which deal specifically with lynching, not all violence is considered criminal, particularly when perpetrated by privileged white men and the state. Much of this sort of violence has not been considered criminal, and in many cases it has been encouraged by institutions like religion, the family, and education. Schoolyard violence has long been considered a "normal" rite of passage for white heterosexual boys. Even in the wake of highly publicized school shootings in the late 1990s, only the most exaggerated forms of bullying have come under attack.

The process whereby certain acts were punished by the state, while others were either overlooked or rewarded, can best be described as one of criminalization. In the USA, various institutions and agents have waged long, bitter struggles over the power to define crime—to criminalize various acts to the exclusion of others. Where common sense might lead us to believe that the judicial system has primary responsibility for defining crime, the reality is rather different. Police, for example, often decide what kinds of crimes to "crack down" on and which kinds of offenders to arrest. These decisions are in turn influenced by the relationship between institutions of policing (local, state, and federal) and funding sources. The media, in an uneasy duet with police, make decisions about which victims count as victims—a determination that, as a police reporter for the *Arizona Republic* noted, overlooks those mainly poor "people our society seldom wishes to read about" (Hermann 1996: 109). The media play a pivotal role in processes of criminalization and are often the first to publicize a new category of crime, as in the case of "carjacking," a new social category of crime that first entered the media vocabulary in 1986. In an example of the recursive nature of the relationship between media and the criminal justice system, the term was adopted in 1994 by the Department of Justice's *National Crime Victimization Survey* (Rand 1994).

The state's monopoly over the use of "legitimate" violence places its own institutions beyond the reach of criminalization. Thus, the military's acts of violent imperialism are not crimes, nor are police harassment, torture, brutalization, and murder of African Americans, Latinos, immigrants, and poor and working-class people in general. When yet another young black man is asphyxiated in the custody of police officers (frequently referred to by coroners and medical examiners as "death by exhaustion"), or when an unarmed 12-year-old child is shot in the back as he flees from state troopers, police are always accorded the benefit of the doubt, even in those cases where their actions are evidently racist and, in a more just society, would be considered criminal.[6] Young black men rarely get the benefit of any such doubts; instead (when they survive their encounters with the state), they are more likely to get three strikes. A perfect example of a struggle over criminalization recently occurred internationally, when the USA refused to vote in favor of the International Criminal Court, for fear that US government officials might be held accountable for actions that *others* might consider criminal.

Tracing the origins of cultural narratives about criminals, victims, and processes of criminalization is an imperfect business, since different cultural forms have long borrowed from one another and the lines between nonfictional forms and genres and their fictional counterparts overlap and often blur together. But nowhere is the cultural production of victims as evident as it is in crime news narratives, where victims of all sorts have long been abundant and the lines between the victimized and the victimizer have been strictly policed. Crime news, the premier human-interest story, is a cultural form that depends on the presence of victims for its affective and rhetorical force. A key feature of the inception of a commercial press in the USA, from the 1830s to the present day, crime news has remained an industry staple.

The lines between victims, victimizers, and protectors are often fungible, but crime news is not a genre that equivocates when it comes to these identities. Rather, crime news has long been in the business of policing these very borders and offering up narratives that, as Gresham points out, have long denied the basic humanity conferred by victim status to African Americans. It is no coincidence, then, that from the 1980s onward, the only way that blacks made the news in the USA was as the subjects of crime news, for this is a role that was historically carved out for them and that has over the past three hundred years been reproduced, resanctioned, and reinforced. Although I had originally intended this to be a study of crime news broadly construed, the centrality of race in my primary source materials—the absolutism of categorizations of blacks as criminals and the constant refusal of mainstream news producers even to countenance the possibility of black victimization—inexorably led to a somewhat different thesis: that white supremacy had been built into the very bricks of the institution of commercial news.

As the following chapters demonstrate, the construction of blacks as criminals and never as victims itself depended on dominant ideologies of gender, making blackness inextricable from the gendered meanings attributed to it. Because the vast majority of crimes—nonviolent and violent alike—have been committed by white men, because most of the most heinous crimes (especially those that like slavery, Jim Crow laws in the south, and lynching were never either explicitly or fully criminalized) have been committed by white men—crime news has had to perform various sleights of hand in order to call up threats that did not indict the practices of white masculinity.

In the Jacksonian era that this book takes as its starting-point, the production of ideologies governing appropriate masculine and feminine behavior, the need to produce and establish the doctrine of separate spheres of male and female behavior and activity, was governed by what I describe throughout as a system of racialized androcentrism. In this system, codes of white masculinity premised on aggression and domination of feminized others were not criminalized. Instead, as Lane notes, shared "codes of values, in which to tolerate any kind of 'dishonor' without fighting was to lose the reputation for manhood" (1997: 351) became a defining feature of Jacksonian masculinity. Constructed as the fathers of the country, as adventurous and civic-minded individuals, white men were the protectors of the social order and of the white women whose job it was to reproduce the nation-state.

Dominant ideologies of masculinity drew much of their meaning and force from a contrast with blackness and slavery. White men protected white women from the deprivations and predations of the public sphere; white women civilized white men, tempering men's more aggressive nature through their passive, silent suffering. Black men and women were understood to be everything that Jacksonian ideologies of gender were not. Black men could not serve as public sphere protectors of black women—the fact that they were prevented from doing so by slavery in the south and their marginalized status as laborers in the north was seen as an extension of their racial inclinations and dispositions, rather than evidence of oppression. Black women, moreover, as slaves and wage laborers themselves, could not exert any civilizing influence on black men. Consequently, the injuries visited upon them by white supremacy were transformed into their own pathologies, which included abnormal strength, aggressive sexuality, and manifestations of dysfunctional maternalism. Jacksonian ideologies of gender thus depended on the production of black people as negative contrasts to white people, as others to the social order the era was busily erecting.[7]

Intersections among race, gender, and class in US crime news have not always been transparent or straightforward. Although there are many excellent studies of race and crime reporting, particularly in relationship to contemporary news, these studies focus on race, and to a lesser extent class, to analyze the racist representations that have proliferated in US news media.[8] Following the work of feminist theorists, particularly black feminist theorists like Kimberlé Crenshaw (1991) and Patricia Hill Collins (1990/2000, 2004), this study understands categories of race, gender, and class to be mutually constitutive. In the ideologically charged context of crime news, for example, codes for representing black masculinity as criminal grew out of early nineteenth-century conceptualizations of gender, race, and class that were fundamentally racist and misogynist. From the fears of "amalgamation," or race-mixing, that newspapers used to fan anti-abolitionist flames in Jacksonian New York City, to what Los Angeles police sergeant Stacey Koon described as a white female highway patrol officer's "fear of a Mandingo sexual encounter" (Williams 2004: 287) that precipitated the beating and arrest of black motorist Rodney King, race and gender have shaped reporting about crime in the USA and thus cultural understandings of crime and social violence.

Race and gender are among the most important sites for struggles over the historical meanings assigned to deviance. Indeed, the powerful efforts on the part of social orders to strictly police the boundaries of these categories (through pollution taboos governing contact with such "others," laws restricting marriage or freedom of movement, restrictions on behavior and dress) speak to the strenuous ideological and cultural work required to construct categories of gender and race and manage their meanings. Crime reporting, which began to assume some of its more familiar characteristics in the 1830s, has played a pivotal role in how US society understands, identifies, and punishes behaviors

considered deviant and therefore criminal. As a cultural form, crime reporting has been an extremely porous form of writing that drew from a wide range
of other cultural productions—broadsheets, the gallows genre that flourished
in eighteenth-century America, evangelical literature, popular theater, and a
whole range of novelistic genres. In New York City, urban reporters predated an
organized police force and the production and maintenance of written records.
Police, politicians, and denizens of a whole host of other emerging institutions
probably learned their narrative practices regarding crime discourse from urban
reporters, who had in their turn imbibed these narratives from popular criminal literature.[9]

    In the pages that follow, I understand class to be the wider field through
which other forms of subjectivity are structured in the capitalist economic order
of the USA. But I use the phrase racialized androcentrism to get at how a social
order based on white male privilege, with which white men of other classes were
taught to identify, understood social violence (and the representations of both
criminals and victims upon which constructions of social violence depended) as
somehow originating altogether elsewhere. For despite the materiality of economic privilege, the violence upon which racialized androcentrism is grounded
exceeds narrow understandings of class. As feminist critics have long argued,
family violence crosses class lines, trapping women from very different class
backgrounds in abusive relationships.[10] Violence against African Americans
similarly crosses the lines of class. As Tolnay and Beck (1995) point out, class
ascendancy on the part of African Americans was frequently the immediate,
albeit unacknowledged, cause of lynching. When motorist Jonny E. Gammage
was stopped and killed by police in a suburb of Pittsburgh in October 1995
while driving his cousin's Jaguar, his identity as a young African American man
signified more to police officers than his obvious middle-class status. Racialized androcentrism thus allows us to get at the intricate connections between
race and gender in crime narratives, exposing the shell game that the dominant social order has played in pitting criminalized black male criminals against
white, feminized victims—a shell game that mystifies the real sources of power,
privilege, and oppression. Reexamining the development of US crime news
through a prism that can refract its raced and gendered components can tell
us much about how various forms of threat construction came to be, as well as
shedding light on the hold these forms of threat construction maintain on crime
news today.

    Throughout this book, I consider race and gender to be social constructions,
reflections of the social order that has produced them, rather than biological
givens. While men and women may be born with different skin colors and different sets of genitalia and reproductive organs, it is the cultural meaning assigned
to these differences rather than the physicality of the differences themselves that
makes all the difference. Categories like race and gender are themselves problematic, given as they are by a social order that despises such differences and
freights them with meanings over which scholars have no control. As Barbara
Jeanne Fields puts it,

Anyone who continues to believe in race as a physical attribute of individuals, despite the now commonplace disclaimers of biologists and geneticists, might as well also believe that Santa Claus, the Easter Bunny and the tooth fairy "are" real, and that the earth stands still while the sun moves.

(1990: 96)

As constructed as the category of race is, it remains a fiction and an ideology that results in various forms of action, and I use the term race throughout this book largely because it remains a category that continues to exercise specific effects. At the same time, I am mindful of the arbitrary distinction between race and ethnicity, which assumes, particularly in relation to those of African descent, that African Americans have no ethnicity, despite the vastness of the African continent. Where possible, I have tried to hew to the term "immigrant groups" rather than ethnic identity or ethnicity. Race is likewise a monolithic and analytically unsatisfying category and I have found it helpful, following Thomas Guglielmo (2003: 8), to consider the role that color as a social construct has played in making racial distinctions in the USA.

As this book makes clear, African Americans have been singled out, identified, and criminalized by virtue of skin color in ways that other racial groups simply have not been over the course of US history. Blackness more than any other type of identity has lain at the center of threat constructions. Although, in the first half of the nineteenth century, news narratives understood the Irish to be a hopeless lot, with a propensity for laziness, bellicosity, and excessive alcohol consumption, by the 1880s and 1890s, as many Irish had been assimilated into institutions, and as the Irish vote became ever more important to machine politics in cities like New York, links to such potentially criminalizable behaviors were disappearing. At different historical junctures, various immigrant groups were isolated as public health hazards or criminal threats, but the assimilation of white immigrants into mainstream society effectively moved them out of such demonized but now largely forgotten categories. In the 1890s, the *Chicago Times* claimed that Chicago's Slavic population were "Scythians"—"eaters of raw animal food, fond of drinking the blood of their enemies whom they slew in battle, and [men] who preserved as trophies the scalps and skins of enemies whom they overthrew" (quoted in Gutman 1977: 72), but by the 1920s, few would subscribe to this view. Jacob Riis described New York City's Chinese inhabitants in similarly stereotypical strokes: "He is by nature as clean as the cat, which he resembles in his traits of cruel cunning and savage fury when aroused" (1890/1996: 123). Of course, the discourses about these so-called "dangerous" or "criminal" classes varied regionally, especially before the development of a more nationalized media.[11] In San Francisco at the turn of the nineteenth-century, Chinese immigrants and "tongs" were represented as a significant threat to public safety, while in New York City, with a smaller Chinese population, the Chinese were not viewed as a significant threat to the social order. Representations of African Americans as threats, however, bore no relation to the size of their population or the probability of any threat.

No other ethnic or racial group has been singled out for the wholesale criminalization to which African Americans have been subjected during the last four decades of the twentieth century. Where Jim Crow in the south prevented African Americans from inhabiting the same social spaces as whites and exercising the same political rights, criminalization, especially the incarceration of so many African American men, had much the same effect in the years following the Civil Rights Movement. A central part of this project has thus involved tracing the criminalization of African Americans, both as everyday citizens and as political activists, and the culmination of a revitalized and terrifyingly effective racist discourse in the second half of the twentieth century.

The story this book tells about crime, race, and gender is organized into seven chapters. The first five chapters look at the development and subsequent institutionalization of representations of criminals and victims in New York City newspapers. As Christine Stansell puts it, New York "was a historical stage writ large for encounters that reverberated across the rest of the nation. It was the home of a radical working class and the site of intense class conflicts before the Civil War; it was also at the forefront of middle-class commercial and domestic culture" (1987: xiv). As the center of US (and later world) capitalism, the newspaper industry in New York City was the most technologically and economically sophisticated and it established practices—of production and narration alike— that would be emulated throughout the country. Because of New York City's centrality for cultural production, and the fact that many of the national news outlets subsequent chapters discuss were headquartered in New York, this regional focus allows for a more comprehensive analysis of the emergence of a raced and gendered vocabulary for discussing crime, gender, and race.

Taken together, the first two chapters look at the establishment of journalistic patterns for reporting about criminals and victims in the early years of the commercial press. The first chapter scrutinizes news coverage of crime in the penny press. Focusing on episodic coverage of crime, chapter 1 examines the codes for representing criminals and victims that were being worked out in the early days of the commercial press. Chapter 2 is a companion to chapter 1, exploring how these codes were translated into serialized coverage of high-profile crimes like the murder of prostitute Helen Jewett and the death of Mary Rogers. As these chapters point out, black victims were already a rarity in the penny press of the 1830s and 1840s, where the protection scenarios favored by white urban reporters demanded dead white women.

Chapters 3 and 4 direct attention to two instances where the victimization of African Americans was materially undeniable and therefore elicited some coverage on the part of the mainstream press. News coverage of the 1863 anti-draft riots that occurred in New York City forms the starting-point for chapter 3, which understands the invention of the word miscegenation by two reporters for the *New York World* as the response on the part of white New York culture to the lynching and wholesale victimization of African Americans that occurred during the anti-draft riots. Chapter 4 traces the criminalization of African Americans that the language of miscegenation introduced by analyzing newspaper coverage of lynching in the *New York World*, coverage that denied victim status to African Americans by criminalizing those who had been lynched.

Chapter 5 marks an important transitional moment in narratives about crime and victims, assessing the impact that the rise of objectivity had on the narratives that reporters were constructing about crime in the first decades of the twentieth century. Focusing on the stylistic shift from sentimental crime narratives to objective coverage of crime, this chapter shows how the introduction of a gendered distinction into the practices of crime reporting aided institutions in reproducing racialized forms of threat construction. The focus in the final two chapters is less on relationships among the institutions that served as primary sources for information about crime and criminals, these having become routinized across both print and broadcast media, and more on the reproduction of already-established patterns for understanding the raced and gendered identities of criminals and victims. Chapter 6 addresses a singular moment in representations of crime and victims, in which early television coverage of the Civil Rights Movement, for the first time in US history, represented African Americans not as criminalized threats, but as victims of social violence and discrimination worthy of the active intervention of the state. As chapter 7 and the conclusion make clear, the brief moment that cast African Americans as worthy victims swiftly gave way to the reimposition of strictly racialized threats. Chapter 7 analyzes the twinning of race and gender in the conservative war on crime and the manner in which African American women in particular became the symbolic bearers of criminalized meanings and threats. The book's conclusion brings us full circle to the local crime news with which the project began, examining the explosion of crime coverage in local television news and its reliance on racialized threats to a gendered social order.

According to Stuart Hall, we tell stories that are not of our own making: "We mainly tell stories like we've told them before, or we borrow from the whole inventory of telling stories, and of narratives" (1984). Crime stories, more than other kinds of stories, conform to very traditional and rigid sets of criteria, perhaps because ideologies governing deviance are very slow to change. Crime news is a profoundly conservative form of story-telling that has developed in ways so as to constitute those groups most seriously disadvantaged by US capitalism as its main threats. With few exceptions, the genre represents, as Richard Powers put it, "an utterly predictable routine peopled by predictable character stereotypes" (1983: 86). Because of its stubborn conservatism, crime news also does not conform to a linear historical narrative. In place of a narrative of progress, crime news offers a dogged resistance to change, particularly in its representations of criminals and victims.

Consequently, I am afraid that the story I tell in the following pages offers little in the way of even cautiously guarded optimism about changing these narratives. It would take a wholesale revolution in the ways that the cluster of institutions that serve as gatekeepers for information about crime, criminalization, criminals, and victims think about these topics and act on the basis of those deeply held beliefs to effect meaningful change. Instead, the story I have set out to tell is one of white privilege, and the ability conferred by that privilege to transform its oppressive treatment of African Americans into crime stories that justify the reproduction of such oppression.

For the past three decades, US crime news has conveyed a message told largely through a language grounded in religious fundamentalism. This discourse has argued that the causes of crime are moral ones, rooted in individual pathologies and behaviors: bad families, bad genes, and bad individuals. For all those who have embraced the language of law and order, locating the causes of crime at the level of the immorality of individuals and scapegoated cultures of pathology has served a useful political function during a period of intensified cutbacks in social spending, ongoing privatization, and the build-up of repressive solutions to social wrongs. To assert, tautologically, that natural-born criminals cause crime is to disavow any collective responsibility for social violence on the part of either individuals or the state. Worse still, it is to view significant segments of our citizenry as just plain bad, evil, undeserving, and beyond attention other than isolation and permanent incarceration.

This is a particularly grim and hopeless form of story-telling that brooks no alternatives and has a single chilling conclusion: the prison-industrial complex, the death penalty, and an ever harsher and more punitive response to oppressed communities. In their devastating critique of the war on drugs, former journalist David Simon and retired police officer Edward Burns emphasize the dehumanizing aspects of this type of story-telling:

> That's the myth of it, the required lie that allows us to render our judgments. Parasites, criminals, dope fiends, dope peddlers, whores—when we can ride past them at Fayette and Monroe, car doors locked, our field of vision cautiously restricted to the road ahead, then the long journey into darkness is underway. Pale-skinned hillbillies and hard-faced yos, toothless white trash and gold-front gangsters—when we can glide on and feel only fear, we're well on our way. And if, after a time, we can glimpse the spectacle of the corner and manage nothing beyond loathing and contempt, then we've arrived at last at that naked place where a man finally sees the sense in stretching razor wire and building barracks and directing cattle cars into the compound.
>
> (1997: 478)

Crime news has played a central role in constructing these myths and promoting their requisite lies. By congealing debate about crime into a narrow, polarized set of dogmatic positions that cannot possibly question the racialized androcentrism in which they are invested, the resultant media debate has aggravated people's worst fears and fostered their basest impulses. The very modest goal of this book project is to begin to dislodge the hold that historical narratives exercise on the present: to tell an alternative story about criminals and victims and in so doing to offer up a different way of understanding social violence and its victims.

1 "The most disgusting objects of both sexes"

Gender and race in the episodic crime news of the 1830s

Thomas Carlyle, the great Scotchman, looked up to the starry midnight and exclaimed with a groan, "'Tis a sad sight!" What would have been his exclamation had he stood, reader, where you and I now stand—in the very center of the "Five Points,"—knowing the moral geography of the place,—and with that same midnight streaming its glories down upon his head! *This* is, indeed, a sad, an awful sight—a sight to make the blood slowly congeal and the heart to grow fearful and cease its beatings.

(Foster 1850/1990: 120)

George Foster, a reporter for Horace Greeley's *New York Tribune* and author of the best-selling *New York by Gaslight and Other Urban Sketches*, understood that urban reporters importantly provided a "moral geography" of the city.[1] More than any other form of the urban reporting that was taking shape in 1830s New York City, crime reporting was actively drawing divisional lines that marked the raced, gendered, and classed parameters of safety and danger, and virtue and vice. Although urban crime narratives were attentive to class and immigrant status in their construction of danger zones, race was already forming the starkest of boundaries. On one side of the line stood victims, native born white people; while on the other was a mix of immigrant groups rendered threatening in their proximity with a small black population that loomed large in the androcentric imagination. To understand the purchase that ideologies of race and gender exercise over contemporary crime narratives, we need first to turn to the genesis of modern crime news and reporting in the penny press of the 1830s. To do so, this chapter scrutinizes the foundational role that ideologies of race, class, and gender played in the establishment of the moral geographies constructed by crime news.[2]

News production in the 1830s

On the face of things, penny papers like the *New York Sun* did not look all that different from the six-cent newspapers that had preceded them (although they were shorter in column width and length). Like the papers that preceded them, the penny papers also relied on advertising for revenue. These new papers were not avowedly partisan, but the penny papers were never shy about expressing what to readers of the time would have been identifiable political affiliations. The main difference between the penny press and the papers that had preceded it involved less of a quantifiable change in newspapers themselves and more of a shift in how newspaper owners, editors, and reporters began to think of themselves and their role in the industrializing city.[3] Alexander Saxton points out that six of the seven men identified "as founders of pioneer penny dailies . . . began as artisans" (1996: 99), but printers like Benjamin Day and Moses Beach (first and second owners of the *Sun*) had no abiding loyalty to the artisanal classes from whence they came, but aspired to a new, professionalizing model of newspapermen (featuring owners, editors, and reporters), one that combined both political and economic power and, importantly, one that addressed advertisers, businessmen, and other members of an emerging middle class.[4]

In addressing an audience that was further understood to be more local than regional, the penny press featured what Saxton describes as "local news par excellence: crime, violence, humor, sex in a single package" (97–98).[5] Crime news began to assume two main forms in the pages of the penny press during the 1830s: episodic and serialized. In writing about journalistic narratives, Shanto Iyengar (1987: 2, 14) distinguishes between "episodic" and "thematic" news coverage, a distinction that began to take firm shape with the rise of the commercial press, the earlier mercantile press having been more broadly epistolary in format.[6] Episodic stories were short, capsulated narratives that appeared only once. Traces of episodic coverage persist today—directly, in the police blotters featured in local dailies and campus newspapers and less obviously in the flow of crime news used on slow news days in both local television news and local and national newspapers.

Serialized coverage, in contrast, narrated an event or issue over the course of days, weeks, months, and sometimes even years. I use the term "serialized" rather than "thematic" because it gets at the intercourse between literary form and news production that more accurately describes serialized crime news. Where "thematic" implies a kind of intention or coherence which was often absent from crime news—themes tended to develop haphazardly over the course of serialized coverage, rather than motivating or framing the coverage itself—"serialized" further stresses the simultaneously ideological and economic benefits of more durable forms of coverage.[7]

Scholars typically trace the origins of modern urban reporting, the human interest story, and crime news to penny press papers. According to Helen MacGill Hughes,

> The practice of printing amusing anecdotes in the newspaper began in the police-court reports that were one of the great attractions of the early penny papers. "The vulgar, degrading police reports" of the cheap press were recognized by the outraged editors of sixpenny papers as the principal cause of its success.

> (1968: 187)

The *New York Sun* and the *New York Herald* regularly featured columns on news of a criminal justice system undergoing waves of reform during the 1830s and both newspapers avidly covered several high-profile murder cases during their first decade of existence.[8] The *New York Sun* is credited with originating journalistic crime reporting, in the shape of the Police Office column written by George W. Wisner. In September 1833, Wisner, an unemployed artisanal printer, approached Benjamin Day, offering to attend the police court that began at 4 a.m. and to write an account of the proceedings for the *Sun*. In exchange, Day—already concerned about generating enough news to fill the pages of the paper—agreed to pay him four dollars a week.[9] Wisner's Police Office columns, which appeared without a by-line (these were not commonly used in New York city newspapers until the final years of the nineteenth century), sometimes extended for two or more columns.

Founded two years after the *Sun* in 1835, the *New York Herald* did not devote an entire section of the paper each day (or what would later be known as a department) to crime news, as did the *Sun*, but included sections on police news (under the heading either "Police" or "Court of Sessions") on slow news days. Like the *Sun*, episodic crime news in the *Herald* was more comedic than tragic in tone:

> Two young men, named Alexander Van Vort and Archibald Davis, took it into their heads on Sunday night last, to visit the Methodist Church, in Green street, and there began "praising the Lord"—not "with harp, lute, dulcimer and sacbuts," [a type of trombone] but with two "penny whistles." The audience, unaccustomed to this novel method of devotion, took umbrage and handed our melodists over to the watch.
>
> (19 January 1837: 2)

Unlike serialized coverage, these stories were not knit into a larger narrative about the role of crime in modern society or the immoral behavior of its citizens.

In contrast to the religious narratives about crime that appeared in the execution sermons, broadsheets, printed confessions, and the other ephemera that Daniel A. Cohen (1993) writes about, episodic crime reporting was light-hearted, often sympathetic to those who stood accused, and generally not moralistic in tone.[10] In fact, Wisner's column focused on the details of the crime and the accused's narrative (elements of what would later be described as human interest stories), rather than the wider social or moral significance of the crime itself.[11] More often than not, Wisner's columns chronicled the life of the city in a colorful style, causing a later writer to describe him as "the Balzac of the daybreak court" (O'Brien 1928: 17; Wisner 1918: 171).

In contrast to the serious and moralizing tone of serialized crime coverage, or the reporting of a later, more "objective" era, the reporter belonged properly to the "we" viewing the proceedings, sometimes moved to sympathy for the many destitute women and men who appeared before the magistrate, charged with vagrancy like Ann Scott, who "had no money—no home—no friends"

(*Sun*, 3 September 1833: 2), sometimes with sarcasm, and often with humor.[12] The reporter's "I" constantly asserted the presence of the narrator as a spectator at the court and not as the final arbiter of unruly behavior, a reader of police reports, or a chronicler of police activities, as he would later become: "Whether Sally was offended at the circumstance of having the pantaloons presented to her, or at the husband for his immodesty, our reporter could not say" (*Sun*, 31 December 1833: 2). Unconstrained by devotion to a higher power—call it "God," "Law," or merely protecting one's sources—penny press reporters wrote about their own immediate perceptions of these cases.

In the shifting cultural and political milieu of Jacksonian America, where rapid industrialization was causing seismic shifts in understandings of class, gender, and race, crime news was an important and influential means for communicating appropriate behavior for bodies marked by class, sex, and race. By depicting that which was becoming deviant and often illegal in the eyes of the state, crime news came to play a significant role in articulating the new ideologies and social practices that were to accompany republican understandings of gender and race.

Class and criminalization

Chiefly concerned with the borderlands between the criminal and the non-criminal, the normal and the abnormal, the acceptable and the execrable, early crime reporting was preoccupied with race and gender. Of course, economic privilege has always literally meant the difference between life and death in terms of deviance and punishment across a range of societies. In the USA of the 1830s, class privilege meant that the wealthy and the emerging middle classes could consume alcohol in private or secluded places, where they were less likely to encounter people who angered or displeased them and into which working-class watchmen were reluctant to enter. Working-class people and the poor, on the other hand, consumed alcohol in the streets or in public spaces, where the likelihood of social conflict was greatly increased, as was the risk of being arrested and, like James Stewart of Pike Street, "charged with being drunk" (*Sun*, 7 January 1834: 2).

Class privilege often allowed a man who had been accused of a crime to avoid publicity because a sympathetic magistrate (who may or may not have been acquainted with the defendant's family) recognized him as a reasonable and upstanding man. Wisner wrote, "At the particular request of one or two very respectable citizens, we omit the name of —— ——, charged with insulting a respectable female in Broadway last night" (*Sun*, 31 December 1833: 2).[13] Even in more dire circumstances, where class privilege did not enable the convicted to cheat the hangman, it could allow him to smuggle a knife into the prison and commit suicide, thereby sparing his family the shame of a public hanging, as was the case with convicted murderer John Colt (brother of gun manufacturer Samuel Colt) in 1842. And, of course, class privilege meant not being driven to commit a whole range of petty property crimes, from the theft of a piece of beef, stolen by Barney M'Kelley, because "my mouth hadn't tasted a sweet bit of roast bafe [*sic*] for many a day," to the offense of vagrancy committed by one John Williams, because he "had no home—no clothes—no money—and nothing to eat" (*Sun*, 16 June 1834: 2).

In keeping with the secular tone of episodic crime news, and also bearing in mind that these narratives appeared before the emergence of a more properly scientific language for justifying racism, people who appeared before the magistrate and Wisner were not depicted as inherently evil or depraved.[14] Instead, the accused were generally cast as unfortunates and described in comic rather than rigidly moralistic terms: "Christian Williamson, took an extra glass last evening, and every thing still appeared double to him. Committed, till himself again" (*Sun*, 11 September 1833: 2). In November 1833, "Andrew Smith, and Jane Wiggins, were found enjoying themselves over a bottle of apple jack, near Peck Slip—both the prisoners declared they were respectable people, and moreover had a right to drink when they pleased—committed" (*Sun*, 11 November 1833: 2). While Wisner never explicitly condoned such drunken revelry, working women's and men's declarations about their right to drink in public were a constant theme in his reporting.

Odd fish, cowardly boobies, and sharp-tongued nymphs

In the crucible of a rapidly industrializing capitalist society, class played a principal role in identifying criminal behaviors and in punishing them. But these class-based narratives about crime were at the same time stories about gender: about the meanings of masculinity and femininity. In early nineteenth-century America (as in early twenty-first century America), the terms of masculinity—of what it meant to be the privileged subject of US capitalism—were an abiding theme in crime narratives. This fixation on masculinity makes sense, in light of the fact that men have long committed the vast majority of violent offenses. Moreover, given the role that violence has played in US culture as a defining feature of "normal" masculinity, it also makes sense that crime narratives were central locations in which the often fine distinction between acceptable male violence and unacceptable male violence got worked out.

The propriety of norms of masculinity and femininity was a constant theme in episodic crime reporting in the 1830s and 1840s, typically understood by reference to the distinctly abnormal. Wisner and other reporters demonstrated a fascination with such behaviors, as in Wisner's account of one cross-dresser, entitled "An Odd Fish":

> An animated article of the masculine gender, who called himself *John Roach*, took occasion to escape from his watery element, and to steep his appetite so deeply in brandy that he became quite literally drunk with the liquid he had imbibed. In this state he took occasion to supply his scanty wardrobe with a number of articles of female wearing apparel, furtively as was supposed, with which, near midnight, he went swimming like a man

mermaid along the street. The watchman, Inkster, supposing Mr. *Roach* to be a fish out of water, kindly took him into custody, impounded him in the watch-house, and in the morning sent him to be *salted* down in the cell of the bridewell, as he had been only temporarily *corned* before.

(*Sun*, 17 September 1835: 2, original emphases)

In this and similar vignettes, cases where people either did not conform to gender norms or flouted them were used for comedic effect in order to validate a deeply seated derision, as Pierre Bourdieu (2001) put it, toward all things female. These stories were intended to be funny, little being considered funnier or more ridiculous than a man dressed as a woman, but at the same time they hinted at the anxieties that resulted from transgressive performances of gender.

Coverage of family violence featured similarly incongruous reversals of gender roles.[15] Sally Jane Winthrop, for example, was charged with throwing a pair of tongs at her husband John, an act that was provoked, she argued,

when the husband, getting out of all patience with her, very deliberately took off his pantaloons and presented them to his wife, telling her, "there, bad luck to your ill natured soul, you've been wanting to wear the breeches for a long time—now take them and be hang'd to ye!"

(*Sun*, 31 December 1833: 2)

Reporters' attitudes toward women like Winthrop suggested that cases that defied codes of both classed and gendered behavior (a "true" woman would never disobey her husband, much less strike him) were treated dismissively by both the court and the reporter, indicating that such behavior was not to be taken seriously. The very title of one such case of domestic violence, clipped from the *Boston Morning Chronicle*, "Queer Notions of Honor and Law," illustrates that cases involving transgressions of gender norms were framed as deviant and sometimes criminal (*Herald*, 9 March 1837: 1).

Occasionally, episodic crime coverage offered insights into how women themselves participated in family violence, sometimes fighting back (however violently and ineffectively) against lovers and husbands. Jane Williams

struck her husband on the side of the head with a stick of wood. The poor man had his head tied up with a pocket handkerchief as he gave in his testimony against his unruly rib. He said he didn't like to quarrel with his dear—and he wouldn't quarrel if she killed him. His wife turned to him and called him a cowardly booby—told him he hadn't the spunk of a louse, or he would have given her battle.

(*Sun*, 7 January 1834: 2)

Mary Lawler told the magistrate about her encounter with her former husband:

You see, I was down to the market, selling some mead and spruce beer, to get a little money to support my children with. Last night the brute came down where I was, and, says he, Mary, says he, will you go and live with me again. And says I, go long you divil, for you know I gave you a divorce. And then says he, if you don't go and live with me, I'll break every damned bottle of made [mead] that you've got. Then says I, John Lawler, if you touch my made I'll break your head.

(Sun, 21 July 1834: 2)

Eliza Wallace, who appeared before the magistrate with her elderly mother, also complained of her husband's lack of support for their family: "O, the lying booby. He don't work one jot—but he drinks like a salmon, and his nose is as red as a boiled cabbage all the time" (*Sun*, 26 July 1834: 2).

Stories like these also warned about negative manifestations of masculinity, wherein men could not even exercise control in the so-called private sphere.[16] More frequently, though, crime news condemned the effects of drink and deviance on women in particular. Miss Lydia Ann Swartwout, for example, was described as "one of the frail tabernacles of corrupt morality, who had reveled in the luxuries of so many riotous enterprises, that she had become a wandering object of vice and disgust" (*Sun*, 17 September 1835: 2).

In contrast to such objects of "vice and disgust," specific groups of white women were coming to play more visible ideological roles in crime reporting as victims of crime. Despite the overwhelming parade of victims of family violence through the court system and the pages of crime reporting, abused women were not represented as victims per se until later in the century, when reform movements were more successful in their attempts to publicize the effects of male abuse of alcohol on women and children. Proper female crime victims, then, were not subject to abuse in the private sphere but, in the pages of both episodic and serialized reporting, they appeared as the objects of "insults" from men in the streets, as the occasions for moralizing about proper codes of gendered conduct for both men and women, and as the beautiful, dead white victims whose deaths could teach others about the dangers of various forms of transgression. If white women's role as crime victims was not as evident in the episodic crime reporting of the emerging penny press as it was in serialized coverage, it nonetheless appeared in the distinction that was being drawn between worthy and unworthy female victims: between those women who acceded to masculinist control and those who rebelled against it or just could not afford to pay its price. Rendered through the sentimental codes that scholars like Cathy Davidson (1986), Ann Douglas (1977), and Jane Tompkins (1985) describe, worthy victims were tragic figures who knew their gendered places in society and succumbed to their fate passively.

Again, class played an organizing role in the rendering of the distinction between worthy and unworthy victims in crime news. The white women who appeared as criminals before the magistrate in the *Sun*'s "Police Office" from 1833 through 1836 were overwhelmingly poor or white women. Although middle-class or bourgeois white women (the distinction is difficult to make from newspaper accounts) were occasionally referenced as the objects of "insults" and thus as cautionary tales about the dangers women encountered in the streets, the majority of female criminals and crime victims were clearly not drawn from the upper classes. As Christine Stansell describes in a brilliant chapter on women and the street, the streets were considered unsuitable places for respectable, orderly women, particularly as the ideology of separate spheres gained cultural legitimacy.

Indeed, a white woman who was accosted or assaulted in the streets risked being considered indecent and responsible for her own victimization. Hewlet Piersol "was charged with seizing hold of a young lady in Chatham street, at the hour of 11 last night. The complainant, Mrs. Smith, said she was a married lady—her husband was a tailor, and had sent her of an errand last night at the hour of eleven" (*Sun*, 23 December 1833: 2). On the same date, "Barnet H. Hone of 337 Grand Street, was charged with putting his arms around the necks of Maria Rogers and Eliza Rogers, her sister." And "On Sunday evening as a respectable and well-dressed lady was passing along the street, she stooped down to tie her shoestring which had become loose, when a decently dressed German, named Diedrich Baldwin" (*Sun*, 29 September 1835: 2) accosted her. These accounts emphasized the respectability and status of the victims (one was both married and a lady, another was in the street with her sister, a third was both respectable and well-dressed) in order to demonstrate that the streets were no place for even the most respectable and morally upstanding white women. In this fashion, women were criminalized for the aggressive and often openly violent behavior of the white men of all classes that they encountered in the streets.[17]

The streets were also places where unprotected women might encounter potential seducers, and episodic crime news frequently featured stories of seduction and ruin, narratives that were common in nineteenth-century popular culture and that often served to delineate the attributes of worthy white female victimhood. In one such story, Wisner described a distinctly undeserving victim as a "nymph from the Five Points" (and both "nymph" and "the Five Points" underscored the lowness of her character) who told of "the ill luck" that led her "to meet with a gallant gay deceiver in the person of Mr. Pat M'Graw, a laboring miner, with whose physiognomy she fell in love" (*Sun*, 27 November 1833: 2). Quoting Shakespeare and Sheridan in her appearance before the magistrate, this woman's conversance with popular drama was yet another reminder of her degraded status.

In contrast, "Sally ——" was treated with slightly more sympathy, underscored by the unusual omission of her last name. After her parents died in a cholera epidemic

> a clever young journeyman jeweller invited her to walk out, she accepted the invitation and he took her to one of those 'virtue-destroying hells,' in which males and females who are utter strangers to each other promiscuously assemble—a Philadelphia dance house.
>
> (*Sun*, 30 December 1833: 2)

The orphaned Sally, alone in the world and without protection, was a more sympathetic figure than the sharp-tongued nymph from the Five Points, who blamed her fall from virtue on "ill luck" and demonstrated a shocking absence of contrition.

Crime reporters thus distinguished between tragic and comedic criminals: those who merited sympathy and those who did not. Such distinctions in tone divided along the lines of respectability or the presumption thereof, based on the accused's conformance to standards of womanly behavior. For example, the deserving poor appeared in the guise of an anonymous white woman, who showed up at the respectable hour of 9 a.m. "with a little infant sleeping on her bosom." The wife of a first mate "on board one of our well known merchant vessels, who is now absent on a long voyage," she had used up most of her monthly allowance because of illness and was turned out of her boarding house. Remarking on "the undeserved barbarity with which she had been treated," the magistrate wrote her a check for $20.00 (*Sun*, 20 February 1836: 2). Wife and mother, to all outward appearances a paragon of respectability, this woman's story, unlike most others, merited sentimental attention, as well as unprecedented charitable action.

The sympathy extended to certain poor and white women (as well as white men) resulted from the economic precariousness of the middle class that Stuart M. Blumin (1989) described in nineteenth-century Philadelphia. But where the white middle-class men who wrote crime narratives could imagine themselves in the place of sad and ruined white women and men, race formed the limit of their empathy and racism prevented newspaper reporters from imagining themselves in the place of former or current slaves. Although poor and black women appeared in the crime reports of this era, almost all accounts featured them as perpetrators of thefts and assaults on other black women and men. No offenses committed by white men against black women appeared in the pages of the penny press, although a few cases involving black female criminals did appear. One such case described the stabbing of a man who had "unintentionally incurred the hot displeasure of two colored women named Hetty Joseph and Catharine Searles, two notorious black prostitutes" (*Sun*, 22 July 1834: 2), while in another case, "Antoinette Jackson, a black girl, was brought up from Duane street and charged with an assault and battery on a small boy" (*Sun*, 31 May 1834: 2).

Only a single tragic black female victim appeared in crime reports in the *Herald* and the *Sun* between 1833 and 1841. Not surprisingly written by Wisner, the narrative told of a "black girl by the name of Floranthe Wilson," whose

> features were very pretty—and her dress of the most expensive kind. The gold chain around her neck—a huge pair of gold ear-drops—the sparkling stones with which her hair combs were set—and her lofty, dignified look, gave her the appearance of an African princess.
>
> (*Sun*, 21 April 1834: 2)

The daughter of "a wealthy citizen of the government of Hayti," Wilson had been seduced and then abandoned by an English sea captain and had subsequently gone mad. Of course, Wisner's tale featured a wealthy young woman from Haiti: an exotic "African princess," rather than a child born to slaves in the USA. As an exotic from a distant land, Wilson bore no resemblance to the uniformly unworthy victims of African descent who lived closer to home.

The unworthiest of victims

Both class and gender concerns influenced crime narratives in the early years of the penny press, but race was beginning to take center stage in relation to the forms of threat construction that accompanied these short disquisitions on crime. The presence of even a small population of free blacks (slaves born before 1799 had gained their freedom in New York City in 1827) was a source of consternation and fear for white New Yorkers. Racist ideologies, which simultaneously saw blacks as lacking the drive required for success in an industrializing society and as criminally acquisitive, meant that blacks (freed or not) continued to be viewed as a potentially troublesome population; a view quite likely exacerbated by the constant worry on the part of whites that at some point blacks would revolt against white supremacy.[18]

Blacks' employment status in northern industrializing society, first as chattel slaves and then as a reserve army for labor, continuously shored up white supremacist understandings of the determinative nature of racial identity. Where white New Yorkers and recent immigrants could at least aspire to class mobility, blacks could not. Of the distinction emerging in the 1830s between "hirelings" and "slaves" and "servants" and "help," David Roediger observes that, "The white hireling was usually a political freeman, as the slave, and with very few exceptions the free Black, were not" (1996: 46–47). White workers' status as political freemen exceeded their status as wage laborers, but black women and men's race delineated the entirety of their identities. That black women had to labor outside the private sphere further signified their deviation from republican notions of true womanhood.

Papers like the *Herald* and the *Sun* came into being within the context of increasing anti-abolitionist sentiment and racist ferment—a backlash, some have claimed, against the liberalizing tendencies of the revolutionary era. Day and Bennett considered themselves Democrats and were open supporters of slavery. Bennett had quit his job as associate editor of the *Courier and Enquirer* in order to edit a campaign paper that supported Jackson and Van Buren (Mott 1941: 229–30), while Day, and later Beach, held what historian Frank Mott described as "democratic, but moderate views" (1941: 227). Despite differences in how they may have understood their audiences, as well as their respective positions within the Democratic Party, both newspaper owners shared the racist sentiments that fueled their deep distrust of abolitionism.[19] Although the penny press did not invent racism, it was perhaps the most important purveyor of racist sentiments in the New York City of the 1830s, as evidenced by the role that the mainstream press played in fomenting anti-black violence throughout the nineteenth century.

Penny papers like the *Herald* and the *Sun* mainly distinguished themselves from their predecessors around issues of class, particularly in terms of the anxieties that Alexander Saxton (1996) and Sean Wilentz (1984) have linked to a changing artisanal culture. But while some rifts between the anti-elitism of artisanal culture and the views of the elite class may have been vast, white artisans and the ruling class shared a deep vein of sexism and racism. The bonds of class were weakest when it came to issues of both race and gender. In penny press crime reporting, for example, the primacy assigned to skin color over other forms of identity manifested itself as a convention, where those of African descent were consistently identified as black (without reference to their status as workers), while white immigrants were often multiply identified—as workers, as members of ethnic groups, and as family members.[20] Thus we read of "Edw. Hackett, a gentleman of color" (*Sun*, 9 September 1833: 2), "Luner Brown a Negro" (*Sun*, 24 October 1833: 2), that "A row was kicked up at the Five Points last night, among a parcel of negroes" (*Sun*, 2 November 1833: 2), and that "Wm. Morris, black, was tried on an indictment for bigamy" (*Sun*, 15 November 1833: 2). William Bray, a white man tried for assault and battery was a "seaman," but James Johnson, tried for stealing a $10 bill, was "black" (*Sun*, 17 April 1836: 2). Laboring in the most reviled and contingent of jobs, black people's identities were never linked to employment, as were white people's identities. In the penny press, skin color rather than employment status circumscribed the boundaries of identity.

White criminals were occasionally identified by reference to immigrant identities: "twenty Germans were arrested for kicking up a row at a Dutch Tavern in Mulberry" (*Sun*, 18 September 1833: 2). The use of surnames further contributed to such identifications, especially in the case of the Irish. But "black" was a more ominous shorthand for reporters and their imagined audiences; one that denoted a commonsense connection to crime, especially sexual deviance, and that was to accrue ever more meaning as the century progressed. In the *Herald*, one entry read, "*A black action.*—Catherine Johnson, a negress, dark as the ace of spades, was arrested by officer Welsh on a charge of stealing three silver spoons" (21 June 1837: 2). The *Sun* similarly featured "*A Black Crime*: Catharine Wilson, a colored woman, the wife of James Wilson, of 38 Orange st. was charged with stabbing Wm. Jackson, a man of color, in the breast with a jack knife" (31 December 1833: 2). Not content with merely identifying the race of the accused, each report referred to race three times during the course of a single sentence. The use of "black" in the titles of both reports further suggests that crimes committed by blacks, as well as crimes committed against blacks, differed in some fundamental way from other types of crime.

While the republicanism of this era extolled the virtues of working people and their importance to the new nation, at the same time blacks were seen as opposed to everything this new order stood for. As Roediger puts it, "republicanism had the advantage of reassuring whites in a society in which downward social mobility was a constant fear —one might lose everything but not whiteness" (1996: 60). Making a similar distinction, one prisoner indignantly told the magistrate, "Well, Ise don't know who does support the family if I doesn't—for I works like a black niggur" (*Sun*, 26 July 1834: 2). James Gordon Bennett of the *Herald* plainly embodied the contradictory nature of this project of distinction between white workers and blacks. Bennett was, as Dan Schiller puts it, "relent-less in his assault on class-structured justice and unbending in defense of all men's natural rights" (1981: 65), but his defense of all men's rights never even brooked the possibility that "blacks" might occupy the same category as "men."

Roediger cautions us that categories of racial identity and the terms of racist discourses were far from stable during this era. However unstable these were, few accounts of blacks as victims of crime made it into the penny press. While there are numerous accounts of Irish victims of crime, only rarely do black male victims of crime appear. The case of an anonymous black businessman, owner of a victualling house in which Alfred Parker upset a table of "pickled lobsters and peaches" was a rare exception (*Sun*, 3 September 1833: 2). Wisner's abolitionist politics did make possible critiques of the slave trade and racism more generally understood. One brief article, entitled "The Slave Trade," began: "It is astonish-ing to what an extent this abominable traffic is carried on, notwithstanding the efforts made by Great Britain to prevent it, and the pretended but unreal efforts made by this and other countries to the same effect" (*Sun*, 17 April 1836: 2). And only Wisner was to publish a sympathetic comment on a black victim of the anti-abolition violence that swept through New York City in 1834. As in the case of the Haitian princess, however, the subject of this account was not considered black. Napoleon Francois, "a colored Frenchman," recounted his terror at being chased by an anti-abolitionist mob during the riots of July 1834. When the mag-istrate suggested that the mob didn't want to hurt Francois, Wisner recorded Francois' indignant response: "Hurt me, begar! Yes, begar! They hurt you too, if your skin was colaired like one dam African" (*Sun*, 15 July 1834: 2). These atti-tudes toward blacks would have been decidedly out of place in the *Herald*, where Bennett's invectives against the *Sun* frequently took a racist form, as when he criticized the *Sun* as "our estimable niggar friend" (11 August 1841: 2), elsewhere referring to it as a "decrepit, dying penny paper, owned and controlled by a set of woolly-headed and thick-lipped Negroes" (quoted in Saxton 1996: 104).[21]

While the penny papers often represented the Irish in broad stereotypical strokes—as "splendid specimens of the loafer tribe" (*Sun*, 17 September 1835: 2) and "Adam's degenerate kind" (*Sun*, 29 May 1834), the Irish were not singled out for the specific vitriol and fearful hatred reserved for blacks, castigated by Bennett as "the hordes of free people of color who crowd into this city, and who live, for the most part, by thieving and prostitution" (*Herald*, 13 January 1837: 2).[22] Nor were the Irish constructed as sexualized threats to the status quo in the ways that blacks were. There were no laws forbidding the Irish from marrying native-born women and the Irish were never represented as being particularly desirous of white women, since by and large they were considered white themselves when it came to sexual matters. That the small and disen-franchised black population of New York City could be constructed as a threat attests to the power of racist fears about blacks and crime and how fears of black crime and sexual deviance (and the two were inextricably linked) were already being manipulated during the early part of the nineteenth century to criminalize them in the pages of the newly born commercial press.

Amalgamation and white fear

In the end, Wisner's less racist (and I say less racist because abolitionists often endorsed both taboos and laws against interracial unions) reporting was not to survive beyond his two years as reporter for the *Sun*, while Bennett's proved far more durable. In Bennett's eyes (as well as papers like the *New York World* that were later to take up the Democratic standard), people of African descent were criminalized not strictly for their actions, or for what they had done. They were criminalized for the crimes that white men imagined that they wanted to commit. Reports of criminal activities thus focused ever more on "amalgamation," a word that in the 1830s had come to denote interracial relationships.[23] News coverage of the Five Points neighborhood (so named by the press in 1829, when the *Evening Post* first called for police intervention in the neighborhood) is a case in point. Five Points was "the lower Manhattan neighborhood named for the five-cornered intersection of Anthony, Orange, and Cross Streets" (Anbinder 2001: 14). Until the Five Points was destroyed in the 1890s, the press and representatives from other institutions periodically visited the area for news and information about crime.

In the pages of the penny press, the Five Points was regularly condemned for its sexual excesses. One of the *Sun's* reports on the Five Points observed:

> There, a number of idle blacks, mulattoes, and whites, many of them just released from imprisonment on Blackwell's Island, continually congregate, to carry on their incantations, and in the afternoon of each day, when drunkenness is at its height, the most disgusting objects, of both sexes, are exhibited in the eyes of the examiner. Indecency, squallid [*sic*] poverty, intemperance and crime, riot and revel in continued orgies, and sober humanity is shocked and horrified, at the loathsome spectacles incessantly presented.
>
> (27 May 1834: 2)

The Five Points' signature crime was its untoward mingling of races. The panoply of decadence and licentiousness that greeted delegations from the respectable center was made more shocking and confusing by the residents' lack of respect for racial and ethnic boundaries:

> There, were found sturdy negroes, lying drunk, and almost naked; colored women, also drunk, and in a state of the greatest indecency:—white women, and black and yellow men, and black and yellow women, with white men, all in a state of gross intoxication, and exhibiting indecencies, revolting to virtue and humanity.
>
> (*Sun*, 29 May 1834: 2)

Charles Dickens echoed this revulsion during his visit to Five Points seven years later, describing "cramped hutches full of sleeping negroes"—a place "Where dogs would howl to lie, women, and men, and boys slink off to sleep, forcing the dislodged rats to move away in quest of better lodgings" (1842/1934: 88). Economic and racial boundaries were routinely transgressed in the brothels, taverns, and oysterhouses of the Five Points; transgressions that further underscored the criminal licentiousness of the area.

In reporters' emphasis on the sexual excesses of the Five Points, we vividly glimpse the forging of the link between race and gender in US crime reporting, bound together by the anxiety about amalgamation expressed in the popular culture of the 1830s and 1840s. The intertwining of race and gender lay at the heart of this specifically masculinist form of threat construction that projected fear of overly sexualized and masculinized black people onto what were considered (at least ideologically) to be the most prized possession of white men: vulnerable white women. In an article entitled "Abolition Developed," Bennett observed of one sample of abolitionist oratory:

> There can be no mistake in the meaning of these burning, impassioned sentiments—"witherer of our prospects"—"new life and energy bursting forth"—"waste places begin to bud and blossom." This is a new language— the language of a love that burns to the very heart. It is the passionate aspirations of one race burning to expand its affections to the arms or on the bosoms of another. It is the race of Africa making love to the race of America. It is a general consuming fire that pants for a social level of the two races . . . Under the cry of the gospel, and of liberty, the black rascals want to press to their bosoms white wives, and the colored wenches to be caressed by handsome white husbands. This is the ultimate and only object of the abolition movement at the north.
>
> (*Herald*, 4 March 1837: 2)

That Bennett saw in these metaphors only the most sexualized and, to his thinking, depraved desires testifies to the power and imagination of an emerging racist discourse about crime, fear, and race. Black men, this logic suggested, wanted nothing more than white women—an argument that would be used again and again to justify horrific acts of racist violence in the centuries to come. White men's desire for—and privileged access to—black women was of course unmentionable. During the period in question, there was a single, brief entry on the case of a white man "who had recently been united in holy matrimony to a fine fat Negro woman" in Chrysanthemum Street, a working-class area of the city. The mob that had gathered was prevented from demolishing the couple's home and administering "the law Lynch to the offender" by the arrival of a justice (*Sun*, 11 September 1835: 2). But no one would mention white men's brutal assaults on black women, a reality that was culturally unthinkable within the framework of racialized androcentrism.

In the pages of the penny press, fear of amalgamation was hopelessly and often contradictorily bound up in attacks on abolitionists, who even when not female were seen as a contemptible, feminized lot. Particular ire was reserved for female abolitionists who in addition to opposing slavery were, as Rosenberg remarks, openly challenging "the subservient role of women within the American family" (1985: 124). In another report, this time on his visit to the Capitol, Bennett rendered the link between abolitionism and racial and gender transgression even more transparent. On this particular "blue Monday" (thus named because it was the day in which petitions were presented to Congress), John Quincey Adams "presented a petition signed by several female fanatics, praying for the abolition of slavery in this District." Bennett proceeded to deride the petitioners in the following gendered terms:

> It appears to me to be a great piece of impudence in those petitioners to attempt thus to interfere with the rights and property of others. The people of the District do not take it kindly, I assure you, and denounce these foolish women and crazy philanthropists who are perpetually stirring this thing, in no measured terms. They say they have already lost enough in being deprived of the elective franchise and obliged to suffer taxation without representation.—They would be much more satisfied if these silly women and men would petition for the total exclusion of the hordes of free people of color who crowd into this city, and who live, for the most part, by thieving and prostitution.
>
> (*Herald*, 13 January 1837: 2)

Impudent, foolish, and silly, white women clearly had no business writing petitions, much less protesting the property rights of privileged white men. Bennett concluded by offering the following advice to his readers: "Beauty, you observe, is much more attractive than politics; and the young legislators pour into the gallery to feast the eye and enjoy the fascinations of the sex, rather than be bored to death by the prosing of the honorables below." While generally more circumspect on the race issue, the *Sun* reported that one magistrate "very gravely advised" a dissatisfied young woman brought before him to "go home, call her associates about her, and organize an Anti-wear-a-frock-with-the-bosom-below-the-bosom-society" (*Sun*, 27 May 1834: 2).

According to Bennett, female abolitionists were especially foolish insofar as they—unlike the white men whose role it was to protect them—did not recognize the true motives of African Americans. As Bennett put it, "There is no idea more preposterous and false than the equality and liberty of the black and white races in one and the same community, unless the purpose is to mix the breeds and *Colonel-Dick-Johnson* all the present races and colours of mankind" (*Herald*, 28 January 1837: 2, original emphases).[24] Political efforts on the part of white women were consistently mocked in the penny press, more oblique references to white women's political activity were subjected to ridicule, and the abolitionist alliance between whites and blacks was rendered a nefarious, sexualized one with which white abolitionists proved incapable of coping.[25]

Increasingly, newspapers linked republican debates about sex and morality with abolitionism, lambasting both for their alleged promotion of amalgamation. Thus framed, the issue and the problem focused on interracial relationships involving black men and white women. Few white abolitionists shared the courage and conviction of William Lloyd Garrison and Lydia Maria Child, who publicly campaigned to repeal a Massachusetts law that banned interracial marriage. Instead, racist newspaper editors like Manuel Mordecai Noah, Webb, and Bennett used the threat of amalgamation to discredit the motives and actions of female reformers and abolitionists.

White fear, black villains

As we have seen, the poor and working classes formed the general reservoir for a constant stream of crime reporting. Although whites conformed to the letter of an emerging republican understanding of citizenship, they did not (or could not) always conform to its law. They drank to excess, beat their wives, abandoned their families, were often able-bodied *and* unemployed, and they fought and sometimes killed themselves or each other. While some of these activities were considered both immoral and illegal, many were overlooked or even dismissed as unfortunate by-products of a necessarily aggressive white masculinity. Episodic crime reporting in the 1830s and 1840s never suggested that white men—be they native-born or immigrant—constituted a criminally dangerous group of people or a class of criminals, despite the fact that the majority of property crimes, family violence, other forms of assault, and homicides (not to mention nineteenth-century urban riots) were in fact committed by single white men.[26] That the ongoing formulation of hegemonic masculinity was the real threat to society and its members' well-being—the true cause of social violence—was an idea that could not be countenanced in a social order so deeply dependent on the production of male subjects appropriate for a newly industrializing nation and the expansionism that breathed life into it.

Women, of course, were no threat to society as criminals, although some of them were to prove threatening in other ways. White women's appearance in episodic crime news served mainly to remind readers of the boundaries of republican womanhood and the social cost of transgressing those. Yet even in these short episodic reports, hierarchies of victimization were being established and women's role as passive objects of social violence was being subtly reinforced. Although the rhetorical potential of passive, feminized objects in constructing racialized threats to the social order would not be fully realized until after the Civil War and the emergence of discourses about miscegenation, tales of seduction and abandonment in the penny press foreshadowed the rise of the figure of the dead white woman that was to become a staple of crime reporting.

What emerges most forcefully in the crime reporting of this era is a powerful sense of fear about the black population, specifically black men—a fear as vicious as it was groundless—a fear that tells us more about the construction of white republican masculinity and its insecurities and fault lines than it does about the material realities of the period. A form of masculinity inherently suspicious of women (who could not be trusted to resist the blandishments of even the most improbable seducers), republicanism projected its own anxieties about sexuality, industrialization, and a rapidly changing social order onto the figure of the predatory black man, intent on securing that most ideologically prized possession—a white woman.

The resulting anxieties about amalgamation, the expression of a white masculinist fear, ran throughout crime reporting even in the early days of the commercial press. Again, while the Irish, German, Polish, and other immigrants may have been viewed as nuisances, they were not seen as the threat that black men were, a threat constructed from the gossamer imaginings of white men. Roediger argues that the "violent and sexually menacing black male of the post-Civil War 'coon song' is largely absent" from the early minstrelsy that was becoming popular in the 1830s (1996: 121). But while such a figure may not yet have dominated some forms of popular culture in the 1830s, he was already making an appearance in the pages of newspapers like the *Herald* and the *Sun*. Wisner's column and its abolitionist sympathies were the exception rather than the rule in the penny press. Eventually, Day, who later said that where he "was rather Democratic" in his politics, Wisner "was always sticking in his damned little Abolition articles," quarreled with Wisner, subsequently buying out Wisner's share for $5000 in cash (quoted in Mott 1941: 223), and thereby putting an end to any further "little Abolitionist articles."

That newspapers shared conventions of threat construction based on fears of amalgamation underscores the emergence of a consensus among urban elites about the nature of social threats—a consensus that directly reflected their economic and political interests. The mainstream commercial press was produced by and for white, more privileged men who imagined an audience that looked much like them. The narratives that they produced thus reflected their own standpoint, their own interests, anxieties, and preoccupations. Those who did not look like them, or behave in ways that they deemed appropriate, or whose presence challenged ideologies of republican masculinity were demonized in the pages of their papers. These forms of demonization allowed newspapers to serve up folk devils to whom all manner of social and moral woes could be attributed and upon whom they could heap various social anxieties. And since white editors and reporters never considered blacks to be part of their audience (or even an audience at all), they never risked alienating any part of the community of consumers they wanted to attract.

Ultimately, the construction of a social threat in the form of black men served to undermine tentative and already fragile alliances among black people, white women of all classes, and white working-class men by suggesting that the motivations for such alliances were fundamentally impure and tainted by sexual desire. By thus setting those particularly disenfranchised by the peculiar androcentrism of US-style capitalism against each other, crime reporting actually functioned to divert attention from the actual causes and sources of social violence and to create hierarchies of victimization that could be quickly mobilized in the interests of elites. Episodic crime news of this era thus participated in projecting fears originating in the minds of anti-abolitionist white men onto a small and embattled population of African Americans.

In addition to constructing blacks as a fearsome population, crime reporting in the 1830s also participated in the broader project of developing narrative codes through which worthy victims could be juxtaposed against villains who were considered absolutely distinct from them in the gendered, raced, and classed vocabulary of the era. For in terms of cultural understandings of gender, no two figures could be as diametrically opposed as those of the proper white female subject of the cult of true womanhood—that repository of the civilizing impulse, the broodmare of white European civilization—and the sexually menacing black man who was scarcely a generation away from the jungle. These white and black poles of the field of crime reporting had already begun to determine cultural understandings of criminals and victims.

2 The cult of dead womanhood

Protectors, villains, and victims in the origins of serialized crime news

As blackness was coming to define the basic contours of criminality in the penny press, so white femininity was assuming center state in emerging economies of victimization. Although most violent crimes, including murder, have been committed by men and have involved male victims, across the nineteenth and twentieth centuries murder cases involving white female victims (and a few female murderers) have traditionally received a disproportionate amount of press attention. The murder of Elma Sands in 1800, Lizzie Borden's trial for the murder of her parents in 1892, the murder of Nicole Simpson at the end of the twentieth century, and the murder of Laci Peterson at the beginning of this century are only a few examples.

The belief that sex (or violence, since the two frequently appear interchangeably) accounts for the media's preoccupation with stories involving women is a form of common sense—often invoked as an explanation for this preoccupation, but seldom itself questioned. In order to understand why gendered narratives were so important to the formation of serialized crime news, we need to question the axiom "sex sells." Instead, invoking a feminist truism, we can say that "gender sells"—that gendered narratives about crime were popularized because they reflected a wider preoccupation with gender systems and the changing meanings of gender, rather than the materiality of biological categories of sex or even sexual acts themselves.

When I say that "gender sells," however, that is not to say that race was secondary to emerging codes of victimization, or that narratives about crime and victimization were not at once tales about the meanings of whiteness and blackness. Here, rather than using a feminist lens, as some critics have suggested, in order to understand the interrelationship of gender, race, and class in the making of white male protectors and white female victims, the metaphor of the prism, a device that can refract social constructions of whiteness into their constituent elements, is more appropriate. In serialized crime news, white male editors used dead white women as a medium in order to rearticulate and reconsolidate an androcentric regime fearful that its power and cohesiveness were slipping away. Both "whiteness" and "womanhood" were key parts of the formula that emerged during this period. The stories about crime—and about the vibrations and waves of gender and race that went into the making of whiteness—that comprised the cult of dead womanhood reflected a racialized androcentric system that maimed and killed when it felt its dominance was threatened. At the heart of the moral or family values that this form of masculinity used to mask its basic violence were very visible dead white women and less visible African American women and men against whom white victims were contrasted and judged worthy.

The following analysis specifically follows the waves of gender, race, and class that went into the making of serialized crime coverage in the 1830s and 1840s, particularly in terms of the development of narrative codes for representing victims and victimization. Just as the axiom "sex sells" has come to be a form of common sense, so we live in a culture that has so naturalized narrative codes of victimization that the resultant constructions appear natural and, for many, divinely inspired. We forget at some cost that the codes of victimization invoked in today's crime coverage once were made by cultural producers working in specific historical and economic contexts. The struggles over who would count as worthy victims, who would be dismissed as unworthy victims, who would be demonized as villains, and who would be canonized as protectors were being worked out specifically in the pages of nineteenth-century newspapers. The status of news as non-fiction guaranteed that the results of these struggles over villains and victims in the pages of the press would have wide-ranging consequences, not only for the media themselves, but for institutions like the police and, as Laura Hanft Korobkin (1998) points out, for the kinds of stories the criminal justice system was also developing about crime, criminals, and justice.[1]

Serialized crime coverage as narrative form

Shipping news, financial news, and crime news were initially covered episodically, in part because such news occurred in discrete segments (ships arrived and departed, the market went up or down, criminals were jailed, sentenced, or released). Initially covered episodically, early crime news more accurately reflected what Eric Monkkonen has described as the "episodic, personal violence" (1990: 525), that was descriptive of the realities of actual social violence.

Print media have long understood the advantages of serializing literary works, but it took more time for news producers to understand that news could also be packaged and serialized like fiction, thereby providing more durable forms of coverage than episodic coverage did. Not only did serialized coverage allow editors to build circulation, it also allowed them to develop and utilize narratives that directly benefited newspapers as both cultural and economic institutions. And where the brevity of the episodic form constrained the stories that journalists could tell, the extended duration of serialized coverage allowed journalists to experiment with both form and content.

Early serialized crime news reflected its immediate cultural and political context. By the 1830s, republican culture in New York City was beginning to fully register the impact that industrialization was having on everyday life. Ironically, as Evelyn Nakano Glenn points out, the ideology of separate spheres was emerging at the very moment that households were becoming ever more dependent on market forces (2004: 73). Poverty was taking on a distinctly feminine cast, as the exigencies of urban life coupled with expectations about female dependency made women particularly vulnerable to market forces. As Christine Stansell demonstrates, working-class women were being thrust into the industrializing labor force, as shop girls and factory workers in the formal economy and as piece workers in the homework economy. As Stansell and other feminists have observed, not all the changes associated with urban life were negative for women. Urban living allowed young, single white women to escape—however temporarily—from rigid patriarchal households in which they ceaselessly labored at housework and child care. Earning wages also allowed these women to enjoy some modest leisure time activity, like Sunday trips to the Elysian Fields in Hoboken, New Jersey.

In an androcentric culture, however, changes that allowed for any modicum of female independence are always viewed in strictly negative terms, for individual women and society alike. Thus, emerging ideologies of female nature and femininity, particularly those traits associated with what historian Barbara Welter (1966) first described as the "cult of true womanhood," reacted negatively to any potential for female independence. Ideologies like this sought to reinstate what proponents referred to as traditional female virtues, but what were in essence fairly novel ideologies of femininity. According to Welter, the cult of true womanhood depended on four key virtues: piety, purity, submissiveness, and domesticity. Submissiveness in this context almost seems redundant, because the general thrust of beliefs about true womanhood was that it was right and natural for women to submit to men, providing their submission allowed them to remain pious, to protect their purity, and to remain in the domestic sphere. Women's "natural" submissiveness necessitated the presence of male heroes to protect them from those individuals and social forces that might jeopardize their purity.

That republican ideologies of femininity, like the periodic calls for a return to some mythic form of "family" or "moral" values that have since followed from these ideologies, excluded more women than they included was really the point, since the purpose of these discourses was to erect boundaries around those traits said to comprise female virtue and proper female behavior. By virtue of both race and class, black women never conformed to the mandates of true womanhood. As women of color, they could not conform to an ideology of femininity premised on whiteness. As laboring women, along with all those immigrant and native-born women laboring in the waged economy, they were excluded as well, for having transgressed the mythic line separating public from private. In the pages of mass circulation newspapers, true womanhood was more often than not defined by reference to negative examples in which fallen women displayed a shocking lack of regard for the virtues of true womanhood. Not pious or pure enough, unwilling to submit to the more ridiculous demands of androcentric culture (such as not appearing on public streets), the women who appeared in both episodic and serialized crime culture served as warnings to those women who lived and labored in more public spaces and ways about the dangers of the lives they had no choice but to lead.

The ideologies associated with true womanhood also functioned as explanations for the increases in female poverty. Of the sentimentalism that was an intrinsic part of true womanhood, Ann Douglas observed, it "was an inevitable part of the self-evasion of a society both committed to laissez-faire industrial expansion and disturbed by its consequences" (1977: 12). Thus, if women strayed from the path of virtue, they had no one to blame but themselves— an explanation for indigence that dovetailed neatly with a growing evangelical emphasis on redefining "the material needs of the poor" as "spiritual ones" (Dorsey 2002: 51).[2]

Serialized crime coverage also borrowed liberally from a variety of novelistic forms. As we will see, Edgar Allen Poe and *New York Herald* owner and editor James Gordon Bennett shared an interest in dead white women, the gothic, and the novel of detection. In narrating the life and death of prostitute Helen Jewett, Bennett drew on British romances like Jane Porter's *The Scottish Chiefs* (1810) and Richardson's *Pamela* (1740/1914) and *Clarissa* (1748/1930). The themes of abandonment, seduction, and ruin that ran throughout serialized crime coverage were generic characteristics of sentimentalism. The framework that held these variegated elements together in serialized crime reporting was the protection scenario, which imbued newspaper crusades with a sense of high-mindedness and purpose that went well beyond the delivery of information.

The cult of true womanhood as protection scenario

Welter and critics who have since adopted her terminology focused on the strictures placed on female behavior by the cult of true womanhood, thereby overlooking the centrality of male protection to it. A precondition of true womanhood was protection from the bustling public sphere, where would-be seducers abounded. Women further had to be protected from themselves, since they were by nature weaker. Women's dual need for protection thus also dictated a role for white men, who were the protectors and heroes who allowed women to blossom, orchid-like, in their parlors and bedrooms.

The cult of true womanhood was a variation on the protection scenario that has long played a central role in US popular culture. The terms "captivity narrative" and "protection scenario" are often used interchangeably, although these are more effectively understood as historically consecutive narrative forms.[3] Captivity narratives corresponded to an earlier era of mercantile capitalism, where they made sense to audiences living with or near colonized (not, notably, enslaved) populations.[4] The possibility that the colonizers might be captured and enslaved by savages provided the impetus for the type of threat construction favored by captivity narratives, in which the hostile actions of the colonized ironically provided justification for ever more aggressive acts on the part of the colonizers. Protection scenarios, on the other hand, were a product of industrializing, or industrialized, societies and constructed threats based on a wide-ranging set of internal challenges to the existing social order, rather than on threats that issued from without.

Richard Slotkin (1973), Judith Hick Stiehm (1982), and Susan Jeffords (1991) have argued that in the USA, captivity and protection scenarios depended on a gendered cast of characters. First, among these was a "worthy" female (or where necessary a feminized) victim, preferably a wife, mother, or daughter whose relationship to the patriarchal family underscored her worthiness. Unable to act or even speak on her own behalf, the victim required the services of a male protector, whose ability to represent and act on behalf of the victim defined him as heroic. The second element of these scenarios demanded the presence of a villain, preferably not white, although even white villains could be darkened if the need arose. In the hands of imperialist propagandists, written and visual captivity narratives organized around female victims were popularized as early as 1682, with the publication of Mary Rowlandson's *The Narrative of the Captivity and Restoration of Mrs. Mary Rowlandson.*

Race was a central feature of early captivity narratives, where racist distinctions often were evoked through the visual connotations associated with civilization and light, and barbarism and darkness, as in James Fenimore Cooper's *The Last of the Mohicans* (1826/2001), in which the fair-skinned Alice and Cora Munro were taken captive by the dark and bloodthirsty Canadian Huron Magua.[5] Within this narrative frame, it was unthinkable that European colonists (women as well as men) might choose to live with Native Americans, whose cultures and social orders were seen as uniformly violent, repressive, and uncivilized.[6] White male protection of white female victims, or, to adapt a phrase from Gayatri Spivak (1988), white men protecting white women from brown men, was a theme that came to predominate in the Americas.

Whiteness determined the worthiness of victims who conformed to the strictures of true womanhood and therefore deserved the intervention of masculinist protectors, while cultural constructions of black masculinity underwrote understandings of villainy. As we saw in the previous chapter, journalists were primed by racist ideologies about the nature of African men and their sexuality to identify villains as black. But in 1830s New York, the realities of urban life did not always allow for threat constructions based on black menaces.[7] Either black men were entirely absent from the scenes of homicides or violent deaths, in other words, or the facts of the cases so clearly eliminated them as suspects that no amount of narrative sleight-of-hand could present them as credible threats. In the penny press, black women were entirely invisible within the protection scenarios that proliferated in the mainstream press, either as victims or as villains.[8] Conforming to categories of neither threat nor threatened, black women simply disappeared.

In the versions of protection scenarios that unfolded in early to mid-nineteenth-century US culture, as in some earlier captivity narratives, protection came to refer not to white women's physical well-being, but, in keeping with the ideologies associated with true womanhood, to guardianship of their virtue, which was being linked ever more narrowly to virginity. The culture of the time focused on young, beautiful, vulnerable girls—orphans in particular—who had been seduced, cast aside by society, and ultimately ruined. But by the 1830s, the word "ruin" had taken on an entirely different inflection, referring not to impoverishment or death, but to the loss of the purity or virginity that was coming to define young women's value as literal commodities in the marital marketplace and as icons in the nation-building efforts of the still new republic. A mere three decades before-hand, murder victim Elma Sands' premarital relationship with the man who murdered her raised very few eyebrows, belonging as it did to "a late eighteenth-century system of courtship that tacitly tolerated premarital sexual intercourse between betrothed couples" (Cohen 1997: 291). By the nineteenth century, such tolerance had been withdrawn. By 1844, editor, journalist, and novelist George Lippard reflected the new value placed on virginity in the preface to his best-selling novel, *The Quaker City*: "the seduction of a poor and innocent girl, is a deed altogether as criminal as deliberate murder. It is worse than the murder of the body, for it is the assassination of the soul" (1844/1995: 27). That the loss of virginity was seen as more horrid than murder says much about the misogyny of a culture that valued intact hymens over women's lives. It also speaks to a construction of female sexuality in which virtue was defined by the absence of desire.

In the penny press' protection scenarios, thefts of women's virginity were similarly seen as more tragic than their actual deaths. Male crusaders of both religious and secular types shared the belief that death was preferable to the loss of virginity. In the hands of newspaper editors like Bennett, women became the occasion and the grounds for moral panics about vice and prostitution, while men's selfless love and admiration for virtuous women and their desire to protect them provided a moral center. Women who had lost their virginity had forfeited protection, although their sentimentalized stories could be used to justify the wider social need for male protection. The two cases that garnered the most attention in the penny press of this era foreground the utility of dead white women to the protection scenarios being constructed within the pages of the penny press. The murder of prostitute Helen Jewett in 1836 and the "mysterious death" of Mary Rogers in 1841, the first two instances of serialized crime coverage, offer unique insights into the raced and gendered economy of victimization set in motion by newspaper editors and journalists.[9]

Falling from virtue: the murder of Helen Jewett[10]

> "What is the reason, Helen, that after a woman falls from virtue she never gets up?"
>
> (Letter from "Wandering Willie" to Helen Jewett,
> quoted in the *Herald*, 13 April 1836: 1)

For early to mid-nineteenth-century writers of all stripes, the death of a beautiful woman was coming to be, in Edgar Allen Poe's words, "the most poetical topic in the world" (1850b: 265). Dead women could be exemplars of the cult of true womanhood, saintly creatures who had accepted their submissive lots and whose miserable, sinless deaths offered models to which all women were to aspire. Dead women could also serve as cautionary tales about what happened when women did not protect their virtue and descended into madness or worse. Journalists were no exception to the strange attraction exercised by the cult of dead womanhood. Both Helen Jewett (murdered in 1836) and Mary Rogers (who died in 1841) were young women whose lives did not fit into an older geography of gender norms. Prostitute and shop girl, they defied the codes governing appropriate female behavior and instead symbolized the pleasures and attendant dangers that awaited women in the new city, where older forms of patriarchal protection no longer had purchase.[11]

By all accounts a beautiful, generous, and intelligent woman, Helen Jewett defied the stereotypes of disease and abject dissolution typically used to represent prostitutes. Jewett and Richard Robinson, the man accused of murdering her, were part of the massive migration of people from rural New England to New York City that was then occurring.[12] Jewett and Robinson's lives dramatically reflected the radically different paths available to men and women in the new urban culture. Jewett's brief biography provided perfect grist for the penny press and the large market for ephemera based on nostalgic renderings of agrarian life (see Figure 2.1).

Born Dorcas Dorrance in Augusta, Maine, Jewett was orphaned at an early age. In spite of her background, Jewett was educated along with the daughters of her adoptive family and raised in a respectable, middle-class household. Had Jewett not been a native-born white woman, with the specific advantages conferred by her upbringing and education, it is unlikely that she would have attracted much attention. Since no case involving a black female murder victim garnered more than a mention in the police office or the court of sessions columns from 1836 until 1841 in either the *Herald* or the *Sun*, we can say with empirical certainty that, had Jewett been black, there would have been no crusade at all.

In addition to her racial and educational attributes, Jewett's death also appealed to the necrophiliac desires that were a largely unsung part of republican ideologies of femininity. As an other-worldly being—too civilized and devout for the trashy public world of men, too pure to be touched or moved by corporeal desires—the ideal woman was passive, cold, and for all intents and purposes dead to the bustling, passionate world of the public sphere. Her very passivity was sexually attractive, moreover, since women who exhibited any sexual desire were understood by this culture to be unwholesome and dangerous. Bennett's *Herald* provides the most stunning illustration of this. Jewett's dead body, Bennett somewhat breathlessly wrote:

> looked as white—as full—as polished as the purest Parian marble. The perfect figure—the exquisite limbs—the fine face—the full arms—the beautiful bust—all—all surpassed in every respect the Venus de Medicis according to the caste generally given of her . . . The left side down to the waist,

Figure 2.1 " Helen Jewett at her childhood's home," from George Wilkes, *The Lives of Helen Jewett and Richard P. Robinson* (1849). Reproduced by permission of the New-York Historical Society.

where the fire had touched, was bronzed like an antique statue. For a few moments I was lost in admiration at this extraordinary sight—a beautiful female corpse—that surpassed the finest statue of antiquity.

(11 April 1836: 2)

As literary critic David Brion Davis observed, Bennett "used the image of statuesque nudity to evoke erotic interest . . . [and] there was a disturbing similarity between a cold, sculptured ideal of Venus and a cold, naked corpse, helpless and frozen before the gaze of men" (1957: 163). If live women were problems to be managed, policed, and protected, dead women were classical objects of serene contemplation and desire, fixed by the admiring gaze of the appreciative republican man.[13] Dead women had an added advantage in terms of the construction of protection scenarios—they could be counted on to not contradict the protector's representation of their lives, needs, desires, and deaths. As Jane Caputi has pointed out, moreover, a focus on dead women directs attention not to the perpetrator of a given crime. Instead, by taking "the burden and the focus" off perpetrators, "the question centers not on how the man could have done this rape, batter, murder, incest, and so on, but on how the woman could have let him" (1989: 443).

But where republican man's literate appreciation of dead women's bodies was cause for no comment, Jewett's literacy served to underscore her tragic rejection of one of the tenets of true womanhood: her lack of piety. According to Welter, magazines of the period offered women "a bewildering array of advice. The female was dangerously addicted to novels . . . She should avoid them, since they interfered with 'serious piety'" (1966: 165). The *Herald* traced Jewett's demise directly to her reading habits. From a very young age, Bennett observed, "she occasionally gave indications of a wild, imaginative mind" and her "education only gave additional power to her fascinations." "Her great intellectual passion," he wrote in the same article, "was for reading the poems of Byron, and particularly Don Juan" (12 April 1836: 1). If penny press accounts are to be believed, one of Jewett's additional shortcomings was that she loved the poetry of Byron, but hated men. George Wilkes, editor of the *Police Gazette*, the popular magazine devoted to the annals of crime and the predecessor of the true crime genre, wrote that Byron's poetry "fevered her veins, and made her pillow the confidant of yearnings, which had they received fruition, would have rendered her ineligible to have hunted in the train of Dian" (1849: 6).[14]

The line between fact and fiction was also blurred in Jewett's own life. While in Portland, she was said to have "assumed the name of Helen Mar, from a popular character in one of the young lady's novels." According to Bennett, Jewett had cynically assumed the name of Helen Mar, the lovely, chaste, and virtuous heroine of romance novelist Porter's *The Scottish Chiefs*. In a more tragic parallel, Jewett's "private correspondence" (letters and diaries recovered from her room) resembled that of the tragic and "infamous Abellard and Eloisa" (12 April 1836: 1) and the manner of her demise found a parallel in "Richardson's Clarissa Harlowe" (14 April 1836: 1). This link between licentiousness and literacy in women frequently surfaced during the first half of the nineteenth century. Cathy Davidson, for example, writes about an 1802 jeremiad titled, "Novel Reading, a Cause of Female Depravity" (1986: 45).

While Jewett's literacy tapped into wider cultural anxieties about the effects of new media like novels on women's tender minds and bodies, it accounts only for part of the journalistic fascination with her. Another part of this fascination with Jewett was due to the physical proximity of "her degraded caste" (*Herald*, 11 April 1836: 2) to editors and reporters themselves, a proximity that played an important role in newspaper producers' growing understanding of themselves as protectors of women. Journalists were no strangers to establishments like that of Rosina Townsend, whose brothel was located in Thomas Street, not far from Press Row. Indeed, at least one reporter was on intimate terms with Jewett. Two years earlier, in June 1834, William Attree (then crime reporter for the *Transcript*, later for Bennett's *Herald*), the "Wandering Willie" of the letter quoted at the beginning of this section, interviewed Jewett for a story he was writing about prostitution. Attree became Jewett's ardent admirer and client. After her murder, the *Herald* republished both the interview and excerpts from love letters Attree had written to her.

In his 1834 interview, suggestively entitled "The Fruits of Seduction," Attree demonstrated his facility with narratives of seduction, echoing what Karen Halttunen describes as "the popular version of the life-course of the fallen woman" (1998: 200):

> In order to convince our readers of the misery resulting from the villainous artifices of those whose sole aim in life, seems to be the seduction of a young and innocent girl, and then, abandon her to the sneers and insults of the heartless, and despicable; we will give a brief sketch of the history of this young girl.
>
> (*Herald*, 13 April 1836: 1)[15]

Attree's public condemnation stood in stark contrast to the letters he later wrote to Jewett, where, as Patricia Cline Cohen points out, Attree promptly dispensed with the artificial framework of the moral crusade (1998: 41–42). In a letter he wrote to her shortly after the interview, he demonstrated no remorse for Jewett's ostensibly miserable condition, but rather envy for her seducer:

> DEAREST ELLEN.—Most lovely and enchanting creature! I shall never forget the moment I saw your fair form in the Police Office. You are fit to be a princess—a very queen. What a prize the villain had who seduced you at the Boarding School! How I should have liked to have been in his place!
>
> (13 April 1836: 1)

While urban reporters and other spokespersons for republican ideologies of femininity publicly espoused the language of the protection scenario, Attree's private correspondence illustrates the mendacity that lay at the heart of this language. Men did not always conduct themselves in accordance with republican codes of virtuous male behavior, nor did they always like passive, passionless women.

Female nature was again called upon as an alibi for male practices that contradicted dominant ideologies. Caught in the act of seducing a woman or engaging in non-procreative sexual acts, men could always plead that they had been overwhelmed by female charms. Publication of Attree's letters thus bore testimony to Jewett's "power" over men, who could not help but be enchanted by such an incredible specimen of femininity. As Bennett put it,

> [S]he was a fascinating woman in conversation, full of intellect and refinement, but at the same time possessed of a very devil, and a species of moral antipathy to the male race. Her great passion was to seduce young men, and particularly those who most resisted her charms. She seems to have declared war against the sex. "Oh!" she would say, "how I despise you all—you are a heartless, unprincipled set—you have ruined me—I'll ruin you—I delight in your ruin."
>
> (12 April 1836: 1)

Attree's correspondence with Jewett also emphasized the need for women to have virtuous male protectors, to guard them from a male sexuality that republican ideologies saw as naturally uncontrollable and lustful, when lacking in the proper discipline.

The contradictory nature of ideologies about male sexuality, and the need for certain white men to protect white women like Jewett from other white men, illustrated the fundamental instability of the protection scenarios being constructed by urban journalists. How could white men be both protectors and villains, crusaders for justice and perpetrators of injustice? How was this fundamental contradiction to be reconciled? As we saw in the case of episodic coverage, when given the opportunity— in the shape of a black suspect— Bennett's newspaper was swift to criminalize on the basis of race. But the construction of those of African descent as *de facto* threats occurred unevenly during this period. Later accounts attributed Jewett's fall from virtue to the corrupting influence of a "negress" who encouraged her affair with her first lover (Wilkes 1849: 9) and later to her maltreatment at the hands of "a den of negro thieves" (see Figure 2.2), which suggests that subtle connections between race and criminality surfaced even in a case where both the victim and the murderer were known to be white.

When the facts militated against threat constructions based on a black menace, reporters could not yet call upon a fully formed inventory of discourses constituting blacks as threats to the social order, particularly in the decades before the Civil War. In the Jewett case, for instance, Rosina Townsend's brothel was not a Five Points whorehouse that admitted blacks and other people of color, whether as workers or as customers. Instead, "The City Hotel," as it was known, catered for privileged white men who could appreciate Jewett's literacy and taste and, just as importantly, who could afford her services. The journalists who wrote the penny press papers identified with this elite clientele (even though they did not typically share their class position), which was also the very audience to whom the penny press was addressed.

Still, Richard Robinson's arrest for Jewett's murder caused ripples of suspicion and incredulity among white New Yorkers. How could a young man with a decent job, from an important Connecticut family—a young man with whom other native-born white men could easily identify—frequent a whorehouse, they asked? How could a white native-born man commit such a reprehensible crime? Although the *Sun* conspicuously avoided expressing any opinion about the identity of the murderer until after the trial ended, instead providing verbatim accounts of the trial proceedings, the *Herald* immediately rallied to Robinson's defense, repeatedly declaring his innocence.[16] Pointedly ignoring the abundant evidence presented at the trial (the murder weapon, for example, came from Robinson's place of employment, his cloak was found at the crime scene, and he was identified by both Townsend and other prostitutes as the last person to be seen in Jewett's room), Bennett obviously sympathized with this "remarkably handsome and intelligent young man" (11 April 1836: 2).

According to Bennett, it was impossible to even consider that such a man

Figure 2.2 "Descent of the police upon the negro den," from George Wilkes, *The Lives of Helen Jewett and Richard P. Robinson* (1849). Reproduced by permission of the New-York Historical Society.

might have struck a woman he loved with a hatchet and then set her bed on fire. "Would a young man of intelligence and refinement," Bennett growled, "barbarously slay a lovely and accomplished female, that adored and idolized him, as he would a wild beast of the forest?" (13 April 1836: 1). But in this case, none of the usual scapegoats would suffice. In response to acts of violence against female-owned and operated brothels, Rosina Townsend had been forced to adopt stringent security measures that narrowed the pool of possible suspects. Testimony by Townsend and other women who worked at the brothel confirmed that anyone who looked out of the ordinary would have attracted attention.

It being unthinkable that a white man like himself would have committed such an atrocity, Bennett turned his attention to the only other possible suspects: women themselves, who could be endowed with villainous racial attributes when the occasion warranted. Perversely, the protection scenario fosters this kind of misogyny, for the protector often harbors significant condescension toward the feminized victim—a condescension of the powerful toward the powerless that can easily be fanned into contempt, suspicion, and open hatred. Worthy or not, in other words, victims can also be despicable, particularly insofar as they can be represented as contributing to their own victimization. Viewing that always-suspect "female sexuality" as the true perpetrator of the crime" (Halttunen 1998: 203), Bennett argued that Jewett ultimately bore the responsibility for her own murder. After all, as Bennett put it, when Jewett was seduced, "in a moment of love and passion" to which women were likely to succumb, she had given up "the only ornaments and value of female character" (13 April 1836: 1). From the theft of her only ornaments and value, it was but a short step to her murder at the hands not of a man who both desired and detested her precisely because of her valueless status, but, according to Bennett, at the hands of some "deep laid conspiracy of female rivals —of the vengeance of female wickedness— of the burnings of female revenge" (13 April 1836: 1). The true cause of what he acknowledged to be an odious crime lay in the hazardous vagaries of female nature: jealousy, vengeance, and uncontrollable female anger. So intent was he on the theory of a female murderer, Bennett even speculated that the murder weapon—a hatchet—suggested a female perpetrator: "If a young man did compass the death of his paramour would he use a hatchet—coldly and deliberately? Would he not use poison or a dagger much more likely?" No, such a horrible act could only be attributable to "female vengeance or female design" (14 April 1836: 1); thus the murder of Helen Jewett was too "cold-blooded" to have been committed by a man. "The deliberate setting fire to a house," he fumed, "has more the character of female vengeance in it than that of the heedless passion of a youth of nineteen" (13 April 1836: 1).

Bennett, a major player in what David T.Z. Mindich describes as "the race and gender wars" (1998: 20) that typified Jacksonian democracy, drew upon a vast repertoire of stories from popular culture in scapegoating Jewett and other prostitutes, using widely available themes and motifs to support his indictment of female nature. On 11 April, he wrote: "The murdered girl was one of the most beautiful of her degraded *caste*. She was a perfect Millwood" (1836: 2). "Millwood" referred to the character of Sarah Millwood from George Lillo's morality play, *The London Merchant, or the History of George Barnwell* (1776), a play itself based on a popular seventeenth-century ballad, "The Ballad of George Barnwell." George Barnwell was an innocent youth drawn into a literal orgy of consumerism by "A gallant dainty dame" named Sarah Millwood, whose heartless pursuit of money led to both their executions. Like Millwood, Bennett implied, Jewett had spitefully sought to ruin her lover, whose singular failing was not malevolence, but weakness—the "heedless passion" of a youth of nineteen—in the face of sophisticated and scheming female charms.[17]

To articulate more clearly the link between female nature and brutality in his version of the protection scenario, Bennett drew a direct comparison between Jewett and dark-skinned savages, racializing gender in the process. In his third visit to Jewett's room in Thomas Street, he

> made a curious discovery of a painting in one of the corners. It was a piece of Indian history. It represented a beautiful female, in disorder and on her

knees, before two savages, one of them lifting up a tomahawk to give her a blow on the head.

(14 April 1836: 1)

The painting, which Bennett claims to have first noticed on his third visit to Jewett's room, was John Vanderlyn's painting, *The Murder of Jane McCrea* (1803–4) (see Figure 2.3). En route to join her fiancé (a Loyalist officer) in 1777, McCrea's party was ambushed by Native Americans. McCrea was shot and her body (purportedly found scalped and naked) was buried on "the morning of her intended marriage" (Colley 2002: 228).[18] In the painting, the crouching, pleading McCrea's pallid white skin forms the central visual contrast with the dark, muscular, and menacing Native Americans.

Bennett argued that Vanderlyn's painting was a spur to the vile imaginations of women like Rosina Townsend and Helen Jewett. What if, Bennett speculated,

a woman who had borrowed money or jewels of Ellen—if a rival in the same line of life, wanted to make away with such a troublesome competitor, would not that picture, perpetually hanging there—visible at all hours—suggest to female vengeance or female design—the very act that was perpetrated?

(14 April 1836: 1)

According to this logic, Vanderlyn's painting had, like novels and other forms of media, negative effects on women, in whom this visual representation cultivated a latent strain of malice. In a tortured metonymic process, women identified not with the victimized Jane McCrea, but with the dark savages about to murder her. Victim and victimizer were ultimately conflated, eliminating white men entirely as villains. To the androcentric imaginary, then, at the murky heart of female nature lay darkness as vicious and uncivilized as that of people of color. In fact, without the firm, civilizing hand of white androcentrism, women's primal nature threatened to trump the goodness and virtue assigned to whiteness.

The contradictions and inconsistencies within Bennett's argument were typical of the illogical nature of androcentric thought, particularly as this was expressed through the cult of dead womanhood. Women were too hot-blooded and too cold-blooded, they were too passionate and too calculating, too out of control and too controlling. Native-born white men, despite abundant evidence to the contrary, were heroic protectors, whose job it was to protect women not only from villainous non-white men, but also from their own natures.

In choosing between misogyny and racism, the racialized androcentric culture of the first half of the nineteenth century would time and again side with the gender of its own race. But in the absence of an appropriate male villain, unworthy or undeserving white women could easily be darkened and thereby transformed into the agents of their own demise. Thus, both victim and villain in the Jewett case, according to Bennett, were female. To his thinking, women

Figure 2.3 John Vanderlyn, *The Murder of Jane McCrea* (1803–4). Reproduced by permission of Wadsworth Atheneum Museum of Art, Hartford, CT. Purchased by subscription.

risked descending into savagery and barbarism when male supervision and control were absent and could not provide the stabilizing influence of "fixed principles" (12 April 1836: 1). No longer subject to the patriarchal controls exercised in earlier settings, women owned boarding-houses and brothels, they worked in factories and in shops, and young women did not always reside in male-headed households.[19] When bad things happened to these women, blame could be laid at their feet, for their having transgressed the social order, rather than at the feet of a social order and economic system that was at once placing increased demands on female labor and at every turn reinforcing women's dependency on men.

The *Herald*'s coverage of the Jewett murder foregrounded the contingency and misogyny inherent in the twinned notions of white masculine protection and white female true womanhood that formed the foundations for moral crusades in serialized news coverage. White journalists and cultural producers often went to the most extraordinary narrative lengths to produce crime suspects that looked nothing like *them* in order to suggest that the line between protector and villain was an inviolable one. For protectors can never be villains—to even hint that these categories may be interchangeable is to destabilize the entire protection scenario, not to mention the cult of true womanhood. To Bennett's thinking, and given the relatively fixed racial identity of the male villain in the Jewett case, the proper protector, he who could protect women both from their inherently flawed nature, as well as from the machinations of one another, was none other than the newspaperman. Bennett argued that newspapers could protect future victims through the magical power of publicity and its ability to force society to better monitor a social order now lacking the proper familial mechanisms. Of his newspaper, he wrote, "We shall follow the even tenor of the law as much as the Police. Police Justices are put into office for the purpose of ferreting out crime, and aiding to bring criminals to justice. Editors are just as useful in their day and generation." "We are the *avant-couriers*," he argued, whose duty it was to expose the sorry "state of society and morals—look at the hells and gambling houses permitted by this very Police—look at these houses of abandonment, protected by some of the very officers of justice, look at the whole frame of society which debauch young women and young men, and root out virtue and morality from among us" (15 April 1836: 1).

But Bennett's use of the protection scenario in the Jewett case was too contradictory, not to mention too divergent from the widely held belief among other penny papers that Robinson had in fact killed Jewett, to provide a solid foundation from which to launch a moral crusade. And the use of white women as both victims and villains further destabilized the ideology of whiteness that knit these protection scenarios together. Although the Jewett case in many ways made the reputation of the *Herald*, it was not until the death of Mary Rogers five years later that Bennett's moral crusade came into its own.

"Bruised by the mangling clench of Lust": The Death of Mary Rogers

Who that has loitered up Broadway,
    But mark'd her mid the evening light,
(Encircled by the young, and gay,)
With face that said her soul was right.
Ay—she was beautiful, in form,
    More than beautiful, in mind,
Affections, more serene and warm,
    We seldom in *her* station, find.
That form, so delicate and ripe,

Was bruised by the mangling clench of Lust,
The bosom that was virtue's type,
  Bedaub'd with slime, and foam, and dust.
Time will the bloody mystery bare—
  Lift the curst hand that grip'd her throat—
There did the foul Infernals lay her
  When they dragg'd her from the clotted boat.

(from "The Beautiful Segar Girl: A Sketch of Violation
and Murder," *Herald*, 21 September 1841: 2)

The youngest child of older parents, Mary Rogers and her mother Phebe left New London, Connecticut after the death of Rogers' father in a steamship explosion in 1834.[20] Following the migratory path of Helen Jewett, they moved to New York City, where they boarded with John Anderson, owner of a tobacco store at Broadway and Liberty, not far from Press Row. Hired by Anderson to work as a sales clerk, Rogers was one of a rare new breed of "butterfly catchers"—"beautiful young girls in cigar and confectionery stores" who were used "to attract an exclusively male clientele" (Srebnick 1995: 52). In 1839, Rogers stopped working for Anderson and she and Phebe set up a boarding-house at 126 Nassau Street.

Like Jewett, Rogers did not have the rudder of patriarchal guidance to help her navigate the waters of her new urban environment. Although she was not an orphan, her mother—and news accounts all emphasized Phebe's age and feebleness—proved unable to protect her beautiful young daughter from the unfamiliar dangers of the city. It was unlikely that Mary was a prostitute, but it was true that the Rogers lived at the margins of respectable New York culture. Boarding-houses operated by women ran the gamut from quasi-respectable middle-class establishments to brothels. By this reckoning, the Rogers establishment was barely respectable, since it catered mainly to sailors and working-class men, rather than the new category of more socially acceptable middle-class workers like Jewett's murderer, Richard Robinson. Contemporary accounts suggested that Mary moved freely among this class of men, which hinted that her behavior was not entirely reputable. To further call into question her social status, shop girls were a novel sight in the 1830s and certainly Rogers' presence in Anderson's cigar shop (and the phallic connotations of this were not lost on nineteenth-century observers), surrounded by journalists, city workers, and members of the less respectable sporting culture of the time, defied contemporary codes of proper sexual conduct and female behavior.

The *Herald*'s reporting alluded to Rogers' employment status, as well as a previous unexplained disappearance, but it took pains to stress that "the mother of Mary kept a respectable boarding house," where Mary Rogers "was the main stay of her mother. She did all the marketing, and conducted herself with the utmost propriety" (3 August 1841: 2). References to Rogers' virtue ran throughout coverage in August and September. On 8 August, the *Herald* observed that Alfred Cromeline, a boarder in Phebe Rogers' house, testified "during the whole time the witness has known her, [she has] borne an irreproachable character for chastity and veracity" (8 August 1841: 2). Rogers' fiancé, Daniel Payne, insisted that he never "knew of Mary keeping company with any person but himself, nor of any male person calling on her carnally. Her habits were domestic, and she was not in the habit of leaving the house except to visit her relations" (12 August 1841: 2). Bennett vigorously defended Rogers' honor and reputation, even going so far as to claim that an autopsy report had proved that "previous to this shocking outrage, she had evidently been a person of chastity and correct habits" (17 August 1841: 2). Cognizant of the fact that a moral crusade demanded a worthy victim, Bennett overlooked evidence and testimony to the contrary in his efforts to represent Mary Rogers as a virtuous and chaste young woman.

This focus on Rogers' purity also meant that she was not accorded the erotic interest devoted to Jewett. There was, of course, the now obligatory description of the dead body, but this one was printed nearly three weeks after the corpse had been discovered. And this description did not include poetic musings or erotic contemplation, focusing instead on the violence that ostensibly could be read off her corpse:

> The first look we had of her, was most ghastly. Her forehead and face appeared to have been battered and butchered to a mummy. Her features were scarcely visible, so much violence had been done to her. On her head she wore a bonnet—light gloves on her hands, with the long, watery fingers peering out—her dress was torn in various portions—her shoes were on her feet—and altogether, she presented the most horrible spectacle that eye could see.
>
> (*Herald*, 4 August 1841: 1)

This shift in focus—from prostitute to innocent and unambiguously worthy victim; from the corpse as object of erotic contemplation to the corpse as the text from which violence could be read—afforded the *Herald* a measure of respectability and credibility that it had lacked in its coverage of the Jewett murder. Rather than presenting eroticized descriptions of a prostitute that verged on the improper, thus permitting other editors to condemn Bennett's reporting, in covering Mary Rogers' death, the *Herald* fully adopted the language and style of a moral crusade in which the newspaper and its editor appeared as protectors of worthy white womanhood.

Rogers' line of work, like Jewett's, brought her into contact with many of New York City's literati: "she was said to have been admired by James Fenimore Cooper and Edgar Allen Poe [whose "Mystery of Marie Roget" was based on her death], among other luminaries" (Lardner and Reppetto 2001: 18) and she was well known to journalists in nearby Press Row. This familiarity heightened journalists' sense of outrage about her death and led them to emphasize their role as protectors. Rogers' social visibility accounted for some of the publicity that followed the discovery of her body on the banks of the Hudson River three days after her disappearance in July 1841. Ironically, Rogers' body was discovered on the banks of the Elysian Fields, a popular recreational destination for young women and men from New York City. The significance of the location would not have been lost on readers for whom this death would have appeared a morality tale about the dangers of leisure time activities for single women. Of course, the discovery of a floating body (female or male) was not an unusual occurrence, particularly in the hot summer months, when the combination of drinking and the proximity of saloons to the waterfront often proved lethal for working-class people.[21] Although the pages of the penny press frequently included brief notices about such unpleasant discoveries, Rogers' reputation as "the beautiful cigar girl," and her contact with journalists, writers, and politicians from her job at Anderson's tobacco shop, guaranteed a level of publicity beyond the obligatory mention of the recovery of a dead body.

When Rogers disappeared on 25 July 1841, Bennett situated this occurrence within a broader field of social anxieties about what could happen to women when the old patriarchal forms of protection were no longer in place. Rather than changing the attitudes and behaviors that encouraged violence against women, Bennett and his culture sought to apply more stringent behavioral codes to women and to fortify measures for male protection.[22] As he had in covering Jewett's murder, Bennett attached added cultural significance to Rogers' death by comparing it to the celebrated murder case of Elma Sands earlier in the century: "Nothing of so horrible and brutal a nature has occurred since the murder of Miss Sands, which murder formed the basis of the story of Norman Leslie" (*Herald*, 3 August 1841: 2).[23]

The Rogers case may have afforded Bennett a victim more worthy than Jewett, but the search for an identifiable villain proved equally complex. Numerous folk devils were offered up as the assassin of Rogers' virtue and her life: "'rowdies'—such men, for instance, as hang about the doors of low gaming public houses, wear flat brimmed hats, and affect an air of vulgar devil-may-care gentility" (12 August 1841: 2); "soaplocks or volunteer fire rowdies" (14 August 1841: 2); and "gamblers, blacklegs, soaplocks, and wicked portion of youth" (18 August 1841: 1). Those suspects conjured by Bennett were clearly drawn from the lowest ranks of the male social order: "soaplock," a term of condemnation typically applied to working-class youths for the hairstyle they sported, was linked to "rowdies" and "negroes." By 21 August, the racial elements of the mysterious suspect came into sharper focus: "The Lower Police have arrested a Negro, said to know something about the murder of Mary Rogers by a gang of negroes, and he is now in jail." Nothing came of this lead, and by September the *Herald* had settled on a suspect who was "a dark complexioned young man" (17 September 1841: 2).[24]

Where the Jewett case could not sustain a fully fledged crusade, coverage in the Rogers case was much more clearly organized around demands for reforms that purported to protect women from similar fates. According to the paper, institutions like the police were supposed to substitute for more traditional forms of patriarchal authority. Bennett had criticized the police during the trial of Richard Robinson—they were, he claimed, literally and figuratively in bed with the brothel owners—but in the Rogers case, the police were targets of his critique from the start. On 4 August, he wrote: "How utterly ridiculous is all this! It is now nearly a week since the dead body of this beautiful and unfortunate girl has been discovered, and yet no other steps have been taken by the judicial authorities" (2). Two days later, Bennett explicitly called for reforms to the police not merely to apprehend suspects, but to protect women from such a fate in the future: "Our Police department needs to be entirely changed. We want a different system, a new organization entirely" (5 August 1841: 2).[25]

In the name of Mary Rogers and the protection of women, Bennett launched a major crusade against a system of policing based on rewards and watchmen, arguing that "the true administration of public justice is shamefully neglected" (10 August 1841: 1). Not only should the public subscribe for a reward to find the killer of Mary Rogers, Bennett expressed the hope that "citizens will take the matter up, and call a meeting in the Park or elsewhere" (1). Throughout, the paper encouraged citizens to "take such measures as they shall deem proper . . . to effect the detection of the murderer or murderers" (12 August 1841: 1), at one point proclaiming that New York City had fallen into a "savage state, a place without law—and without order of any kind" (quoted in Srebnick 1995: 88). Such assertions may have flirted dangerously with vigilantism, but they also shored up the role of newspapers in society: "Really—really, the newspapers are becoming the only efficient police, the only efficient judges that we have" (9 August 1841: 2).

As a response to calls made in its own pages on behalf of a public for which it claimed to speak, the *Herald* organized a Committee for Public Safety, which held its first meeting on 11 August 1841. Two of the members of the Committee of Public Safety were crime reporters: William Attree, whom we encountered earlier as one of Jewett's clients; and Richard Adams Locke, crime reporter for the *Sun*. The Committee of Public Safety condemned the reward system upon which investigations were conducted. This system, the *Herald* raged, "offers an impunity to the rich ruffian, it holds a shield over the violator of female virtue, and in but too many cases, acts as the stimulant to outrages at which humanity shudders" (9 August 1841: 2). In the same editorial, Bennett ominously predicted that if Mary Rogers' alleged murder was not solved, "no woman will be safe, even under the protection of a husband or brother," citing other reports to prove that such attacks were on the increase.

A second crusade also followed from the Rogers case—this one eerily similar to the crusade against female brothel owners that emerged from the Jewett case. The discovery of Rogers' body had coincided with general social concern about the controversial practice of abortion. Indeed, that very July saw the first trial of Ann Lohman, who went by the professional name of Madame Restell. Lohman was a well-known abortionist who frequently advertised in the *Herald* (see Figure 2.4). In the fall of 1842, the woman who had kept the house in Hoboken where Mary Rogers was last seen made a deathbed confession that Rogers had died as the result of an abortion. Although a link between Restell and Rogers has never been established, the possibility that Rogers had had an abortion when

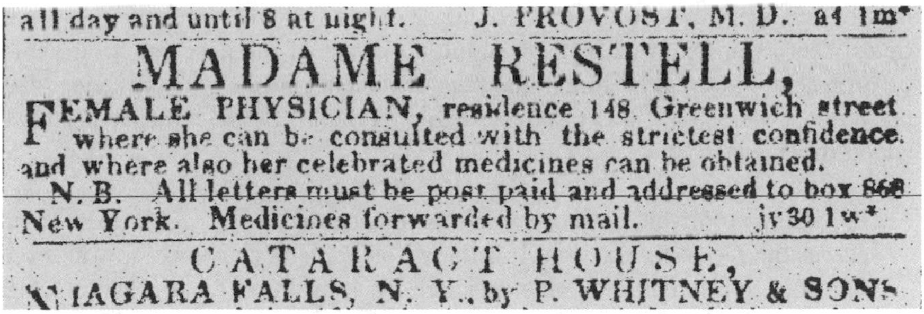

all day and until 8 at night. J. PROVOST, M. D. a4 1m*

MADAME RESTELL,

FEMALE PHYSICIAN, residence 148 Greenwich street where she can be consulted with the strictest confidence. and where also her celebrated medicines can be obtained.

N. B. All letters must be post paid and addressed to box 868 New York. Medicines forwarded by mail. jy30 1w*

CATARACT HOUSE,

NIAGARA FALLS, N. Y., by P. WHITNEY & SONS

Figure 2.4 Advertisement for Madame Restell, *New York Herald*, 4 August 1841.

she disappeared in 1837 and that she died as the result of a second abortion in 1841 was enough to connect Restell, Rogers, and abortion in the pages of the penny press. Rogers' name was invoked in public discussions about the law and Rogers' Connecticut relative Frederick Mather aided in its passage.[26]

As in the Jewett case, having failed to identify a non-white male suspect, the crusade against abortionists served up a female villain in the shape of female abortionists.[27] Again, anxiety converged around the sexual conduct and behaviors of women—who in an androcentric culture had little choice but to cater to male desires for non-procreative sex—rather than the sexual conduct and behavior of "respectable" white men like tobacco store owner John Anderson, who almost certainly had been Rogers' lover in 1836–37. In their history of the New York Police Department, Lardner and Reppetto observe that "Of all the statements taken by the magistrate's office after Rogers' death, his [Anderson's] was the only one never quoted or cited" (2001: 20), a suggestive oversight.

In the end, and as weeks turned into months, it gradually became clear that a murder might not even have been committed in the Rogers case. Rumors that Rogers' death may have resulted from an abortion began to circulate as soon as one month after her disappearance, and a deathbed confession a year later lent additional confirmation to this version of events. But Bennett did not let facts deter him from the moral crusade that followed Rogers' death. On 25 August, the *Herald* conceded that "Many people now begin to believe that Mary has not been murdered," but as late as 24 September the paper continued to describe it as a murder, on 17, 21, and 24 September publishing a series of woodcuts that purported to represent "the scene of the murder" (24 September 1841: 1). Having ascribed legitimacy to his coverage of Rogers' life and death even in light of evidence that contradicted his narrative framework, Bennett insisted on pursuing this particular moral crusade; one that would prove central to understandings of the role of newspapers in society and to the future of his paper in particular.

Institutionalizing protection

In justifying their secular acts of voyeurism and titillation in covering crime, journalists had to find a substitute for the language of redemption and salvation used by evangelicals to validate their attention to violence and other prurient topics. Editors and journalists were painfully aware of the need for a rationale for protracted coverage of individual acts of violence in their newspapers. The day after Jewett's body was discovered, for example, Bennett tacitly acknowledged these issues:

> We know no private circumstance that has caused such a sensation in our city as the recent transaction. It is the whole topic of conversation wherever one goes. It is horrid. It creates melancholy. It produces horror. Will it work a reform? Will it make the licentious pause?
>
> (12 April 1836: 1)

This passage brilliantly foregrounds the contradictory nature of crime news and the problems that serialized crime coverage posed for newspaper editors. Crime news was seen as being tremendously popular: "it is the whole topic of conversation." Helen MacGill Hughes later conceded that penny press crime news may have had "a salutary effect, but it is evident . . . that the entertainment, not the edification of the readers, was the reporter's intention" (1968: 188).

Like reading novels in particular, crime news was believed to have deleterious effects on readers, the least of which were melancholy and horror. At the same time, Bennett craftily linked his paper's coverage of this melancholic and horrible topic to what he argued were the positive effects of newspaper coverage: publicity and, presumably, prevention.

Newspapers were by no means the most respectable forms of communication during this era and readers of the penny press (rather like viewers of television at the end of the twentieth century) were frequently represented as an uneducated mass or mob. That serialized crime coverage had economic benefits for newspapers could not be denied. Intent on gaining political and cultural legitimacy and distinguishing their newspapers from the wider field of print media, newspaper owners and editors had to downplay these economic benefits in order to facilitate an understanding of newspapers as important cultural and political institutions, rather than as mere businesses intent on profit. Extensive coverage of crime and other "sensations" threatened to undermine the very public image that newspaper editors were cultivating. Expressing a sentiment that was by no means new in the 1850s, one critic of the penny press said that it "answers the purpose of a pepper-box for diseased or slow stomachs, but it affords very little food to a healthy organization" ("The Press": 1852: 365). Edgar Allen Poe used the occasion of Mary Rogers' death to criticize newspapers for creating "a sensation" rather than furthering "the cause of truth," adding that much newspaper writing "is of the lowest order of merit" ("The Mystery of Marie Roget" 1850a).

For a swiftly growing industry, badly in need of cultural legitimacy, episodic crime coverage lacked the seriousness and depth of purpose that the industry needed to attach to itself.[28] But where episodic crime coverage could not inform, educate, or uplift, serialized crime coverage followed the inspirational example of the evangelicalism from which it drew and argued that attention to crime in the pages of newspapers was somehow tantamount to prevention. As Stansell observes, "From its beginnings, the evangelical movement had concerned itself with urban poverty" (1987: 64). "Religious duty," moreover, "lay not just in responding to need—or vice—when it presented itself, but in actively ferreting out opportunities to minister to or struggle with the benighted souls hiding away in those dark urban places" (65).

Although newspaper editors were not interested in saving souls, they quickly recognized the narrative possibilities and economic incentives afforded by actively investigating, or "ferreting out," "those dark urban places." A narrative about a dead prostitute could make the most of the prurient elements of the story, while at the same time imbuing its fetishization of these details with a sense of higher moral purpose: identifying the murderer or publicizing the sinister path that had led Jewett to such a terrible end. Moral crusades that used dead women to call for the protection of the living thus allowed newspapers to use a widely devalued and hugely successful formula, elaborating on all the lurid and gruesome aspects of a crime, while at the same time masking the business imperatives that motivated such coverage. Rather than turning one's eyes from darkness and evil, newspapers insisted, one must confront them squarely. Thus exposed to the caustic light of public scrutiny, the horrors associated with industrialization would evaporate.

Writing from an androcentric perspective, for a white, largely native-born audience, editors and reporters like Bennett imagined a community of readers that was increasingly cohering around threats embodied by certain "others" (people of African descent, immigrants, and "fallen" women). The trick for editors and reporters was to prove that they were part of the solution and not part of the problem. They had to convince their imagined audience that they were protectors of that most vulnerable and valuable segment of the population (white women), rather than crass merchants who would sell the woes of others in order to make money. Protection scenarios and the resultant moral crusades allowed newspapermen to enhance their cultural role—to promote an understanding of journalists as acting in the interest of an imaginary public. The cult of dead womanhood allowed them to express their concern about the vulnerability of women, suggesting that rather than catering to the most vulgar and debased appetites in the name of profit, they were actually performing a public service.

The struggles over legitimacy that accompanied the emergence of serialized crime reporting thus used compromised dead white women to advance newspapers' own interests. The Jewett and Rogers cases both provided a platform for newspapers to promote a fairly grandiose view of the cultural and social role that they played in society, at times when the penny press was under attack from other, more established newspapers. Of his visit to the Jewett crime scene, Bennett wrote:

> I knocked at the door. A Police Officer opened it stealthily. I told him who I was, "Mr. B. you can enter," said he, with great politeness. The crowds rushed from behind seeking also an entrance.

"No one comes in," said the Police Officer.
"Why do you let that man in?" asked one of the crowd.
"He is an editor—he is on public duty."

(11 April 1836: 2)

The editor of the *Herald*, Bennett suggested, was a man of stature—a far cry from how the universally disliked Bennett was normally dealt with in New York society as well as from how the penny press was received by more respectable newspapers and magazines.

The debased status often conferred on the penny press appeared most dramatically in repeated attacks on the *Herald*, whose coverage of the Jewett case gave it a firm foothold in the field of newspaper production in 1836. As Elliot King (1994) has pointed out, the attacks in 1840–41 on the *Herald* that came to be known as the "moral wars" had their origins in earlier news coverage of the Jewett case, when the fledgling *Herald* first successfully and quite aggressively competed with Day's *Sun* and Webb's *Courier and Enquirer*. In May 1836, when coverage of the Jewett murder peaked, the penny press as a whole was being attacked by other papers in the city, as well as "the country papers," on the grounds of its immoral coverage of the crime. The *Commercial Advertiser* wrote:

We would rather see their columns filled with the dullest common places, or the most trivial records of overgrown beets and turnips—with wearisome disquisitions on anything or nothing; aye, or even with dull speeches on the floor of Congress, than with such matters however entertaining or exciting they may be, &c. &c.

(Quoted in the *Herald*, 29 April 1836: 1)

Bennett included this excerpt in his own column, where he offered the following tart response: "No doubt you would—no doubt whatever you would like to see us penny rascals, as dull and stupid—as flat—as lazy—as indolent—as insolent—as ridiculous as any of the larger papers in country." Rather than ignoring these critiques or defending his paper from attacks, Bennett turned insults like these into publicity stunts that allowed him to boast to his most valued audience: "TO ADVERTISERS.—The rapid increase of the *Herald* outstrips all calculation. We this day begin to strike off nearly *fifteen thousand copies per day*" (15 April 1836: 1). Instead of disguising the profit motive, Bennett flaunted it in the face of both his critics and his direct competitors.

When the *Montreal Morning Courier* observed "that the editors of that city, (New York) were feasting most gloriously upon the circumstances relating to the murder" (30 April 1836: 1), Bennett dismissed the writer as an "impudent blockhead," bragging that the *Herald's* city circulation had increased to 15,000 copies per day, and justifying coverage of Jewett's murder by pointing to its economic benefits. Within a week of initial coverage of the Jewett murder, the *Herald* "was selling out print runs of between 10,000 to 15,000 copies" (Cohen 1998: 28).

Although other reporters and editors soundly criticized Bennett's style and coverage—one described his second visit to Jewett's bedroom as the act of a "vampire returning to a newly found graveyard" (quoted in Lardner and Reppetto 2001: 13)—a desire to replicate Bennett's circulation figures left his critics in a somewhat awkward position. Since the *Sun* and the *Transcript* were devoting as much space to the story as the *Herald* (by 21 April, the *Sun* was boasting of 1,300 new subscriptions for home delivery), their criticisms smacked more of professional jealousy than any real ethical outrage. In a field driven by the dual needs for cultural legitimacy and profit, newspapers had little choice but to follow Bennett's lead.

However graphic or sensational his coverage may have been, had Bennett stuck to the business of reporting about crime, it is unlikely that the moral wars would have escalated to the extent that they did. But his persistent and frequently mean-spirited attacks on revivalism, Catholicism— the newspaper once dismissed the pope as "a decrepit, licentious, stupid, Italian blockhead" (quoted in Fermer 1986: 22)—and especially other newspaper editors escalated the tension between him and other newspaper editors, ultimately proving provocative in the very physical, masculinist terms of his day. In October 1835, Peter Townsend, an editor for the *Evening Star*, administered a public beating to Bennett (Crouthamel 1989: 26). A year later, Bennett was knocked down and caned by James Watson Webb, the editor and proprietor of the *Courier and Enquirer* and Bennett's former boss. And on 10 May 1836, in the midst of the coverage of the Jewett case, Webb assaulted Bennett for a second time.[29] Again, Bennett used the occasion to tout his paper.

> I am positive Webb is insane. From the remarkable success of the *Herald* and the visible decline of the *Courier & Enquirer* in popularity, influence and circulation, it is highly probable that he has lost his senses as rapidly as he ever lost his money in stock operations.
>
> (10 May 1836: 1)

The hatred other penny press owners and editors felt toward Bennett was expressed perhaps most eloquently by Day, who described Bennett as "the notorious vagabond Bennett; the veriest reptile that ever defiled the paths of decency' whose 'only chance of dying an upright man will be that of hanging perpendicularly upon a rope,'" (quoted in Fermer 1986: 28).

Just over a year before the death of Mary Rogers, in May 1840, tempers flared again, when Bennett described the disabled Parke Benjamin, the *Evening Signal*'s editor, as "half Jew, half infidel, with a touch of the monster," further asserting that Benjamin's lameness was the result of a "curse of the Almighty" (quoted in Fermer 1986: 97). Benjamin and Webb led a new attack on Bennett.[30] Inveighing against Bennett in their editorials, they also established committees to convince advertisers to withdraw their subscriptions, as well as to have the *Herald* removed from public reading rooms.

The moral wars that followed were really a clash between "the traditional and the new establishments—the old elite, on the one hand, and the new middle class and the would-be plutocrats, on the other"—a clash that was played out on the grounds of taste and morality (Tucher 1994: 119), specifically in regard to crime coverage.[31] The charge of moral turpitude leveled against Bennett was a familiar one. His competitors portrayed Bennett as a scandalmonger who subordinated his public duty as a newspaperman to the pursuit of profit. The moral wars did not immediately silence Bennett, but they did affect business. According to Mott, the *Herald*'s circulation dropped by a third in the wake of these attacks (1941: 237).

Mary Rogers' death thus occurred at an opportune moment for Bennett, allowing the *Herald* the chance to recover some legitimacy and, through its championing of a young, white, dead woman, perhaps regain some of the circulation it had lost. The *Herald*'s calls for improvements to public safety further shifted attention from its dubious reportage to the inefficacy of the police as an institution. And if it was never clear as to how improvements to the police would have prevented Rogers' death, that was beside the point, since saving young women was the excuse for, but hardly the point of, the crusades that followed.

Native-born victims

The at once ideological and institutional advantages of serialized crime coverage involving dead white women proved numerous. These protection scenarios tapped into very real anxieties on the part of their male audiences. Serialized crime coverage permitted newspapers to construct scenarios that featured editors and reporters as protectors of both the public and the public interest. Bennett's coverage of the Helen Jewett murder and the death of Mary Rogers illustrated that newspaper editors were eager to promote protection scenarios, as long as these included victims and villains that provided a suitable complement to the heroism of the newspaper as institution. According to this logic, women and any other worthy victims could be protected from the ravages of an industrialized society that threw them into dangerous proximity with darkened villains only through the combined and coordinated efforts of the police, who would detect and arrest criminals, and the press, who could publicize both crime and punishment as a warning to both the wicked and those who dared to think of wickedness.

As we have seen, women made for more popular subjects in murder cases than did white men. Although the 1841 murder of Samuel Adams by John C. Colt (brother of Samuel Colt, inventor of the revolver) was covered in some detail by the penny press, it did not fit into the narrative framework of the protection scenario and while it garnered much sentimentalized coverage it never developed into a moral crusade.[32] But dead women could be framed through narratives of protection that extolled the virtues of white masculinity on the part of both newspapers and the audiences they imagined for their cultural products. Dead women could be used to elicit sentimental responses from newspapermen and audiences alike. Better still, they could not talk back to their protectors, much less ever suggest that the protector and the villain were interchangeable. Live women, like Rosina Townsend and Ann Lohman, on the other hand, eking out livings outside the boundaries of a legal economy that excluded them, provided an androcentric culture with convenient scapegoats when the need arose: "criminals" whose actions were generally tolerated, but very swiftly criminalized when the occasion dictated. Hostility toward these women and people of color in general runs throughout the popular culture of this era. It was hardly coincidental that the riots of the 1830s were directed at two groups: black people and women who owned brothels.

As had by this time become conventional, only certain kinds of white, native-born women qualified as worthy victims in crime reporting, a tendency that still structures crime reporting of victims today. In the heterosexist universe of US culture, married and widowed women did not qualify as the subjects for crusades, probably because they were assumed to be under the protection of their husbands. And if their husbands murdered them, and then as now women were more likely to be murdered by intimates than by strangers, this particular challenge to the very foundation of masculine protection would not appear in the pages of the penny press. The central dogma of this culture was that white men were the protectors of white women. To call this into question was to open up a series of other questions about the victims of this social order. To even imagine, much less wage, a crusade against those who claimed protector status was thus impossible within this ideological framework.

As we saw in chapter 1, fears about interracial relationships, or amalgamation, caused anxiety in the episodic crime coverage of the 1830s and 1840s, thus hinting at the more overtly racist forms of threat construction that were to come. Although serialized crime coverage could not as yet produce black threats to white femininity, scenarios of protection organized around white male protectors contained a built-in tendency to blame people of color for corrupting white women and to seek non-white suspects for violent crimes. Thus, African Americans appear as the agents of corruption in Helen Jewett's biography; as the gangs of "negroes" who may have killed Mary Rogers; or as swarthy suspects as in the Rogers case. Perhaps because their acts of aggression and hostility toward women and people of color required some justification, the racialized androcentrism that came to flourish in the USA consistently represented communities of color in particular as bearing responsibility for their oppression. Although this victim-blaming tendency is more pronounced with regard to gender in serialized coverage of the 1830s, the general applicability of this to racialized others became more pronounced as the century wore on.

In the end, white newspapermen and the male audience they addressed in their papers had neither reason nor motive to question a worldview that predisposed them to think ill of women and people of color—to sentimentalize dead women, while criminalizing those who were alive. And although we tend to view crime news and other tabloidesque forms of news as feminized products aimed at a female audience, the *Herald*'s emphasis on financial news and political reporting showed that Bennett believed his male audience to be as interested in this sort of serialized crime news as it was in the goings-on on Wall Street or in Washington, DC. The racialized androcentrism upon which nineteenth-century culture was based, and the centrality of a protection scenario featuring white male protection of "worthy" white female victims, worked to ensure that neither black women nor men could be considered victims within this narrative form, no matter how innocent or how worthy they might be.

3 "The innocent cause of all these troubles"

Black victims of the 1863 anti-draft riots

In the fall of 1863, African Americans made destitute by the anti-draft riots that had occurred earlier that year filed claims for damages with the New York City Special Commission on Draft Riot Claims in an attempt to procure some restitution for the destruction of their belongings, their homes, and in some cases the lives of family members. Many recounted terrible stories about their encounters with racist mobs. James P. Black told of being stoned near his home by a mob that stole his valise and "called me a 'black son of a bitch'" ("Claim filed by James P. Black" 1863).[1] Charles Geichard, a sailor whose trunk was stolen, filed a claim for $50, reporting that "a large crowd armed with clubs took possession of the cart [upon which his trunk had been placed] and drove us off" ("Claim filed by Charles Guihard [*sic*] " 1863). Catherine Nichols, "the wife of Alfred Nichols who is at the war fighting for his country," filed a claim for ten dollars for the destruction of her property ("Claim filed on behalf of Alfred Nicholson [*sic*]" 1863). George Spriggs of 124th W. 19th street recalled being turned out of his home:

> the landlord told us on Monday that if we didn't get out of the house the mob would burn the house. My clothes were taken away from me in the street—a mob of 15 or 16 came up and two men snatched the clothes out of my hand—Then they said let's kill him—I ran away.
>
> ("Claim filed by George Spriggs" 1863)

Eugenia Brown, who also filed a claim for lost possessions, described how she was driven from her home by an armed mob. She had just enough time to gather her possessions "to take them away to a place of safety, but the same mob with others took them away from me on Grand and Baxter" ("Claim filed by Eugenia Brown" 1863).

Still clipped to these yellowed claims is stark evidence of the institutional reception granted to these narratives of victimization, in the shape of handwritten evaluations of individual claims. F.R. Lee, the claims officer who had been assigned to evaluate the validity of these cases, carefully labeled all claims made by African Americans as "coloured," subsequently dismissing them as "fraudulent" in a language that was moralistic and hostile to blacks. Of one case involving a white woman with a black husband and "two molatto [*sic*] children," Lee wrote, "This is a revolting case . . . In upon going in to the house I found an Irishwoman bloated with rum who claimed to be the mother of the black children . . . This claim should be rejected" ("Claim filed by Mary Cisco" 1863). George Spriggs' claim was rejected because:

> The testimony of this class of persons I confide should be received with much caution. In this case he fails to show that he was attacked by Rioters. In my opinion it is nothing more than a case of Highway Robbery (if he was robbed at all) and ought to be rejected.

Lee expressed the same skepticism about the claim of another, more affluent black, who had requested $121.00 for destruction of possessions and property: "He having gone to two different lawyers, and notwithstanding he is well recommended I believe him to be a great rogue, from the fact that he has sworn to a cool and deliberate *lie*, and he knows it" ("Claim filed by Robert N. Van Dyne" 1863), the lie being that his possessions had been stolen in the first place.

In case after case involving black claimants, Lee drew stark lines between rioters and those whites whose testimony contradicted African Americans' claims for compensation, despite the fact that rioters and looters were often the same. If Elizabeth Dewitt's articles were stolen, Lee observed, "it was not by rioters as it had been satisfactorily proven that none of the mob entered the premises" ("Claim filed by Elizabeth Dewitt" 1863). Similarly, Gilbert Mapes' statement, which asserted that he and his family had fled their home without taking their clothing because a large mob had gathered in the street, was dismissed because "there is no proof whatever of the rioters entering the house" ("Claim filed by Gilbert Mapes" 1863). In response to Catherine Nichols' claim on behalf of her soldier husband, Lee scoffed, "This is a sham . . . All the coloured people in the house left but during their absence, no mob attempted to enter the house . . . She is an associate of Emily Rell from the same house who got paid one claim and then put in the second" ("Claim filed on behalf of Alfred Nicholson"). Lee never entertained the possibility that rioters and neighbors were often one and the same.

Although some white women filed claims for damages based on the loss of wages of husbands who had been killed during the riots, only one black woman applied for damages she sustained as a result of her husband's lost wages. "The house was attacked by the mob," Mary Frazer wrote, "I was in the house when they commenced throwing bricks and stones. I then left and run for my life—my husband is a mulatto man afraid to come back" ("Claim filed by Mary Frazer" 1863). Frazer's claim for $15.50 was denied with no comment, although white woman Ann Garvey's claim for $5,000 for the death of her Irish husband, shot by rioters as he "was peaceably attending to his usual business avocations," was granted in full ("Claim filed by Ann Garvey" 1863).

Other institutions charged with aiding victims of the anti-draft riots shared this claim officer's hostile attitude toward black victims. A new ordinance was passed to raise $2 million to pay for substitutes or cash so that working-class New Yorkers could avoid the draft, but no public aid was offered to the black victims of the riots. A Merchants' Relief Committee, which received a great deal of self-congratulatory publicity from the mainstream press, raised $42,600 for black refugees, but the fund ran out before the onset of what was to be one of the coldest winters on record, leaving a black, largely female homeless population in dire circumstances. As for the criminal justice system, as Cook points out, "Only one of those who attacked or murdered negroes during the riots received a heavy sentence" and that single, heavy sentence was incurred solely because the defendant had also been charged with robbery (1974: 180).

The previous chapters have demonstrated how norms of race and gender were an integral part of both episodic and serialized crime coverage in the nineteenth century. In contrast to the predilection for dead white women that typified serialized crime coverage, this chapter shifts analytic focus onto how newspapers understood and covered victimization of African Americans. Since mainstream, mass-circulation dailies uniformly ignored black victims of the often violent life of the city, the following account turns to incidents and sources dealing with the collective victimization of African Americans in order to analyze how black victims were represented in the few instances where their victimization could not be ignored. Thus, this chapter looks at New York City newspapers' coverage of the violent crimes against African Americans that occurred during the 1863 anti-draft riots. Because of the extent of this criminal violence against blacks, the anti-draft riots constitute one of the few moments in the history of mainstream news where white editors and reporters had to cover African Americans as victims of widespread violence, rather than as potential villains and perpetrators of crime. In addition, because charges were brought against some rioters, and claims filed by those injured by the riot, the historical record of the riots offers one of the few instances in which African Americans' accounts of the violence can be compared to accounts that appeared in mainstream news.

New York City is not typically understood to be a place where terrorist crimes against African Americans occurred.[2] Even those scholars who study lynching do not include the black victims of the anti-draft riots as victims of lynching, although "the traditional definition of a lynching is a murder committed by a mob of three or more people" (Aptheker 1977: 9). The hangings, beatings, and drowning deaths of black people that occurred on those hot, awful days of the week of 13 July 1863 certainly fit that definition. This most violent riot in nineteenth-century America claimed at least 105 lives, 11 of which belonged to black men who were beaten to death, drowned, or lynched (Bernstein 1990: 5).[3]

The following pages draw from coverage of the riots that appeared in three New York City mainstream, mass-circulation newspapers: the *World*, the leader of the anti-abolitionist press at the time; the *Evening Post*, a paper with abolitionist sympathies that catered to New York City's elites; and the *Tribune*, which, under the editorship of Horace Greeley, was the most staunchly abolitionist of New York City mainstream newspapers and was itself singled out for physical attack by rioters. The *World* and the *Tribune* understood themselves to be direct political and economic rivals. As such, they effectively illustrate the conceptual parameters of cultural understandings of black victims in the mainstream. The *Evening Post* also supported abolition, but in a restrained manner more in keeping with the tastes of their affluent audience. The *Evening Post* further published at least three daily editions during the anti-draft riots and offered the greatest quantity of coverage.[4]

By way of conclusion, the chapter scrutinizes an ideological outgrowth of newspaper coverage of the anti-draft riots: the invention of the term "miscegenation." Although, as we will see, there were significant variations in how each of these three newspapers understood and framed black victims of violence, the limits of their comprehension appeared in their shared opposition to "amalgamation," or the procreative union of blacks (typically understood to be male) and whites (typically represented as female). Even those newspaper accounts most sympathetic to African American New Yorkers shared with their more blatantly racist counterparts discernible concern about this. This shared concern came to a head several months after the 1863 anti-draft riots. Although we tend to see the worst excesses of white supremacy (both material and ideological) as occurring in the south, just five short months after the anti-black violence of July 1863, two northern journalists employed by the *New York World* fanned the flames of racist sentiment that had driven the anti-draft riots. The anonymous pamphlet, *Miscegenation: The Theory of the Blending of the Races, Applied to the American White Man and Negro* (Croly and Wakeman 1863), that resulted from their efforts launched the word "miscegenation" into public discourse and disseminated it throughout the USA, where it became a central issue in the 1864 presidential election. In it, the two anti-abolitionist journalists posed as proponents of abolitionism, arguing throughout the document that "miscegenation," a neologism they had created, was the real and noble goal of the abolitionist movement and the Republican Party alike.

Analyzing these two events—victim narratives about African Americans and a discourse that invidiously sought to criminalize African Americans—allows us to make some important qualifications about how the dynamics of class, gender, and race were being developed by cultural producers in the field of newspaper production in the USA of the 1860s. Most importantly, in using dead white women to sell newspapers, journalists were not deliberately or even consciously constructing new gender norms and ideologies. Instead, this focus emerged from the wider ideological and cultural context in which reporting occurred—a context that disposed white men to take up positions as protectors of white women. In a culture so steeped in the logic of androcentrism, gender invisibly percolated through all aspects of social life. Like fish in water, journalists (and other members of society for that matter) affirmed and reproduced gendered social relations in largely unconscious and practical ways.

But if journalists reproduced gendered social relations, so to speak, and without even thinking about it, they were very much aware of race and racial distinctions, particularly during the Civil War. Where representations of women and African Americans in the case of both episodic and serialized coverage had effects that may have been unintentional or at least not directly planned, representations of African Americans in the anti-draft riots and the miscegenation hoax itself were calculated by racist newspapers like the *World* to have specifically racist ideological and material effects. This incident reveals newspapers and reporters to be knowing and seminal agents in the production and distribution of one of the most virulently racist discourses in US history, one that transformed the often inchoate logic of the rioters into a scientific discourse that became the foundation for the lynch narratives examined in chapter 4.

Bound by the racist logic that made the suffering of black women invisible, that saw in black men the consummate threat to the social and sexual order of things, newspaper accounts of the anti-draft riots and the miscegenation hoax that followed illustrate the cancerous institutionalization of a view of black masculinity that continues to plague US culture. Far from reflecting a public opinion or sentiment that they were in any case in the process of inventing, New York City newspapers played a determinative role in the origins and national dissemination of the racist logic used to justify white supremacy and white violence for years to come, constructing the oversexed black savage of white supremacist myths that concealed the all too practical savagery of white racism.[5]

Victims, blame, and silence in the *New York World*

With the exception of the *New York Daily News*, the *World* was the most pro-slavery, anti-abolitionist paper in New York City in 1863.[6] Originally begun as a religious daily by Alexander Cummings, in 1861 it bought Webb's *Courier and Enquirer* and was subsequently purchased by financiers belonging to the Democratic Party. Financed by pro-slavery owners, including the former pro-slavery mayor of New York City, Fernando Wood, edited by Democrat Manton Marble, the paper expressed open scorn and derision for the party of Lincoln. On the Sunday immediately preceding the riots, the *World* published an inflammatory anti-draft polemic, which would later be blamed by the *Evening Post*, the *New York Times*, and the *Tribune* for starting the riot. Casting the conflict as one between the "laboring population" and the federal government, a front-page story in Tuesday's *World* reported that there was careful and well-organized opposition to the draft: "It was generally understood throughout the district, on Sunday, that a forcible resistance was to be made to the draft. All the laborers who were liable to be drawn from 'the wheel of fortune,' volunteered their services" (14 July 1863: 1).

The immediate cause of the riots was the passage of the first federal conscription bill in US history, which ordered that all male citizens be enrolled for the draft in two classes.[7] Most controversially, a man could be exempted by paying a $300 fee or by providing a substitute. In New York City, which had a strong anti-war faction (the Peace Democrats), anti-abolitionist newspaper editors, known pejoratively as the Copperhead Press, had been fanning the flames of anti-abolitionist sentiment for months before the rioting began.[8] In New York

City, the first lottery was held on Saturday, 11 July 1863. For twenty-four hours, the city simmered quietly, but early on the morning of Monday, 13 July, the quiet was shattered. For the five days that followed, rioters took over the streets of the city. During the first hours of Monday morning, 13 July, rioters attacked government and police officials, looting buildings that housed munitions, but their attention swiftly turned to African Americans.

The *World* and other anti-abolitionist newspapers could not entirely ignore rioters' violent attacks on African American men. On Tuesday, a front-page story in the *World* admitted that "The riot also took the form of a crusade against negroes, and wherever a colored man was observed, he was chased, stoned, and beaten" (14 July 1863: 1). The *World* did not call for unprovoked attacks on blacks. Instead it sought to explain the rioters' behavior by arguing that abolitionists had indiscriminately and irresponsibly stirred up anti-black sentiment. According to the *World*, it was wrongheaded to think that blacks were fit for citizenship and, by arguing for such "unnatural" rights, the abolitionists had endangered the lives of all blacks.

The *World*'s treatment of violence against black men in particular fore-shadowed the arguments it would make in defense of lynching nearly three decades later. Reporting on two lynchings that occurred between 7 and 8 p.m. on 13 July, for example, the *World* hinted that African Americans had caused the violence against them. Of one lynching, the *World* observed, "a negro living in Cornelius street, near Bleecker, was set upon by the crowd, and, to protect himself, drew a revolver and shot a white man" (14 July 1863: 8). Pursued by the mob, according to the *World*, he was overtaken and then hanged. Immediately following this account, the *World* reported a second lynching under the subheading, "A Negro Shoots a Rioter and Is Himself Killed." These cases, grouped together in the pages of the *World*, suggested that armed blacks were roaming the city, shooting and injuring whites and thereby provoking lynching.

But other eyewitness accounts dramatically diverged from the *World*'s version of events, suggesting that even when the *World* reported attacks on blacks, the result-ant stories were made to conform to a narrative framework in which black men were made to bear responsibility for the violence against them. "A Negro Shoots a Rioter and Is Himself Killed," which referred to a case in which three blacks were walking home from work and specifically identified an African American as the cause of the ensuing violence, is a case in point. In contradiction to this arti-cle, and according to an eyewitness account of the crime, three black men were "coming along Varick Street, in a quiet manner, with their dinner kettles in their hands").[9] As they passed a liquor store, John Nicholson (an Irish bricklayer) and two other men suddenly attacked them. Two of the black men successfully evaded the mob, but men yelling "Kill the nigger!" and "Kill the black son of a bitch!" repeatedly beat one of the men ("Testimony of Mary Keirny, 1863"). In a final attempt to escape, the terrified man shot at Nicholson, slightly wounding him (Nicholson survived and was later arrested for his part in the lynching), thereby giving the last of the original trio enough time to flee the scene. At that point, a fourth black man, William Jones, also on his way home from work and unaware of what had transpired, tragically happened into the path of the mob. Jones was beaten and hanged, and then his body was set on fire by rioters. In direct contradiction to the *World's* report, the black man lynched by the mob was not even the same man accused of shooting and wounding Nicholson.

Framing these stories in terms of armed black resistance, the *World* portrayed a skewed picture of the ongoing violence. In place of the reality of a situation in which laboring men and women of color were being stripped of their possessions, driven from their homes, tortured, and then brutally murdered, the *World* depicted armed and dangerous black men who were lynched because of their attacks on white men. By falsely reporting that the mob had killed black men who had attacked whites first, the *World* sought to restore reason to acts of white violence and torture.

In the few instances where the *World* depicted black victims, they were described in the broadest journalistic strokes. During the week of the riot as well as the week following it, the *World* avoided describing black victims of the riot, who remained both nameless and faceless and were referred to only as "negroes" or "colored people." It was true that many black men fled the city, never to return. As Harris observes, "By 1865, the black population had plummeted to just under ten thousand, its lowest since 1820" (2003: 286). Yet newspapers had ample access to a significant population of African Americans, who had sought refuge in police station-houses throughout the city.

Nor did the *World* carry a single story about the widespread looting and destruction of black property and institutions serving black people, although there were brief references to these acts: "the colored church, corner of Marion and Prince streets" was attacked by a mob of two hundred, the Good Shepherd's Home for "the accommodation of aged and infirm colored people," between Sixty-fourth and Sixty-fifth Streets and between First and Second Avenues was similarly assaulted, and a crowd gathered menacingly in front of "the colored public school in Raymond Street" (15 July 1863: 1). Beyond these brief descriptions, the paper did not comment on the racialized nature of these assaults on black property and institutions, nor did it knit these interrelated accounts into a coherent narrative about anti-black violence as it did in the case of attacks on the military or thematized coverage of mob attacks on the *Tribune* building. In fact, in a number of cases, the *World* did not even mention why rioters had attacked particular buildings. In the case of attacks on the Thirty-fifth Street station-house, for instance, stormed by rioters seven times on Tuesday, the *World* never mentioned that these repeated attacks occurred because of the presence of African American refugees in that station-house.

By the third day of rioting, the *World* conceded that, "No negro is safe anywhere. Negro houses everywhere are sacked, straggling colored men murdered, and in one or two instances they have been chased off the docks" (16 July 1863: 1).[10] Yet even this brief acknowledgment of the targets of the violence was accompanied by a statement that laid blame for acts of violence at the doorstep of the abolitionist press "whose shoulders bear the guilty burden of inciting these riots" through their provocation of "the popular passions." "Negroes," Marble fulminated on the editorial page, "are cruelly beaten in New York because mock philanthropists have made them odious by parading them and their emancipation as the object to which peace first and the Union afterward, with the lives of myriads of Northern men, are to be sacrificed" (16 July 1863: 4). According to the *World*, African Americans were victims not of the mob, anti-abolitionists, or white supremacy, but of the

> radical presses, whose lawless, reckless speech, and whose [hold?] upon the President at Washington to protect pernicious doctrines have been the cause of the great civil struggle waging on other soil, and the forment [*sic*] and cause of the riot raging among our homes.
>
> (15 July 1863: 4)

The abolitionist press, according to Marble, had created the mob and, by provoking the white laboring population beyond countenance and belief, was singularly responsible for the resulting pogrom against blacks.

For the *World*, the conflict boiled down to a struggle over the manner of white masculinity capable of protecting a social order grounded in white privilege. In this ideological combat among those groups of white men who would claim social status as protector, the *World* repeatedly held papers with abolitionist sympathies to blame for the violence against African Americans. This logic was plainly at work in another editorial, entitled "Fighting for the Negro," in which Marble compared Republican calls for freeing the slaves to arguments made during debates about the annexation of Mexico. The annexation of Mexico, he argued, was rejected, because "the addition of a mongrel race, part Indian, part negro, and part Spanish, to the population of the United States would, it was thought, be a fatal error, as it was not fitted for, nor capable of self-government" (14 July 1863: 4). Similarly, suffrage for blacks in the USA was doomed to fail, first because of "the incompetence of the negro" and "second, the refusal of the white man to fight for such an object." According to Marble, "The instincts of the people are never wrong, and the instinct of this people is unalterably fixed in placing government in the hands of the white race alone." The editorial forebodingly concluded, "We therefore warn our Republican friends not to let the 'nigger' in the fence poke out his head too soon" (14 July 1863: 4).

This sort of argument quickly became a theme in the *World*'s coverage of unfolding events. One eyewitness saw a crowd chasing an African American on the first day of rioting. Members of the crowd were shouting "'Down with the bloody nigger!' 'Kill all niggers!'" This passerby continued,

> Never having been in New York before, and being totally ignorant of the state of feeling with regard to negroes, I inquired of a by-stander what the negro had done that they should want to kill him? He replied civilly enough—"Oh, sir they hate them here [because] they are the innocent cause of all these troubles."
>
> (quoted in Cook 1974: 77)

The belief that blacks were the "innocent cause of all these troubles" reflected a racist common sense that would be repeated again and again in the century to come. This logic suggested that because African Americans were understood to be the passive vehicles for abolitionist politics (all agency being ascribed to whites, a move that effectively erased blacks from the multiracial abolitionist movement they in fact led), they could not be held accountable for white abolitionists' political views and agendas, although some white men could understand why other, less well informed white men might be angry at blacks. Blacks being understood as incapable of self-determination, moreover, the cause of the troubles had to be those white men who supported abolition and the war effort. Blacks, and therefore sentiment against them, had been "stirred up" from the outside —from what would again and again be described as external or outside agitators. In the century that followed, arguments denying black political agency were to be invoked constantly, blaming abolitionists, socialists, communists, student organizations, civil rights activists, and lawyers in their turn for having agitated a population of blacks that racists considered to be inherently passive, docile, and incapable of organizing on their own behalf.

Incompetent, unfit for self-governance, the *World* depicted blacks as having been led astray by Republicans who "seem to think that the negro race in the Southern States is either more advanced or more capable of improvement than the Mexican" (*World*, 14 July 1863: 4). Blacks should not be blamed, the editorial argued, because to think them capable of making any kind of rational political decision was a categorical error—the instincts of white people were right (in contrast to abolitionists, "the people" were "strictly philosophical reasoners"). "A phrenologist might as well attempt by a thump to develop a boy's reverence," the *World* continued, "as an abolitionist to argue this belief [in white supremacy] out of the community (14 July 1863: 14). Blacks thus were victims not of the mob, but of white abolitionists who only pretended to care about their freedom and their rights.

The depiction of the rioters as having some justification for their violence was reinforced by the *World*'s efforts to downplay the violence against blacks that was occurring on the streets around it. On Tuesday, the paper included a single, brief mention of attacks on African Americans:

> Three negroes were killed by the boys about the Fulton market, and left dead upon the pier adjoining Fulton ferry. In the districts where negroes live most numerously crowds went through the streets stoning the colored people.
>
> (14 July 1863: 1)

This reference was immediately followed by justification for these attacks, as well as the abolitionists' culpability for provoking the mob's ire. One member of the crowd, the *World* reported without comment, said

> I don't know that the niggers themselves is responsible for this here trouble, but by God there is a war aboat 'm, damn 'm, and we'll pound 'm. It's the

abolitionists that have been pushing matters eternally, and we won't stop it. We'll pound the God damn abolitionists as well as the niggers.

(14 July 1863: 1)

Blacks may have not been directly responsible, the report suggested, but a war waged on their behalf was. In this twisted scenario, blacks (rather than the institution of slavery) were held directly responsible for the draft and indirectly for their own suffering. If they had not been so impossibly simple-minded, the *World* suggested, they would have understood that advocates of slavery—not those who sought to abolish this institution—had their best interests at heart.

The abolitionists, the *World* concluded, had promised African Americans protection, but had delivered hatred and violence. Abolitionists, by this calculus, were false protectors and the radical press was staffed by cowards, feminized would-be protectors, who hid behind the victims of their reporting:

> It might have been supposed that the editor of the *Tribune*, trembling all day long in the safe umbrage of a friendly restaurant, and escaping at last under cover of the darkness to his home, might have been led by these hours of seclusion to fling away the torch he had so long and so thoughtlessly brandished. It might have been supposed that the editors of the *Evening Post*, making their office a fortress, and cowering under the shelter of policemen detailed to protect their press and persons at the expense of the poor orphans of a humbler race, who were thus abandoned to the rage of a furious mob, would have learned how perilous a thing it is to persist in injustice, in calumny, and in slander.
>
> (15 July 1863: 4)

In effect, it was the abolitionism expressed by the *Tribune* that "has done more than any other agency to incite the antipathy to the negro race which is working out such terrible results in the streets of New York to-day" (15 July 1863: 4).

That "the poor orphans of a humbler race" were unsafe because of the racist proclamations of pro-slavery newspapers was a thought never entertained by the *World*. Neither Marble nor his reporters were at all aware of the irony of their argument: one that at once condemned violence against blacks, while in the next breath gave that same violence new life. Through its openly racist reporting and inflammatory editorials such as "Fighting for the Negro," the *World* persevered in giving voice to racist fears about the threat posed by the dwindling black population in an unapologetically racist language. On Friday, for example, the paper described the "hegira of negroes from the city" in the following fashion:

> In some parts of the city, however, where they are thickest, they are to be seen still in large numbers. On West Broadway there are apparently so many that they have little fear of a mob. During the afternoon they were not so careful to secrete themselves, in the lower part of the city.
>
> (17 July 1863: 1)

The language of this report bears witness to the *World*'s attitude toward the black population. These were not worthy victims, its language suggested, but a kind of infestation that like locusts or some other undesirable insect thickly covered certain areas of the city and was so bold that it did not even bother "to secrete" itself in the lower, more abject regions of the city.

Rioters, who attacked specific sites in the city that symbolized black reproduction, shared the belief that the black population was some kind of noxious infestation. At four o'clock on Monday afternoon, a crowd had gathered outside the Colored Orphan Asylum at Fifth and Forty-third. The 237 children who lived in the Asylum were evacuated through a back door, while the rioters yelled, "Burn the niggers' nest" and "Down with the niggers" (quoted in Cook 1974: 77). Not a single mainstream newspaper reported these epithets, although they were repeated by a number of eyewitnesses deposed at the indictment of rioters.

The burning of the Colored Orphan Asylum posed some problems for the *World*'s framing of events. First of all, the violence of the mob was directed at terrified children, none of whom was older than twelve. The property destroyed, moreover, was owned not by the demonized anti-slavery government, but by a charitable institution that had been specifically organized to care for orphaned African American children, who were not accepted by the mostly Catholic-run orphanages in the city.

In the case of the burning of the orphanage, the *World* further could not resort to stock arguments about the cause of the riots. The *World* defended the rioters by arguing that the draft was forcing white men to fight for an Emancipation that "would compel the white laborer to *leave his family destitute and unprotected while he goes forth to free the negro, who, being free, will compete with him in labor*" (*World*, 13 July 1863: 4, original emphasis). To the *World*'s thinking, white workers were being forced into poverty and debt in order to protect black workers who would then travel northward to steal their jobs. According to this line of anti-abolitionist discourse—soundly debunked by historians like Iver Bernstein and Leslie Harris—attacks on black men were an inevitable if undesirable outcome of the draft, but even the *World* could not incorporate the attack on the Colored Orphan Asylum, not to mention attacks on small children, into such a line of reasoning. The *World* could not, for example, argue that attacks on orphaned children resulted from the righteous anger of wronged white working men and women without revealing the genocidal logic of those who supported slavery and those who would burn an orphanage. Nor could it argue that the burning of the orphanage was in any way a response to the Conscription Act. Instead, when confronted with an event that so directly contradicted its ideological position on the nature and causes of the riots, the *World* brushed it off with a single sentence, noting tersely at the end of one paragraph, "The Colored Orphan Asylum was burnt" (14 July 1863: 2).

"Men who had no fault": The *New York Evening Post* and black victims

> To-day the proudest city in the land
>> Has been convulsed with riots! It is true
>> That men who dared their simple duty do
> Met arson, death, rapine on every hand;
> And men who had no fault, save that their God
>> Had given them a skin of dusky hue,
>> Under the feet of reckless fiends were trod.
> And treason shakes the city through and through.
> And this the greeting that we send to those
>> Who've fought and bled on many a gory field,
>> And now at last in triumph have appealed
> For help, that they may surely crush our foes,
> What damning blots are these upon thy name;
> For shame, New York! Ten thousand times for shame!
>
>> (*Evening Post*, 14 July 1863, first morning edition: 1)

The *Evening Post*'s coverage differed in important ways from that of the *World*. On the second day of rioting, the newspaper prominently placed this poem on its front page, casting the rioters not as wronged laboring men and women, but as "reckless fiends." From the first day of rioting, and in distinct contrast to the *World*, the *Evening Post* cast blacks as victims of the violence: "About nightfall a negro was seized by the mob and hanged in Clarkson street [William Jones]; and other colored citizens were assailed in various parts of the city and roughly used" (second edition, 14 July 1863: 1). The *Evening Post* understood the causes for blacks' suffering to be twofold: a mob for which the newspaper offered no apology and the anti-abolitionist papers' inflammatory discourse about blacks as the cause of economic and social problems that had been exacerbated by the war. The *Evening Post* did not blame "the unoffending negroes of the city" (first morning edition, 17 July 1863: 4) and, itself sympathizing with abolitionist politics, did not see abolitionism as the cause of the riots.

The *Evening Post* devoted more coverage than the *World* or even the *Tribune* to those blacks who had fled to police station-houses to avoid the mob. A reporter from the *Evening Post* visited a police station-house in order to talk to black refugees about their plight. Even here, the newspaper shared a wider cultural condescension toward blacks. In an article entitled "The Colored Refugees of New York: A Visit to the Police Headquarters," of the roughly 200 African Americans crowded into the Police Headquarters at 800 Mulberry Street, the reporter noted: "The majority of these were women and children. Many families being apparently represented only by the female portion and the 'pickaninnies'" (first morning edition, 18 July 1863: 1).[11] Not just women or children, the refugees are comprised of a "female portion" and "pickaninnies," a word used exclusively (and derisively) in the USA to refer to African American children.

The reporter, however, did not see these refugees as wholly unworthy: they were "remarkably calm and cheerful in their demeanor." "We doubt," continued the reporter, "if whites of any race would be capable of bearing with such equanimity what has fallen to the lot of these poor people." This equanimity resulted from their contact with Western religion: "The secret of their contented appearance must be found in the Christian resignation to misfortune and trustful hope in the future, characteristic of the African race." As a result of the combination of Christian values and intrinsic African cheerfulness, "Their gratitude to those who have protected them is boundless." Not surprisingly, this reporter did not register the despair that underlay what one elderly minister of the African Methodist Bethel Church on Thirtieth Street told him, after expressing a "gratitude [that] was unmeasured." When the white reporter conveyed his belief that "we thought his race had a hopeful future before them," the black minister responded, "Yes . . . in the next world" (first morning edition, 18 July 1863: 1).

Where the *World* saw blacks as victims only insofar as their white protectors (abolitionists) were really villains, and even given this scenario, the constant emphasis on armed resistance made their innocence always already suspect, the *Evening Post* saw blacks as worthy victims because of their docility, their thankfulness, and their lack of "anything like vindictiveness towards the authors of their troubles" (first morning edition, 18 July 1863: 1).

[One] old man could hardly find words to express his gratitude to those who had afforded him protection. Over and over again did he speak of the kindness with which he had been treated by the officers and men since he had been at the station house.

(first morning edition, 18 July 1863: 1)

Like the title character of *Uncle Tom's Cabin* (1852/1966), African Americans were worthy victims insofar as they repeatedly performed their gratitude.

Despite its less plainly racist language, the *Evening Post* carried even fewer reports about attacks on black men than did the overtly racist *World*, despite the fact that it published three daily editions during the riots.[12] Moreover, although the *Evening Post* featured news reports about African American refugees, not a single reference to blacks appeared in its editorial pages. On the second day of rioting, editor William Cullen Bryant spoke of the humiliation caused by "the black deeds which yesterday disgraced the city" (third edition, 14 July 1863: 4), although he did not elaborate about the nature and object of those deeds. Condemning the *New York Herald*'s championing of the laboring classes —its assertion that the riot represented "*Popular* opposition to the enforcement of the conscription"—and the *World*'s claim that the riot was "a tremendous uprising against the draft"—the editorial instead depicted the rioters as "scoundrels who went about insulting women, robbing houses and turning little innocent children out of doors" (third edition, 14 July 1863: 4). The political debate carried out in the *Evening Post*'s editorial pages thus excluded any reference to the role that skin color played in the riots.

"Why are negroes indiscriminately assailed and beaten?" The *New York Tribune*

Having already earned the longstanding enmity of anti-abolitionist editors like Manton Marble, editor Horace Greeley and the *Tribune* became targets of the rioters' wrath during the riots. The *Tribune* building was stormed by rioters on Monday and, along with the nearby *New York Times* building, had to be protected by troops for the remainder of the week.[13] In contrast to the *Evening Post* or the *World*, the *Tribune* alone provided serialized coverage of the mob's violence against African Americans. Beginning with its first day of coverage, the *Tribune* chronicled what one column heading described as "Assaults upon Colored People":

> As if by preconcerted action an attack was made upon colored men and boys in every part of the city during the day, crowds of from 100 to 500 persons hunting them like bloodhounds. Several inoffensive colored men were dragged off the city cars and badly beaten, while a number were taken from carts and drays which they were driving and terribly maltreated. A small colored boy, about 9 years old, was set upon and hunted at the corner of Broadway and Chambers street by the mob. He jumped on a two-horse wagon that was passing by, when stones and sticks were hurled at him from every quarter. We believe the poor little fellow escaped.
>
> (*Tribune*, 14 July 1863: 1)

Unlike anti-abolitionist newspapers, the *Tribune* did not interpret the attacks on blacks as being unorganized, spontaneous, or somehow accidental. Rather, the paper understood these attacks as part of a broader, more systematic assault on the rights and persons of African Americans. The *Tribune*, moreover, reported on black victims in a language that stressed their innocence: "inoffensive colored men were dragged off," they were "terribly maltreated," a "poor little fellow" was "hunted" by an angry white mob. The *Tribune*'s depiction of black refugees was similarly less racist than that of rival papers:

> Many refined and well-educated women (we might say ladies, if the title was not so often abused), with their bright and intelligent children were brought down from the neighborhood of West Forty-eighth and Fifty-first streets, and Sixth and Seventh Avenues.
>
> (21 July 1863: 8)

Unlike the happy-go-lucky "female portion" and "pickaninnies" of the *Evening Post*'s coverage, these were "refined and well-educated women"—ladies, in fact—with "bright and intelligent children."

Nevertheless the *Tribune*, like the other newspapers herein examined, overlooked black female victims and their dire economic circumstances, as did many later historians, who accepted the belief that the mob "demonstrated a certain savage chivalry. Only black men were beaten or killed; black women were usually not molested" (Cook 1974: 83). Yet black women suffered most acutely in the aftermath of the riots. Stripped of their possessions, homeless, often left to care for children and the elderly (black men having been driven off during the riots, many of them never to return), black women were the most marginalized fraction of a marginalized, impoverished labor force. No newspaper invoked a protection scenario or any wider language of protection around black women, and this absence, more than any other aspect of anti-draft reporting, underscored the racism at the heart of a white protectionism invested solely in white female victims.

In contrast to other mainstream newspapers, the *Tribune* did report assaults on black children. Where the *World* ignored and the *Evening Post* downplayed the symbolic and material significance of the destruction of the Colored Orphan Asylum, the *Tribune* not only gave the event its own column heading, it also provided a more detailed description of the attack: "The infuriated mob, eager for any outrage, were turned that way [toward the Asylum] by the simple suggestion that the building was full of colored children. They clamored around the house like demons, filling the air with yells" (14 July 1863: 1). The *Tribune* also hinted that rioters knew that their behavior was particularly execrable in this case—"a few of the less evil disposed gave notice to the inmates to quit the building"—and that "The sight of the helpless creatures stayed, for a moment, even the insensate mob," giving the children enough time to escape.

As the first reported act of violence against blacks in the city, the highly symbolic nature of the attack on the Colored Orphan Asylum was not lost on Greeley. Where both the *World* and the *Evening Post* very briefly mentioned the burning of the Colored Orphan Asylum, the *Tribune* issued the following critique:

> The catalogue lacked but one atrocity to prove itself matchless in brutal villainy in the whole world's history of even mob atrocity and violence; and so this mob—these amiable gentlemen—before they were content to rest their tired heads upon their innocent pillows, added this last and crowning item to the Christianlike list of their Good Samaritan deeds—*they deliberately set on fire, over the heads of the terrified and screaming children, an Orphan Asylum.*
>
> (14 July 1863: 1, original emphasis)

For the *Tribune*, this act of violence against innocent, orphaned children and what victims could be more innocent and deserving of protection than parentless children?—defined the essence of the mob.

Greeley was alone in arguing that the understanding of the violence as being anti-draft was fundamentally incorrect:

> It is absurd and futile to attribute this outburst of ruffianism to anything else than sympathy with the Rebels. If, as some pretend, it results from dissatisfaction with the $300 exemption, why are negroes indiscriminately assailed and beaten almost or quite to death? Did *they* prescribe this exemption? On

the contrary, are they not almost uniformly poor men, themselves exposed to the draft, and unable to pay the $300. What single thing have they done to expose themselves to this infernal, cowardly ruffianism? What can be alleged against them, unless it be that they are generally hostile to the Slave-holders' Rebellion?

(15 July 1863: 4)

According to Greeley, the riots were plainly "a diversion in favor of Jeff. Davis and Lee," an opinion confirmed by the epithets of "'nigger,' 'Abolition,' 'Black Republicans'" declaimed by the orators addressing the crowd.

Like the *Evening Post*, the *Tribune* also depicted the human cost of the riots by reporting on the "colored refugees."[14] But in contrast to the *Evening Post*'s focus on the behavior and conduct of the refugees at the police station-house, the *Tribune*'s story about "The Colored Refugees" recounted individual tales of victimization and narrow escapes from vicious mobs. Nevertheless, it shared the *Evening Post*'s view that the suffering of the black refugees was ennobling, a view popular during the era, but only possible from the perspective of those who can choose not to suffer: "He who reflects upon the situation of the negroes during the week of riot, cannot fail to see something of sublimity in their carriage, something of grandeur in their undaunted tranquility" (23 July 1863: 4). Offering further elaboration of this point, the account continued:

> Notwithstanding their misfortunes, sufferings and losses they are calm and cheerful. They are not unconscious of the dangers from which they have escaped, nor of the difficulties which surround them, but they have a strong faith in the power and justice of God. While they express the deepest gratitude to their benefactors, they show no spirit of vindictiveness toward the rioters, who with torches, halters, and firearms drove them from their homes.

(21 July 1863: 2)

For blacks and women alike, suffering could have positive effects, and in this instance, blacks were appropriately generous in their forgiveness and grateful for their rescue.[15] Of course, housed in police stations, hunted by mobs, African Americans had no choice but to appear forgiving and grateful.

Its understanding of the riots as being specifically anti-black and its depiction of black victims as in fact victims distinguished the *Tribune*'s coverage from that of other mainstream newspapers. Yet however progressive the *Tribune*'s coverage may appear when contrasted to other dailies, it shared underlying assumptions about whiteness and sexuality that prevented it from understanding the sexualized nature of the violence aimed at blacks, a theme that ran throughout African Americans' and other eyewitnesses' accounts of the violence.

"Then They Built a Fire in the Street to Burn Him"[16]

Despite important differences in the field of newspaper reporting, as well as the politics of the newspapers themselves, the system of racialized androcentrism operative in the north meant that deeply racist conventions of reportage cut across political and ideological divides in newspaper coverage of the anti-draft riots. Most important among these conventions was the absence of accounts that represented the extent to which opposition to interracial relationships of all kinds lay at the heart of the violence. No paper referred to the fact that the mobs consistently attacked symbolic and material sites of interracial social life. "All the hotels and restaurants in that section [the Second Precinct] having colored help were threatened"; cars and omnibuses (which were not segregated) were "scarched for colored people, and any discovered were set upon and beaten" (Barnes 1863: 34); and houses like those owned by Mrs. Johnson in the Fourth Ward, and which were rented "to negroes" (Barnes 1863: 39) were stormed, looted, and burned. Boarding-houses, dancehalls, and bars that catered to black customers also were attacked, as were more respectable businesses like hotels and restaurants that hired black employees. Referring to the fact that "the mob seemed to have vented all its anger" on Monday "between Twenty-eighth and Twenty-ninth Streets" (third edition, 14 July 1863: 1), like the *World*, the *Evening Post* neglected to mention the reason for such awful deeds: the area under assault was home to a significant population of blacks. Rioters thus "took advantage of the chaos of the Draft Riots to attempt to remove all evidence of a black and interracial social life from the area near the docks. White dockworkers attacked and destroyed brothels, dance halls, boarding houses, and tenements that catered to blacks" (Harris 2003: 283). These attacks on interracial social life underscored the fact that the riots were as much about what whites perceived to be the effects of abolition as they were about the draft itself.

The *World*, which had the greatest stake in representing the riots as "anti-draft" rather than anti-black, only hinted at some of the sexual anxieties that motivated attacks on what Harris calls "black and interracial social life." At one point, the paper observed in passing:

> Not only the negroes, but the Chinese who vend bad tobacco and poor cigars, have become obnoxious to the mob, and in the Fourth ward, where the Chinese congregate, their quarters have been sacked and ruined. Some were married to white women, and this sort of amalgamation was not considered much better by the rioters than that of the out-and-out blacks.
>
> (15 July 1863: 1)

The theme of amalgamation was more evident in coverage of the arrest of "Mr. Andrews, of Virginia," who was arrested for his role in exhorting the mob to violence. While the *World* described Andrews as a "rank secessionist and a copperhead of the worst order," its harshest criticism was reserved for his personal life: "Andrews came to this city almost five years since, most of which time he has lived with a notorious negro courtesan known as Josephine Wilson,"

Andrews "was known to be living with a negro wench," and "Had the crowds whom he offered to lead known the facts, the practical amalgamationist would probably have met with a very different reception" (17 July 1863: 1).

Aside from these and other similarly cryptic references to amalgamation, no mainstream newspaper reported that the first attacks on black men involved those married to, or living with, white women. On Tuesday night, a shipbroker who had left his home to get a pitcher of ale was approached by a white man with a gun, who said, "There is a nigger living here with two white women, and we are going to bring him out and hang him on the lamp post, and you stop and see the fun" (quoted in Cook 1974: 134). This white man, William Cruise, led the mob to the home of William Derrickson, a black man married to a white woman (a young white woman, Ellen Foose, also boarded with them). Fearing for his life, Derrickson escaped through a window. The mob broke into their home, where white Mary Derrickson had hidden her younger son "under her petticoats." William Cruise beat her nine-year-old son Alfred with a cart-rung, while Moses Greene struck him in the back of the head with an axe. They then dragged the unconscious child into the street. According to Foose's testimony:

> Best [another rioter] struck the boy with the cart-rung—the mother threw herself before him and said not to kill the boy but to kill her. Every stroke they gave they struck her. She had a cut on the side of the head where they struck her.
>
> ("Testimony of Ellen Foose" 1863)

When a white grocer intervened by firing a pistol-shot that dispersed the crowd, the child was rescued from the mob that had been intent on lynching him and then burning his body. Mary Derrickson, however, died within the month from injuries she had sustained while protecting her children. This incident and its aftermath were not reported in the *World*, the *Evening Post*, or the *Tribune*.

In another such case, Ann Martin, married to a black man who owned a bar, was confronted by rioters who had made their way to her house, shouting "kill the God Dam negroes." One of the rioters, she testified, "kicked my dog, saying it was a nigger's dog and to kill it," adding that "they would kill all the damned negroes in the house" (quoted in Cook 1974: 203). Asked by one rioter, "What made you marry a nigger?" Martin responded that "I could marry who I liked—That he could marry who he liked," whereupon the rioter demanded liquor, saying that she "was married to a god damned nigger and he meant to smash him" (quoted in Cook 1974: 203).

The absence of coverage of attacks on the Derricksons and the Martins fits into a wider pattern of ignoring victims of racist violence. Having married black men, these white women had forfeited the privileges assigned to white female victims of crime. Moreover, in marrying black men, these women unequivocally challenged the central premise of the protection scenario. Why would these women deserve protection, when they had consented to unions considered deviant? In marrying black men, white women had violated the central tenet of white, androcentric ideology: the belief that interracial sex went against "nature" and that no white woman would freely choose to engage in such an act.

A further dimension of the coverage of attacks on interracial social life lay in newspapers' representations of the mob as anonymous, unidentified strangers caught up in the violence of the moment, selecting random black strangers for attack. Although randomness factored into a number of the attacks near the docks, Alfred and Mary Derrickson, as well as Ellen Foose, knew the men who attacked the family. Ann Martin knew the men who had come to her husband's bar demanding liquor and threatening to set the premises on fire. Evidence suggests that in a number of cases working-class whites took advantage of the riots to exact revenge on those black men who had attained some measure of economic success, with the possession of a white woman seen as a central indicator of such success.[17] Here again, mainstream newspapers downplayed the intentionality of white violence, instead producing a mob that far from evincing systematicity in its persecution of blacks was rendered faceless, irrational, and unaccountable.

Anxieties about maintaining sexual boundaries between races were also evident in the *Evening Post*'s coverage of the refugee situation, which placed mostly African American women in close proximity with white police officers. The author of the 18 July 1863 story about refugees emphasized that there was nothing untoward in these black female refugees' relationships with the white police who were housing and protecting them. Younger women were seen "chatting gaily, but decorously, with the soldiers and policemen, who seemed troubled by no senseless superstitions on the subject of 'nigger equality'" (first morning edition, 18 July 1863: 1). These women "all seemed of cleanly habits," and were represented as high-spirited, but without sexual liaisons on their minds. Anticipating wider social concern on the part of their readers about the racial mingling that was taking place in the station-houses, the reporter assured his readers that this mixing was a matter of necessity rather than any desire:

> To ease the consciences of those who are apt to be horror struck at the thought of an exchange of courtesies between the races, we will state that we did not observe the slightest infringement of propriety or politeness on either side, nor was anything said or done that would have been incongruous at the most select party on Fifth Avenue.
>
> (first morning edition, 18 July 1863: 1)

The contact between the races in police station-houses, the author thus reassured his audience, was restrained, polite, and asexual.

As further evidence of newspapers' collaboration in downplaying the at once racialized and sexualized dimensions of the violence, none of these newspapers reported about specific injuries to blacks, beyond words like "hanging" or "beating," although the *World* featured descriptions of wounded and dead white rioters and bystanders.[18] Even *Metropolitan Police: Their Services During Riot*

Week. Their Honorable Record, an account praising the police force that was published six weeks after the riots by *New York Times* reporter David Barnes, carried no information about the frenzy of violence visited upon black male victims. In particular, no newspapers referred to the sexualized dimensions of the violence against blacks, or what Bernstein refers to as the "sexual policing of black men" (1990: 31). Victims of the mob repeatedly told stories of being beaten and stripped naked: Mrs. Margaret Robinson watched as her young son and daughter were stripped naked. John Brown, owner of a black sailors' boarding-house, "was caught in the street, robbed, and stripped of his clothes" (Cook 1974: 79). Naked, he ran the few blocks to the ferry. William Green, a black saloon owner, was similarly stripped naked and was rescued by a white man moments before the crowd was going to hang him. Even young Alfred Derrickson was stripped of his clothes ("Testimony of Ellen Foose" 1863). Charles Jackson testified that "They throwed me overboard; my clothes was all off me" (quoted in Cook 1974: 144). Victims who were hanged had their clothing removed either before or after they were killed and the bodies of victims were also mutilated. After another hanging, the crowd cut off its black victim's fingers and toes, in an act of symbolic castration, or the "sexual conquest of the black male community" (Bernstein 1990: 29) through violent symbolic acts.

Castration figured more graphically in the lynching of Abraham Franklin, a disabled black coachman who lived with his sister in a house at Twenty-seventh Street and Seventh Avenue. George Glass, leading a group of rioters, broke into Franklin's house on Wednesday afternoon. Both Franklin and his sister Henrietta were dragged into the street and beaten. Franklin was kicked and dragged by the mob for a block and then hanged on a lamppost. After rioters had cut down his lifeless body, according to court transcripts, an Irishman named Patrick Butler:

> Maliciously, scandalously, and indecently did inflict violence upon a corpse then and there lying and being, to wit upon the dead body of a negro man, and did then and there indecently kick and indecently and scandalously pull about the said negro corpse by its private parts.
>
> ("Indictment of Patrick Butler" 1863)[19]

When queried as to whether he had "anything to say . . . relative to the charge here preferred against you," Butler answered: "I am not guilty. All I done was to take hold of his private parts" ("Indictment of Patrick Butler" 1863).[20] Like other instances of sexualized violence, this one was referred to only in passing by the mainstream press and so understood to be just another mob-related beating death.

While the suppression of information about the kinds of injuries inflicted on African Americans may have resulted from the restraint exercised by editors and reporters in describing social violence or sexuality, as we will see in later coverage of lynching (as well as in cases of family violence in the nineteenth and early twentieth centuries), newspaper accounts of injuries in particular were much more graphic than they are today. Rather than modesty, the silence resulted instead from the interest that white men and, increasingly, white women shared in a worldview that equated whiteness with heroism and protection. As numerous scholars of violence have noted—from criminologist Lonnie Athens (1992) to historian Roger Lane (1997)—the intensity and excess of the violence against African Americans suggested a level of hatred and personal involvement typically seen in murders involving intimates rather than strangers. The violence against blacks was furious, savage, and monstrous. To depict it in any accurate fashion was to countenance a vision of whiteness that contradicted the logic of racialized androcentrism and white protectionism. Featuring individual black people as innocent victims of white racism, understanding the attacks on them as being in large part attacks on any attempts at racial integration (sexual or otherwise), was to challenge this vision of white heroes and protectors.[21]

Perhaps more threatening from the perspective of white newspaper editors, to acknowledge the sexualized nature of the attacks on black people was to undermine the racist logic that was gaining legitimacy in the north during this time period. According to this logic, black men—not white men—were considered to be inherent sexual monsters. Only black people and other "savages," that is, could be capable of the behaviors exhibited by the mob. More to the point, sexualized violence on the part of the white mob disrupted both the gendered and raced dimensions of the protection scenario, suggesting that victims were not always, or necessarily, women, and that powerful white men, rather than powerless black men, were sexual monsters. To remember the anti-draft riots as what Cook describes as a "black pogrom" that had as its centerpiece white fears about interracial relationships was thereby to introduce a discordant note into the narratives of protection used to frame deviant and criminal behavior in US popular culture.

"The condition of all human progress is miscegenation"

However unacknowledged the link between black men and white women in the reporting of the anti-draft riots, the anti-amalgamationist sentiment held by even abolitionists implicitly accepted the belief that black men were a threat to white women. And this link was evident enough for two reporters for the *New York World* to use it to perpetrate a hoax that, by inflaming racist sentiment and galvanizing resistance to politics that had anti-racist dimensions, intended to undermine the 1864 presidential election. The biography of the word miscegenation began during the anti-draft riots, when the *World* warned its readers that "this administration has not waged this war for the Union, but for the abolition of slavery and the equality of the negro with the white," understood by anti-abolitionists to be amalgamation. In a more ominous vein, the editorial continued, "The full conviction of that idea has not yet come to them, but the proofs are accumulating, and before six months the issue will be made" (18 July 1863: 4). Indeed, slightly more than five months after the riots swept through New York City, the issue of just what abolitionists meant by the "equality of the negro with the white" was made clear in a pamphlet sold along with newspapers on newsstands throughout New York City.

Entitled *Miscegenation: The Theory of the Blending of the Races: Applied to the American White Man and Negro*, the pamphlet that introduced "miscegenation" was published anonymously because, the authors argued, they wanted to direct attention to the merits of the argument put forth in the pamphlet, rather than the merits of the author himself. The real reason for this anonymity was more sinister. In the first place, the authors wished to conceal their connection to the *World* (Marble had been appointed to the 1864 Democratic national campaign committee), as well as anti-abolitionism writ large. They wanted instead to suggest that the pamphlet was the work of abolitionists who celebrated the promise of "miscegenation," a neologism that connoted a new understanding of race mixing—one that blended science and politics in legitimizing white fears about the interracial unions that white supremacists saw as lying at the center of the larger Union goals.

Prior to 1863, the word "amalgamation" was used to refer to interracial unions. Where the word originally referred to the combination of two elements into an alloy, by 1775, the word began to be used in reference to the blending of two races or ethnicities into one new whole. Amalgamation did not refer to black and white unions alone before 1863 and its connotations were not always negative. The transformation of this previous discourse of amalgamation, one that corresponded to a different era of threat construction, into the more modern and ostensibly scientific discourse of miscegenation marked an important moment in the development of modern racist understandings of black sexuality and related processes of criminalization. As long as blacks were enslaved in the south and perpetually fearful about their status as free blacks in the north, it was difficult to construct them as significant and credible threats to the social and political order, especially in the north. The discourse of miscegenation, coming as it did in the midst of the Civil War, changed this, breathing new life into the forms of apartheid that were being developed in the north and generating support for the reign of terror that followed the Civil War. Blacks, this discourse suggested, threatened the sexual order of the world and, in so doing, were more threatening to it than any civil war.

The pamphlet purported to have been written by a proponent of abolitionism, but the reality could not have been further from the truth. Instead, it was authored by two anti-abolitionist journalists who worked for the *World*: David Goodman Croly, managing editor of the *World* who was an early advocate of positivist sociology, and George Wakeman, a young staff reporter.[22] Invented by two reporters for the *World*, at the behest of the newspaper's anti-abolitionist owners and editor, "miscegenation" was used exclusively to describe the sexual union of blacks and whites, with the express intent of insisting that this form of union was what was really being fought for in the Civil War.

The argument laid out in the pamphlet was inflammatory even by nineteenth-century partisan standards. Blending scientific and ethnological language and citation style, the authors argued that the "pure" races (by which they meant Anglo-Saxon) were decaying. Mining a deep vein of Anglophobia (not to mention misogyny), they suggested that such a decline was readily apparent in the British context:

> even the English race itself is beginning to decay. This is shown by the excessive number of females born in that country. They are known to exceed the number of males by over one million. It is a well-known law, that an increase of female population is a symptom of weakness and effeminacy. In the effete races of Northern Mexico, it is remarked that six or seven females are born to one male.
>
> (Croly and Wakeman 1863: 16)

Only a literal infusion of new blood, the authors emphasized throughout the pamphlet, could save the USA from a similarly awful, feminized fate. If masculinity was to remain central to the construction of the USA as a nation-state, the solution was clear: "the dark races must absorb the white" (17).

The pamphlet cites a succession of "experts" who attest to the "physiological equality of the white and colored races" (iii). Not only were the races equal, the authors proclaimed, but also "wherever, through conquest, colonization, or commerce, different nationalities are blended, a superior human product invariably results" (9). Indeed, the authors continued, the "lowest people . . in the scale of civilization in Europe," the Irish and Sicilians, "are brutal, ignorant, and barbarous, lacking in everything which goes to make up a prosperous and enlightened community" precisely because they "had no such chance of interchange of blood" with other races (10) and thus lacked the valuable opportunity miscegenation presented. According to "Dr. Hancock, writing in South America, 1837," it is "a well-known fact that the Samboes of South America, the progeny of blacks and Indians—are remarkable for their physical superiority over their progenitors of either side" (13).

According to the pamphlet, Americans had the unique historical opportunity to make themselves "the finest race on earth" if they would just heed the call of nature and

> Engraft upon our stock the negro element which providence has placed by our side on this continent. Of all the rich treasures of blood vouchsafed to us, that of the negro is the most precious, because it is the most unlike any other that enters into the composition of our national life.
>
> (11)

Setting racist common sense on its head, *Miscegenation* cast blacks not as primitives, parasites, or potential sexual predators, but as a precious genetic resource: "we must become Miscegens," the pamphlet declared, "if we would attain the fullest results of civilization" (20).

For a culture invested in a white supremacy based on the purity and piety of white women, the pamphlet offered what could only be interpreted as further insults. According to its authors, not only would miscegenation benefit the nation, to resist it was to resist an urge as deep and primal as the urge to copulate. Over the course of time, "It will be our noble prerogative to set the example of this rich blending of blood." Indeed, the authors continue, linking miscegenation to the Civil War:

> It is idle to maintain that this present war is not a war for the negro. It is a war for the negro. Not simply for his personal rights or his physical freedom—it is a war if you please, of amalgamation, so called—a war looking, as its final fruit, to the blending of the white and black.
>
> (18)

Hinting at the ideology that underlay its inversion of common sense, at one point, the pamphlet observed: "Our police courts give painful evidence that the passion of the colored race for the white is often so uncontrollable as to overcome the terror of the law" (28).

The pamphlet's most inflammatory element lay in its repeated assertions that miscegenation was not only natural, but also greatly desired by women and men of all races. Rather than being a crime against nature, "the yearning of the brunette and blonde to mingle" (18) was entirely natural. The sympathy that Horace Greeley was said to feel "for the negro is the love which the blonde bears for the black; it is a love of race, a sympathy stronger to them than the love they bear to women." Interracial attraction, therefore, was stronger and more natural than heterosexuality. Turning racist taboos on their heads, the author postulated that "it is desirable [that] the white man should marry the black woman and the white woman the black man . . . The next step will be the opening of California to the teeming millions of eastern Asia" (19), a thought that could only horrify nineteenth-century defenders of racial purity and proponents of anti-Chinese immigration policies.

Miscegenation reserved special treatment for white southern women. A section titled "Heart-Histories of the White Daughters of the South" argued that white women were "thrilled with a strange delight by daily contact with their dusky male servitors" (42). The southern woman was for this reason more reluctant than southern man to give up slavery, because abolition would "separate her forever from the colored man" (43). Fully cognizant of the ways in which southern women's charm, virtue, and honor were used to legitimize the violence of southern society, the pamphlet sought to antagonize those who shared such a viewpoint by casting southern women as experiencing a "frenzy of love" for black men and asserting that "It is safe to say that the first heart experience of nearly every Southern maiden—the flowering sweetness and grace of her young life, is associated with a sad dream of some bondman lover" (44).

That the pamphlet's aims were political rather than scientific was evident in the larger argument it purported to make, as well as its subsequent distribution. Abolitionism, the authors asserted, was the party of miscegenation and the Republican Party would not rest content "till it throws aloft the standard of (so-called) Amalgamation" (49). The authors claimed to see miscegenation not just as positive, but also as the only means for the nation's salvation: only miscegenation could prevent the USA from falling into a state of feminized genetic decrepitude.

Miscegenation, the pamphlet concluded, was natural and desirable. It was, moreover, the real aim of the Republican Party and the desired outcome of abolitionist politics: "When the President proclaimed Emancipation he proclaimed also the mingling of the races. The one follows the other as surely as noonday follows sunrise" (49). The abolitionists had swallowed the Republican Party, according to the logic of the pamphlet, and that absorption was a positive thing because it merely followed the dictates of nature and the natural, inevitable, and desirable evolution of the white race into a darker one.

Biographers have since described the pamphlet as a hoax, a term that renders the work of these two journalists waggish or slyly tongue-in-cheek, but there was no mistaking the malevolent purpose for which they had coined the word "miscegenation." On Christmas Day 1863, copies of the pamphlet were mailed to would-be supporters of its content—well-known abolitionists and supporters of abolition like Horace Greeley. The cover letters that accompanied the pamphlet recommended miscegenation as a crucial and forward-looking component of the Republican platform for the 1864 election and requested endorsements of its contents from supporters of Lincoln. In early 1864, additional copies of the pamphlet were sent out for review to magazines and other newspapers and, on 17 February, Samuel Sullivan Cox, a strident anti-abolitionist, invoked the pamphlet in an attack on Republican members of Congress. Croly and Wakeman had forwarded the letters they had received from abolitionists in response to their original mailing to peace democrat Cox's hands. Cox used this correspondence as evidence that "The more philosophical and apostolic of the abolition fraternity have fully decided upon the adoption of this amalgamation platform" (quoted in Kaplan 1949: 296).

For the entire month of March, the editorial pages of the New York press were filled with debates about miscegenation, which, in typical newspaper fashion, devolved into name-calling, and angry gesticulations about which papers in fact advocated miscegenation. The *World* took full advantage of the outrage *Miscegenation* provoked in 1864, using it to cudgel Horace Greeley, Lincoln, and abolitionists like Lucretia Mott and the Grimké sisters. Although in an editorial published shortly after the 1864 election, in which he revealed the pamphlet to be a hoax, Marble observed that it "was very likely that the writers of the book will never be discovered," his knowledge of the composition of the pamphlet ("In order to familiarize themselves in a degree with the subject, they 'crammed' at the Astor Library") and his identification of the authors as "two young gentlemen connected with the newspaper press of New York both of whom are obstinate Democrats in politics" suggests that Marble had been very much aware of the production of the pamphlet (*World*, 18 November 1864: 1). Of all New York city papers, only the *World* remained uncharacteristically agnostic on the issue, likely because it had already accomplished—via Croly and Wakeman—its goal of creating a new word to launch as a campaign issue against the Republicans (Kaplan 1949: 309). Although the word "miscegenation" spread like wildfire among newspapers, no mainstream New York City newspaper questioned the veracity of the pamphlet, its authorship, or the sudden invention of this ugly and awkward-sounding word. Through the cunning of newspapermen who understood the fundamental mechanics of publicity, a miscegenation platform was thrust upon Republicans during the election year of 1864.

Although the articulation of this new word, which came to replace the less consistently negative term "amalgamation," did not achieve its goal of preventing the re-election of Lincoln in 1864, it helped to usher in a new era of racism in the USA, by achieving a number of political and ideological goals. As John D'Emilio and Estelle Freedman observe in their history of sexuality in America, those who transgressed the sexual rules used to police racial boundaries "challenged not only a set of cultural values but also the basis of an emerging system of racial control" (1997: 35). By turning the rules governing racialized sexual boundaries upside down—by claiming not only that black men desired white women, but that white women desired black men—the pamphlet sought to provoke hysteria over the effects of abolition and to reassert the system of racial control in the USA. By deftly conflating African Americans' demands for political rights with demands for sexual rights, the authors of *Miscegenation* further sought to erase the memory of those innocent victims of the riots and, indeed, of the institution of slavery, and to shore up the image of the predatory and sexually aggressive black male.

Perhaps most nefariously, *Miscegenation* put abolitionists and those who supported the cause on the defensive by forcing them to publicly articulate their opposition to interracial relationships and thereby expose the racism they shared with anti-abolitionists. Some supporters of abolition who received advance copies of the pamphlet may have privately agreed with its arguments, but they understood all too well its inflammatory nature, and thus kept silent on the issue. Others were forced into publicly admitting a deep opposition to interracial unions. In an editorial published in March 1864, Horace Greeley said that while no one had the right to interfere with interracial unions, he would not call them either "wise" or "moral." Dodging the issue of black masculinity altogether, he asked, "If a man can so far conquer his repugnance to a black woman as to make her the mother of his children, we ask, in the name of the divine law and of decency, why he should not marry her" (*Tribune*, 16 March 1864: 2). Proponents of abolition like Greeley thus were complicitous if not in directly contributing a word to the American vocabulary that, cloaked in the rhetoric of science and positivism, shored up and gave new life to racist discourses of white supremacy, then in tacitly endorsing its underlying sentiments (see Figure 3.1).

Miscegenation succeeded in crystallizing the worst fears of white men: fears about their own virility, about their desirability (both genetic and sexual), and about some not-so-distant future in which the effects of miscegenation— presumably a generation of mostly female children of color—would rise up

Figure 3.1 "Live coon sandwich," *National Police Gazette*, 4 November 1882.

against them. One could scarcely imagine a more horrifying vision from the perspective of a racialized androcentrism. In this fashion, the victims of anti-black violence were eclipsed by an articulation of gender and race that served to unite white men in racist fear of over-sexualized others. The fear generated by this articulation, in turn, would serve as the alibi for renewed white supremacist violence against African Americans that would continue unabated for decades to come. There would be, in effect, no black victims in the mainstream: only those black men who, like the victims of the anti-draft riots, were made to bear the responsibility and the social costs of their own victimization.

The suspicion white men harbored about the secret desires of black men and white women (not to mention the "truthfulness" and "honor" assigned to whiteness) predisposed them to be suspicious of black people's narratives of victimization. When it came to crime in northern cities, black victims of a whole range of crimes undeniably existed in New York City during the first half of the nineteenth century, but white editors and reporters, as we have seen, did not cover these victims. As Paul Gilje points out, the flipside of the suppression of these victim narratives is the suppression of stories about the "efforts by African Americans to protect themselves and members of their community from slavery." Gilje further observes that information about such acts of resistance "is so hard to come by that it almost seems as if news of these incidents was suppressed. White Americans preferred not to discuss action taken by blacks in the name of freedom" (1996: 88).

In effect, black people and women were robbed of the ability to express their experiences of either resistance or violent repression by news discourses. And although a focus on victim status tends to detract from the victim's agency, victim narratives remain a crucial avenue for empathy and for criminalizing acts deemed socially unacceptable. Worthy victims are protected, memorialized, and sometimes "compensated" for their victimization. Unworthy victims are either ignored or blamed for the violence inflicted upon them—a point that will become even more glaringly apparent when we turn our attention to northern narratives about lynching. To divulge the existence of systematic violence against black women and men in the anti-draft riots and other instances of widespread violence against people of color was to acknowledge the instability residing at the center of white narratives of protection: that perhaps white men rather than black were monsters and that perhaps masculinity as a whole, rather than black men, was intrinsically savage and violent.

4 "The malicious and untruthful white press"
Lynch narratives and criminalization

> The problem on their hands is immeasurable. The colored race multiplies like the locusts of Egypt. The grog-shop is its center of power. The safety of woman, of childhood, of the home, is menaced in a thousand localities at this moment, so that the men dare not go beyond the sight of their own roof-tree. How little we know of this, seated in comfort and affluence here at the North.
>
> (Frances Willard quoted in Wells 1892/1997: 142)[1]

Anyone familiar with the annals of nineteenth-century crime reporting will recognize the name of Helen Jewett. Most conversant with popular crime literature will be familiar with the Lizzie Borden case (if only because of its gruesome popularity as a children's rhyme), as well as the kidnapping of the Lindbergh baby. But few indeed will recall the name of Edward Coy, burned at the stake in Texarkana, Arkansas for having "feloniously assaulted Mrs. Helen Jewett [sic]" (*World*, 21 February 1892: 1). Nor will they recognize the names of "Eph Grizzard, a Negro, Hanged for Assaulting a White Woman" in Nashville, Tennessee (*World*, 1 May 1892: 3), of Robert Lewis, who was lynched in Port Jervis, New York, again for allegedly assaulting a white woman (*World*, 3 June 1892: 1), or of Zachariah Walker, lynched in Coatesville, Pennsylvania in 1911.[2] The elisions, silences, and omissions regarding the terrorist regime of lynching and the denial of the historical presence of black victims were seminal in institutionalizing a racial economy of victimization in US crime reporting.

As we have seen, the link between blackness and crime had long circulated within commercial crime news. The introduction of the word "miscegenation," however, ushered in a new era of racist language and threat construction, bringing together elements of a wider racist discourse that had until the Civil War been comparatively inchoate and disorganized. As we saw in the previous chapter, the introduction of the word "miscegenation"—and despite the acknowledgment that the neologism itself had been invented as a hoax, the word was quickly incorporated into the US lexicon of race—offered a scientific-sounding label that naturalized racist stereotypes about black male sexuality, thereby providing justification for the intensified racist violence of the antebellum era. Where earlier forms of threat construction had balanced racist representations of African American men as "shuffling, obsequious, and harmless 'darkies' who deserved paternalistic protection," with nascent forms of criminalization, in the decades following the Civil War, black men were transformed into "threatening, atavistic animals who posed a threat to the security of white society, especially to white womanhood" (Tolnay and Beck 1995: 254).

Disproving the belief that distance (be it physical or intellectual) facilitates objectivity, New York City newspapers played an important role in reproducing and culturally disseminating the androcentric logic that motivated lynching. Although the New York City press understood both racism and the crime of lynching to be products of the economically and culturally backward south, in reporting on a northern lynching that occurred in nearby Port Jervis, the *New York World* editorialized that the case did not express "a manifestation of any race prejudice" (4 June 1892: 4) since it occurred in the north and not the south. Having forgotten entirely the lynchings that had occurred less than three decades earlier in its own streets, New York City newspapers cast lynching and racism as purely southern issues. Nonetheless, newspapers like the *New York Times* and the *New York World* consistently sought to justify lynching, the most violent manifestation of "race prejudice" in the south.

The following chapter considers the construction and dissemination of lynch narratives in the *New York World* during 1892, a year that saw the highest number of reported lynchings in US history. During that single violent year, a year that also marked the onset of a severe economic crisis, a total of 129 people were lynched in the USA, 106 of them African American (Tolnay and Beck 1995: 271). (See Figure 4.1). First and foremost, the chapter analyzes the extent to which lynch narratives in the *World* were selected in such a way as to include lynchings that would conform to a protection scenario featuring worthy white female victims who had to be protected from murderous and sexually violent black men. These lynching narratives underscored the role that race played in constructing crime waves, especially in this case the lack of fit between media discourses about crime and the realities of social violence. The National Association for the Advancement of Colored People (NAACP), founded in part to combat lynching and other forms of racist violence, determined that only 28.4 percent of blacks who had been lynched had been accused of rape or attempted rape (Zangrando 1980: 8), but the news' concentration on lynching as a response to black male assaults on white women promoted an understanding of violence against blacks that directed attention not to the white perpetrators of these crimes, but to the criminal actions of the victims themselves. The chapter concludes by analyzing the role that race played in determining which violent acts would henceforth be considered criminal, as well as the establishment of patterns for how race and gender would hitherto determine the identities of both criminals and victims in the media.

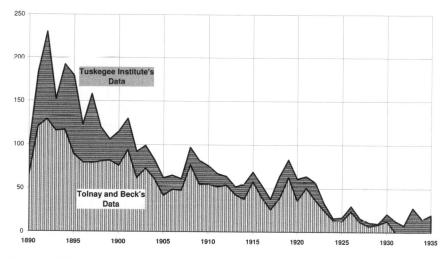

Figure 4.1 Tolnay and Beck's data on lynching statistics in the USA (1890–1935) compared to the Tuskegee Institute's data.

Victims, villains, virtue, and vengeance

It may be granted that the offense is one that is especially and with reason dreaded in the South, and one to which the African race is particularly prone. That is a reason for visiting it with the utmost penalty of the law.

(*New York Times*, 23 February 1892: 4)

Not as openly racist as it had been under the editorial control of Manton Marble in 1863—it no longer used the word "nigger" when referring to African Americans—under the ownership of Joseph Pulitzer (who, as an immigrant, had fought for the Union during the Civil War), the *New York World* remained as staunch a supporter of the Democratic Party as it had been in 1863. During the 1890s, the *World* included immigrants (particularly the Irish—the paper often devoted a whole page to coverage of Ireland's domestic affairs and politics) and women (it was the first newspaper to establish a "women's" page) among its readership, and on occasion it even provided sympathetic coverage of trade unions.[3] In 1892, the *World* had the largest circulation of any newspaper in the USA (the *Times* would not exceed its circulation until the first decade of the twentieth century). The combined circulation of the *New York World* and the *Evening World* was 374,741 that year, making it the largest of the New York City papers (Mott 1941: 435). Its coverage of lynching likely reached more readers and listeners throughout the USA than indicated by circulation figures.

The *World*'s success in a fiercely competitive market was generally credited to the paper's news policy, which featured eye-catching and colorful crime news and staged events; the liberal use of illustrations (especially diagrams of crime scenes); its innovations in departmentalizing news (it featured the first sports section, as well as the first women's pages); and its frequent crusades. Although the *World* is often considered one of the first modern newspapers in terms of its business practices and organizational structure, at the end of the nineteenth century its coverage of crime remained faithful to the general pattern of crime coverage established by the penny press, with serialized coverage of high-profile crimes, like the 1892 Lizzie Borden case and the 1895 trial of serial killer H.H. Holmes (who killed an estimated thirty people in 1893, targeting women who were visiting the 1893 Chicago World's Fair), and episodic coverage, particularly of family violence.[4] In the *World*, crime reports regularly dotted the front page (unlike the *Sun* and the *Herald*, the *World* carried no advertising on the front page), although on slower news days some episodic stories would show up on pages 2 or 8 when necessary.

New York City newspapers reported on lynchings in the 1890s, but they did so sporadically and episodically, invariably underreporting the violence that was then taking place against African Americans.[5] According to Tolnay and Beck, the highest number of recorded lynchings occurred in 1892, a year when the *New York Times*, easiest to track because the newspaper is indexed, featured 31 articles on lynching (see Figure 4.2).[6] The *World*, which ceased publication in 1931 shortly before the *Times'* highest coverage of lynching, featured more crime news than the *Times*, but in 1892 carried only 45 articles on lynching. This represented one-third of the reported lynching of blacks, particularly when we consider that a good number of these stories were devoted to follow-up articles on specific lynching. In the *World*, five of the total lynching stories involved lynching of white men.[7]

Most of the lynchings the *World* covered in 1892 occurred in the south. In other matters, the south was treated like a distant land, which would have made a crusade against southern white men easier, insofar as the region appeared to be economically, politically, and culturally distinct from the north.[8] But in the case of lynching, the *World* tended to condone rather than criticize southern violence against African Americans. Just as the racism of northern mainstream newspapers had been revealed by the miscegenation hoax, insofar as even newspapers with abolitionist sympathies sided with anti-abolitionists against interracial relationships, so lynching narratives illustrated unquestioned beliefs about race shared by whites in the north and south alike. For northern newspapers, criticizing southerners for lynching meant criticizing a system of racialized androcentrism of which northern newspaper owners and editors were fundamentally a part. To criticize the logic of lynching—that it was revenge for assaults on white women's honor—meant that northern newspapers like the *World* would have had to make two arguments that ran counter to its own racial privilege and interests. First, openly opposing lynch narratives would have meant challenging the very basis for white masculinity and its exclusive claims to honor, truthfulness, and justice. Second, it would further have required questioning the veracity and virtue of the white femininity used to bolster white masculinity's exclusive claims to paternalism and protection.

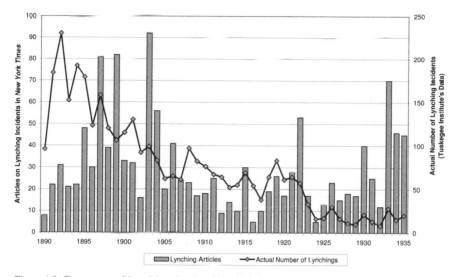

Figure 4.2 Coverage of lynching in the *New York Times* compared to actual numbers of lynching, 1890–1935.

The selection process that governed northern newspapers' representations of lynching as the unfortunate yet comprehensible communal response to the most horrible crime imaginable to white men was based on the narrative frame of the innocent and helpless white woman and the sexually monstrous black man. As we will see, lynchings that did not fit into this framework were either ignored, or the stories were twisted in such a way as to force conformity to this frame, largely through the suppression of specific details about the crimes for which blacks stood accused, as well as a refusal to consider alternative motives for white violence. In order to maintain fictions of white masculinity that resorted to violence only when forced to by attacks on white women, as in its anti-draft riot coverage, the *World* also omitted details about the violence of lynching (especially torture), as well as economic causes for lynching, which would undercut the chivalry white masculinity ascribed to itself. And perhaps most importantly, the *World* did not cover any of the lynchings of black women, which directly challenged the foundations of a protection scenario that purported to protect female victims.

In addition to the selection process that determined which details of individual lynch narratives would get reported, another element of selection was at work in the *World*'s choice of which lynching cases would be covered at all. According to the NAACP (1969), 155 African Americans were lynched in 1892, yet in that same year the *World* only featured 45 total articles on lynching. Both the Tuskegee data and the NAACP data used newspaper reports of lynching to arrive at their totals, which means that the *World* would have had access to clippings that had appeared in other newspapers about most of these crimes.

Significantly, the *World* allotted no coverage on otherwise slow news days to cases that foregrounded economic rather than "chivalrous" motives for lynching and therefore had the potential to call into question scenarios of white protection. On 11 February 1892, Hamp Biscoe, a well-to-do black farmer in England, Arkansas, drove away a white farmer who had driven through Biscoe's field without permission. The white farmer secured a warrant for Biscoe's arrest. When the constable and deputies arrived at Biscoe's house, he "warned them he would shoot if they persisted in their attempt to arrest him" (Wells 1892/1997: 89). Biscoe wounded the constable and both he and his very pregnant wife were shot in the ensuing fight. Along with their infant and 13-year-old son, the Biscoes were arrested and put under guard. That night, husband and wife were executed (the lynchers stopped long enough to steal $220 that Mrs. Biscoe had concealed in her stocking), the infant wounded, and the son fatally shot, although the child lived long enough to tell authorities about the murders and the robbery.

The Biscoe case threatened the general alibi whites offered for lynching on a number of different levels. This case involved a married couple, not a single black man. As such, it contradicted the widely disseminated belief that those who were lynched were male, as well as the "chivalry" upon which the protection scenario was founded. This crime resulted in the murder of a father, a pregnant woman, and a young child, as far from the stereotypical rapist of lynch narratives as one could get. Moreover, white defenses of lynching depended upon notions of chivalry, in which white men were forced to defend the honor and virtue of white women. To admit to an economic motive was to undercut the related sense of "noble" purpose.

According to Wells, Biscoe had become "a confirmed imbecile" (1892/1997: 88) because of a quarrel with a white man over a debt Biscoe refused to pay, but Biscoe's paranoia about white men planning to steal his farm was well-founded in light of subsequent events. As Tolnay and Beck's analysis confirms, charges of sexual assault and other crimes were often pretexts for retaliation against African Americans who were perceived to be more successful than whites, particularly during economic downturns. Before his death, their son told officials that his pregnant wife had begun to cry, telling her family's assailants, "You intend to kill us to get our money" (Wells 1892/1997: 89). This lynching laid bare the economic motivation behind many lynchings: the theft of African American property and capital. Unable to frighten Biscoe off land that they desired, the lynchers killed him and his family instead.

The lynching of Thomas Moss, Calvin McDowell, and Wil Stewart on 9 March 1892, outside Memphis, Tennessee, also pointed to economic motives for killing blacks. Business partners in a successful grocery store that directly competed with a white-owned store in the area, Moss, McDowell, and Stewart were arrested in the wake of a shoot-out instigated by W.T. Bartlett, a white store-owner who competed with them for customers. Taken from their jail cells, transported north of the city by train, the men were literally shot to pieces.

At the time of this lynching, journalist Ida B. Wells edited the *Memphis Free Speech and Headlight*, a newspaper affiliated with the Baptist Church. She was a close friend of the murdered Thomas Moss. When the white press published a series of articles arguing that lynching was an understandable and legitimate reaction to African American men's rape of white women (despite the fact that in this case no such allegations had been made), the *Free Speech* published an editorial that criticized this argument and hinted that white women were not the innocent parties white newspapers made them out to be. Shortly after publication of this editorial, the newspaper's office was attacked while Wells was away on business, and white community leaders made it clear that if Wells were to return to town they would not vouch for her safety.[9] These events caused Wells to understand how lynching was being used as what Angela Davis has described as "a weapon of mass political terrorism" (1983: 24), against those blacks who seemed to be achieving a measure of success. As Wells put it in her autobiography, the lynching of her friends was "what opened my eyes to what lynching really was. An excuse to get rid of negroes who were acquiring wealth and property and thus keep the race terrorized and 'keep the nigger down'" (quoted in Wells 1970: 64). Northern newspapers did not reach the same conclusion. Confronted with a story that so directly contradicted the racist and sexist logic of lynching it upheld, the *World* carried no account of the lynching of Moss, McDowell, and Stewart.

The *New York Times* did carry a single article on this lynching, mentioning that the white grocery store-owner had initiated the violence, but it immediately followed this statement with the observation that Moss, McDowell, and Stewart "were recognized as 'bad niggers' by the respectable people of both races, and had they been killed in the fight with the Deputy Sheriffs there would have been few regrets for them." Not only did this clash with Wells' description of the three victims as solidly middle-class and thoroughly respectable citizens, it also directly contradicted the *Times*' own description of the collective funeral held for all three, which "was attended by a great crowd of negroes, many of whom quit work for the day in order to be present" (11 March 1892: 4).

A few brief accounts of lynching covered by the *World* referred to direct attacks on the social and economic order of white society in the shape of African Americans lynched for having murdered police; town, county, or state officials; or prominent citizens. In Shreveport, Louisiana, an African American man allegedly shot a plantation lessee and was immediately lynched (9 January 1892). In Acadia, Florida, "Walter Austin, colored, was lynched near here last night for the murder of Bert Hard, a white man, foreman of the Moorehead Phosphate Works" (17 February 1892: 1). These short one-paragraph accounts never questioned the veracity of the charges against African Americans (in the cases where charges were even made before the lynching occurred), nor did any of the articles speculate about motives African Americans might have had for such crimes. Indeed, newspapers threw up their editorial hands when it came to understanding lynchings that had all too obvious economic explanations. Referring to the terrible lynching of Dennis Cobb, "a well-to-do negro" in the impoverished Bienville Parish near New Orleans, the *World* noted, "No reason has been given for the desire to lynch him" (28 March 1892: 1). Refusing to recognize the link between black economic success and white violence, the *World* left it at that.

On the whole, the majority of cases covered in any detail by the *World* strictly conformed to dominant ideologies of white masculinity (as brutal, but just) and black masculinity (as savage and lustful). This linchpin of the protection scenario—the casting of two diametrically opposed forms of masculinity—did not allow for any representation of the victims of lynching *as* victims, for this would cast doubt on the legitimacy of the protection scenario itself. By mainly including accounts of lynching resulting from allegations of either sexual assault of white women or murder—crimes, as we have seen, viewed as being equally heinous by nineteenth-century androcentric culture—the *World* reified the racist logic used to justify such acts of terrorism.

In this way, the majority of cases covered by the *World* implied that infractions of the racialized sexual order were the cause for lynching. In Acadia, Florida, "A negro named Henry Hinson used offensive language in the presence of ladies." When ordered away by "W. Jefferson Chitty, a prominent young white man . . . Hinson went, but returned with a pistol and deliberately shot Chitty, killing him almost instantly" (13 January 1892: 1). According to the *World*, "Both whites and negroes justify the lynching," although black citizens would have had little say in the matter. In the case of the burning of Ed Coy, the justification for the savagery enacted upon him was his "felonious assault" upon Mrs. Jewell; in Anniston, Alabama, Will Carter and Jim and Berry Roden were lynched for having "brutally beat Mrs. Bryant and then assaulted her while she was unconscious" (17 May 1892: 3); the *World* also reported an attempting lynching near Nashville, Tennessee of "the negro who attempted to assault Mrs. Mairty" (21 May 1892: 1); "Bob Lewis, a negro, who had assaulted Miss Lena McMahon, daughter of John McMahon," was lynched in Port Jervis, New York (3 June 1892: 1). Later that summer, near Birmingham, Alabama, "An unknown negro attempted to assault two white women in the outskirts of Jasper yesterday. He was pursued by almost the entire male population of the town, and this morning he was caught in a swamp and lynched" (5 July 1892: 1).

The *World* reported on extreme instances of brutality in some detail, although these accounts too were rife with contradictions. In the case of Edward Coy, burned at the stake in Texarkana, Arkansas, the *World* observed, "That Coy ought to have been hanged or shot is generally admitted, but burning the poor wretch at the stake was a disgrace to civilization" (22 February 1892: 1).[10] As in all other lynch narratives it reported on, the *World* viewed Coy as indisputably guilty—the opening sentence described him as "the negro who feloniously assaulted Mrs. Henry Jewett [*sic*]" (21 February 1892: 1).[11] Coy's guilt being assumed from the opening sentence of the article, there was no other mention of the assault or of Coy's having even been charged in the columns that followed, which described the awful manner of Coy's death. Although the article described the lynching as an "awful spectacle," and in a follow-up article that appeared the next day observed that "A reaction in public feeling has set in and people are beginning to realize that the horrible affair of yesterday, the burning of Ed Coy at the stake, will do irreparable damage to the reputation of the city" (22 February 1892: 1), even here concern devolved around the city's reputation and not the barbarity of the deed itself.

Although the *World* could not avoid reporting that Coy had been burned at the stake, as in the case of anti-black violence in 1863, they never referred to the vicious forms of torture that preceded his execution. For example, the *World* never reported that, before being burned, Coy was tortured by boys and men, who cut flesh from his body before pouring coal oil over him. By projecting savagery onto racialized others, newspapers suppressed details that might reveal the savage practices of white lynch mobs.

Indeed, despite its initial condemnation of the mode of execution, the very next day the *World* sought to rationalize the violence by devoting a full column to an ugly diatribe centering on white female justification for racist violence that was headlined, "Mrs. Jewell Has No Regrets":

> I could have cut the scoundrel's heart out when he was first brought into my presence after his capture. I had been told before that I should have the naming of his mode of death. I had plenty of time to think about it, and after the fullest deliberation I decided that death at the stake and by fire was the proper punishment for his crime as well as the only death that would be certain to teach his race a lesson, and thus tend to save others of my sex from the horrible experience through which I have passed.
>
> (23 February 1892: 1)

Since women were assumed to be peace-loving, nonviolent creatures, for a member of the cult of true womanhood to propose such an awful manner of death, the original crime must have been terrible indeed.[12] According to the *World*, Mrs. Jewell enacted a dreadful and feminized rationality: she engaged in "the fullest deliberation," deciding that death by fire "would be certain to teach his race a lesson," and she was motivated by the altruistic desire to save other white women from her "horrible experience."

Here again, Wells' account is distinct from that of the *World*. According to Wells, one witness suggested that Mrs. Jewell "was of bad character" because she had been sexually involved with Coy for more than a year before the lynching. Forced to bring charges against Coy, "When she came to apply the match Coy asked her if she would burn him after they had 'been sweethearting' for so long" (Wells 1892/1997: 123). The *World*'s report did mention some hesitancy on the part of Jewell, "who looked at the negro, then the torch, and then the spokesman, and falteringly turned to the crowd. 'No, no! Apply it,' was the cry, as the woman was seen to falter. Then she applied the torch and immediately turned and made her way through the crowd" (21 February 1892: 1). In the *World*, Jewell's reluctance and her flight from the scene were understood to be the result of womanly restraint and modesty and not the behavior of someone who, unlike Edward Coy, who was robbed of any choice whatsoever, had two narrow "choices": to participate in the execution of her lover or to be lynched herself.

The denial of any form of consent or agency on the part of white women was an important part of lynch narratives. On one hand, it allowed white women to scapegoat black men for relationships that may have been consensual. On the other hand, it allowed white women to offer up African American scapegoats when unauthorized sexual relationships with white men had been discovered. White women were thus complicitous in the commission of crimes against African Americans. In July 1863, Irish women played an important role in goading rioters to beat, torture, and lynch African American men, while they robbed fleeing black women and children and looted the homes of those who had sought refuge elsewhere. In numerous instances of lynching, even when innocent of making accusations, women played a similarly important role in these communal acts of violence. As Kathleen Blee's (1992, 2003) research reminds us, white women's involvement in racist social movements has long been a crucial component of such activism.

While the silences and contradictions that appeared in the *World*'s coverage of the burning of Edward Coy might be explained by the paper's reliance on clippings from other newspapers and its geographical remoteness from the scene of the crime itself, the lynching of Robert Lewis in Port Jervis, New York, shows how an identical framework was utilized in a story that occurred much closer to home. The lynching of Robert Lewis was covered widely in the New York City press because of its geographical proximity to New York City.[13] The *World*'s version of the story asserted that, on 2 June 1892, Robert Lewis was hanged "for an outrageous assault." The account continued,

> The crime, a most heinous and revolting one, was committed about noon to-day on the outskirts of the village, on the banks of the Neversink River. It was witnessed by two young girls, who stood about fifty feet away, and also by two young negroes, who would have interfered on the girl's behalf, but were kept at bay by a revolver.
>
> (3 June 1892: 1)

As in the case of Coy, Lewis' guilt of committing "a most heinous and revolting" crime was considered unquestionable, witnessed as it was by at least four people.

Like the lynching of Coy, other accounts of the incident sharply diverged from the version depicted in the *World*. The *World* placed numerous eyewitnesses at the scene; some of whom it reported were kept at bay with a revolver. No weapon was mentioned in other accounts. It later asserted that several children were playing nearby, but in the same report it stated that there were no witnesses to the crime itself save the unconscious victim. According to the *World*, the victim was walking along the banks of the river, accompanied by two children. Putting her in the company of two children accorded her a measure of reliability and respectability, thereby dodging the question as to what the unaccompanied single woman was doing at the river's edge. Here again, no other account suggested that the victim was accompanied by anyone but Peter Foley (who she had been dating) and Robert Lewis.

The story of the alleged rape was more complicated than the *World* let on.

The victim, 21-year old Lena McMahon, had been dating Peter Foley, an itinerant worker, until January 1892, when he was arrested for failure to pay a hotel bill. She continued to see Foley against her middle-class parents' wishes. Three days before the alleged assault, McMahon had argued with her parents and left their home, returning to Port Jervis on the day of the attack. Upon her return, she met Foley and the couple went for a walk along the banks of the Neversink River. When Foley went to town to get them lunch, Robert Lewis (whom McMahon later charged had been encouraged to assault her by Foley) attacked McMahon, who fainted. While she was insensible, Lewis allegedly raped her.

A 1955 account of the lynching, which also accepted that Lewis raped McMahon, offered the dubious assertion that Foley had put Lewis up to the crime by telling him that, "You can take her. She might kick up a little fuss, but don't let it worry you. Just take her. She'll give in" (Friedman 1955: 47). While the *World* also hinted that Foley may have played a part in the crime, Foley's participation was limited to his urging Lewis to rape McMahon. According to the newspaper, after having been caught by members of the lynch mob, Lewis "confessed the crime and implicated William [*sic*] Foley, a white man." "Feeling against him in this community is so strong," the *World* continued, that Foley would likely meet the same fate as Lewis (3 June 1892: 1). Needless to say, although Foley was later imprisoned on extortion charges, he was not lynched. In fact, less than a week after Robert Lewis was lynched, a white man was arrested and charged with sexually assaulting a 9-year-old girl. The suspect was deemed to be intoxicated and sentenced to two months in jail.[14]

Like the *New York Times* and the *New York Tribune*, the *World* was close enough to Port Jervis, New York, to send a reporter to the town. Still, the newspaper got several key facts wrong, facts that favored the actions of the lynch mob. The newspaper never mentioned McMahon's argument with her parents and subsequent unescorted departure from Port Jervis, instead suggesting that she was assaulted as she innocently played on the banks of the Neversink with two children. Nor did it refer to her relationship with Foley, beyond saying that he had "been paying attention to the girl against the wishes of her parents," a statement that emphasized parental protection and middle-class respectability.

Moreover, by reporting that McMahon was in critical condition, the *World*'s account accentuated the putative viciousness of the attack on her. The headline the day after the lynching claimed that the female victim was in "a critical condition," having been left insensible by the violence of the attack, "with injuries which will probably prove fatal" (3 June 1892: 1). Yet McMahon's life was never in danger. After awakening from the attack near the Neversink River, she was "discovered" by her erstwhile seducer Foley and then escorted home by another Port Jervis resident, to whom she was said to have recounted the story about being raped by Lewis. A few days after the lynching of Lewis, McMahon was said to have further admitted, "They hung the wrong man. William Foley was the one they really should have strung up, for he was at the bottom of it" (Friedman 1955: 47), but this was interpreted to mean that Foley had urged

Lewis to rape McMahon and not that Foley had framed Lewis for an act he had committed.[15]

McMahon was known to suffer from "fainting spells" and "inexplicable lapses of memory" (Friedman 1955: 47) that in this case corresponded to key moments in her story. According to a later account, Robert Lewis, the biracial son of a Port Jervis resident, was a "good-natured husky young man," who, when he was not driving a bus for a local prison, "spent most of his days plucking fat fish out of the rivers that girdled the town" (Friedman 1955: 47).[16] Why would a young black man, who had no previous history of violence and who was apparently in full possession of his faculties, rape a young white woman on the banks of a river in broad daylight in front of witnesses? Why did townspeople and newspaper reporters alike so easily accept the secondhand testimony of a young and possibly mentally ill white woman, who had been romantically involved with Foley?

By reporting that a white female victim lay near death, the *World* upheld a scenario that validated the actions of the mob. Because Lewis was deemed guilty of assaulting a white woman, he was beaten, bound, dragged through the street by his neck, stoned, hanged, cut down, and then hanged again, in a terrible process that took some three hours. The *World* conceded:

> From the time the negro was brought to town up to the time that the mob pounced upon him he was handled most savagely. He was dragged by the neck up one of the principal streets, kicked, beaten and otherwise maltreated. In fact the man was practically dead before he was hung up to the tree.
>
> (3 June 1892: 1)

Judge William Howe Crane, the father of journalist and author Stephen Hart Crane, lived across from the church where Lewis was hanged. At the inquest, Crane testified about his futile attempts to intervene in the lynching. Lewis had been beaten so badly, Crane testified, that he "did not recognize him as Bob Lewis" (Wertheim and Sorrentino 1994: 73).

The *World* published an editorial after its initial news coverage that confirmed its fundamental agreement with the lynching. The Port Jervis lynching, the editorial argued, had nothing to do with race. Rather, it expressed that "popular sentiment regards this particular crime, when committed by a negro against a white woman, as one deserving of death. The law does not provide a death penalty for it, and so the people take the matter into their own hands" (*World*, 4 June 1892: 4). In this, the *World* again endorsed the logic of the lynch mob by refusing to accord black suspects the right to due process accorded to whites. Black men who were even accused of assaulting white women should be sentenced to death. Assuming that white men and women would not lie about such an attack, the mere rumor of such a crime was proof enough to carry out this sentence. The *World* conceded that:

> Lynchings are always criminal outbreaks, but after all it is difficult in any community to arouse public opinion against a lynching done for such a

cause as this. The brutal assailant of a helpless woman is a person for whom American manhood has very little sympathy indeed.

(4 June 1892: 4)

What this account does not—and cannot— state is that although the same pages of the *World* carried innumerable stories of family violence, beyond lurid front-page coverage, there was no evidence that "American manhood" much cared about the wretched conditions and miserable deaths of working-class and immigrant white women, not to mention the assaults on black women that had long been disregarded by the mainstream press.[17]

"Ask any man who has a wife, a daughter, a sister"

> If America would not hear the cry of men, women and children whose dying groans ascended to heaven praying for relief, not only for them but for others who might soon be treated as they, then certainly no fair-minded person can charge disloyalty to those who make an appeal to the civilization of the world for such sympathy and help as it is possible to extend. If stating the facts of these lynchings, as they appeared from time to time in the white newspapers of America—the news gathered by white correspondents, compiled by white press bureaus and disseminated among white people— shows any vindictiveness, then the mind which so charges is not amenable to argument.
>
> (Wells 1892/1997: 131)

The editor of the *World* was a firm believer in the value of the newspaper crusade.[18] In a letter to managing editor Charles Lincoln, Joseph Pulitzer gave a thumbnail sketch of his journalistic credo (quoted in Juergens 1966: 32), which began with these two points:

1 What is original, distinctive, dramatic, romantic, thrilling, unique, curious, quaint, humorous, odd, apt to be talked about, without shocking good taste or lowering the general tone, good tone, and above all without impairing the confidence of the people in the truth of the stories or the character of the paper for reliability and scrupulous cleanness.
2 What is the one distinctive feature, fight, crusade, public service, or big exclusive? No paper can be great, in my opinion, if it depends simply upon the hand-to-mouth idea, news coming in anyhow. One big distinctive feature every day at least. One striking feature each issue should contain, prepared before, not left to chance.

Pulitzer further demanded that crusades feature prominently in the *World*'s coverage of the city's affairs: "'It is Mr. Pulitzer's wish,' one of the editors reported after an interview with him, 'to have constantly on hand and waged vigorously a campaign, crusade or battle directed on proper lines; this is a fixed principle.

Subjects of wide interest should be taken always" (Juergens 1966: 50). In an undated memorandum, Pulitzer bemoaned the fact that

> the great lack both in the Sunday and Daily Editions is a continuing and great mystery, a great romance, or a great cumulative exposure, feature, crusade story of any sort deeper and deepening which can go on from day to day with sustained interest (not merely one day flies).
>
> (Juergens 1966: 53)

Pulitzer did not invent the journalistic crusade, but he did transform it into a routine journalistic practice. News production should not be "left to chance," he declared, thus formally articulating that which James Gordon Bennett had understood at an intuitive level: that a good reporter did not merely cover police courts, he created stories, understanding that, "It is an axiom of journalism that a story which takes several days, or weeks, to reach a climax is more exciting, and sells more newspapers, than one which can be reported in a single issue" (Juergens 1966: 53). The *World* was the main innovator in the area of crusading coverage in the 1880s and 1890s, reflecting a broader journalistic movement toward investigation and reform. The newspaper crusaded to raise funds to erect the Statue of Liberty, it campaigned for police reform, and it crusaded for reform of prisons and mental institutions. It never, however, featured a crusade against lynching.

The most benign meaning we can assign to the absence of a crusade would be to say that, like other mass-circulation newspapers of its era, the *World* simply did not consider African Americans of interest to an audience that they understood to be white. In the eyes of newspaper editors, the public sphere involved white men. White women were included only insofar as they were of interest or political use to white men or as potential consumers. Lynching was therefore not considered to be a "subject of wide interest." A more likely explanation for the absence of a journalistic crusade about lynching, however, is that the white men who produced the *World* shared the wider cultural skepticism and bias against the very possibility of black victims. Structurally disposed to consider African American men as criminals rather than victims, although some northern whites decried lynching for its violation of due process, many shared the belief that blacks must have done something in order to warrant such a response on the part of white communities understood to be genetically predisposed to rationality.

Indeed, until the murders of civil rights workers James Cheney, Andrew Goodman, and Michael Schwerner in 1964, lynching never inspired the investigative or prosecutorial zeal associated with other acts of individual violence in US culture. Where moral crusades about white slavery in the early years of the twentieth century, the kidnapping of fascist Charles Lindbergh's son in 1932, and the moral panic over child stranger abduction in the 1980s were all constructed as widespread social threats on the basis of little or no empirical evidence, lynching elicited no such outrage. Laws were passed in the wake

of crusades featuring white victims, and institutions like the FBI were granted
extended powers and funding because of alleged increases in these categories
of crime.

Historian Evelyn Nagano Glenn makes a useful distinction between formal
citizenship, based on formal law and legal rulings, and substantive citizenship,
which "involves the actual ability to exercise rights of citizenship" (2004: 53).
While black people may have been granted formal citizenship after the Civil
War, terrorism against people of color denied them the substantive citizenship
that would have given them recourse against racist crimes like lynching. The
absence of substantive citizenship, moreover, demonstrates how difficult it was
for African American reform movements, representing black victims of violence,
to get a hearing in the white, mainstream press. As we saw in the Jewett and
Rogers cases, the presence of reform movements helped generate serialized coverage of crime. Such coverage of reform movements and their demands was
effective in attracting supporters, as well as pressuring institutions to address
social problems. Yet despite the strenuous efforts of anti-lynching activists like
Ida B. Wells and organizations like the NAACP, until the 1930s, with the exception of the African American press, lynching was not accorded the crusading
coverage that came to be associated with other crimes.[19] Even muckraking journalists remained largely silent about the issue of lynching.[20] The mass media
thus proved unresponsive to the voices of black citizens, either as individuals or
as organized social movements.

Despite lynching's violation of almost every aspect of democracy that the
USA purported to value, the police, the media, and institutions of government
(at both state and federal levels) not only refused to intervene, but in many
ways and places such institutions encouraged this violence, if only through their
refusal to condemn it. A Pennsylvania anti-lynching bill, drafted after the lynching of Zachariah Walker in 1911, and introduced to the general assembly in
Harrisburg in March 1913, was not signed into law until May 1923, at a time
when there were reports that the Ku Klux Klan had hanged another African
American man in Beaver, Pennsylvania (Downey and Hyser 1991: 155). The
US Congress failed to pass the Dyer Anti-Lynching Bill in the early 1920s (156).
In fact, despite several attempts, no federal anti-lynching law was ever passed,
although a federal kidnapping law passed easily in 1933, after the abduction and
murder of the Lindbergh baby.[21]

In the end, there would be no anti-lynching crusade in the pages of mainstream, mass-circulation newspapers because to do so would have involved
mounting challenges to dominant understandings of American manhood that
white newspaper editors, reporters, and audiences were creating and upholding.
Constructions of white masculinity in the USA, as we have seen, were grounded
in protection scenarios that were organized around white men's duty to protect
white women from threats they had themselves constructed. In these scenarios, the privilege of being protectors was a fundamental condition of whiteness.
Black men appeared only as threats, never as men desirous of protecting their
wives and children. In the name of protecting their (white) women, white men

sought to justify violent practices that were at every level antithetical to the ideological order they had constructed. Indeed, it is difficult to imagine a form of violence more directly opposite to the protection scenario than lynching in which women, men, and children were kidnapped from the supposed sanctity of the private sphere under cover of darkness, then tortured, mutilated, and murdered, their bodies often left as a warning to others.

Criticizing the rationale behind lynching would have directly challenged the deep investment in reproducing an understanding of white men as rational, civilized, and eminently reasonable creatures. Moreover, challenging what Wells called "the old thread bare lie that negro men rape white women" (1892/1997: 52), would have further entailed challenging allegations of sexual assault either made by white women or ventriloquized by white protectors on behalf of injured white women. Finally, and as we have seen in this chapter, sexualizing lynching—suggesting these crimes were somehow "chivalrous" responses to attacks on white women—masked the all too real economic, ideological, and political motivations behind lynching as a terrorist tool. The *World* and other newspapers could not deny that lynching was a criminal act, but they routinely represented black men as the agents provocateurs of mob violence. The real problem, as they understood it, lay in the failure of the criminal justice system to mete out swift and severe punishment for the sexualized crimes black men had undoubtedly committed.[22]

The *World* went to some lengths to sexualize motives for lynching. Of the 45 articles reported by the *World*, only a dozen referred to rape or assault and three of those involved the case of Edward Coy. Yet the editorial page was swift to use cases purportedly involving sexual assault—Coy and Lewis, for example—to tacitly condone lynching on the whole. One editorial approvingly cited racist South Carolina Governor Ben Tillman's assertion that "There is only one crime that should bring on lynching. I, as Governor, would head a party to lynch any negro that would assault a white woman" (8 June 1892: 8). A few weeks later, the *World* repeated this central point: "Ask any man who has a wife, a daughter, a sister, or any other woman near and dear to him, whether he would rather have her killed or criminally assaulted, and the answer will be quick and emphatic in favor of death" (28 June 1892: 4). Of course, southern discourses of lynching were more open in laying out the racialized terms of protection. Thus, Governor Tillman specified that he would lynch any *negro* who had assaulted a *white* woman—he did not call for lynching any man who had assaulted any woman.

Mainstream newspapers accepted the assumption that lynchings were responses—however misguided or unjust—to the rape of white women by black men, what Wells was later to criticize as a logic that saw lynching "as the desperate effort of the Southern people to protect their women from black monsters" (quoted in Addams and Wells 1977: 29). In mainstream news, no one questioned the veracity of charges against African Americans. And there was widespread consensus that execution was an appropriate punishment for African American men accused of rape, even though white men thus charged often did not even serve prison time. By the end of the nineteenth century, patterns for representing both criminals and victims had been established and crime news became invested in notions of miscegenation that represented black men as criminally desirous of white women, white women as objects over which white and black men were to struggle on a profoundly uneven playing field, and black women as the contradictory and therefore invisible part of this scenario.

Forbidden membership in the cult of true womanhood, black women qualified neither as women in the sense demanded by a racialized androcentrism nor as victims. Where some white women were worthy victims and others were not, black women simply disappeared. As Lisa Lindquist Dorr puts it, "White men's discussions about a victim's complicity in her violation indicates that whites believed that certain kinds of women, and potentially all women, were untrustworthy, either because they were irrational or because they were deceitful" (2004: 11–12). Yet as we saw most clearly in the lynching of Edward Coy and Robert Lewis, even the words of the least trustworthy of white female victims could, in 1892, be trusted over the protestations of innocence made by blacks. Even the culturally most dubious of white female victims—Helen Jewett and Mary Rogers, to take two examples—could be elevated to worthy victimhood when the occasion arose. But black women could not be so elevated. Wells cited a South Carolina journal that made this racial and gendered economy of victimization shockingly clear. "It is not," the journal observed, "the same thing for a white man to assault a colored woman as for a colored man to assault a white woman, because the colored woman had no finer feelings nor virtue to be outraged" (quoted in Wells 1892/1997: 127).

Thus lacking the requisite finer feelings and virtue central to entry into true womanhood, black women did not appear in the *World*'s coverage of lynching. Between 1889 and 1918, 61 women were lynched in the USA, 50 of whom were executed for "crimes" like "racial prejudice." In 1892 alone, six women were lynched: four for "racial prejudice" and two for well poisoning. The *World* reported on none of these cases. Wells documented numerous cases in which black girls and women were the victims of sexual assaults by whites. Wells told of one case in which a gang of white men raped a black girl, while they held down the black man who had been out walking with her (1892/1997: 128). In Nashville, Tennessee, the city that had seen the brutal lynching of Ephraim Grizzard for allegedly raping a white woman, a white man had raped an eight-year-old black girl. Sentenced to jail for six months, the white man was released and later became a police detective in that city. Although, as Wells pointed out, "colored women have always had far more reason to complain of white men in this respect than ever white women have had of negroes" (1892/1997: 127), in case after case, the myriad indignities and violations visited upon black women were completely ignored.

Newspapers also ignored African American women's political mobilization against lynching during this era, a mobilization that turned the logic of the protection scenario on its head. As Hazel Carby put it, the shape of this challenge "reassessed the mythology of the founding fathers in terms of rampant lust, greed, and destruction" (1985: 265). Wells in particular criticized miscegenation laws that "pretended to offer 'protection' to white women but left black women the victims of rape by white men and simultaneously granted to these same men the power to terrorize black men as a potential threat to the virtue of white womanhood" (1982: 268). Living as they did outside the parameters of scenarios of protection, African American women and the club movement that produced the first Congress of Colored Women of the United States defied paternalistic authority by speaking out on behalf of themselves and their communities. It was no wonder that mainstream newspapers, invested in protection scenarios and the forms of white masculinity and femininity these women were contesting, chose not to hear them.

If depictions of black male sexual monsters were a form of threat construction that facilitated the production of white scenarios of protection, denial of the victimization of African American women, as well as the challenges they were mounting to racialized androcentrism, was also central to the reproduction of racialized androcentrism. As Angela Davis points out, the demands of the economic exploitation of African Americans (from slavery to the current time) did not allow blacks to conform to the ideological mandates of nineteenth-century androcentric culture. Among chattel slaves in the south and wage slaves in the north, as Davis continues, "the promotion of male supremacy among the slaves might have prompted a dangerous rupture in the chain of command" (1983: 8).

By failing to challenge this logic, news narratives accepted a view of black men and their sexuality as being monstrous, and reproduced a racial economy of victimization that saw black men as being predisposed—both socially and genetically—to violent crime. Coverage of lynching in both 1863 and 1892 further illustrated the tendency on the part of the US mainstream press to deny African Americans victim status, despite the obvious magnitude of the crimes committed against them. The absence of coverage devoted to violence against African Americans confirms that even given the most horrendous and heart-wrenching circumstances—an African American mother who threw her body over that of her nine-year-old son in order to protect him from a racist mob only to be kicked to death herself, African American men burned alive because of relationships with white women—journalists consistently sought to rationalize and provide alibis for these and other acts of racist hate. When confronted with evidence that so directly contradicted the protection scenario upon which white masculinity was erected, the press and white society as a whole simply ignored it.

The discourse of miscegenation—its focus on lustful black monsters and its erasure of black women who had no choice but to labor—aided in the wider cultural project of ensuring that black men would have no access—ideological, political, or cultural—to the role of masculine family head, provider, and protector. Cast solely as the black villain intent on defiling the white victim, black men were ideologically relegated to the role of criminal, while black women were exiled from this narrative framework altogether.

The case of lynching demonstrates how the race of criminals and victims affected a whole range of institutional practices. In newspapers, white criminals in the shape of lynch mobs were understood to have complicated and often legitimate motives for their criminal acts. Blacks accused of crimes were cast as motivated by a primal and simple sexual desire for white women. In terms of the criminal justice system, the US government cared so little about lynching that it never collected statistics on it. Thus, the existing statistics on lynching come from African American organizations like the NAACP and the Tuskegee Institute.

Finally, lynching constituted a wider refusal either to criminalize or to prosecute particular kinds of crimes against people of color, especially when white people committed those crimes. No statistics exist on how many men were ever accused, much less convicted, of taking part in lynching. Had white men been charged with the lynching of blacks, that itself would have been considered newsworthy. The absence of such coverage can only mean that few if any white men were ever charged with such crimes. Certainly, there is no evidence that suggests that any white men were convicted of these crimes. Because the victims were black, newspaper accounts of lynching (which, along with photographs circulated from the south, were the only accounts of lynching that northern whites were likely to encounter) consistently represented lynching of black men as justifiable and at some level socially acceptable punishment for crimes they had unquestionably committed against white women's virtue.[23] Had the victims of these crimes been white, lynching undoubtedly would have been criminalized and those responsible for such criminal acts would have been punished and condemned.

It should not be difficult, from our historical vantage point, to see the homologies between the racialized threat constructions that emerged after the Civil War and more recent genocidal logics in economically ravaged, war-torn countries, where the perpetrators of the most hideous crimes against humanity have blamed their victims for provoking the outrages visited upon them. Congolese, during the reign of Belgian King Leopold between 1893 and 1909, were said to be reproducing at a rate threatening to white colonists, who were dying at an alarming rate; and Tutsis in Rwanda were repeatedly described as "cockroaches," whose rates of reproduction directly threatened Hutu control.[24] The racialized and gendered discourse of miscegenation that emerged in the USA during the Civil War similarly enabled a reign of terrorism based on fears about racial purity. By criminalizing desires projected onto black men by white cultural producers and politicians, the discourse of miscegenation set the stage for a succession of moral crusades in the years to come, all of them dependent upon the construction of a threatening and sexually predatory black man whose sole purpose in life was to reproduce with white women and whose very reason for being was to undo the "white" race.

In the 1890s, the USA stood on the verge of an era of institution building, record keeping, and data collection; an era that was to change relations among institutions producing information about crime and criminals. White women's political mobilization for suffrage would gain momentum in the years ahead and an increasingly female immigrant labor force would become more militant. As white women in general began speaking on their own behalf, scenarios of protection organized around white female victims began to yield gradually to those involving white children. Nevertheless, the dynamics of black criminality and the erasure of black women set in motion by lynch narratives and the threat of miscegenation would guarantee that white supremacy would itself remain a sturdy and resilient strand in crime news for decades to come.

5 Monopolists of reason

The demise of sentimental
crime reporting

Where the previous chapters considered reporting of crimes that were denied to
be such, and the raced and gendered character of coverage of acts of violence
against victims deemed unworthy by mainstream news, this chapter directs
attention back to crime reporting itself. Being an obstinately conservative form
of reporting, insofar as its mode of narration remained fairly constant across
the nineteenth century, by the end of the nineteenth century the style and content of crime reporting had changed very little. But between 1900 and 1930,
crime reporting was to undergo a series of changes that transformed it, in terms
of both style and content. In the 1890s, the vast bulk of crime reporting in New
York City's mass circulation dailies featured sentimental stories about family violence, or violence against intimates that occurred in the so-called private sphere,
and thus directly engaged with ideologies of gender and class. By the late 1920s
this form of crime reporting had disappeared in favor of stories about street-
based crime, organized crime, and a narrative focus on institutions created and
staffed by white middle-class men, represented as heroic defenders of a public
sphere experiencing an onslaught from the street.

The change in news coverage was striking. During the final decade of the
nineteenth century, and into the opening of the twentieth, New York City newspapers routinely covered cases of family violence—murder-suicides, wife-killings,
infanticides, and myriad forms of intimate assault. The widowed James Forshay
(known as "Christian" Forshay because of his fondness for "church-going"),
"crazed by grief for his wife, shot his child and then himself," in a story headlined "Killed the Boy He Loved" (*New York World*, 19 June 1894: 1). In another
story, "Murder This Boy's Mania," an 11-year-old boy, "crazed" not by grief
but by a blow to the head, attempted to kill his mother, himself, and his infant
twin brothers (*New York World*, 2 July 1894: 1).

These were stories that did not skirt the reality of family violence, but
covered it directly, replete with language freighted with emotion and sentimentalized details. Of course, family violence is a more recent category of crime that
nineteenth-century journalists would not have recognized as such. In addition,
prone to under-reporting, family violence has always been a notoriously difficult category of crime to track. Given the erratic collection of data on crime in
New York City at the end of the century, we have no way of knowing whether

the abundance of crime reporting about what we would now describe as family violence resulted from some actual increase in these forms of crime during the period, whether the efforts of the temperance movement and the new profession of social work had sensitized journalists to such crimes, or whether there was a sudden increase in police attention to family violence. We do know, however, that in the decades following the end of the nineteenth century, family violence did not magically disappear from US society, which makes the disappearance of reporting of crimes against intimates by the late 1920s of particular interest to those concerned with how gender and race have shaped accounts of crime.[1]

The change in style and content of crime reporting corresponded to changes sweeping other institutions assigned responsibility for surveying and interacting with the poor and destitute, those groups historically understood to be inclined to violence. As such, the change with which this chapter is concerned reflected a wider shift in approaches to social problems, wherein the sentimentalized representations of the poor long invoked by religious charities were replaced by the "objective" representations of the poor favored by modern institutions intent on establishing their political and cultural credentials. For crime reporting, this change involved a significant departure from earlier sentimental forms of story-telling that frequently took familial relations as their starting-point, to crime narratives in which women and the home barely figured. In response, the protection scenario subtly shifted from an emphasis on the protection of actual women to the protection of a consumer-oriented, feminized public.

This chapter looks at the impact of the introduction of a gendered distinction into crime reporting and the resultant rejection of sentimentalized crime reporting in favor of the objective crime reporting that was to devalue and replace it. Beginning with the institutional ferment that contributed to this shift, the chapter turns to crime narratives that were sites of progressive-era struggles over gender and objectivity. It concludes by considering the institution that emerged from this conflict as the primary definer and popularizer of crime narratives, the Federal Bureau of Investigation, whose first public war on crime was one from which any overt mention of gender and race had been expunged.

From the feeling heart to the trained eye

The system of racialized androcentrism that developed in the USA, like the capitalist economic order it has served, is a spectacularly flexible one, capable of absorbing challenges to existing ideologies of gender and race and mounting challenges of its own during periods of economic and social upheaval. Susan Jeffords (1989) has spoken of the "remasculinization of America" that occurred after the Vietnam War, but the process she describes, or any putative crisis in masculinity for that matter, is a more continuous one, in which ideologies of white masculinity are posited as constant and unchanging in relation to the shifting shadows from the various threat constructions it projects to reinvent and reconsolidate its power. In writing about the manifestations of androcentric reinvention that were occurring between 1890 and 1930, Donna Haraway notes

"Conventional western ambivalence about 'civilization' was never higher than during the early decades of monopoly capital formation" (1989: 54).

If the Jacksonian manifestations of masculinity that had been very much at stake in the penny press' crime reporting devolved around a frontier that then seemed boundless and an investment in whiteness shored up by the institution of slavery, ideologies of masculinity in the progressive era confronted a different set of challenges. Heightened competition between robber barons, and the recessions, labor strife, and widespread social unrest that followed from this, were effecting changes in ideologies of masculinity. The rough-hewn adventurism of Davy Crockett, predicated as it was on exploring the contours of an expanding nation-state, was giving way to the rough riding of Teddy Roosevelt and a shift from internal colonization to imperialist adventurism. As the nation-state itself began to settle into its more modern geographical cartography, attention turned to building both institutions and institutional practices oriented toward modernization and a new era of industrial expansion.

During the progressive era, the news industry, like other institutions governing modern life, was changing in response to wider economic and political forces. If James Gordon Bennett was the Davy Crockett of his day, baiting and battling with other editors and reporters in the streets of New York, so advocates of journalistic professionalism like Joseph Pulitzer, who may not have practiced what he preached during the Spanish-American War but was at the same time a great proponent of a professionally trained news corps, and Adolph Ochs, owner and editor of the *New York Times*, stood at the symbolic forefront of massive changes in the way that newspapers conducted business, as well as themselves. Ochs and his newspaper, in particular, have come to be most closely associated with a change in stance and style in news reporting that would come to be known as objectivity and that positioned itself in opposition to the sentimentalism of an earlier era.

The literary style known as sentimentalism refers to a style of writing associated with emotion, a faith in humanity rather than "reason," and a narrative slipperiness in identifying victims and protectors. Some critics of sentimentalism, like Ann Douglas, dismiss the sentimental as "an inevitable part of the self-evasion of a society both committed to laissez-faire industrial expansion and disturbed by its consequences" (1977: 12). Jane Tompkins argues, in contrast, "for the positive value of stereotyped characters and sensational, formulaic plots" particularly insofar as these challenged the existing social order (1985: xvii). According to Cathy Davidson, the sentimentalism expressed in the nineteenth-century American novel "tended to proclaim a socially egalitarian message. It spoke for—often even in the title—orphans, beggar girls, factory girls, or other unfortunates, and it repeatedly advocated the general need for 'female education'" (1986: 73). Sentimentalism was at once associated with both a style and a subject matter: both would come to be identified with women, the feminine, and the subjective, and both would be denigrated as objectivity gained institutional hegemony.

Just as the penny press of the 1830s had borrowed liberally from literary genres and contributed to both literary and institutional forms of writing like police narratives, so the press at the turn of the nineteenth century included a good amount of traffic across cultural forms. The mainstream press of the late nineteenth century featured a style of crime writing that was emotionally descriptive when speaking of victims, intrigued by the relationships that underlay social violence, and attentive to the economic circumstances in which social violence took place. In terms of style, sentimental news reporting—like the social movements that it covered and that often inspired it—sought to invoke feelings and passions about its subject. As in literary sentimentalism's emphasis on human relationships and emotional loss, late nineteenth- and early twentieth-century crime reporting typically offered elaborate descriptions of the emotional states of both criminal and victim and often described its subjects in prose that sought to overcome rather than reinforce the distance between reporter and reported and readers and victims.

Altogether different from the abstract, passive, and emotionally detached style of writing valued as objective by modernism, sentimental crime narratives shared a number of characteristics. First, nineteenth-century accounts of crime favored emotionally charged and often speculative language, as opposed to the technical and clinical language of objectivity. The following account, for example, included an elaborate reenactment of the crime itself, rather than a recounting of the "facts" of the case:

> Directly after breakfast Mrs. Noyes prepared a dose of aconite in some sweetened water and forced the children to take it. The girl, suspecting something wrong, ejected the last mouthful when her mother was not looking. The boy was seized with vomiting, and threw the poison up. Mrs. Noyes took about a drachm of the poison herself, and then took a razor and drew it across the girl's throat. Then she tried to cut her own, but did not succeed in severing the windpipe. The girl grasped her mother's hand and held on until assistance arrived.
>
> (*New York World*, 25 May 1892: 1)

Even if the reporter did not include himself in the crime scene, this description still had more of a resemblance to Bennett's account of the murder of Helen Jewett some six decades before rather than to the crime news that was to follow.

A second characteristic of sentimental crime reporting involved the perspective of the reporter himself. Unlike the writing of Wisner and Bennett in the 1830s and 1840s, in the 1890s reporters were frequently absent from the narrative as well as the scene of the crime. But omniscience did not presuppose emotional distance. While the perspective of the reporter had begun to shift, it remained rooted in a sentimental and sensual form of writing, replete with vivid adjectives and grisly descriptions. The text of one very typical murder story from the 1890s, for example, included the following description:

A horrible odor prevaded [sic] the apartment. In the far corner of the squalid kitchen lay the body of a woman face down. The feet were stretched under the supper table one corner of which touched the wall. A case knife with dark stains upon the blade, lay near the head. There was also a broken lamp standard close by. Broken bits of glass were scattered about the floor. A large hole had been burned in the tablecloth.

Officer Berman turned the body upon its back, and he and the neighbors saw the distorted and swollen features of Philip Cunningham's dead wife. The face had been terribly burned.

(*New York World*, 26 April 1892: 1)

Here again, the writer's attention to seemingly inconsequential details (shards of shattered glass, a broken lamp) and senses like smell were more typical of thickly descriptive sentimental crime reporting than they were of objective reporting that focused chiefly on details related to the crime itself.

Appealing straightforwardly to the reader's senses, the *World*'s crime reporting included an attention to domestic detail further associated with more sentimental and feminized forms of writing: the squalor of the kitchen, the supper table that partly concealed the victim's feet, the broken lamp, and the hole in the tablecloth. Reports of family violence devoted careful attention to those feminized, often mundane details that constituted the background, and that seemed to have little to do with the crime itself, particularly from the later perspective of scientific and objective police work, concerned primarily with the ostensible empiricism of detective work and the trained eyes of police detectives.[2]

In contrast to later "harder" coverage of crime, whose use of proper names and official titles considered both criminals and victims in isolation from their social networks, these narratives stressed relationality as opposed to the abstract individualism of objectivity, using language that called attention to relationships among victims, perpetrators, and witnesses. These crime narratives underscored the abject nature of the private sphere, as well as the intimate nature of relations among the actors involved in such tragedies. Mrs. Noyes was a mother, and despite her assaults on her children, her dying little girl "grasped her mother's hand." Banner headlines further capitalized on this sentimental formula by distilling highly emotional storylines into a few eye-catching headlines:

Shot the Girl He Loved
Her Mother Sprang to Save Her and Was Hit by Another Bullet
LEIFSHOFTS THEN PUT A BULLET IN HIS OWN HEAD.

(*New York World*, 4 July 1893: 1)

SHOT HIS WIFE'S HEAD OFF
She Upbraided Him for Spending His Wages for Drink, and He Killed Her before Their Son.

(*New York World*, 17 June 1894: 1)[3]

These stories, readers were repeatedly reminded, involved mothers, sons, lovers, daughters, fathers, wives, and husbands, not cold and distant strangers who had no relationship to the people they had harmed. These were crimes, moreover, that did not present the abstract threat of stranger dangers, but the violence that could transpire in a private sphere that an androcentric culture elsewhere presented as sanctuary.

However much sentimentalism may have reproduced dominant ideologies of gender, it is also true, as Andrea Hibbard and John Parry (2006) have pointed out, that sentimental crime narratives allowed for discussions of women's oppression at the hands of husbands, lovers, and fathers, while at the same time acknowledging the reality of a society in which the family and the private sphere were not the safe havens that proponents of moral or family values made them out to be. Sentimentalism's emphasis on relationality further accorded some sympathy to both victims and victimizers alike, stressing a context that "made" otherwise decent people go bad, rather than the genetic determinism and isolated individualism that were beginning to shape narratives about criminal "classes."[4] In place of the Calvinist understanding of human nature as depraved that was morphing into genetic understandings of crime, sentimental crime narratives accentuated the inherent goodness of human beings.

For example, the following headlines anchored a story that offered a remarkably sympathetic depiction of the murderer:

> Death at a Mother's Hand
> Mrs. Korn Poisons and Shoots Her Children and Shoots Herself.
> HER LITTLE GIRL DEAD, BUT THE BOY WILL LIVE.
> (*New York World*, 6 May 1893: 1)

The remainder of the two column, front-page story, complete with a sketch of Mrs. Korn, contained an elaborate and heart-wrenching description of the crime:

> Then Mrs. Korn caught her golden-haired little daughter to her bosom, held her there for a second and, with the child still in her arms, fired the revolver into her little daughter's side. Then she laid her tenderly on the couch near the doorway and, pointing the revolver to her own breast, fired.

This description of the crime itself, complete with adverbs and adjectives that imbued the murderer's actions with maternal affection and care, also included the full text of Mrs. Korn's suicide note, which blamed her actions on her 45-year-old husband: "If I had never met this man, my husband, this would never have happened. He is the cause of it all. I have no rest anywhere I go. I am afraid of him, he acts so queer."[5] In their affinity for the downtrodden, sentimental crime narratives had the capacity to understand that the line between victims and villains was a permeable one, even when it came to a husband whose duty was protection and a mother who had done the culturally unthinkable.

The institutionalization of objectivity fundamentally altered the style of crime reporting. As Mindich (1998), Dan Schiller (1981), and Michael Schudson (1978) all describe in detail, many of the journalistic routines and practices that later came to be associated with journalistic objectivity had been experimented with in different places and times beforehand, with mixed results. From Benjamin Day's claims to be non-partisan to the increasing use of interviews and official sources at the end of the nineteenth century to Joseph Pulitzer's assertions that his paper represented a disembodied public (as opposed to personal) opinion, the detachment, non-partisanship, and omniscience later to be associated with journalistic objectivity had all been disparate practices within sometimes widely ranging journalistic routines. The widespread adoption of objectivity as both a journalistic ideal and a style of writing is best understood as a response to the various pressures that were being brought to bear on the newspaper industry during a period in which its routines were cohering into a more uniform whole. In the newspaper industry, the institutionalization of objectivity occurred alongside changes in the relationship between institutions of policing and media industries, as well as increasing levels of coordination among them; changes in the very notion of sources for journalistic narratives; and the use of "scientific surveys" to measure social violence.

Objectivity was, as numerous feminist critics have observed, a ruse of power; a strategy that mystified the social locations of those producing information and knowledge.[6] In order to effect a stylistic disembodiment whose most powerful effect was to detach power from its sources, and in order to maintain the claim to be perspectiveless while at the same time presenting perspectives that less and less frequently included the voices of working-class men and women, sourcing of information became more narrowly controlled.[7] As Gretchen Soderlund has pointed out, this entailed a shift from "'street-based' information" to "'institution-based' sources," from a form of sourcing increasingly associated with "the crowd, emotion, gossip" (2002: 442) and therefore femininity, to masculine sources understood to be objective, rational, and emotionally detached.

While these emergent, masculinized sources also included politicians and agents of various institutions of criminal justice, it was at this point that police began to emerge as the single most important source for information about crime. In the USA, journalists have always had a symbiotic relationship with the police who provided them with information about crime, criminal activity, and the "dangerous classes" as a whole. Lardner and Repetto describe the New York Police Department as the offspring of newspapers, a statement that was particularly true insofar as crusading journalists like Thomas Gordon Bennett played an important role in bringing down the old watch system, thereby giving birth to a more organized, modern police force (2001: 23). Throughout the nineteenth century, newspapers' criticisms of the police and crusades against police corruption resulted in major reforms to institutions of policing and police practices. Nevertheless, relations between child and parent institutions developed unevenly and antagonistically across the nineteenth century. Where the *New York Times* sang the praises of the police department and its comportment during the 1863 anti-draft riots (the police were the only state institution to emerge from the riots politically unscathed), by the 1890s, newspapers like the *New York World* once again waged acrimonious campaigns against police corruption and, with the assistance of reform-minded politicians, successfully ousted police officials believed to be corrupt. As late as the 1890s, newspapers like the *New York World* were calling for the use of qualifying examinations for police officers in order to curb corruption and promote professionalism within the police force. In the 1880s and 1890s, crusades against the unprofessional behavior of police officers like Alexander "Clubber" Williams, renowned for his skillful and eager application of that weapon, were common.[8]

Until the end of the nineteenth century, both police and newspapers were concerned with internal organization—with trying to maintain order within their own ranks and to establish professional and institutionally reproducible codes of conduct and behavior. There was significant disagreement and open conflict among journalists over the role of newspapers in society, as well as the routines and practices that should govern their behavior. Police were in a similar state of flux.[9] Just as police station-houses had accommodated refugees during the 1863 anti-draft riots, so they served as shelters for the homeless, the destitute, and the unemployed in the 1890s, the last of whom could consult police station-houses when in need of information about employment opportunities.[10] In the 1890s, police still had primary responsibility for a number of functions that would soon be taken over by new institutions devoted to social welfare. But where before the progressive era police had housed the homeless (in some years, the number of overnight lodgings provided by police exceeded annual arrests), and "felt the initial responsibility to the poor" (Monkkonen 1981: 102), modernization effectively replaced such service and protection with punishment. Between 1880 and 1920, the nature of police work was to change dramatically, "from an informal, even casual, bureaucracy to a formal, rule-governed, militaristic organization" (Monkkonen 1981: 31).

Journalists did not consider police—who were not yet "professional" enough or committed to the scientific enterprise of crime prevention—to be the most credible authorities on crime itself. In reporting on crime, for example, reporters were as likely to consult eyewitnesses for their insights as they were to confer with police officers. Even if the words of police officers were occasionally given more credibility than the words of people on the street, crime reports were not narrated surreptitiously through the institutional lens of the police. Access to prisoners, moreover, was not as tightly controlled as it would later become and, like earlier crime reporters, journalists often included the testimony of those accused of crimes in their accounts of criminal activity. Muckraking journalist Lincoln Steffens recalled in his autobiography that well into the 1890s detectives, prisoners, and reporters freely mingled in station-houses, where "Sometimes a prisoner would give his version of his crime and his capture after the detective who had caught him told his" (1931: 285) and there are many other accounts of comparatively open access to prisoners housed in the Tombs in New York City.[11] As a result, reporters were more likely to hear competing versions of events, told from multiple perspectives.

Professionalization of police and crime reporters distanced both groups of men from the poor and working-class subjects of their work. By the beginning of the twentieth century, fewer reporters came from poor or working-class backgrounds, and professionalization, and the mechanisms of distinction that underlay it, combined to encourage reporters to identify with other professionals. Jacob Riis, for example, may have been an immigrant, but he brought a middle-class reformer's sensibility to his work, as did the native-born Lincoln Steffens. This more privileged class status meant that reporters often had more in common with police and other officials than they did with other sources. As reporters began to rely on institutional sources like the police for their information about crime—sources that were unlikely to stray from elite understandings of the causes and solutions to crime—so they less and less frequently consorted with "street" sources that had the potential to trouble their narrative frameworks. Seen ever more frequently as subjective, unreliable, and unpredictable, the "street" shifted from a source of information to the locus of criminal activity. The ostensible impartiality of institution-based sources was a central precept of the narrative structure of journalistic objectivity. Since information and perspective did not emanate from a now invisible narrator, it was important that the sources did not appear individual, subjective, or representative of any particular set of economic, political, or ideological interests.

Until the beginning of the twentieth century, then, police had little to offer journalists in the way of incentives to cooperate with them, whether in terms of access to information or of political influence. In the first place, police records in New York City were irregular and haphazardly maintained. Police blotters began to be used in New York City in 1845 and boroughs maintained irregular and informal records about categories and increases in crime before the Civil War, but it was not until 1898, during discussions about incorporating the boroughs, that individual police departments began to publish annual reports, initiating the publication of formal, citywide annual reports in 1900.[12] This meant that police had neither the credibility nor the monopoly over information about crime that they were soon to possess and reporters had not yet become dependent on police and police records for their information about crime or increases in criminal activity. Indeed, the very idea of "objective" information or sources had yet to be institutionalized.

Each of these changes—the growing intimacy between police and journalists, the monopolization of perspective and information flow, the increasing hegemony of institutional sources—contributed to the rise of objectivity during the progressive era and its integration into the everyday lives and routines of a whole host of institutions, institutional practices, and the narratives that institutions were telling themselves and one another about their function and purpose. More uniform forms of record-keeping on the part of institutions combined with survey methods to further facilitate the institutionalization of objectivity, allowing police to better control information about crime waves and affording them greater control over defining crime, both in terms of individual acts and in terms of categorizing specific acts as significant social problems.

With the advent of better-organized and more accessible records about crime, officials could point to supposedly incontrovertible evidence of increases and decreases in categories of crime, as well as of social violence itself. In place of the words of individual city or police officials, which were often questionable, reporters began to support their assertions about crime and society with the concreteness of numbers, the testimony of professional experts, and the objectivity conferred by institutional credentials. As dubious as collection methods were and are, as unreliable as police records have been historically, these measurements came to lend further power to "objective" coverage of crime. If street sources were unpredictable, experientially based, and feminized, so numeric calculations were seen to provide hard-edged, incontrovertible evidence of criminal activity and increases in categories of crime. In turn, these forms of evidence were understood to originate from perspectives interested in measurement alone and not in the political uses of increases or decreases in crime rates.

The distancing mechanism that was a key part of objectivity was also at work across other institutions assigned responsibility for managing the poor and attempting to explicate their plight. Karen W. Tice, for example, describes how the use of case records served to professionalize the nascent profession of social work during the progressive era by rejecting "flimsy notions of benevolent femininity" and replacing these with "muscular scientific professionalism" (1998: 48). Although the professionalization of social work proceeded differently than that of journalism, since the latter was a largely feminized enterprise beforehand, the growing emphasis on authorial distance and "factual" writing was strikingly similar. In both crime reporting and social work narratives, writers were being trained to adopt a specific set of strategies for eradicating their perspective from the narrative itself. In both forms of writing, authors were taught to use quotation marks, so that their subjects could "speak for themselves" without the interference of authorial bias. Before the professionalization of their respective institutions, both social workers and journalists had more direct experience with the poor and with poverty than most other members of the middle class. The rise of objectivity, and what Tice describes as "the gendering of professional proximity" (1998: 11), taught both social workers and journalists to distrust emotional responses to their subjects and to view the poor clinically and impassively, rather than with compassion and proximity.[13]

Sentimental writing existed on the wrong side of the divide introduced by the gendering of professional proximity. To be professional and objective meant being cool, distant, and masculine. One could not write about poor or oppressed peoples with sympathy, because that would imply nearness rather than distance, passion as opposed to dispassion, and bias as opposed to a god's eye view of the proceedings capable of presenting "both sides" of the picture. In contrast to the popular, sentimental writing used to describe the lot of a feminized poor, objectivity symbolized the hard-edged scientism and rationality of modern institutions, whose power would be hitherto concealed behind a style of writing and a mode of interaction that purported to be disembodied and disinterested. Where in the nineteenth century and into the early twentieth, the reporter described crime scenes, victims, and criminals in graphic and melodramatic detail, by the late 1920s he would no more use the language of sentiment than he would appear at the police station-house wearing a dress.

Struggling over objectivity

It is right to show up vice where vice exists, but it is outrageous to create vice. What we need is the reformer who uplifts and is happy when he finds nothing wrong.
(Charles O'C. Irwin, President of the Employment Agents' Society of New York, Inc., quoted in the *New York Times*, 8 May 1910: 20)

The struggle over objectivity vividly appeared in the contrast between two high-profile cases from the early twentieth century that appeared at each end of the chronological boundaries of the moral panic around white slavery.[14] The first was the 1907 trial of Henry Thaw for the murder in 1906 of architect Stanford White. The second was the murder of 15-year-old Ruth Wheeler in 1910. The former was one of the last great sentimental crime narratives in mainstream newspapers, while the latter bore the imprimatur of the new brand of objective reporting.

In the first case to be called "the Trial of the Century" in a century that was to have a number of other similarly branded crimes, on 25 June 1906, Pittsburgh industrial magnate Henry Thaw and his wife, former showgirl Evelyn Nesbit, were watching "Mamzelle Champagne" at the Roof Garden theatre of Madison Square Garden, when Thaw suddenly arose, walked over to the table where prominent architect Stanford White was dining, and shot him in the face. The narrative that ensued was an intricate progressive-era fable about gender, wealth, and power, with newspaper coverage of White's murder and Thaw's two trials (the jury was hung on the first) threatening to expose the violence that lurked at the heart of constructions of white masculinity. During Thaw's trial, Nesbit testified that White had "seduced" her at the age of 16 by drugging a glass of champagne and then having intercourse with the unconscious girl. Although Thaw triumphed culturally and legally, insofar as he was widely believed to have been justified in avenging Nesbit's honor and was ultimately acquitted by reason of insanity, testimony revealed that Thaw was a violently misogynistic man, who had beaten Nesbit so badly on at least one occasion that she was bedridden for a week.[15] Although both men sought to claim the status of protector, during the course of the trial, it became clear that both were abusers of women.[16]

Nesbit's youth, beauty, and staunch and tearful defense of her husband on the stand afforded her much positive coverage, but newspaper accounts agreed that she had been ruined by White. In a culture so singularly unsympathetic to women in general, so predisposed to suspect them of "gold-digging," Nesbit's responses were culturally illegible. She had continued to accept money from White long after the affair was over, for example, and she had confessed to

White that Thaw had whipped her and she had even given a deposition to a lawyer regarding Thaw's violent behavior. That she was a victim was undeniable, but the identities of victims, murderers, and protectors were hopelessly muddled in this case, with the open sentimentalism of the reporting yielding some noteworthy ambiguities.

Although the phrase "white slavery" did not appear in news coverage of the White case, the themes introduced at the trial did set the stage for the moral panic about white slavery that shortly followed. Nesbit became the paradigmatic victim of sexual exploitation at the hands of powerful men. Sexuality, rather than economics per se, was understood to be at the heart of women's exploitation and society was understood to have a responsibility to protect young white women from a crime that transformed private sexual labor into a commercial exchange. According to Soderlund, during the course of the panic over "white slavery," the *New York Times* discernibly shifted from a more sentimental form of coverage to a form of skeptical rationalism that "reflected elite concerns about the muckraking press' potentially disruptive role in a capitalist democracy" (2002: 443). The moral panic over white slavery, Soderlund continues, marked a transitional moment in such crime narratives—a noteworthy instance of the growing divide between sentimental and objective coverage, the dwindling importance of gender in crime narratives, and the elision of overt references to race in northern coverage of crime.

The moral panic about white slavery began to take a more direct form in 1909, with the publication of an article by journalist George Kibbe Turner on the "white slave traffic" in *McClure's* magazine. The *New York Times* picked up on the term in July 1909, in its coverage of the trial of Ella Gingles "the Irish lacemaker," accused of having stolen lace from Miss Agnes Barrette, her former employer (12 July 1909: 1). Gingles, backed by several prominent Irish organizations, claimed that Agnes Barrette had "attacked her and mistreated her in the Wellington Hotel on two occasions last winter and that the object of these attacks and of the theft charge was to force her to be sold to an unnamed man in French Lick Springs, Ind." (*New York Times*, 20 July 1909: 4). Although Gingles was ultimately cleared of all charges, the jury said that they did not believe her story about white slavery. After the Gingles case, eight stories appeared in the *New York Times* about white slavery, for a total of twelve in 1909. Coverage peaked in 1910, which saw the passage of the Mann Act (prohibiting the transportation of women from one state to another "for immoral purposes"), with a total of 38 articles, and then ebbed in 1911, when only six articles appeared on white slavery.[17]

Although the white slavery panic had all the makings of a moral panic about women, the *New York Times* in particular was uncharacteristically skeptical when it came to the claims being made about some ostensible epidemic in the sexual enslavement of white women. In part, this had to do with competition between the magazines that had broken the story and the newspapers which then went on to provide serialized coverage of it, but it also owed to the fact that New Yorkers were extremely defensive about Turner's charges that New York City was the epicenter of all vice. Moreover, as Soderlund points out, the very subject matter of the white slavery panic linked it to sentimentalism, and to a rather outmoded type of captivity narrative, with young girls being taken from their homes, drugged (like Evelyn Nesbit), and ruined.

Another link to the sentimental inhered in the fact that many of the social movements agitating under the banner of white slavery were throwbacks to feminized religious charities instead of the scientific charities that were gaining importance and political legitimacy during the progressive era. Coverage of family violence and episodic stories that explained crime in terms of environmental as opposed to biological causes were indebted to reform movements like the temperance movement, rather than the scientific reform movements that were to take the place of religious charities during the first decades of the twentieth century. Charitable organizations run by women were seen as neither credible nor objective reformist movements in the eyes of an establishment ever more invested in the institutionalization and containment of reform.[18] The subject matter was women, the movement agents were either female or feminized, and its fully blown sentimental style conflicted with the growing imperatives of objectivity. In response to the moral panic about white slavery, the State of New York appointed a Grand Jury on White Slavery, led by industrialist John D. Rockefeller, Jr., which reported in 1910 that it had not found evidence that organizations existed for "the traffic in women" (Langum 1994: 36).[19] Where films, which had no obligation to objectivity, exploited the white slavery panic in a wholly melodramatic and sentimental style and continued to do so for years after the panic ended in the press, newspapers did not.[20]

The growing power of institution-based sources and reformers over alternative sources like social movements was further illustrated by a case that had all the trappings of a sentimentalized narrative, one that in an earlier era would have generated powerful crusades of its own. On 25 March 1910, 15-year-old Ruth Wheeler, a recent business school graduate who had gone to her very first interview for a position as a stenographer, disappeared. Two days after her disappearance, "The police were startled at finding the burned body and the sudden turn it gave to what they had considered an abduction case" (*New York Times*, 27 March 1910: 1). After Wheeler's charred and dismembered body was found on a fire escape platform of a tenement house at 222 East 75th Street, Albert Wolter, an 18-year-old German immigrant, was swiftly charged, convicted, and then executed for her murder. Wolter never confessed, insisting until he was electrocuted that he was innocent of the crime, but police officials speculated that he had advertised for a stenographer. Wheeler had applied at his apartment, and when she refused his advances, he strangled her and then tried to dispose of the evidence by burning her dismembered corpse.

The murder of Wheeler had all the makings of a sentimental narrative. Wheeler was young, white, and "a maiden." She was one of four children being raised by a dressmaker mother who had had no choice but to enter the waged economy when her husband was killed by a railroad locomotive while working. Thus lacking in paternal support and protection, like Mary Rogers, Wheeler had not chosen to enter the waged economy, but had been abandoned to it. Like both Jewett and Rogers, Wheeler was a new breed of female wage earner, a business school graduate and a stenographer, in a city undergoing massive changes.

Throughout the investigation and the trial, efforts were made to insert this case into the ongoing panic about "white slavery." Wolter, the newspaper claimed, was believed by police "to be an east side cadet" (cadet then being slang for the Caucasian version of what would later be known as a pimp) who was "in the habit of writing regularly to business colleges saying that he was in need of a stenographer so that he could get into correspondence with young girls" (27 March 1910: 1). Wolter was a cadet, moreover, who was being supported by another girl he had seduced (Kate Müller, who was later to bear his child). Despite her indiscretion with Wolter, Müller was working in a bakery and not the sex trade to support them and efforts to locate other trafficked girls fizzled out early on. By the third day of front-page coverage, "The police have abandoned the idea that Wolter was engaged extensively as a 'white slave' dealer, as he was living in very poor circumstances, and had even pawned his overcoat and a pair of shoes a week ago" (29 March 1910: 1).

Although the first article that appeared on the Wheeler case referred to the emotional state of the Wheeler family—"Both the mother and the dead girl's sisters were in a pitiful state last night. Mrs. Wheeler, sitting in a rocking chair, repeated her youngest child's name over and over again" (27 March 1910: 1)—aside from this reference, reportage evinced a distinct lack of interest in the death of the victim, the motives for her murder, and the emotional state of anyone but Wolter himself, the focus being on his evident lack of contrition. Where in the Jewett case, almost obsessive attention was paid to the everyday activities and habits of Helen Jewett, in coverage of her death, Ruth Wheeler remained faceless and without substance.

Reluctant to drop the story altogether, attention subsequently shifted from Wolter himself to the employment agencies said to be responsible for Wheeler's death: "The tragedy of Ruth Wheeler has aroused social workers to a new sense of the danger, physical and moral, which surrounds office workers" (*New York Times*, 10 April 1910: 20). In response to what was being described as "the problem of the stenographer and the office girl," it was proposed that the labor law in question be amended so that employment agencies would have "to file with the Police Department the names of all girls they have directed to positions, and the names and addresses of prospective employers, names and addresses of girls placed, and the names and addresses of their employers" (*New York Times*, 16 April 1910: 20). The crusade ultimately died out, since it was unclear as to how this amendment could prevent such a crime from happening in the first place. After Wolter's execution on 29 January 1912 the story concluded with assertions about the efficiency of a criminal justice system which had apprehended and dispatched the man responsible for this crime in short order, rather than the need for further reform.

The white slavery panic did not take hold in newspapers owing to the largely disorganized state of the institutions responsible for generating panics. In the first place, relations between social movements and institutions like the police, local government, and the press were antagonistic during this period, as social movements seen as being outdated and ill advised vied with institutional reformers over setting the agenda for reform. Consensus among institutions was increasingly critical to the success of moral panics in the age of objectivity, since institutional agreement and the expertise conferred by institutional status could effectively substitute for empirical evidence. Officials were just learning to speak in a single voice about issues of wider social and political significance. In the near future, their ability to produce such an institutional consensus would allow them to continue to create moral panics out of little more than their own paranoia, but now in the authoritarian tones of objectivity.

The Federal Bureau of Investigation's first war on crime

By the first decades of the twentieth century, police officials, politicians, policy-makers, and reporters could, as in the case of white slavery, disprove the existence of crime waves. But they still lacked the data increasingly necessary to prove that particular types of crime were on the rise, as well as the ideological necessity for such proof, which objectivity would come to furnish.[21] The lack of uniform crime reporting procedures at the local and state levels made national crime reporting and a national police agenda impossible, since experts did not yet exist who could be called upon to attest to national trends and problems. More than any other institution, what was to become known as the Federal Bureau of Investigation played a determinative role in organizing and monopolizing information about crime and overseeing the shift from earlier sentimental crime news to the objective reporting of crime exemplified by the first "war on crime" in US history.

The genealogy of the first war on crime began with the panic over white slavery. Even though the basis for the crusade was ultimately rejected by the *New York Times*, the ensuing panic was sufficient to generate passage of the Mann Act in 1910, which marked the rise of the Bureau of Investigation (the predecessor of the Federal Bureau of Investigation), securing "the Bureau's first major field office, in Baltimore, and a dramatic increase in manpower" (Langum 1994: 49). The Bureau of Investigation that took shape between 1910 and 1933 (the name was formally changed to the Federal Bureau of Investigation in 1935) reversed the relationship that had previously existed between journalists and police by establishing a police monopoly over information and its distribution. By the 1920s, the FBI was offering statistics as well as an endless flow of stories about kidnappers, extortionists, and abortionists to a press that now covered police narratives about crime rather than criminal activities viewed from the perspective of multiple sources. Where journalists and social movement actors had previously set news agendas through the creation of moral panics in often sentimentalized tones, the FBI's first war on crime was to reverse this flow, ensuring that institutions of policing would have primary responsibility for defining crime and for setting crime-fighting agendas.

Although most institutions are not reducible in any meaningful sense to the individuals who created them, the FBI as an institution bore the indelible stamp of one man: J. Edgar Hoover. Creator and director of the FBI for over 50 years, Hoover was the product of a segregated southern city, Washington, DC. Hoover was hired by the Justice Department shortly after being admitted to the bar in 1917, just as the Bolsheviks were preparing to take control of the Russian Revolution. As a clerk and then, shortly, an attorney, Hoover had no direct decision-making power during this period, but he was in a position to participate in the war on dissent that was materializing in response to calls for beefed up national security.

Attorney General A. Mitchell Palmer promoted Hoover in 1919 to head the Justice Department's anti-radical drive, which culminated in the Palmer Raids, or the "Red Scare," that followed the end of World War I, during which 10,000 "radicals" were indiscriminately arrested. The first Palmer Raids quickly came under widespread criticism and congressional investigations soon followed, as the extent of the arrests and police tactics became known, casting a pall over the reputations of the Bureau of Investigation and the Justice Department. The very failure of the Palmer Raids afforded Hoover an initiation into the world of press and government relations, allowing him to refine his information-gathering strategies, to learn from the mistakes that had been made, and to fine-tune his public relations strategy. Taken as a whole, the Palmer Raids and, later, the failure of national Prohibition enforcement taught government officials invaluable lessons about managing news and the flow of information.[22] In fact, the Wickersham Report, a survey conducted in 1929 to formulate public policy on the 18th Amendment, concluded that media debate about crime and crime policy did nothing more than create "suspicion in the minds of its readers and hinders the effective enforcement of the law by officials" (quoted in Potter 1998: 27).

Objectivity, progress, and science were Hoover's stock in trade and he used the veneer these provided to mask his myriad prejudices. A devotee of objectivity, he insisted on facts, professionalism, research, and scientific evidence that could empirically establish criminal identity, such as fingerprints. The Radical Division that Hoover established to wage his novice campaign against foreign-born dissidents was primarily a research operation, the first evidence of Hoover's lifelong romance with a form of objectivity underwritten by selective information gathering and analysis.[23] The practices and routines he instituted to gather information during these early years would become standard operating procedure during his lengthy tenure at the FBI. The Radical Division collected information on radical publications, organizations, and individuals. These central files were then used to identify "over 60,000 'radically inclined' individuals" (Powers 1987: 68).[24] Hoover also implemented ongoing monitoring of radical periodicals. This research-intensive procedure enabled the FBI to become the foremost expert on radicalism, thus giving it "a semi-monopoly over a sort of information so difficult to obtain, so extensive in coverage, and so commonly inaccessible as to make its independent verification almost impossible" (Powers 1987: 69). Hoover also acquired a thorough appreciation of how both alternative and mainstream media functioned in the USA; this understanding enabled his clever manipulations of information and media in the decades that followed.[25]

Above all, Hoover was a public relations genius. During the first two decades of the twentieth century, and along with the transition from street-based information to institution-based information discussed earlier in this chapter, the public relations industry was also taking shape. Better known for its effects on news sources, particularly insofar as it served to undermine journalistic objectivity's emphasis on "credible" public sources by privatizing and concealing corporate sources, public relations had a significant impact on crime news and representations of victims as well.[26] Not just a tool for corporate interests, public relations techniques and strategies were also used by government institutions to control the flow of information to the press. Public institutions like the government and police were learning that they too could benefit from objective news coverage that permitted them to manage and control the flow of information to media outlets from behind the scenes.

In the years following the Palmer Raids, Hoover crafted one of the first public relations campaigns conducted by a federal agency, and perhaps the most successful. It began as an effort to rehabilitate the image of a Bureau of Investigation tarnished by the Palmer Raids, a rehabilitation that was necessary to transform it into a national crime-fighting powerhouse. One former FBI agent claimed that the FBI's central duty from the beginning "was not investigations but public relations and propaganda to glorify Hoover" and the FBI (Sullivan 1979: 80). The media campaign for this public relations gambit pioneered two broad strategies that became the foundation for later FBI dealings with the media; strategies reflective of a sophisticated assessment of a rapidly integrating culture industry.

The first strategy, cultivating friendly contacts within media industries (newspapers, film, radio, book publishing, and later television), entailed identifying editors, reporters, producers, directors, and others responsible for cultural production who sympathized with the FBI's politically reactionary views on crime and society. These friendly contacts were then used to disseminate information sympathetic to the FBI's point of view, as well as to distribute cultural representations and fictionalized accounts of the FBI favorable to the public image Hoover was constructing. The second strategy, often illegal and unconstitutional, involved overt repression, in which immediate action (both legal and illegal) was taken against those cultural workers who refused to comply with, or dared to criticize, the FBI and the crime narratives it was constructing.

In cultivating its friendly sources, the FBI relied on services and free publicity provided by journalists, writers, and broadcasters who were willing to reproduce the FBI's point-of-view in exchange for a combination of ideological, personal, and professional gains.[27] Hoover and his staff identified friendly sources like *Washington Star* reporter Rex Collier and columnist and radio personality Walter Winchell through personal contact and extensive reviews of media and then made sure that these personal contacts were commended and rewarded. The

Bureau of Investigation maintained a "list of persons to receive various releases and documents" (Theoharis and Cox 1988: 127), a list of those to whom information would be "leaked."[28] Invariably, these leaks "went to what an internal FBI memo called the 'anti-Communist writers who have proved themselves to us'" (Schrecker 1998: 216). This information highway ran in two directions. As historian Ellen Schrecker observes, some journalists volunteered information directly to the FBI. Hearst columnist George Sokolsky was so accommodating, in fact, that the FBI had to create a special procedure for dealing with the volume of information he generated.

The FBI's "Crime Records Division" directly managed news coverage, but this management was but one aspect of a broader public relations strategy that was fought and won not only in news coverage of crime, but in op-ed pages and across the wider field of cultural production in the 1930s.[29] If cultural memories of the 1920s and 1930s have long involved images of G-Men combating "organized" crime, this was in large part the legacy of "reality" radio programs like "The FBI" and "The FBI in Peace and War", the series of G-Man films, and the popularity of pulp and hardboiled detective fiction that glorified law enforcement, rather than the effects of newspaper coverage alone. In fact, one could say that Hoover perfected the infotainment genre in the 1920s. Fully cognizant of the importance of myth-making in entertainment media, Hoover encouraged numerous cultural representations of the FBI across media and genres, a form of thematic integration enabled by the overlapping institutional and economic structures of the industry and Hoover's elaborate network of industry contacts, as well as his archive of information about them.[30] The Hollywood film industry enshrined Hoover and the G-Man as cultural icons through a series of films released in 1935: *G-Men; Public Enemy's Wife; Public Hero No. 1; Whipsaw; Mary Burns, Fugitive;* and *Show Them No Mercy!* (Powers 1987: 200–1). As Powers puts it, "Popular entertainment, with its enormous influence on public opinion, helped make J. Edgar Hoover and his FBI into an independent force on the national scene" (1987: 201).[31]

The symbolic framework of the war on crime waged by the FBI from 1924 to 1936 (Potter 1998: 2–3) was a far cry from the sentimental coverage of crime that had preceded it. Hoover used a discourse of crime that was hardboiled, devoid of lurid descriptions, and strictly opposed to sentimentalism. Even those cultural producers friendly to the FBI complained that the FBI's control often resulted in boring narratives, lacking in dramatic appeal. Along with this pared-down language of detachment came a concomitant shift in focus from feminized and female victims whose lives bridged public and private spheres to crime scenarios in which the only characters were white men. As a cultural icon, the G-Man embodied a version of racialized androcentrism deemed more appropriate by modern standards. Featuring only white men as both protectors and villains, with a feminized public as the potential victim, the G-Man was the expression of a perfect homosocial universe, ruled by reason, rationality, and scientific logic. The crime-fighting apparatus Hoover was busily promoting required a villainous, criminal genius worthy of the strenuous scientific endeavors of the protector. Race and gender were expunged from Hoover's scenario, speaking as they did of contentious questions about social justice and equality, not to mention having the potential to direct attention to the covert war on crime that Hoover was then waging against African Americans. This was a crime-fighting agenda set not by social movements or moral reformers who invoked worthy victims in a distinctly sentimental fashion, but by a federal crime-fighting institution not interested in pathos, or the white women and children who were its main vehicles.

The discourse of this first war on crime was governed not by sentiment or emotional appeals on behalf of female victims, but by constant mention of rates of crime and increases in categories of crime. In place of the sentimental crime news that had saturated the front pages of even the *New York Times* in the first decade of the twentieth century, readers were treated to stories about underworld quarrels (*New York Times*, 5 January 1925: 23) and other forms of organized crime that threatened the public sphere; numerous articles on ever-rising crime rates[32]; and more cries like that of General Sessions Judge Otto A. Rosalsky, "We need more police. We need a Secret Service, new laws investing the authorities here with more power" (*New York Times*, 6 January 1925: 1). Overall, the *New York Times*' coverage of what we would now describe as family violence decreased from 34 articles between 1900 and 1909 to five in the 1940s, a decrease that reflected its wider retreat from covering crime as it took place in the so-called private sphere (McGucken 1987: 263). Instead, "a disproportionate emphasis on violent street crimes" (McGucken: 192) emerged in the years following World War I.

Of course, this focus on street-based crime and white public enemies also stemmed from the effects of Prohibition, which criminalized previously legitimate and enormously lucrative business transactions owned by white men. Nevertheless, Hoover and the FBI did not participate in the Prohibition Bureau's crusades against gangsters like Frank Costello and Lucky Luciano, or what Repetto describes as "'Get Mr. Big' drives" (2004: xiii). Instead, the FBI went after less powerful criminals like John Dillinger, who were then inflated to mythic proportions.

Although the FBI was not alone in effecting changes in news content and style, it was the most successful in harnessing broader cultural currents to its project of constructing a national crime-fighting agenda. Powers notes that even before the murder of Charles Lindbergh's son in 1932, "Kidnapping [by strangers] was the most highly publicized crime of the pre-Roosevelt depression because it was a direct attack on the home, the country's grassroots symbol of security and traditional values at a time when both were threatened" (1983: 31). The FBI used the case, and the Bureau's involvement in it, to gain passage of the Lindbergh Law in 1933, which gave jurisdiction to the Bureau of Investigation in cases involving kidnapping if the kidnapper crossed a state line (Ungar 1976: 72–73). This was followed in 1934 by passage of legislation that was to dramatically expand the FBI's powers by, as its sole critic (Senator William H. King, a Democrat from Utah) put it, "substituting a Federal criminal code for the criminal code of the States" (quoted in Ungar 1976: 75). This broadening of federal police powers

> put a whole host of new crimes under federal jurisdiction for the first time: the robbing of a national bank, the flight of a defendant or a witness across state lines to avoid prosecution or giving testimony; the transmission of threats by any means whatsoever; racketeering practiced on businessmen engaged in interstate commerce; transporting stolen property across a state line; resisting a federal officer.
>
> (Cook 1964: 155)

Kidnapping became the most highly publicized crime not because of dramatic increases, but because kidnapping was a crime that the FBI had found useful since the Mann Act in granting it expanded powers over investigating and prosecuting crimes. Increased attention to kidnapping was a windfall for the FBI, which depended on Congressional perceptions of such threats for continued funding and expansion.[33]

The FBI had a key stake in presenting a picture of steadily increasing crime, but at the same time, and lest it look incompetent (like the Prohibition Bureau), the FBI had to show that it was winning the war against particular categories of crime. Until the late 1920s, local crime data collection was notoriously unreliable and no infrastructure existed for this collection; nor was there any apparatus designed to collect and analyze crime trends on a national scale. The FBI changed this. According to Christopher Wilson,

> the Uniform Crime Reports [UCR], initiated in the late 1920s by Vollmer, Smith, Hoover, and others, were explicitly designed to circumvent not only the suspicious bookkeeping of local precincts, but what Fosdick called the "hysterical headlines" of the press.
>
> (2000: 68)

Wilson adds that the "UCR were not, as they are so often cast, simply empirical registers against which images of crime or policing can be debunked" but were rather the "by-product of both management science and public relations" (68). Small surprise then that, from their inception, the FBI's UCR have never reported an overall decline in crime, but rather served to control what had hitherto been a politically unmanageable procession of crime waves and crime news. Teamed with the myth of the G-Man, the hard data and incontrovertible reporting provided by surveys like the UCR offered a public image of police and police work as objective, scientific, and above all rational, untarnished by the irrational violence and corrupt politics of earlier cultural representations of the police.

If the focus on empirical evidence was one indicator of the FBI's modern manliness, the first war on crime's construction of public enemies as white men was a second aspect of the FBI's bid for institutional credibility and authority when it came to crime. It would make no sense to have such a highly organized, scientifically proficient, federal police force, and to continue to pour resources into that police force, if the opponent it faced was not formidable. Although in the past, the protection scenario demanded a villain who posed a significant threat to the victim, the FBI's version required the creation of criminal masterminds and geniuses capable of eluding the FBI, for a time at least. The FBI even transformed its own incompetence in cases like that of John Dillinger into cultural myths about criminal cunning. Although immigrants played a role in the construction of a few public enemies (mainly of the more politicized variety, like Sacco and Vanzetti), most cultural representations of the leaders of organized crime—John Dillinger, Bonnie Parker and Clyde Barrow, Pretty Boy Floyd— were native-born citizens of English or Irish descent.[34] The war on crime framework highlighted a masculinized field of struggle in which both attacker and attacked were seen as powerful and worthy opponents, since making war on a powerless, feminized opponent could be mistaken for bullying.

These white male criminals were crucial to the FBI's myth-making. In addition to providing villains worthy of the FBI's best and most costly efforts, these criminal geniuses also elevated police and other law enforcement officials. Hoover's myth-making had to counter longstanding cultural depictions of police as objects of derision and comedy (as in silent film stars' Charlie Chaplin and Buster Keaton's hilarious depictions of police high jinx) or as agents of brutality and corruption. In order for the dramatic and heroic representation of the G-Man to become dominant, these previous images of police had to be superseded by the handsome, professional, and deadly serious figure of the G-Man. The careful recruitment of FBI agents illustrated Hoover's awareness of the importance of public image, especially when it came to G-Men. For thirty years, applicants had to be at least 5 feet 7 inches tall; agents were denied promotions because of hair loss, obesity, or other forms of non-conformance to the image Hoover believed an agent should project. By 1930, examiners who interviewed candidates were using a form that contained categories like "Personal Appearance," "Dress" ("neat," "flashy," "poor," "untidy") and "Features ("refined," "ordinary," "coarse," and "dissipated') (Potter 1998: 50–51). Melvin Purvis, the agent credited with killing John Dillinger, became the model for the new FBI agent. Purvis was clean-cut, reserved, and apparently adept in utilizing information and scientific policing methods to capture criminals. Hoover approvingly referred to him as "the Clark Gable of the service" (Summers 1993: 70).

The homosocial universe that developed as a result of this institutional framework was mirrored in its narratives about crime. Ruled by objectivity and the head rather than sentiment and the heart, aside from occasional gun molls, mothers, and the girlfriend-turned-informant, women had no place in narratives about the war on crime, whether as victims, repositories of national identity, or agents. The FBI offered protection, but for abstract American values in need of police surveillance and protection rather than identifiable female victims.

African Americans were also noticeably absent from the first war on crime's white homosocial universe. The white slavery panic that had given birth to the

Mann Act invoked the issue of color, if only through its metonymic replacement of African Americans with white women, but race appeared erratically and not thematically in coverage of white slavery. One of the early arrests in New York City was Belle Moore, "an extremely light mulatto" (*New York Times*, 1 May 1910: 1), who was accused of having sold two 15-year-old white girls into slavery. But the figure of the black pimp had not yet been conjured as a folk devil and any attempt to attribute the traffic in white women to a powerful organized crime syndicate run by African American women would have been scoffed at. Perhaps the figure of a black organization selling white girls was simply too ludicrous given the obvious powerlessness of blacks as a collective force in northern society; perhaps objectivity and the empirical turn imposed some limits on the imaginings of a racialized androcentric order. Whatever the case, no longer slaves, no longer victims, African Americans largely disappeared from the pages of northern newspapers.

Narratives of white protection and black threats, however, remained powerfully operative within the two institutions that would hitherto serve as gatekeepers for information about crime: the police and the criminal justice system. Although newspaper coverage of white slavery only rarely referred directly to race, the Mann Act, passed in 1910 in the wake of the panic about white slavery, was specifically used against two groups of people: white women (as in the moral panics of the 1830s, prostitutes in particular) and African American men involved with white women. The Mann Act, and those police agencies responsible for enforcing it, kept earlier racist ideologies of crime alive, adhering as they did to the logic that had previously appeared in newspaper lynching narratives. In this, individual white women had no agency, sexual or otherwise, and individual black men, like boxer Jack Johnson who was arrested in 1912 for violating the Mann Act by abducting a white woman were motivated solely by their desire to possess white women.

However repressed the link between blacks and crime may have been in newspapers during this era, institutions like the FBI continued to *act* on the racist beliefs that had made such a link possible in the first place.[35] Hoover's private hatred of African Americans was legendary. As Powers notes, Hoover "surrounded himself with blacks in menial service positions" (1987: 323) and his refusal to hire African Americans as special agents later led to a major rift with the Kennedy Administration. Hoover believed that people of color were among the most significant threats to his understanding of what it meant to be "American." Hoover's suspicions about, and surveillance of, African American individuals and communities were built into the very institutional fabric of the FBI. The war on crime that publicly featured white men protecting society from other white men provided cover for Hoover's unpublicized crusade against African Americans. This crusade began in 1919, when he initiated an investigation of black nationalist Marcus Garvey's Black Star Steamship Line, and was to include all major African American leaders active during Hoover's lifetime.[36]

In the 1920s, the FBI initiated intensive monitoring of the African American press. To his superiors in the Justice Department, he wrote: "something must be done to the editors of these publications as they are beyond doubt exciting the negro elements of this country to riot and to the committing of outrages of all sorts" (quoted in Theoharis and Cox 1988: 57). Beginning in 1919, Hoover began routinely reporting to Congress on the seditious activities of various "negro" publications.[37] In 1920, Hoover prepared and distributed a pamphlet entitled *Radicalism and Sedition among the Negroes as Reflected in Their Publications* (Powers 1983: 128). Like the Klan and other white supremacist organizations, the FBI reserved particular ire for those white organizations that were crossing race lines to organize black workers or to oppose Jim Crow, like the Industrial Workers of the World and the Communist Party.[38] The FBI's treatment of these organizations and their media— constant surveillance, routine harassment arrests, and so forth—stood as a lesson to others who might want to organize across racial divides. The FBI's long-standing practice of recruiting agents heavily from southern states guaranteed that such racist attitudes would not be challenged within the agency.[39]

Hoover had learned from the fall-out of the Palmer Raids (a lesson reaffirmed by his skirmishes with critics in the 1940s and 1950s) that while overt racism and xenophobia might be acceptable during times of war, during a manufactured peacetime crusade these could turn into political liabilities. One could fight communists with impunity, a lesson so crucial to the ideology of the Cold War, which was actually quite a nasty, hot war for the people of color it rendered invisible. And if Hoover's ghostwriters sometimes suggested a link between communism and the Civil Rights Movement, this was not really about race, but about fighting a communist menace that preyed on the simplicity of black people. The problem with the NAACP, according to the FBI, was not that it was an African American organization, but that it was a communist front organization. The problem with Dr. Martin Luther King, at least initially, was that communists like Bayard Rustin controlled him.[40] In private, Hoover could refuse to hire African Americans as anything but domestic servants, he could continue to conduct massive investigations of African American political organizations and leaders (who did not yet have the political ability to confront him), but in public it was best to suggest that his problem with civil rights organizations was that they were communist rather than that they were led by African Americans.

In these ways, the FBI's first war on crime was a screen for the private war being conducted against African Americans, a war whose seeds were sown in the 1920s, but which escalated in the 1960s and was institutionalized in the 1970s. Where, in the first war on crime, African Americans were not visible as either victims or criminals, in this second war on crime they figured prominently as criminals, deviants, and, eventually, the cause of a whole range of social ills. When African Americans began to mobilize on their behalf in the post-war period to challenge both formal and informal apartheid in the USA, institutions like the FBI, now well versed in the camouflage that objectivity could provide them, were well prepared to begin their own mobilization against what they viewed as insurrection.

6 From the war on poverty to the war on crime

> We cannot condone riots, looting, and the inflammatory talk of black extremists, but how much have we done, voluntarily, to meet the legitimate demands of black citizens? We can shake our heads and tell ourselves that the black American is pushing us too fast. We can wring our hands and say we would be willing to help black Americans, if only they didn't riot and demonstrate. We can insist, as some do, that police power be used to keep the black man in his place. We can thus choose to turn away, in fear and hostility, from the problems that black America has pressed for equality. If we do, we cannot expect that we or our children will live in peace.
>
> (Democratic Vice-Presidential Candidate Edmund Muskie, *ABC Evening News*, 15 October 1968)

As the FBI was staging its inexorable rise to power, the ideological link between African Americans and crime lay largely dormant in northern news reporting. In the 1930s, the Prohibition Bureau (previously the Narcotics Division of the Bureau of Internal Revenue) generated a minor moral panic around drugs like marijuana and cocaine, using the racialized threat of crazed black drug fiends to criminalize these drugs, but this bureau had neither the media savvy nor the staying power of the FBI.[1] Moreover, domestic problems like Prohibition and the Depression combined with increasingly dismal news from Europe to push crime news to the side, where it would largely remain until after World War II.[2]

Like chapter 3, which examined mainstream news coverage of the anti-draft riots, this chapter turns to the flip side of portrayals of crime and criminals: the cultural identification of victims in whose names criminal justice policies are enacted or reformed. The post-World War II era was the only period of news production in which African Americans were seen as victims of white rage and oppression and as heroic political actors—leaders of a movement they had inspired, organized, and led. This shift in framing African Americans in the news media resulted from their self-mobilization in the post-war era, the movement's aptitude in exploiting the new medium of television, and the way in which the nationalization of this new medium thrust northern and southern cultures of journalism into conflict. The criminalization of African Americans on national television that was completed at the end of the 1960s thus began not in the grainy realm of televised crime news, but rather as a response to the powerful and evocative ways in which blacks first began to appear on television screens throughout the USA. In spite of their effective banishment from televised entertainment programming, African Americans marched onto television screens as participants in a well organized and growing Civil Rights Movement.

Civil rights and the birth of television news

Born of years of hard struggle, the Civil Rights Movement did not begin in the years following the end of World War II, but had multiple origins in the activism of anti-lynching organizations, black trade unionism, black communism, black nationalism, and black church and civic organizations. The growth of a mass movement accelerated in the immediate post-war period, as African Americans were yet again confronted with the contradictory nature of US democracy. Although temporarily and reluctantly embraced as soldiers and workers during the war years, blacks were the first to be dismissed from well-paying jobs to make room for returning white soldiers. For those African American servicemen who had experienced less segregated institutional and cultural spaces during World War II, the return to a south still ruled by Jim Crow and a north where they continued to be treated as criminals rather than returning heroes was particularly jarring.[3]

As black institutions and organizations began mobilizing for the series of massive legal and political challenges they would shortly mount, white media institutions were preparing for the advent of the era of television. Broadcast industry leaders like David Sarnoff of RCA and William Paley of CBS anticipated that television would alter the political and cultural landscape of the United States, but no one could predict the nature of the changes to come. In the years following World War II, when corporations began to redirect their attention from war-related production to consumer production, the Federal Communication Commission and businesses turned their attention to existing broadcasting practices, beginning to sort through the knotty array of problems that stood in the way of mass production and distribution: UHF versus VHF, which color specifications to adopt, licensing assignments and agreements, and so forth. In 1948, the FCC stopped issuing licenses for a four-year period that came to be known as "the freeze," thereby allowing media powerhouses like CBS and NBC (which was owned by RCA) to consolidate their power and to work through the nuts and bolts of the new industry.[4]

Originally seen as an unlikely medium for news, television rapidly became the central agenda-setter for news production, despite critics who thought that television news would never supplant either radio or print. The broadcast industry viewed television mainly as an entertainment medium that promised to deliver millions of viewers daily to advertisers on an unprecedented national scale. Industry magnates predicted that the vast audience for television desired escape rather than education or information, fiction and entertainment rather than realism and news, and leisure rather than the labor of thought. In part, their predictions were based on an emerging Cold War ideology of the nuclear family which, like its nineteenth-century predecessors, insisted that the family and the domestic sphere were distinct from the public world of politics and work. As such, industry leaders reasoned, families would reject the intrusion of any real-world unpleasantness into their domestic havens. Advertisers eagerly sponsored entertainment programming, but they were reluctant to have their products associated with an unpredictable and often bleak sequence of news events.

Existing limitations on camera technologies and transportation of film further contributed to skepticism about television's ability to surpass either radio or print in quickly delivering news. In the era before hand-held cameras, video cameras, and satellite transmission, the time-consuming tasks of shipping and developing film meant that images for news items became available days after events had occurred and well after print and radio had already covered those events. These technological obstacles made it seem even more unlikely that news would ever deliver audiences to advertisers with the same regularity and reliability as entertainment programming.

These assumptions led industry leaders and observers alike to consider television news as "an unpromising child" in 1953, "the schizophrenic off-spring of the theater newsreel and the radio newscast . . . confused as to its role and future course" (Barnouw 1970: 40). Journalists working in print and radio shared many of these reservations about the new medium. In addition to technological problems with the transmission of information, the ideological emphasis on the visual nature of the medium suggested that infantilized viewers would be mesmerized by the images flitting across the screen. This further cast doubt on the legitimacy of television as a news medium, particularly among serious-minded reporters. Even journalists who had earlier made the transition from print to radio resisted the move to television, believing that television's emphasis on entertainment programming precluded a commitment to providing serious news coverage. Journalists and producers, many of whom had enjoyed a remarkable degree of autonomy and creative control during World War II, had additional worries about retaining control over news production, especially in the face of powerful corporate sponsors.

Aside from longer, documentary-style programs like *See it Now* and *CBS Reports*, the type of news analysis that emerged in television news was a headline service that used a rip and read format, featuring an announcer doing little more than reading news items taken from the Associated Press' radio wire (Kaniss 1991: 102). Analysis, which Barnouw described as a "staple of radio news in its finest day," was rejected for its potentially controversial content, as well as for being "non-visual" (1970: 43) and thus unlikely to maintain viewers' interest.

These structural factors were reinforced by the political climate of the 1950s, which engendered a form of timidity that left indelible marks on the structure and practices of the industry itself. Networks' desire to deliver the largest possible audience to advertisers, as legendary reporter Edward R. Murrow observed in 1957 and in 1958, led to the avoidance of any content that could be construed as controversial. Television news producers were thus admonished not to "offend some section of the community" (Murrow 1958: 33). Anything that might possibly be considered controversial in the eyes of advertisers had to be eliminated.[5] The Red Scare and resultant boycotts made sponsors more and more intent on avoiding any form of controversy that might annoy or disturb some section of the consuming public. These forces dovetailed nicely with network and sponsor arguments against the news "commentator" and for the news "analyst"— the former, it was said, was "an opinion-pusher," while the latter was "a newsman who analyzed the news but promoted no view" (Barnouw 1968: 135). In this climate, "controversial" became a code word for "liberal," and "sponsor troubles" became the euphemism for the blacklist and resultant industry purges.

However concerned the industry was about intrusions into the private sphere and controversial content, the new medium of television needed news and other ostensibly public service programming to temper the crass commercialism of so much of its content.[6] The real issue was how to minimize costs, even though, as the networks swiftly learned, news was incredibly cheap to produce and extremely profitable. Indeed, television news was born into a perpetual state of downsizing, nearly four decades before that term entered a popular vocabulary. When James T. Aubrey, Jr., took over CBS's programming division in 1959, for example, among his first decisions was to cut back on the News Division.[7] Within two years, CBS's net annual profits had doubled, but Aubrey still complained that they would have been higher had CBS "not wasted so much money on public affair programs" (Halberstam 1979: 252). Aubrey's job was to increase profit margins—as Fred Friendly later recalled, to "get the ratings, and make as much money as you can" (quoted in Barnouw 1970: 244). In order to do this, businessmen exercised ultimate control over news production, and their condescension toward creative cultural producers, as well as the public, was becoming increasingly evident. As Aubrey himself put it, "The trouble with the creative people is that they don't know the public. The people out there don't want to think" (Halberstam 1979: 254). One of Aubrey's subordinates summarized Aubrey's philosophy to a writer: "Your job is to produce shit" (quoted in Barnouw 1970: 244).

As was the case with the rise of the penny press in the 1830s, television news' desire to reach a broad audience and not to offend its advertisers led to an early predilection for disaster and crime coverage, particularly for local stations. But certain factors combined to prevent crime news from dominating national network newscasts in the 1950s and the early 1960s. In the first place, news crews were small and stringers (cameramen in various locations who were willing to do some shooting on the side) were too thinly dispersed to cover "breaking" crime news. Television news favored planned or even staged events that could provide reliable footage. The fifteen- and thirty-minute formats of news programming exercised more serious constraints over the presentation of information than any other aspect of production, since such analysis as there was had to be made to fit into these time limits.[8]

Furthermore, as members of a new and not entirely legitimate media indus-try, reporters and camera crews had yet to develop a working relationship with police forces, who had reason to be concerned about the presence of cameras. Where police were familiar with print media, and comfortable with their abil-ity to control the flow of information and representations of themselves, the addition of a visual dimension that was unpredictable and uncontrollable made police wary of television. The wider, national police agenda was further focused on other forms of deviance: communism, juvenile delinquency (said to lead to communism or drugs), and the Cold War.

Anxieties about the new medium's visual intrusion into the home further curbed crime coverage and displays of violence. The endless replaying of the Zapruder film of the Kennedy assassination opened the door to major changes in visual conventions for covering violence. The unrest of the 1960s and the Vietnam War institutionalized these changes. But in the 1950s, producers were uncertain as to whether advertisers and audiences would embrace news pro-gramming at all, much less representations of conflict and violence.

In terms of visual representations of African Americans, although black actors appeared on television in its earliest days, after 1952 they were effectively banned from entertainment programming. The link that institutions like the FBI had sought to articulate between blacks and all that was threatening to the "American" way of life had made race a lightning rod for controversy and alle-gations of un-American activity. In the wake of the publication of *Red Channels*, which listed a significant number of black actors, writers, and other anti-racist cultural producers deemed to be communists and therefore unemployable, sit-coms featuring blacks like *Amos 'n' Andy* (1951–53) and *Beulah* (1950–53) were cancelled. These programs were cancelled not because they were racist depic-tions that might offend African Americans, but because race itself had become a forbidden topic, both visually and verbally.[9]

Censorship of images of African Americans abounded during the early years of commercial television. A drama produced for the Westinghouse *Studio One* series on CBS drew its material from an incident in which white suburbanites in Cicero, Illinois drove an African American family from their neighborhood. The network and sponsors told writer Reginald Rose that "The black family would have to be changed to 'something else.' A negro as beleaguered protagonist of a television drama was declared unthinkable. It would, they said, appall south-ern viewers" (Barnouw 1970: 34). When Rod Serling wrote about the lynching of Emmett Till for a *U.S. Steel Hour* program, he had to change the identity of the victim from a teenaged African American visiting relatives in the Mississippi Delta to "an old pawnbroker" who lived in New England (Barnouw 1970: 35). Although the industry routinely invoked the racism of southerners as the alibi for censorship, the networks really wanted to avoid upsetting racist and anti-communist (the two went hand-in-hand) sponsors and advertisers in the north and south alike, for whom any mention of race had come to mean that some threat to American values based on whiteness must be lurking nearby.

But news programming was a different ball game, especially in the new era of television, where, as Robert Schakne of CBS News put it, echoing a refrain common among reporters of the era, "The whole process of changing television into a serious medium happened to coincide with the Civil Rights Movement" (1987). Although the captains of industry had invested enormous time and energy in planning the economic infrastructure of television, and despite politically conservative forces' efforts to control the content of entertainment programming, not even the most prodigious and scrupulous planning effort could account for emerging political events, especially new social movements that were too large and well-organized to be long ignored. And as "breaking" news moved ever closer to the occurrence of events themselves, framing and control over the representations of events were increasingly more difficult to manage.

Most importantly, northern journalists considered themselves to be a breed apart from their southern counterparts: more civilized, more professional, and certainly more progressive on issues having to do with race. The extent to which this self-understanding was inaccurate became evident later, but in comparison to the open racism of southern discourses, northern journalists seemed progressive indeed. Tim O'Connor, a Harvard-educated reporter for the *Los Angeles Record, PM*, the *New York Star*, and the *New York Daily Compass*, wrote of the 1946 lynch-murders of two married African American couples in Monroe, Georgia: "When the votes were counted in the July 17 primary, and the minority candidate Talmadge was declared the Democratic nominee, the season on 'niggers' was automatically opened, and every pinheaded Georgia cracker and bigoted Ku Kluxer figured he had a hunting license" (2003: 78). Where black victims in the south were criminalized by virtue of their race, northern news media increasingly considered southern whites to be the criminal elements of an intractably violent, backward society. Northern journalists were often critical of the overt and vicious racism of the rural south, but these two essentially distinct, regional cultures of journalism did not come into direct conflict until the Civil Rights Movement began its mass mobilization in the 1950s.

In addition to their sensibilities regarding race and civil rights, a number of other factors combined to make northern news workers feel alien indeed in the south. In the first place, the broadcast industry's infrastructure was not very well organized in the south, lacking as it did the older structure of sourcing and newsgathering that existed in the north. The news bureau nearest much of the action in the south was in New Orleans, too remote from places like Birmingham, Montgomery, and Selma to effectively cover real-time events. In addition to the absence of a national base, southern affiliates were generally hostile to the northern-based networks. CBS, well known as the most liberal of the networks, was regarded as the Communist Broadcasting System and both print and broadcast journalists were consistently cast as communists and part of the corps of outside agitators said to be responsible for stirring up unrest.

Journalists who traveled to the south to cover the movement thus found themselves in conflict not only with southern officials and institutions, but with their media counterparts as well. Reporters covering the south, who understood themselves to be more professional, more objective, and more civilized than their southern counterparts, experienced an intense alienation from the very institutions they had learned to rely on for information about crime, social disorder, and race relations. Forced to question the institution-based sources they had been taught to consult, journalists turned to sources associated with subjective, biased, and feminized modes of narration and information production: their own, embodied perceptions of events, unofficial or street-based sources, and African Americans.

Covering the movement in black and white

> When you have the pictures, which I saw the last time I visited America, of the dogs biting negro kids, that awakened much good conscience in white America across the country.
> (Gunnar Myrdal, quoted on *CBS News Special Report*, 11 June 1963)

When the news media narrate the story of coverage of the Civil Rights Movement, they mythologize it, exaggerating the individual heroism of northern reporters and their responsibility for training the eyes of the nation on southern atrocities. Really, the self-determination and self-organization of African Americans themselves ensured that they would appear on television news throughout the country. African Americans first appeared on the pages and screens of US mass media after the Montgomery Bus Boycott in 1955–56 and the desegregation of Central High School in Little Rock, Arkansas in 1957. Robert Kintner, then president of NBC, had it wrong in asserting that television "put Negro Americans into the living rooms of tens of millions of white Americans for the first time" (quoted in Donovan and Scherer 1992: 18). Dick Valeriani, a reporter who covered the movement for NBC, expressed a different opinion, when he described the Civil Rights Movement as "a movement whose time had come and if there were no television at that time the movement would have succeeded anyway" (Valeriani: 1987). African Americans gave the new medium no choice but to take note of their resolve and their mobilization.

Just as the captains of industry anticipated the political and cultural power of television, so too did the leaders of the Civil Rights Movement in the south, who believed that the success of their movement depended on their ability to attract the eyes and ears of the national media. Media-savvy civil rights activists geared their strategies of resistance to the imperatives of the new medium, much as abolitionists in the past had adapted their strategies to print media. As Steven D. Classen points out, broadcast representations of civil rights activism were enabled by the early and largely invisible efforts of "a handful of deeply committed integrationists and African Americans who attempted to attract the attention of the national television networks and use local media to attack Jim Crow" (2004: 41). Activists like Medgar Evers and his brother Charles used radio and television to challenge segregation in Mississippi. Evers and the NAACP also made the first legal attacks against Jackson, Mississippi broadcasters for not operating in the public interest: attacks that anticipated the challenge later mounted against the federal broadcast licenses of Jackson television stations.

In addition to regulatory challenges, activists gave great consideration to the images they wanted to project. Although the media memorialized Rosa Parks as the symbol of individual resistance to segregation during the Montgomery Bus Boycott, Rosa Parks was not just a tailor's assistant—she was a leader in her own right. As Jo Ann Robinson, a community activist and president of the Montgomery Women's Political Council, later put it, "We had planned the protest long before Mrs. Parks was arrested" (quoted in Garrow 1988: 16). In fact, just nine months before Parks was arrested in December 1955, a 15-year-old student was arrested for refusing to give up her seat on a Montgomery bus. Although activists thought they might have a test case in this, the student had actively resisted arrest (and had been charged with assault and battery) and she was unmarried and several months pregnant. These image-related problems led local leaders to conclude that she "would be neither an ideal candidate for symbolizing the abuse heaped upon black passengers nor a good litigant for a test suit certain to generate great pressures and publicity" (Garrow 1988: 16).

The strategy of nonviolent resistance used by the Civil Rights Movement and the tactics associated with it were particularly well suited to the visual requirements of the new medium. Indeed, for groups of people and organizations that had been historically singled out for criminalization by agents of the state, nonviolent resistance proved to be an effective strategy for fighting against the imposition of demonization and its racialized threats (Bermanzohn 2001). It was difficult to demonize people who appeared vulnerable and who refused to fight back or even resist.

Nonviolent resistance had the effect of starkly polarizing political forces and providing a visual contrast between nonviolent protesters on one hand, and southern officials and institutions on the other. As Martin Luther King himself put it:

> Nonviolent direct action seeks to create such a crisis and foster such a tension that a community which has constantly refused to negotiate, is forced to confront the issue. It seeks so to dramatize the issue that it can no longer be ignored.
>
> (1963)

In short, nonviolent resistance was a perfect vehicle for the simple, evocative, and short morality tales that seemed so well suited to commercial televised news in the 1950s. Haynes Johnson, a reporter for the *Washington Star* and the *Washington Post*, said "that the south was always a story that was so, in a way, simple. It was the greatest story of our times, I believe, in that you had it right in front of your eyes. It was simple—the idea that all it was about was to go from here to that wall and try to register to vote" (Johnson: 1987). As Nick Kotz, who covered the Civil Rights Movement for the *Des Moines Register* and the *Washington Post* observed: "The players were clearly identified: peaceful black Americans, trying to exercise those American rights, opposed by an official segregationist society that resisted those rights with violence that included every act, including murder" (Kotz: 1987). Activists effectively exploited this contrast as well as television news' thirst for conflict in staging events, relying on the fact that the white, southern establishment would respond with their usual displays of violence and that the resulting polarization would attract the eyes of the news media and, by extension, the attention of the federal government.[10]

In addition to the stark visual juxtaposition of dogs, hoses, and police attacks with images of children and young people dressed in their Sunday best, the careful planning of movement activities conformed to the type of serialization that television news had adopted from print journalism. Television news coverage "influenced northern newspaper and magazine editors to keep playing the story year after year" (Donovan and Scherer 1992: 8). Arlie W. Schadt, covering the south for *Time*, confirmed this tendency: "There's a tendency to want to drop something after a while, but I think that everybody's sense of history was caught as this went along. It really was a tremendously dramatic day-by-day and then week-by-week and even month-by-month development" (quoted in Donovan and Scherer 1992: 8). In this fashion, the Civil Rights Movement became the first major domestic story, or theme, for television news in particular, presenting African Americans for the first time in the history of mainstream news media as victims worthy of attention.

Positive coverage of civil rights activism also grew out of the uncomfortable position in which many northern reporters found themselves. Many journalists had been introduced to the terrorism of southern racism when they covered the trial of two white men charged with lynching eighth-grader Emmett Till in Mississippi in late August of 1955. It was said that Till, who had left Chicago to visit relatives in the Delta, had said "Bye, baby" to a white woman as he left a store, although accounts of the incident itself varied. Later that night, he was kidnapped from his uncle's home and murdered by two white men.[11] Many of the northern reporters who went on to cover the Civil Rights Movement cite the lynching of this 14-year-old as their introduction to southern culture. John Chancellor, David Halberstam, Bill Minor, and other journalists later identified the Till case as the beginning of an emerging national awareness of the incipient movement, although it was a consciousness that had been forced upon the white press. All major networks covered the trial in detail, flying footage from Mississippi to New York City each day for the news. Even so, had Mamie Bradley, Till's mother, not insisted on her son's body being returned to Chicago for burial, where she arranged for an open casket funeral to "let the people see what they have done to my boy!" (quoted in Feldstein 1994: 271), northern news media might not have been so interested.[12] Whatever their motives, for a generation of journalists, the murder of young Emmett Till was their first foray into the south, only three months before the Montgomery Bus Boycott was to send them back into the field.

Of course, it was one thing to cover the trial of Till's white murderers, but it was another matter altogether when journalists began to experience some of the white supremacist violence directed at African American activists. Reporters consistently found themselves on the wrong side of local institutions when cov-

ering events in the south. In 1957, *Life* magazine journalists were beaten up by
white supremacists in Little Rock. Journalist Stuart Loory described the reception given to Freedom Riders in 1961:

> One of the mob hit Moe Levy of NBC across the face. That was their first
> blow. The mob surrounded the cameramen, grabbed their equipment and
> flung it against the pavement until microphone, recording equipment and
> cameras were broken shambles.
>
> (2003: 575)

In a pattern that became routine, journalists were among the first to be
assaulted, in order to prevent any filming of subsequent attacks.

Print and television journalists shared similar experiences. When Dan Rather
arrived in Oxford, Mississippi in 1962 to cover James Meredith's admission to
the University of Mississippi, he and his crew attempted to check into a motel,
only to be greeted by a sign that read "No dogs, niggers or reporters allowed."
Many journalists considered covering the Civil Rights Movement in the south
a "domestic war story" (Rather and Herskowitz 1977: 80). Claude Sitton, who
covered the movement from 1958 to 1964 for the *New York Times* later referred
to Vietnam as "another different kind of war" (1987).[13]

Not only were journalists assaulted, they were also subjected to other violent forms of institutionalized racism. Karl Fleming, of *Newsweek*, recalled that
journalists realized early on that they were under surveillance by the Ku Klux
Klan and local police (the memberships often overlapped) and that both local
law enforcement and the FBI frequently tapped their phones (1987). Northern
journalists' colleagues in southern broadcast industries also reviled them. Local
network affiliates had long worked to squelch information about the Civil Rights
Movement and frequently refused to cooperate with their national counterparts.
While covering the brutal beating of Freedom Riders in Birmingham in 1961,
for example, reporter Howard K. Smith found that "the local station was mys-
teriously unable to patch me through to the network" (1996: 272). Fred Friendly
recounted that the Huntley-Brinkley news program carried by WLBT, the NBC
affiliate in Jackson, Mississippi, was

> occasionally interrupted when it was covering civil rights, and sometimes,
> prior to news reports on the *Today* show, a WLBT announcer would warn,
> "What you are about to see is an example of biased, managed, Northern
> news. Be sure to stay tuned at seven twenty-five to hear your local news-
> cast."
>
> (1976: 91)[14]

According to another source, the coaxial cable was cut the night Ed Sullivan
featured an African American performer on his show, "so that the people of Birmingham could not see television" (Morgan 1987). As late as 1963, CBS "found
two of its southern affiliates refusing to carry an *East Side/West Side* episode

because of its negro roles" (Barnouw 1970: 223). The stereotype of the liberal national news media that became a decisive feature of the conservative backlash grew out of this antagonism between local media that defended white supremacy and a national media that had been transformed by conflict into what SNCC leader John Lewis described as "sympathetic referees" (1987). Just as the charge of un-Americanism was a racist one, so the claim that the media were liberal would henceforth be inferentially racist.[15]

Northern journalists' alienation from institutions and official sources in the south undermined the objectivity that since the progressive era had necessitated a physical and emotional distance between reporters and the stories that they covered. If objectivity had permitted northern journalists to reify white supremacy in the case of lynching, as David Mindich (1998) argues, the breakdown of objectivity—and the passion with which journalists responded to the violence in the south—allowed for the first sympathetic news reporting of African Americans since the Civil War. This breakdown in the logic of racialized androcentrism did not occur through the efforts of individual journalists. Again this took place because of structural factors that forced journalists into sympathetic relationships with the activists they were covering. In the first place, and as Michael Schudson observes, "the further a reporter is from the home office, the greater that reporter's freedom to violate objectivity norms" (2001: 163). Distant from their home offices, alienated from local offices, reporters sympathized with the dignity and determination of the protesters in the face of white violence. Journalists subsequently found the line between reporting and advocacy had become slippery and unclear because, for the first time in their lives, mainly white journalists were experiencing some of the effects of institutionalized racism.

More than twenty years later, Karl Fleming of *Newsweek* recalled that journalists "certainly felt sick, we felt ashamed, we felt certainly frightened, we felt mortified at what we saw our fellow human beings doing to other human beings. So, we felt" (1987). Journalists had not been particularly feeling when it came to covering lynching at the end of the previous century. Distant from the circumstances in which such violence took place, insulated from its effects, journalists could afford to be objective. But when forced by the circumstances in the south to "feel" some of the violence inflicted on African Americans, journalists found it impossible to maintain an objective stance. Hounded by local officials, harassed by local police and the Ku Klux Klan, beaten and attacked by white supremacists, it would be surprising indeed had reporters' perspectives remained the same.

The production history of *CBS Reports'* documentary about race relations in Birmingham, Alabama, "Who Will Speak for Birmingham?" further illustrates the isolation journalists were experiencing. When filming began, in September 1960, Police Commissioner "Bull" Connor refused to speak to reporter Howard K. Smith, even if that conversation was held off-camera. David Lowe, who produced and wrote for the news program, and Smith recognized that "balance" was an impossible fiction in this instance. There were not, in fact, two equally reasonable sides to this story. "Who Will Speak for Birmingham?" ultimately provided a searing critique of southern racism, juxtaposing images of activist Reverend Fred Shuttlesworth and the repeated bombing attempts on his home and church with testimony of white southerners like one Mrs. Pritchett, who lamented the previous

> joyousness of the negro. He was happy and contented. You do not hear that any more. We used to hear negroes singing all the time. They just used to walk down the street singing. The servant in the house would sing, the gardener would sing, like in Spain and Mexico right now. I haven't heard a negro break spontaneously into song in four or five years.
>
> ("Who Will Speak for Birmingham?" 1961)

In another interview on the program, presented without commentary, Lowe (himself Jewish) asked Judge Hugh A. Locke whether Jews could join the Birmingham Citizens Council. "No," Locke tersely responded, "Only Americans."

The documentary concluded with Smith quoting Edmund Burke's famous lines: "The only thing necessary for the triumph of evil is for good men to do nothing." When network executives got wind of the editorial content of the documentary, they called Smith to New York (Smith 1996: 272), where they promptly fired him for refusing to tone down the documentary.[16] Even in covering the south, there were finite limits to what could be said about race and racism: as Smith put it, "CBS was a business; in a crunch it needed bigoted and fair-minded listeners alike, and didn't want to alienate either" (275).

The need to include both racist and anti-racist audiences resulted in further contradictions, not all of them negative from the perspective of those active in the Civil Rights Movement. On 28 August 1963, *CBS News Special Report: March on Washington* covered the landmark event that brought over a quarter of a million protesters to the capitol. CBS decided to pre-empt regularly scheduled programming to cover the event, which was broadcast without commercial interruption because of what was euphemistically referred to as "sponsor" difficulty (white advertisers refused to buy time during the program).[17] Featuring Roy Wilkins, Martin Luther King, Bayard Rustin, and John Lewis, among other activists, the broadcast included speeches that were covered in their entirety (this was in fact the only time that television broadcast the whole of one of Dr. King's speeches), with long shots of the speakers interspersed with tight close-ups of a multiracial crowd. King was introduced as the "moral leader of the United States" and Bayard Rustin's list of demands was covered in its entirety and without commentary.[18]

Even this most peaceful, nonviolent mass mobilization was haunted by the historical link between African Americans and violent crime. The lead-up to the march was full of predictions of mob violence. On *Meet the Press*, "television reporters grilled Roy Wilkins and Martin Luther King about widespread foreboding that 'it would be impossible to bring more than 100,000 militant negroes into Washington without incidents and possibly rioting'" (Branch 1998: 131).

Roger Mudd, who hosted the broadcast, repeatedly remarked on the fact that there were "No reported incidents of violence" and that of "570 casualties," all were marchers who had fainted (*CBS News Special Report*, 28 August 1963). Despite attempts to construct "militant" African Americans as objects of white fear, this was perhaps the last time that the Civil Rights Movement would appear in such an unambivalent light.

However much individual journalists represented civil rights activists in a heroic and deserving fashion, the victim narratives they were constructing had limited effects on the conduct of local, state, and national officials like the FBI, who continued to operate under an older set of narrative assumptions. Journalists may have considered victims of white violence as worthy, but the slow, and in some cases nonexistent, pace of justice underscored the fact that the criminal justice system did not. Northern media presented the death of Medgar Evers in 1963 as a tragic loss to his community and to the movement, but it was not until 1994, over thirty years after his death, that white supremacist Byron De La Beckwith was finally convicted of his murder. And as Jennifer Wood points out, "It would be difficult to find representations of more 'ideal' victims than . . . four little girls in their Sunday finery, blown to bits by a bomb planted in the church they were attending" (2005:14). Yet it took forty years to convict the men responsible for the bomb that killed those four little girls in Birmingham in August 1963. And as much publicity as the murders of Freedom Summer volunteers in Philadelphia, Mississippi garnered in the summer of 1964, four decades later ex-Klansman Edgar Ray Killen was convicted for manslaughter in those slayings. In the end, however positive the televisual spotlight, the narratives produced by northern reporters about civil rights in the south were about to be eclipsed by the very forces that had obstructed justice in the south.

Reverting to racism

> In 1968, I think that we, the media, issued a redefinition of the Civil Rights movement. It was more than a redefinition. I think that we said that it was over. We said that it was over and we didn't really examine what had happened and the redirection that the Civil Rights campaign had taken.
>
> (Alatney 1987)[19]

Too often, we assume that political backlashes are simple and straightforward cultural and social events: forces of conservatism reacting to progressive political and social movements. But like moral panics, backlashes are complicated social phenomena: products of institutional and cultural convergences and specific historical conjunctures.[20] Lane has observed, "in the same 1964 summer that Chaney, Goodman, and Schwerner were assassinated, the term 'white backlash' was coined to describe the beginnings of a paradoxical countermovement up North" (1997: 272). In the case of the transformation of news coverage of African Americans in the 1960s, what Lane describes as "a paradoxical countermovement," or what others might describe as a backlash, might more appropriately be understood as a reversion to form—as the reimposition of very traditional, racist narratives after a short, unprecedented departure from these older narratives.

This process of reversion became distinctly observable as the locus of activism moved north, as unrest and rebellion became evident in the urban centers of the north, and as the leadership among a younger generation of activists became more militant.[21] As early as the coverage of the Harlem uprising in 1964, the general timbre of coverage had begun to change.[22] The reasons for the transformation of news narratives about race and resistance are complex, owing as they do to interrelationships among institutions and social movements. The movement in the north differed in important aspects from that of the south, particularly in terms of political strategies and activist analyses of social problems and movement goals. As the 1960s wore on, for a younger generation, understandably impatient for social change, less religious in orientation than their parents' generation, and less inclined to be polite in demanding rights that should have been theirs by virtue of citizenship, nonviolent resistance was losing its popularity as a movement strategy. Moreover, structures of apartheid in the north, such as redlining, police violence, and employment discrimination, were practiced more covertly than they were in the south. The racism that had been built into northern institutions was less visual in nature, for whites at least, which detracted from the symbolic power of nonviolence as an activist strategy. African American communities in the north, moreover, had very different histories and politics than those in the south, and both working-class and poor African American communities practiced forms of resistance and self-empowerment that were difficult if not impossible to create and sustain in the terrorist regimes of the south.

These differences in political practices and community structures were compounded by the finite limits of the structure imposed by television as a medium and as an industry. Activists in the north were agitating less for the more symbolic rights associated with citizenship and more for equality in housing, education, and employment. The resultant analyses and critiques of economic policies were just as trenchant as those of southern activists, but they were frequently more sophisticated and relied on data and analyses not easily conveyed through a visual medium and in the short one- to three-minute format preferred by television news.

As the movement moved to the north, stark, simple binaries gave way to a much more complex tapestry of economic oppression and disenfranchisement. When questioned about television's role in covering civil rights in the late sixties, Dick Valeriani observed that television "is a picture medium. In large part those pictures are not available anymore . . . It is more difficult for television to deal with the deep-seated problems of poverty and economic issues and that sort of thing" (1987). Cedric Robinson also commented on this dimension of news coverage:

Television, of course, had little capacity to display the divisional and ideological complexities of organizations, but network news producers enthused over the visual possibilities of stark, racial conflict acted out in well-lit public spaces. Television's dramatic canon of simple binaries, good vs. evil, was even more seductive when Blacks symbolized good and whites, evil.

(1997: 145)

Footage of events in the south provided a compelling, visual morality play that required little commentary. Poverty and economic devastation, in contrast, made northern whites uncomfortable, particularly when these occurred in their backyards. From the perspective of producers and reporters, the routine and decidedly undramatic nature of urban poverty also lacked visual interest.

The northern movement, moreover, was an urban one. Unlike the rural black poor, who could be represented as the simple, agrarian black folk so popular in late nineteenth-century culture, or the southern black middle class, whose piety, politeness, and attention to dress rendered them dignified and non-threatening, urban activists in the north were beginning to openly reject white fashion standards, to wear Afro-centric hairstyles and clothing that accentuated their difference, and they were refusing to conform to white middle-class codes of propriety, politesse, and behavior. The middle-class biases and sympathies of white reporters which made for sympathetic coverage of southern farmers and the black middle class, negatively affected coverage of a younger and more militant African American working class in the north.

There was, furthermore, no love lost between northern news media whose historical tendency either to ignore black communities or to demonize them (the latter typically with scant knowledge of the communities they represented) led black activists to rightly understand the news media as just another segregated institution with which they had to do battle. African Americans viewed them as members of the establishment rather than potential sympathizers with good reason. When journalists covered urban uprisings, they traveled with the police and saw events from a perspective structured by the view from helicopters in Watts and Detroit and from police cruisers in places like Harlem and Newark. If their alienation from white southerners had helped to unite journalists with civil rights activists, so their alienation from black communities and activists in the north thrust them back into familiar institutional positions and routines structured by white privilege. Although many of them were fresh from reporting in the south, many white journalists could not understand why African Americans in the north often regarded them with suspicion.[23] After all, they did not consider themselves to be the enemy.

Roy Reed, who covered the Movement for the *Arkansas Gazette* and the *New York Times*, recalled the change in the following terms:

After black power became a reality, some of us white reporters began to see our lives change in a subtle and disquieting way. We'd always been very much at home in our limited ways in the black community . . . After black power and after the first black violence began to erupt and be directed against white people, things changed for us white reporters in ways that you can't imagine. I remember being spat on by a black girl.

(1987)

Reporters' contradictory consciousness of the change in coverage runs throughout Reed's comments, especially in his assertion that reporters had been "very much at home," albeit in "limited ways," as well as the claim that black violence was directed at white people (an example of this that left an impression on him was being spat upon by a girl). Reed acknowledged that white reporters' fear of militant African Americans "might have had a distorting effect" on their coverage of events in the north, a point that the *Report of the National Advisory Commission on Civil Disorders* (Kerner Commission Report) also made in criticizing the media for exaggerating the extent of urban violence in the late 1960s. Few questioned the grounds for their fear.

Instead of identifying with activists as they had in the south, reporters in the north shared the perspective of the very institutions activists were criticizing. The resultant divide between reporters and the communities they were covering partly explains why, as one reporter later acknowledged, "We didn't turn around and look at Harlem to the extent that we looked at the South" (Johnson 1987). However much activists like Jesse Gray of Harlem's Community Council on Housing tried to make the case that there was "little difference between legal segregation in the South and de facto segregation in the North" and "no difference between the Jim Crow system up south and down south" (*The Harlem Temper* 1963), activists' comparisons between the north and the south were ignored as news anchors like Dan Rather focused on "a new militancy on the part of negroes" (*CBS News Special Report* 1963), or what Harry Reasoner called "racism in reverse" (*The Harlem Temper*). Two years before cities like Newark and Detroit were damaged by riots, reporters were already giving short shrift to agitators' demands. Instead, they emphasized the physical threat blacks presented to society.[24]

This growing sense of threat was strengthened by journalists' institutional alliance with the police and criminal justice system, which further prevented journalists from understanding, much less sharing, the perspective of northern activists. In the north, journalists from the networks and major newspapers had a well-organized infrastructure for newsgathering, and often intimate relationships with their official sources. Print journalists had fewer street-based sources than they had had sixty years earlier, and reliance on street-based sources was rare indeed in the more insular world of broadcast journalism. According to civil rights leader Ralph Abernathy:

in the South the press tended to view apologies for the status quo with a healthy skepticism, in the North the same people would accept the explanations of a [Chicago Mayor] Daley and a [African American Congressman William] Dawson without seriously questioning the validity of what they said. As a consequence, the national coverage we got seemed spotty and less sharply focused.

(1989: 367)

The segregated nature of the newsroom, as well as overall societal segregation, meant that few in the news industry had contacts within black communities.

Ultimately, where covering the movement in the south entailed traveling to a culture that seemed alien and exotic, and enabled journalists to extend a sympathetic and sometimes paternalistic hand to members of the movement, when the conflict moved north, it demanded a degree of self-criticism for which reporters were ill prepared.

Northern reporters' sense of superiority to the openly racist forces they encountered in the south further prevented reporters from recognizing their own biases. Criticizing the immorality of southern racism and white "rednecks" was one thing; criticizing the politics and economic infrastructure—the informal apartheid—of the industrialized north was another thing altogether. As Alison Graham observes (2001), the trope of the "redneck," like that of "rogue cops" invoked years later, permitted reporters and northern society as a whole to distance themselves from institutionalized racism as it existed in the north. In retrospect, Ralph Abernathy observed,

> Had Chicago been a southern city I'm certain that the press would have exposed the mayor's duplicity, conducted in-depth interviews with local blacks, and uncovered the racism of the Daley machine. But the story simply didn't please as many people, nor did it appeal to anyone's sense of moral superiority, as stories about Birmingham and Selma did. When you attacked Mississippi, New Yorkers and San Franciscans felt good about themselves. When you attacked Chicago, everybody felt uncomfortable.
>
> (1989: 496)

Years after the events they had covered, reporters were more willing to recognize their failures. For Johnson, "After the high point of Selma . . . Many of us who had covered that period suddenly found ourselves in Newark, in Watts, in Detroit, in the urban centers. We saw the cities burning in the North; they didn't burn in the South. We saw race relations plunge into a very different, more difficult period and we saw a reaction coming" (1987). While northern journalists were not responsible for the shape that this reaction took, they provided unquestioning narrative support for it.

"The whole United States is Southern"

> They all hate black people, all of them. They're all afraid, all of them. Great God! They're all Southern! The whole United States is Southern!
>
> (Douglas Kiker quoted in Carter 1995: 344)

The news frame of the war on poverty, with its emphasis on civil rights and addressing inequality through equal access to education, employment, and housing, gave way to the news frame of the war on crime between 1963 and 1968, with contributions from numerous individual players, institutions, and political forces. The racism that informed this second war on crime was given new life and cover by the fear ascribed to a segregationist "silent majority" and ventriloquized by conservative politicians like Barry Goldwater, Ronald Reagan, and Richard Nixon. As the discourse of the war on crime gained ground, it dramatically altered media representations of African Americans. Undermining the Civil Rights Movement's efforts to portray people of color as worthy victims, protesting with dignity, courage, and conviction, the war on crime combined a discourse about juvenile delinquency with white fears about the anger of African Americans. Heedless of the warnings of activists, as well as the warnings of a handful of politicians like Edmund Muskie, by 1968 the USA had made a decisive turn away "in fear and hostility, from the problems that black America has pressed for equality" (*ABC Evening News*, 15 October 1968).

This second war on crime drew on the language of law and order that had accompanied the federal government's attempts to force southern institutions and politicians to desegregate public institutions in the 1950s. The earliest televised call for law and order came during the struggle to desegregate schools in Little Rock, Arkansas, and juxtaposed a small band of black schoolchildren with a vicious, largely adult white mob. Such calls for law and order were made on behalf of a federal government deeply resented by segregationist politicians and citizens in the south and the north alike. It was a language that was shortly to be appropriated by the defenders of white supremacy, whose resentment of centralized or "big" government was to shape politics in the USA into the next century.

Ever more strident calls for law and order made against African Americans rather than white supremacist mobs appeared as early as 1963, with the political rhetoric of George Wallace, Barry Goldwater, and Ronald Reagan. Wallace in particular sought to set calls for law and order made by the government in order to protect the rights of African Americans on their head. During the bloody Birmingham summer of 1963, Wallace fought integration and helped to stir up white supremacist rage and violence against African Americans by suggesting that actions like closing schools to prevent desegregation actually protected Alabamans by preventing outbreaks of justifiable rage on the part of whites caused by the presence of "outside" agitators (blacks and communists). Whites were victims, he ranted, the federal government was willing to sacrifice the lives of innocent schoolchildren in order to integrate schools, and the problems in the south were reducible to the unrest caused by outside agitators.

Really, Wallace argued, white Alabamans were the victims of a liberal federal government—and it is again worth noting that the demonization of liberalism that was to flourish in the final decades of the twentieth century had its roots in white supremacist defenses of segregation and violence against blacks—in cahoots with a truly unholy alliance between the Civil Rights Movement and

the Communist Party. That the Communist Party's membership had been dec-
imated by the Soviet Union's invasion of Hungary in 1956 did not matter, since
the fight against the ungodly, integrationist forces of communism had become
embedded in the forms of threat construction favored by conservatives. Even
after the bombing deaths of Addie Mae Collins, Denise McNair, Carole Robert-
son, and Cynthia Wesley at the Sixteenth Street Baptist Church in September
1963, and the ensuing riots, which claimed the lives of two more black teenaged boys, Wallace and other prominent whites insisted that black activists had
planted the bombs. Like the federal government, this logic implied, fanatical
blacks were willing to sacrifice the lives of children for a cause aimed at nothing
less than the overthrow of traditional moral values.

Wallace's rhetoric revived the strain of racialized androcentrism that had
long lain at the heart of representations of African Americans in the north, as
well as in the south. Wallace's presidential aspirations led him to tone down the
more overtly racist elements of his limited rhetorical repertoire, but his constant
references to outside agitators, communists, and disorder left no one guessing
who was to blame. Consistent with nineteenth-century ideologies of race, Wallace considered blacks to be genetically less intelligent than whites. As in the
case of abolitionists, blacks were, according to this logic, particularly suscepti-
ble to being "stirred up" by political forces desirous of using them as vehicles
for gains generally linked to the furtherance of communism or socialism. Blacks
were, moreover, intrinsically savage and criminal. Birmingham native William
Pritchard, interviewed for *CBS Reports* in 1961, blatantly voiced this racist logic:
"Substantially, all the negroes in Alabama and perhaps in the States have the
same background. They were all savages in Africa: their parents sold them into
slavery, their chieftains sold them into slavery" ("Who'll Speak for Birmingham?" 1961). The combination of tractability and the essential "criminality" of
the black character, white supremacists argued, made for a hazardous mixture.
Wallace and others successfully used the language of law and order to articulate
black resistance with crime and to convert menacing white supremacists into the
innocent victims of a communist conspiracy. Coverage of Wallace's address to
a UAW convention in 1968 echoed this old racist refrain: "When Wallace talks
about anarchists, working men and women know who he means: social protesters in general, anti-war demonstrators, campus dissidents, and negro militants in
particular" (*CBS Evening News*, 20 September 1968).

In these scenarios, African American resistance was rendered irrational,
devoid of any agency, and inherently criminal, while white resistance to reform
was upheld as virtuous. When a series of riots erupted in protest of integration,
Wallace defended white rioters in terms that would never be extended to African American political movements, especially in the north. White rioters, he
claimed, were "not thugs—they are good working people who get mad when
they see something like this happen. It takes courage to stand up to tear gas and
bayonets" (quoted in Carter 1995: 172). Good working people, courageous in
their defiance of the federal government, white people were again accorded
a privileged status, even when those who died as a result of their words and

actions in places like Birmingham were little girls, dressed up for church, or teenaged boys out riding their bikes, whose only offense was, like the victims of the 1863 anti-draft riots, to happen into the path of a white mob.

In 1963, the language of Wallace and other segregationists had not gone entirely national, a process that began to take place during Wallace's first failed bid for the presidency in 1964. But already, television narratives in the north were beginning to refer menacingly—and contradictorily—to "a negro revolution" and to the machinations of "outside provocateurs" ("Nineteen Sixty-Three: A TV Album" 1963). And when riots wracked cities throughout the north after 1965, the term "law and order" took on a life of its own, as white television viewers were presented with images that suggested that their homes, their property, and their lives were in imminent danger. Dozens of cities were torn by violence during successive years: 34 died in Watts in August 1965; 23 in Newark, NJ; and 43 in Detroit in July 1967 (Lane 1997: 275). But 1968 proved to be the decisive moment in the transformation of the war on poverty news frame into that of the war on crime. Following the assassinations of Dr. Martin Luther King, Jr. and Robert Kennedy, and amid deepening public opposition to the Vietnam War, the contemporary language of law and order really came into its own, having found a congenial host in the medium of television.[25]

Despite the mythology that surrounds John F. Kennedy's assassination, the assassination of Martin Luther King on 4 April 1968 had much more immediate, anguished, and violent effects on the country. In the nation's capital, eight people died in the uprising that followed news of King's murder, 987 were injured, and 4613 were arrested. In Baltimore, four perished and 258 were injured. In Chicago, 6700 National Guardsmen were called in to stop the violence, which continued for three days and left more than 500 people injured and eleven, all black, dead (Abernathy 1989: 453–54).

In the days following Dr. King's assassination, the anguished and desperate uprisings throughout US cities underwent a process of redefinition in the media. Then Governor of Maryland Spiro Agnew chastised a group of African American leaders after an uprising in Baltimore following the assassination of Dr. King. These blacks, Agnew charged, had not taken "a strong stand against black militants like Rap Brown," who promoted "a perverted concept of race loyalty" (*CBS Evening News*, 13 August 1968), "race loyalty" being a phrase that was never applied to white segregationists in the south or the north. Agnew's verbal attack on black leaders in the days following the assassination won him the approval of Republicans throughout the country, as well as the vice presidency. In later years, Nixon spoke in glowing terms of Agnew's response to these riots.

A special local program entitled *We Are All Policemen: A Look at Crime and the Community* and broadcast in New York City less than two weeks after Dr. King's assassination included even more aggressive evidence of criminalization. The program was divided into four sections: "The Crime Problem," "The Police at Work," "Citizens," and "The Challenge of Crime." Repeated shots of and references to Harlem implied that it was the epicenter of violent criminal activity. Potential victims were said to be white women who "arm themselves with tear gas before going into the streets," as well as the members of an all-white Upper East Side community group, who expressed their shared sense of victimization. "Civil disorder" was equated with "mass crime" in the concluding segment: both were referred to as "holocausts." As if this equivalence was not enough, this clip was immediately followed by footage of Anthony Imperiale, an openly racist politician from Newark, New Jersey. Imperiale hysterically and incoherently argued that politicians and the Supreme Court had been passing laws making it possible for "black radical animals to exist and to let the communists into this country and we know communists have got a lot to do with what's going on." Host Edwin Newman interviewed no African Americans. Blacks appeared on the program only as shadowy, criminal threats. Balance, as usual, weighed on the side of the powerful.

The second war on crime

Numerous polls and opinion surveys have been cited to suggest that crime "emerged as an important issue on the public agenda about 1965," not surprisingly at the very moment when the forces arrayed against the Civil Rights Movement were gearing up (Skogan 1977: 1). As Ditton and Farrall point out, the panic about crime in the USA grew out of "the manipulation of the Nixonian silent majority, from right-wing white concern about the extension of rights to the poor and the black" (2000: xvi). Politicians like George Wallace, Barry Goldwater, Richard Nixon, and Ronald Reagan were hardly the authors of the law and order agenda that became ascendant during the 1960s, even though they were among its strongest spokesmen.

The words of politicians committed to maintaining the racist status quo were inspired and supported by the crime-fighting agenda so strenuously promoted by the FBI throughout the twentieth century. This was, as we have seen, a crime-fighting agenda that reproduced itself across the twentieth century by reconstituting threats that were, to more observant eyes, a noxious potion composed of racial stereotypes and gender clichés. In the eyes of this crime-fighting establishment, challenges to the existing social order were criminalized in the name of protecting moral values. Although the worst effects of the FBI's formidable repressive power had long been borne by African American activists and their supporters, the second war on crime allowed the FBI to more openly pursue what was essentially a racist crime-fighting agenda. The social movements of the 1960s outraged Hoover, opposing as they did the very moral values he had championed for the better part of the twentieth century (including racism, homophobia, xenophobia, misogyny, and an abiding intolerance for anyone who dared to disagree with him). But African Americans paid the heaviest price for dissent.

The FBI and Hoover had been experiencing some institutional insecurity since the beginning of the 1960s. John F. Kennedy's election to President in 1960 initiated a crisis for the FBI, as "the country began to move away from the politics of antisubversion," addressing instead "the problems of crime, race, and poverty through proposals to promote health, education, and welfare" (Theoharis and Cox 1988: 325). Although Hoover had had very cordial relationships with both Republican and Democratic presidents dating back to Franklin D. Roosevelt, the Kennedy and Johnson years were difficult. The appointment of Robert F. Kennedy as Attorney General meant that Hoover could not engage in his preferred habit of bypassing the Attorney General and submitting reports directly to the White House. His relationship with Robert Kennedy was frosty at best: Robert Kennedy considered the FBI to be "a very dangerous organiza-tion" and he had made clear his intention to integrate the institution (Branch 1998: 536). Although Hoover's relationship with Johnson was much better, he despised Attorney General Ramsey Clark, publicly referring to him as a "jelly-fish."[26] Among Clark's transgressions was the fact that he insisted that the FBI submit written requests before wiretapping or bugging operations and that the FBI further had to seek reauthorization for these operations every six months (Theoharis 1995: 162). Clark, moreover, was an outspoken critic of the war on crime, later explicitly criticizing the FBI's stake in rising crime rates in his 1970 book, *Crime in America*.

In response to a shift in national priorities that could only have negative effects on an agency whose funding and future depended on perceptions of crime as a significant social problem, Hoover reluctantly "modified his germ-phobic [anticommunist] rhetoric to emphasize a generalized assault on American values" (Theoharis and Cox 1988: 327–88). At the same time, and as he had with dissidents in the past, Hoover intensified surveillance of the Civil Rights Movement, hoping to turn up information that could be used to criminalize its participants.

Hoover had suspected Martin Luther King's "loyalty" since the Montgomery Bus Boycott in 1955 (Theoharis 1995: 96) and harbored a particularly vicious, personal hatred of the civil rights leader.[27] The FBI began to monitor the activ-ities of the Southern Christian Leadership Conference and King in the late 1950s. Rumors about King's associates Stanley Levison and Bayard Rustin's links to the Communist Party (as well as Rustin's homosexuality) were used against the civil rights leader throughout his lifetime. The FBI gained approval from Attorney General Robert Kennedy in 1963 for official, systematic wire-tapping of King on the basis of these rumors.[28] Soon after this, Hoover declared King "specifically unfit to receive death warnings" when the FBI became aware of these. While the FBI's standard practice was to notify potential targets of assassins about death threats, King was never to receive this information (Branch 1998: 198). The FBI treated King not as a political leader, but as a criminal sub-jected to intensified police investigation and counterinsurgency tactics.

When King took the FBI to task for its refusal to address civil rights violations in the south, the FBI's crusade against King began to take the shape of attacks on his character, values, and sexual conduct, with blatantly racist overtones based on the link between blackness and sexual excess. In a 27 January 1964 memo, Hoover wrote: "King is a 'tom cat' with obsessive degenerate sexual urges" (Theoharis and Cox 1988: 359). At a November 1964 press conference with Washington, DC newspaperwomen, shortly before King's acceptance of the Nobel Peace Prize, Hoover called King "the most notorious liar in the country."[29] Later that same month, the FBI sent a tape to Coretta Scott King made of composite buggings of King's hotel rooms that ostensibly demonstrated his participation in a "sex orgy" (Theoharis 1995: 97). Also included in the package was a letter composed by FBI Assistant Director William Sullivan, calling King "an evil, abnormal beast" and concluding, "You are done. There is but one way out for you. You better take it before your filthy, abnormal, fraudulent self is bared to the nation" (Theoharis and Cox 1988: 359). Shortly after this incident, Cartha DeLoach, FBI liaison to Johnson, offered copies of "a purported FBI microphone surveillance transcript" of King's sexual activities to numerous news producers, editors, and reporters, including Ben Bradlee (then with *Newsweek*) and *Los Angeles Times'* Washington bureau chief David Kraslow, while related information, such as transcripts and photographs, was offered to CBS correspondent Dan Rather, *New York Times* reporter John Herbers, *Chicago Daily News* columnist Mike Royko, *Atlanta Constitution* editors Ralph McGill and Eugene Patterson, and *Augusta Chronicle* reporter Lou Harris (Theoharis and Cox 1988: 357). On 21 December, Hoover also sent copies of a specially prepared two-page FBI report entitled "Martin Luther King, Jr.: His Personal Conduct" that presented similar "evidence" of King's sexual excesses to the White House, Vice President Humphrey, Secretary of State Dean Rusk, Secretary of Defense Robert McNamara, and the heads of the CIA, the USIA, and the four military intelligence services (Theoharis and Cox 1988: 359).

Reporters were aware of FBI surveillance of King and the movement as a whole (Donner 1980: 256).[30] Some reporters responded by cooperating with the FBI. Richard Stolley of *Time* recalled

> We also provided the FBI with contact sheets: you know, 35 millimeter contact sheets and photographs so that they could go over them and identify people against whom they could bring conspiracy charges and all the rest. We did that systematically for a number of years.
>
> (1987)

Fred Powledge, then a reporter for the *Atlanta Journal*, more critically remembered, "there were lots and lots of fishy things going on there, but we couldn't find out exactly what and why and who and where—all those things we're supposed to find out" (1987). That journalists largely remained silent about the FBI's surveillance tactics (not to mention about the Bureau's notorious reluctance to intervene in beatings and murders of African American civil rights workers in the south) stands as a grim testimony to the Bureau's power over the press.

In 1968, Hoover made perhaps his most important contribution to the gathering racist storm. Although Johnson and Hoover had established a mutually agreeable relationship, Nixon and Hoover were closer, in both political and ideological terms, as well as in their paranoid, authoritarian personalities. Hoover claimed to have never voted and considered himself to be apolitical and non-partisan, but he shared the 1968 Republican Platform's central belief that "Lawlessness is crumbling the foundations of American society" (*Republican National Platform* 1968: 6). The Republican Platform's emphasis on fighting crime, and its specific commitment to "full support of the FBI and all law enforcement agencies of the Federal Government" (7), boded well for the future of the FBI and was obviously a more attractive alternative than a Democratic Party that in addition to fighting a war on poverty was in a state of disorganization and shock. The FBI stood to benefit from a war on crime that necessitated more funding for police and policing activities. It did not stand to benefit from a war on poverty that sought to prevent crime through education, health, and welfare.[31]

Beginning in September 1968, Hoover lent considerable support to Nixon's burgeoning war on crime. During that month, he began to hold monthly press conferences at which he made grim pronouncements based on the FBI's *Uniform Crime Reports* about dramatic increases in crime rates throughout the country, his presence ensuring intensified media coverage. It was unprecedented for the Director of the FBI to call press conferences for the release of these statistics which were compiled on a quarterly basis and usually released without much fanfare. These press releases continued throughout the fall, suddenly ceasing after Election Day.[32]

Television news gave prominent attention to what appeared to be a consensus that crime was the number one social problem confronting US society. On 19 September 1968, Walter Cronkite reported that "FBI director J. Edgar Hoover said today that the national crime rate for the first half of this year increased by 21 percent. The northeastern section of the country and the larger cities recorded the biggest increases" (*CBS Evening News*, 19 September 1968). One month later, Spiro Agnew, referring to an FBI follow-up report on the crime problem, told reporters:

A report recently released by that great American J. Edgar Hoover, and I'm proud to call that man a great American, indicates that serious crimes have increased 57 percent in seven years. That two-thirds of all the crimes of violence are committed by young people under twenty-one years of age. It tells me that the permissiveness that pervades our society, that's encouraged by those who rationalize and excuse lawlessness of any form, who allow any form of dissent as long as the so-called objective is meritorious, are tearing down America today.[33]

(*CBS Evening News*, 14 October 1968)

Significantly, where the September statistics reported that crime rates had increased 21 percent in the first half of 1968 (an increase that corresponded to the social unrest of 1968 and intensified police activity), the October statistics raised the heat, claiming that serious crimes had increased 57 percent in seven years, seven years that not coincidentally encompassed the Kennedy and Johnson administrations. Still reeling from the impact of Robert F. Kennedy's assassination and the violence at their 1968 convention, the Democrats had no response to Agnew's claim that law and order was in fact a precondition for civil rights—that "no civil rights can be successfully achieved without restoration of order" (*ABC Evening News*, 8 August 1968)—or to Nixon's assertion that "a broadened war on poverty . . . was no substitute for a war on crime" (*CBS Evening News*, 13 September 1968).

In the lead-up to the 1968 election, as well as the years that were to follow, law and order discourses paired news segments on crime rates and calls for law and order with segments covering black activism. On 4 September 1968, CBS ran the following sequence: a lengthy four-minute, ten-second segment on the Nixon/ Agnew ticket and calls for law and order, immediately followed by a three-minute segment on violence at the Democratic Convention, criticizing television for not saying more "about all the injuries heaped on police," and finally a report on an attack on African Americans at a Brooklyn hearing on the Black Panther Party, that expressed utter disbelief about the charge that the group had been attacked by 200 off-duty police wearing "Wallace for President" buttons, a charge that later proved to be true. The Black Panther Party was consistently singled out for the most negative coverage, almost all of which centered on its stand on self-defense, with images of armed black men that were to become iconic for anti-crime warriors, entirely superseding those of the myriad social programs it had instituted in African American communities to alleviate the worst effects of poverty.

On 19 September 1968, NBC broadcast a piece on Black Panther Party leader Eldridge Cleaver and the controversy over his teaching classes at the University of California at Berkeley. Immediately following this clip, David Brinkley noted, "The FBI reported today that the crime rate in this country has risen again, another 21 percent in the first half of this year. The biggest increases were in the cities and in the northeast and the type of crime growing most rapidly was robbery, usually in the streets" (*NBC Evening News*, 19 September 1968).

Framing devices that juxtaposed dissent with pieces on crime and calls for law and order became standard fare during the 1968 campaign. In this, news media followed the logic of the Republican Platform, which acknowledged the need for equality and civil rights only to immediately define the core problem facing US society as "lawlessness." Without appearing overtly racist—no reporter had to say, after all, that black activists were responsible for a crime problem that was visually defined as black—the narrative structure of these news reports made that point anyway. Whether or not producers and editors were intentionally invoking a link between black agitation and crime, or blaming blacks for their own marginalization, is beside the point. For in creating nightly news narratives that had coherence as stories about America, these media narrators were, as Stuart Hall (1984) once put it, telling stories as they had been taught to tell them, in ways deeply influenced by ideologies of race and gender. However temporarily successful the Civil Rights Movement had been in publicizing the racist victimization of black Americans, by the end of the 1960s narratives about the state's need to protect the rights of African Americans had been swept away by a now national discourse of a crime problem that reconstituted African Americans as threats to an American way of life that was implicitly understood to be white.

7　Criminalizing black culture

In late October 1989, a middle-class white man named Charles Stuart dialed 911 from his car, which was parked in the predominantly African American neighborhood of Mission Hill in Boston, Massachusetts. His pregnant wife Carol had been shot in the head, he told dispatchers, by a black man who had carjacked them, and he had been shot in the stomach. News crews rushed to the scene where Carol Stuart lay dying, with her wounded husband bleeding next to her in the car. From the beginning, this was a story made for television.

Boston police immediately initiated an aggressive search of Mission Hill, suspending civil liberties and treating any black man in a jogging suit as a potential suspect. By 15 November, the police had come up with a suspect, William Bennett, who was then duly identified by Charles Stuart as the man who had carjacked the couple and fatally wounded his wife.[1] In a city that had become known for its racism after its violent response to attempts to desegregate Boston South High School in 1974–75, Charles Stuart's account of his wife's murder proved all too believable. Despite the fact that most women are murdered by intimates, that a white man would kill his pregnant wife was unthinkable. The racialized narrative Stuart offered police—one of black male violence against a white female victim—was a plausible one in the minds of whites. Although Boston police officials later claimed that Stuart had been a suspect all along, his story did not begin to fall apart until his brother Matthew identified him as the killer in late December.

Had the media been more critical of Stuart's story, and less predisposed to treat the words of a white victim as gospel, they might have reported that the Stuarts' marriage had been less than idyllic. Stuart had pressured his wife to get an abortion, he had taken out three life-insurance policies worth hundreds of thousands of dollars, and he had made repeated comments to family members about killing her.[2] Yet despite inconsistencies in his story—inconsistencies initially explained by reference to Stuart's own traumatic experience as a victim—it took the word of another white man to convince police and journalists that William Bennett was not the murderer.

When Stuart committed suicide in January 1990, there was no public discourse about a pathological culture of greed and consumption that might have motivated his crime. Whites as a racial group were not blamed in any way for the murder, his mother was not blamed for his behavior, and there was no scrutiny of his family and cultural background, the assumption being that family members had suffered enough. In place of identifying various pathologies that may have caused this crime, Stuart's murder of his pregnant wife was understood to be a shocking yet aberrant act, one that could not have been either anticipated or prevented and thus no cause for a moral panic or crusade.

The contrast between representations of this crime and any number of less heinous crimes committed by blacks could not be greater. Most obviously, a black suspect would never have elicited the sympathetic credulity extended to Stuart; nor would an alibi blaming a white man for the murder of a black woman have been at all believable to whites. Indeed, it is doubtful that the murder of a pregnant black woman would have attracted much media attention, particularly if the crime had occurred in an African American neighborhood. In the unlikely event that it had, certainly the media would have been more aggressive in investigating a husband's testimony, particularly when so much of it was inconsistent. Had Stuart been black, the crime would have been immediately inserted into a framework that held blacks as a group accountable for such violence, and black culture—particularly the behavior of black women—the explanation for any criminal acts perpetrated by African Americans.

The Stuart case was only one of a number of high-profile news stories featuring what Katheryn Russell (1998) calls "racial hoaxes" that proliferated in the late 1980s and 1990s.[3] A mere quarter of a century after the heyday of the Civil Rights Movement, racialized narratives shockingly similar to the lynch narratives of the late nineteenth century reasserted themselves with force and vigor and constructions of black villains and white victims quickly fell back into older, overtly racist narrative grooves. This chapter explicates the processes whereby such reversions were effected by tracking the gendered and raced narratives about crime created by institutions and individuals in the post-civil rights era. Focusing on high-profile crime news themes and cases, increasingly the only occasions in which media attention was directed to issues of race and racial disparities, the explanation for this shift begins with the scapegoating of black women and black culture that began to take shape in the 1960s and then turns to the myriad ways in which stories about criminals and victims worked to confirm the belief that if blacks were victims at all, then they were victims of their own culture. Black culture, and not white culture, was the cause of all the problems that civil rights activists had ascribed to white supremacy.

The cult of true womanhood, sixties-style

By the end of the 1960s, the historical threat that black men were said to pose to white womanhood had been mostly subsumed beneath narratives featuring violent, angry, and armed black men. Nevertheless, the link between black men and crime had expanded from an openly racist one based on fears of miscegenation (and a specific threat to white women) to a now generalized threat to society as a whole. Southern politicians continued to make reference to threats against white women, but this connection was not as easily or openly invoked in northern narratives about crime. In the north, the threat now invoked a discourse of fearful white people menaced by generalized black threats to their families and their property. But the older link between gender and race in crime narratives roiled just below the surface of these wider crime narratives, where it was to be all too easily invoked when the occasion warranted, particularly in high-profile family violence cases involving whites, like Charles Stuart's murder of his wife Carol.

Crime narratives of the post-civil rights era invoked an all too familiar cast of racist stereotypes, constructing scenarios that justified white fear and hatred, and creating a threat that was, like the early nineteenth-century threats used to provoke anti-black violence, mythic in its dimensions. Mass-mediated representations of black and white criminals and black and white victims gave new life to forms of institutionalized racism and reinvigorated an array of racist narrative practices that had lain dormant for a decade. Where the discourse of miscegenation, and its reliance on threatening black masculinity, dominated ideologies of race, gender, and crime in the decades that followed the Civil War, after the 1960s the focus lay not only on interracial unions and their threat to moral values, but increasingly on intraracial relations as well, on the ostensibly pathological nature of black culture, and the threat these posed to the moral or family values that were seen solely as the province of whiteness.

But there was one significant change. Across the nineteenth and twentieth centuries, women as a group were not subjected to the kind of systematic criminalization visited upon black men, mainly because ideologies of femininity and domesticity understood women as being inherently weaker than men, needy of protection, and hardly the powerful villains that protection scenarios required. For women to be constituted as a threat would have been to suggest that the forces of white androcentrism were neither as fully masculine nor as powerful as they understood themselves to be. As we have seen, the deeply seated misogyny that has been a thread in US threat constructions expressed itself in ways other than the criminalization of women (prostitutes being the somewhat unique exception): through protection scenarios that denied white women agency and black women presence, through the over-sexualized representations of black women, and through the distrust, suspicion, and occasionally open hatred with which women in general have been regarded. This is not to say, of course, that deviance in women was not punished, but rather that women—black or white—were not construed as the agents of moral panics in the same way that black men were. Women of all colors may have been despised and considered frail and unreliable, but until the 1960s they were not constructed as rationales for fear.

This narrative terrain was irrevocably changed by the events of the 1960s. Although today we tend to understand women's political organization in terms of the feminist movement that emerged after the Civil Rights Movement and the student anti-war movement, black women activists played a principal, if less historically acknowledged, role in the Civil Rights Movement. Activists like Ella

Baker, Diane Nash, Rosa Parks, Ruby Doris Smith Robinson, and many others offered powerful examples of strong female leadership and political participation both before and after Betty Friedan called attention to the plight of white middle-class women.[4] Their participation, moreover, cut across the lines of class in ways that seldom occurred among white women. The pathologization and subsequent criminalization of black women, the first such widespread criminalization of women in US history, needs to be understood as the second arm of the racist reaction to the Civil Rights Movement and thus as a response to the political mobilization of which black women were a central part.

The criminalization of black women began in the 1960s, with a focus on black mothers receiving government assistance. Although US welfare policies have long found ways to exclude black people, women in particular, from receiving benefits, until the 1960s the discourse that justified these exclusions did not overtly suggest that black women should not receive benefits because of their criminal potential to exploit the system.[5] According to historian Rickie Solinger, as late as the 1950s,

> a poor, resourceless mother, even an African-American one, particularly one with an illegitimate child, would generally have occupied a low, marginal status in the United States. Her status as a mother may have marked her as a slattern or a slut, but probably would have protected her from classification as an aggressor, a villain, an enemy of the people.
>
> (2001: 142)

Solinger further points out that discourses that pathologized African American women for being "unnaturally strong and powerful in relation to their men" (2001: 155) were also a part of this earlier rhetorical terrain, but these were not yet part of a wider, national discourse about crime and the black family.

The nationalization of the discourse that identified the black family as the cause of crime, and black mothers as matriarchs of the crime wave, began to gather steam with the 1964 composition of what was purported to be a secret "internal memorandum" (Gresham 1989: 117). *The Negro Family: The Case for National Action* (hereafter referred to as the Moynihan Report) diagnosed "the deterioration of the fabric of negro society," which it saw as being caused by "the deterioration of the negro family" (1965). A key overseer of the transition from the war on poverty to the war on crime, Daniel Patrick Moynihan had served as an undersecretary of labor for the Kennedy and Johnson administrations, where he played an important role in formulating policy for the social programs that came to be known as the war on poverty. He left the Johnson administration in 1965 and later joined Richard Nixon's White House Staff as urban affairs advisor in 1968.

The Moynihan Report he authored in 1965 bears the imprimatur of this transition. Couched in liberal language about race, each section of the report begins by acknowledging the structural obstacles that racism placed in the path of black Americans, only to immediately undercut the power of the structural with an emphasis on the familial and the individual. The fourth chapter of the report, for example, begins by expressing admiration for the resilience of African Americans:

> That the Negro American has survived at all is extraordinary—a lesser people might simply have died out, as indeed others have. That the Negro community has not only survived, but in this political generation has entered national affairs as a moderate, humane, and constructive national force is the highest testament to the healing powers of the democratic ideal and the creative vitality of the Negro people.
>
> (1965)

Moynihan immediately added, "it may not be supposed that the Negro American community has not paid a fearful price for the incredible mistreatment to which it has been subjected over the past three centuries." In the report, this price lies in the "fundamental fact of Negro American family life," which is "the often reversed roles of husband and wife."

Like the psychoanalytic theory from which the Moynihan Report heavily borrowed, the family that it discussed was abstracted from its wider social and cultural milieu. The report criticized the mass media for creating "an image of the American family as a highly standardized phenomenon," but then immediately reified that image by suggesting that departures from this standardized norm were mainly negative. Arguing throughout that "A number of immigrant groups were characterized by unusually strong family bonds; these groups have characteristically progressed more rapidly than others," the report implied that African American families lacked such "strong family bonds," and that the entirety of the problems facing African Americans in the post-war period could be attributed to a subsequent family disorganization, in which "a large proportion of negro children and youth have not undergone the socialization which only the family can provide." Using a rhetoric that has since become second nature to conservative politicians, pundits, and reporters, the report continued, "disorganized families . . . have not provided the discipline and habits which are necessary for personality development." The report characterized black families as highly dysfunctional social units: disorganized, lacking in discipline and socialization, retarded in terms of personality development; and black culture, governed as it was by women and not men, as a pathological one, since culture was rightly the province of masculinity.[6]

The Moynihan Report saw family disorganization as the primary cause of unemployment and the rationale for the naturalized link between blacks and crime.

> It is probable that at present, a majority of the crimes against the person, such as rape, murder, and aggravated assault are committed by negroes. There is, of course, no absolute evidence; inference can only be made from arrest and prison population statistics. The data that follow unquestionably

are biased against negroes, who are arraigned much more casually than are whites, but it may be doubted that the bias is great enough to affect the general proportions.

Again, this passage exemplifies the shifting terrain of discourses about race in the 1960s. Acknowledging problems associated with bias (particularly the fact that blacks have been historically policed, not to mention arrested, convicted, imprisoned, and executed, with much greater frequency than whites), the report then dismissed these biases, suggesting that they could not possibly be as great as they appeared.

Although the Moynihan Report drew on E. Franklin Frazier's 1939 *The Negro Family in the United States* and Gunnar Myrdal's classic *An American Dilemma: The Negro Problem and Modern Democracy* (1944), where these earlier discussions of black families understood their "pathology" to result from racism, the Moynihan Report adroitly transferred responsibility for the disadvantages blacks faced in US society from a collective responsibility to an individual, or personal responsibility.[7] "Family disorganization" was responsible for "a large amount of juvenile delinquency and adult crime among negroes" and this disorganization was understood to be a direct result of "the failure of the father to play the role in family life required by American society." But it did not stop there. The failure of black fathers was not understood to be an effect of racist violence or the structural disadvantages confronted by black men. Rather, it was the effect of a "matriarchal negro society," in which "mothers made sure that if one of their children had a chance for higher education the daughter was the one to pursue it" and in which historical factors had predicated against "the emergence of a strong father figure," thereby denying "The very essence of the male animal" which "from the bantam rooster to the four-star general, is to strut." That "negro families in the cities are more frequently headed by a woman than those in the country" was the root cause of the problem, according to the report, since women-headed households emasculated men by denying them the opportunity to fulfill their role as breadwinners.[8]

The Moynihan Report turned the very strength and resilience of black women in the face of awful adversity into the source of racial problems, and poverty into the effect not of discrimination, but of pathological family structure. As an institution, marriage had not granted to black women any of the ideological or economic privileges reserved for whites. Historically excluded from the cult of true womanhood which relegated proper women to the domestic sphere, African American women were once again pathologized for not measuring up to a white supremacist standard that excluded them. That "Fifty-six percent of Negro women, age 25 to 64, are in the work force, against 42 percent of white women" was seen not as an effect of economic forces that since slavery had forced black women of all ages into full-time labor, that had forced them to work parallel shifts as laborers in the public and private spheres, but as evidence of their pathological strength and their symbolic castration of their husbands and sons. Ironically, sympathy was for the first time extended to black men, who had been victimized not by lynch mobs, the Ku Klux Klan, or white citizens' councils, but by black women.

The belief that women are by definition weak and in need of white male protection is the centerpiece of racialized androcentrism. Acknowledging black women's strength and resilience undermined the very foundations of that system. In addition, it hardly seems coincidental that in the 1960s, when white middle-class men were beginning to lose control over women's wages and property, and as white women were moving in greater numbers into the full-time workforce, white men began to argue that the very source of the problems faced by black Americans resided in black men's inability to effectively dominate women.[9] In order to strengthen what it described as "the Negro American family structure," the Moynihan Report concluded that the federal government must design programs that had "the effect, directly or indirectly, of enhancing the stability and resources of the Negro American family." Beyond this, and despite its subtitle— "The Case for National Action"—it had nothing to say.

The ostensibly secret Moynihan Report lay fallow until the following spring, when presidential assistant Bill Moyers suggested it to President Johnson as the basis for a major policy speech he delivered, ironically, at all-black Howard University. In the speech, Johnson spoke about the "special nature of negro poverty":

> Perhaps most important—its influence radiating to every part of life—is the breakdown of the negro family structure. For this, most of all, white America must accept responsibility. It flows from centuries of oppression and persecution of the negro man. It flows from the long years of degradation and discrimination, which have attacked his dignity and assaulted his ability to produce for his family.
>
> (1966)

Throughout the summer that followed Johnson's speech, the Moynihan Report was "leaked to selected journalists" (Gresham 1989: 118). But according to Jewell Handy Gresham, "the event that cemented" the impact of the Moynihan Report was the Watts uprising in August 1965 (which occurred less than two weeks after the August passage of the Voting Rights Act), when "in a mad scramble for instant wisdom, journalists turned to the black family report and drew on its conclusions as explanations for the violent civil disorders" (118).[10]

Where the Moynihan Report stigmatized black women for having usurped authority in the domestic sphere, wider social forces were conspiring to criminalize them for taking advantage of the paternal authority of the state. When the state sought to protect black women, this theme ran, they abused its assistance through deceit, connivance, and fraud. Although the soubriquet "welfare queen" was a rhetorical invention of the late 1970s, "widespread hostility to poor mothers receiving public assistance money" (Solinger 2001: 139) on the part of politicians began to emerge in the mid-1960s. In fact, beginning in 1965, "the complexion of the poor turned decidedly darker. From only 27% in 1964, the proportion of African Americans in [news] pictures of the poor increased to

49% and 53% in 1965 and 1966, and then to 72% in 1967" (Gilens, quoted in Solinger 2001: 143) and "widespread hostility to poor mothers receiving public assistance money" on the part of politicians began to emerge in the mid-1960s, as poor women were more and more frequently depicted as black (Solinger 2001: 139). These representations were successful in disseminating a wildly distorted understanding of race, gender, and class to politicians and middle-class viewers alike, neither of whom had contact with many actual poor people. According to political scientist Martin Gilens, when respondents were asked by a 1982 poll, "What percent of all the poor people in this country would you say are black?" their guess was 50 percent (1996: 595).[11]

This racist and sexist emphasis in public discourse was observable as early as 1964 in Ronald Reagan's preliminary attacks on poor black women. At their heart, Reagan's arguments suggested that poor African American women were whores who had sex and then children for ridiculously small sums of money. In 1964 Reagan told a story he was to repeat for years to come: about "a young woman who had come before" a judge "for a divorce. She had six children, was pregnant with her seventh . . . She wanted a divorce so that she could get an eighty dollar raise" (Solinger 2001: 140). In 1971, fortified by the Moynihan Report's linking of a "culture of dependency" with blackness, then Governor of California Ronald Reagan touted his government works projects as a solution to this problem of an inferentially black "dependency" (*NBC Evening News*, 26 February 1971).

Reagan revived these narratives throughout his political career, most dramatically during his 1976 presidential campaign, when he spoke incessantly about "welfare misuse," citing "the case of a Chicago woman who used 80 names to collect money on welfare" (*CBS Evening News*, 7 March 1977). Linda Taylor, an African American woman, was said to have

> eighty names, thirty addresses, twelve Social Security cards and is collecting veterans' benefits on four nonexisting deceased husbands . . . And she's collecting Social Security on her cards. She's got Medicaid, getting food stamps, and she is collecting welfare under each of her names. Her tax-free income alone is over $150,000.
>
> (quoted in Zucchino 1997: 65)

Although a Cook County grand jury only charged Taylor with the theft of $8000 from public welfare in 1976, this dramatically reduced figure was never reported on television news.[12]

In these ways, the Civil Rights Movement's demands for equality were transformed into demands on the part of a now black, undeserving, and female poor for "handouts" and entitlements. The difficulties and hardships of poverty exacerbated by racist ceilings on economic advancement were effectively transformed into a magical feudal economy—the welfare state—where queenly black matriarchs exploited the very system that had so altruistically attempted to help them. The resultant images of female welfare frauds thus reworked the racist ideologies about pathological black femininity and its social consequences presented in the 1965 Moynihan Report in order to instantiate a vision of the poor in the USA as predominantly black, female, and inherently corrupt.[13] Images of black welfare queens gave further support to arguments that, as victims of nothing more than their own isolated shortcomings, these families were patently undeserving of any federal intervention, save in the shape of punishment.

The politics of emboldenment

The election of Ronald Reagan in 1980 marked the culmination of the nationalization of what was, broadly speaking, a white supremacist understanding of the effects of racism on African American communities. Under the sign of the perennially paternal, jovial, and reasonable movie star, who evoked nothing so much as the paterfamilias of 1950s sitcom legend, the Reagan Administration pursued an agenda that was at its very core both misogynist and racist. Although the media was to consistently—and erroneously—proclaim broad popularity for Reagan's presidency and policies, his candidacy made clear where he stood on issues of gender (unlike Carter, he opposed the Equal Rights Amendment and supported efforts to overturn abortion rights) and race (he was a staunch supporter of the racist apartheid regime in South Africa).[14] And Reagan made support of the silent white majority of racists and segregationists now united—north and south—under the banner of states' rights visible from the very beginning of his candidacy. Lest his meaning be unclear, and at the urging of Trent Lott, Reagan made his first campaign speech in Philadelphia, Mississippi, where less than 20 years before, Cheney, Schwerner, and Goodman had been murdered by white supremacists.

Reagan's domestic policies consistently conjured up the specter of race to demonize poor people, although as Manning Marable points out,

> Reagan never used blatantly racist language, because he didn't have to. As sociologist Howard Winant astutely observed, the New Right's approach to the public discourse of race was characterized by an "authoritarian version of color-blindness," an opposition to any government policies designed to redress blacks' grievances or to compensate them for both the historical or contemporary effects of discrimination, and the subtle manipulation of whites' racial fears. The New Right discourse strove to protect white privilege and power by pretending that racial inequality no longer existed.
>
> (2003: 73)

In place of the massive social spending that the *Report of the National Advisory Commission on Civil Disorders* (1968) had recommended as a first step toward addressing racism, Reagan cut federal low-income housing programs by 84 percent, offering up a newly reformulated "war on drugs" as the solution to urban decay, homelessness, and despair.

Reagan made racism and racist explanations for social problems publicly acceptable again, albeit through a more sophisticated language of race hating and baiting than that of George Wallace. Where before the rise of Reaganism racists, fearful of criticism from those quarters that had been sensitized by the Civil Rights Movement, were publicly criticized or self-censored their speech, after Reaganism forms of racialized discourses about crime and welfare became acceptable once more, particularly in the media. Television's visual dimension, and politicians' more skillful use of this medium, enhanced these racialized discourses and contributed to enabling linkages between crime and blackness, since no one had to draw attention to the fact that suspects in crime cases were identifiably black.

As conservatives became increasingly emboldened by their ideological successes in criminalizing African Americans, and in converting black victims deserving of federal protection and intervention into black villains deserving only of prison, their discourses regularly appealed to older, more overtly racist images. In place of the more liberal discourse that characterized the Moynihan Report and the careful coding of the war on crime, by 1988 presidential candidate George Bush, Sr. ran a series of ads featuring William Horton, a convicted murderer, who had been released on furlough only to kidnap a white couple, raping the woman.[15] The ads suggested that Dukakis not only was "soft" on crime, but he favored a revolving door approach to prisons, going so far as to issue "weekend passes" to murderers. Here again, visual imagery foregrounded an unspoken link between race and crime: the ad featured brown and black inmates passing through a revolving door.

According to Susan Estrich, a professor of law who was then working for the Dukakis campaign, the Willie Horton ad campaign

> was very much an issue about race and racial fear . . . You can't find a stronger metaphor, intended or not, for racial hatred in this country than a black man raping a white woman. And that's what the Willie Horton story was. I talked to people afterward, men and women. Women said they couldn't help it, but it scared the living daylights out of them . . . I talked to men who said they couldn't help it either, but when they saw the leaflets later and the ads and the like, they couldn't help but thinking about their wives and feeling scared and crazy.
>
> (quoted in Anderson 1995: 207)

A flurry of news reports followed the ad, as well as protests by civil rights activists like Jesse Jackson. But the news discourse aided in putting Dukakis on the defensive by inserting the controversy into a "hard on crime" framework. *ABC News* began one of its nightly news reports with the following: "The question is 'Where does the Governor stand on crime and punishment and what are the facts of the celebrated Horton prison furlough case, which the Vice President likes to say is proof that his opponent is soft on crime?'" (*ABC Evening News*, 22 September 1988). The report then immediately cut to a newspaper photograph of Horton, while reporter Jackie Judd observed, "Willie Horton has become the symbol of everything that Bush finds wrong with Dukakis on law and order, crime and punishment."

The ads provided the Bush campaign with an enormous amount of free publicity, allowing them to speak for victims writ large. One clip showed George Bush, Sr. criticizing the Democrats because, "When it comes to the plights of the victims and their families, there is what one can only describe as an astounding lack of sensitivity, a lack of human compassion" (*NBC Evening News*, 7 October 1988). During the same time slot, *ABC News* featured a segment on Massachusetts' successful prison furlough program, including an interview with Horton's victims, Angela and Clifford Barnes, who were campaigning for the Republican Party and demanding an "apology from Dukakis" (*ABC Evening News*, 7 October 1988). In response to critics, another report quoted Bush's aides as saying that "they would have used the Horton case even if he wasn't black and it's ridiculous to suggest that talking about law and order is somehow anti-black because blacks are even more concerned about crime than whites" (*NBC Evening News*, 24 October 1988). In distinct contrast to the time allotted to the Bush campaign's offensive against Dukakis, the Democrats and Dukakis never responded to the ad on a network news program.

The contrast between conservative run-ups to the 1968 and 1988 elections is instructive. Where, in 1968, the final months of the presidential campaign were devoted to law and order and war on crime issues that contained a more cautious link between race and crime, by 1988, after the conservative revolution, the link between violence, prisons, and African American men had become a form of common sense. Far from the color-blindness that contemporary commentaries ascribed to Reaganism and the political discourse that followed from it, racialized discourses about crime became important campaign issues by manipulating racist fears. In 1988, GOP political strategist Lee Atwater unapologetically described the Willie Horton ads, and their overtly racist discourse about monstrous black men raping white women, as the Bush campaign's "silver bullet" (quoted in Anderson 1995: 223), suggesting that the campaign ads were responsible for Bush's presidential win in 1988.

The late 1980s also ushered in a whole new lexicon for a range of "black" crimes. Having criminalized African American women and men, attention turned in the last half of the 1980s to a generation of youthful "superpredators."[16] Black gangs gained increasing coverage beginning in 1986, a trend that deepened in the early 1990s. The welfare queen morphed into the "crack mother" bearing "crack babies" in 1988, "black-on-black crime" emerged as a media category in 1989, and the first mention of "drive-by shootings" on television news occurred on September 1990.

In the resurgent racism of the late 1980s and 1990s, even efforts to recall events of the 1960s and to remember the fallen heroes of the Civil Rights Movement were framed in such a way as to deny their victimhood and to reinforce a framework of black pathology instead. To raise issues of race in the final years of the twentieth century was invariably to invoke the specter of black pathology and the link between crime and race, absolving white people of racism in the process. In this fashion, network television frequently used the occasion of newly national celebrations of Martin Luther King's birthday not to talk about the very white supremacy that had caused his death, but to raise the specter of black pathology, testifying to the ways in which any mention of race was to be connected to crime in the last years of the twentieth century. Although televised news routinely reported on the numerous celebrations of King's birth through-out the country, as the 1980s gave way to the 1990s, reports were increasingly less likely to discuss the fact that few of King's goals for racial equality had been met. Indeed, Bill Moyers, the very person who had first brought the Moynihan Report to President Johnson's attention, televised "The Vanishing Black Family—Crisis in Black America" (1986), a special report that featured what the program touted as an "intimate" look at the lives of black teenage welfare moms and criminal black youths, during the week of the first national celebration of King's birthday. The first reference to the new category of "black-on-black crime" was, sadly enough, during a segment on Martin Luther King's birthday. The segment opened with a reference to Dr. King's dream, then cut to "black-on-black crime" in New Orleans and a discussion of why blacks were "prone" to violence (*CBS Evening News*, 15 January 1989).[17]

Credible witnesses

> They were coming downtown from a world of crack, welfare, guns, knives, indifference and ignorance. They were coming from a land with no fathers . . . They were coming from the anarchic province of the poor. And driven by a collective fury, brimming with the rippling energies of youth, their minds teeming with the violent images of the streets and the movies, they had only one goal: to smash, hurt, rob, stomp, rape. The enemies were rich. The enemies were white.
>
> (Pete Hamill, quoted in Hancock 2003)

Between 1969 and 1989, the time-honored tradition of stories involving black threats to white womanhood was thrown into temporary abeyance, as news themes established that black culture rather than white racism was the cause for racial disparities in the USA. By the late 1980s, the tide had changed. The widespread publicity allotted to the Horton case marked the resurgence of a revivified racist discourse on threatening black masculinity and threatened white femininity. The Horton case legitimized the resurgence of the logic that under-lay nineteenth-century lynching narratives: white people's testimony was not to be questioned, black people's testimony was not to be believed, and black victims were not to be represented. Having tested the racist waters, so to speak, and eliciting no public outcry on the part of politicians, social movements, or the media powerful enough to challenge their framework, the emboldened forces of white supremacy were given new voice.

Numerous cases from the late 1980s offer abundant evidence of the revival of the myth of the black male sexual predator. On the evening of 19 April 1989,

Trisha Meili, a 28-year-old investment banker with the Wall Street firm of Salomon Brothers, was brutally beaten, raped, and left for dead in Central Park. Five Harlem teenagers were convicted of the crime, which also contributed a new racialized word, "wilding," to the media lexicon of crime.[18] Thirteen years after the teens were convicted, DNA evidence as well as convicted rapist Matias Reye's confession that he had raped and assaulted the jogger by himself and did not know any of the youths who had been charged, resulted in the dismissal of the case against those who had been convicted.[19] But at the time of the incident news narratives spoke with one voice, as it were, about the criminality of these youths, never questioning law enforcement officials' accounts.

The media became obsessed with the case, in part because the woman known as the Central Park Jogger (Meili remained anonymous until the publication of her 2004 memoir) was one of theirs, in terms of both race and class. Like Helen Jewett, the jogger could have been one of their sisters, daughters, girlfriends, or wives, although unlike Jewett, the jogger had the benefit of being virtuous. What happened to her, reports repeated, could have happened to any one of them and even feminists were swift to argue that gender trumped race in understanding the nature of the crime and the need for prosecutorial zeal in punishing the teenaged perpetrators. Anne Murray, who in 1989 was police bureau chief for *The New York Post*, said that "she was conflicted about how the editors had played the original story. 'I knew the coverage would be very different if the victim weren't white'" (quoted in Hancock 2003). According to feminist Kimberlé Crenshaw, racism explained why the case was on the cover of newspapers and the lead story on televised news for weeks after the attack, not to mention the role that "racial intimidation" played in the interrogation of the youths (quoted in Little 2002b).

As Crenshaw also pointed out, had the jogger been a woman of color, her treatment at the hands of the media would have been quite different, a point made clear by a similar case that occurred during the same time period. On 2 May 1989, just a few short weeks after the Central Park Jogger was assaulted, a 39-year-old African American woman was dragged inside an abandoned building in the Crown Heights section of Brooklyn, robbed, raped, and sodomized by three men, and then thrown down a 50 foot air shaft. Like the jogger, her survival was in question in the days following the crime. Like the jogger, she would also bear the physical scars of the assault for the remainder of her life, although unlike the jogger, she recalled the brutal assault. The rape was reported on the 11 p.m. news the day after it occurred (McFadden 1989: 31; 1990: B1), leading to the identification of the assailants by another victim, but the story was never considered front-page news copy, appearing on page 31 in 1989 and on B1 in 1990.[20] The story never made the national network news.

On the face of it, and save for the race, age, and class position of the victims, the two cases were shockingly similar. Two unaccompanied women were brutally assaulted, raped, and left for dead in the spring of 1989. But in the eighteen months following the incident, the case of the Central Park Jogger elicited an astounding 344 articles in the *New York Times*, while the case of the Brooklyn rape victim resulted in only three, one of which was about the African American minister who was serving as spokesperson for her family (Goldman 1989: B1) and contained a single mention of the Brooklyn victim.[21] The Brooklyn rape was never inserted into the news frame that had emerged following the assault on the jogger—one of predatory males attacking an innocent and vulnerable woman. The obvious reasons behind the disproportionate coverage had everything to do with the intertwining of race and class in late twentieth century New York City. Not only was the Central Park victim, as one newscast put it, a "noted investment banker" (*NBC Evening News*, 24 April 1989), with degrees from Wellesley College and from Yale University, the crime took place in the heart of Manhattan.[22] Moreover, the Central Park case had familiar, identifiable perpetrators of color and a worthy white female victim. Where the attack on the jogger featured a crime and a location that had deep resonance for reporters for mainstream media outlets like the *New York Times* and national broadcast news personnel, a black victim, assaulted by black men in Brooklyn, did not.

If, in the case of the Central Park Jogger, the media provided no criticism of law enforcement, this owed much to the credibility possessed by law enforcement officials. If black victims' testimony has long been seen as suspect and worthy of skepticism, the testimony of African Americans charged with crime has been even more so.[23] Certainly, law enforcement officials and the media were primed by the overall resurgence of racism in the 1980s to uncritically consume the very discourses they were producing. As Barbie Zelizer puts it, journalists are an interpretive community "that are united through their collective interpretations of key public events" (1993: 223). In the case of the Central Park Jogger, law enforcement officials and the media uncritically united around an interpretation of this event that reflected their acceptance of the wider racialized framework of law and order.

In the end, although the crimes themselves were centrally about gender— about the most excessive forms of misogynist violence enacted upon women's bodies, about the sense of entitlement to women's bodies that violent men are encouraged to have—this was not a story that the media or law enforcement were prepared to tell. Instead, the story of the jogger was not one of male violence against women, but of interracial violence and the threat men of color presented to white women. Invested in the frame of "wilding" that supported this version of events, police and media were reluctant to back off from it. Even though another rape had occurred in Central Park just two days before Meili was attacked (and that victim retained a full memory of the event), neither police nor journalists raised the possibility of a link between the two. Instead, as *New York Newsday* columnist Jim Dwyer later observed: "The story was like a centrifuge . . . Everyone was pinned into a position—the press, the police, the prosecution—and no one could press the stop button" (quoted in Hancock 2003).

However self-critical journalists were with the passage of time, a centrifuge larger than this single story continued to exert its influence long after the

Central Park Jogger case. While men of color are not to be believed, other high-profile crimes from the late 1980s and early 1990s attest to the credulity with which the words of white men were greeted during the same period. Not only did the fundamental belief in black criminality affect the behaviors of the criminal justice system as a whole, further legitimizing the use of excessive force against black suspects by police and increasing rates of incarceration, it also gave white criminals convenient scapegoats for their crimes, particularly those committed against women.

The Charles Stuart case with which this chapter began was only one in a series of cases involving violent and greedy white men who attributed their crimes to amorphous and unidentifiable black predators. On 21 April 1992, Jesse Anderson and his wife Barbara were leaving a Milwaukee restaurant when, according to his account, they were attacked by two black men who stabbed Barbara at least 21 times in the face, head, and body. Barbara Anderson died of her wounds the following Thursday and for five days Milwaukee police stopped and detained black men in the area where the crime had occurred, before charging Jesse Anderson with the crime on 28 April 1992 (DeJonge 1992: 3A). A classically abusive husband, Anderson had a history of violence against his wife (the mother of the couple's three children). He had repeatedly expressed anger over his wife's weight gain, and had contacted his insurance company prior to the murder regarding Barbara's $250,000 life-insurance policy ("Weight-Gain Angle Cited in Slaying" 1992: 1B). Four years later, in 1996, Robert Harris told Baltimore police a similar narrative. An armed African American man had shot him and his fiancée, Teresa McLeod, Harris told police. Although Harris confessed within two days (again, the motive was McLeod's $250,000 life insurance policy), Baltimore police initially and aggressively pursued black suspects.

Perhaps nowhere was the credibility attributed to white narratives about black crime more evident than in the case of Susan Smith, a case that of all of these "racial hoaxes" accrued the most national televised coverage. On 26 October 1994, Susan Smith appeared under the headline "carjacked kids" on national television to issue a tearful plea to the black man she claimed had stolen the car containing her two children (*NBC Evening News*). For the first three days, all network news programs reported the case as a "kidnapping/carjacking," invoking a new category of crime to describe what had happened. And although three days after the children had disappeared, South Carolina Sheriff Howard Wells described Smith as both "victim and suspect" (*NBC Evening News*, 29 October 1994) and *CBS Evening News* reported that Smith was being "queried," it was not until 1 November that the carjacking frame finally gave way to the headline "Missing Boys." On 3 November, the children's bodies were found in a nearby lake and Smith was arrested for their murder.

Of course, no one expects violence of white women, particularly toward their own offspring, and this partly accounted for the media's blind acceptance of Smith's story about the boys' disappearance, as well as their venomous response to her once it was revealed that she had lied. Yet as part of a larger interpretive community that has historically attributed its most vicious, culturally illegible crimes to African Americans, Smith understood that her story would at least initially ring true to both law enforcement and the media: that, in effect, the words of a white mother would have force, power, and credibility. These narratives underscore the wider manufacturing and acceptance of nationalized racialized narratives about crime in US society. Stuart, Anderson, Harris, and Smith acknowledged the power of these racialized narratives when they blamed their violent acts on African American men. Counting on the fact that these narratives would be believed and accepted by law enforcement and the media, each of them was aware that they were accorded a belief status not afforded to African Americans. Each of them, in essence, organized their crime narratives around the fundamental connection between blackness and crime and the fact that, as white people, their narratives about violence would be trusted in automatic and often unconscious ways.[24]

Rodney King and O.J. Simpson

"I didn't believe in his [O.J.'s] innocence. But like most black people I knew, I wasn't interested in talking to white people about it unless they had sorted themselves out around the issues. This country just doesn't have the tools for black and white people to have those kind of conversations."

(Linda Burnham, Black Women's Resource Center, quoted in Younge 2005: 17)

Two cases following from the twinned themes of pathological black female hegemony within the private sphere and black male threats to white women came to define race and crime issues in the 1990s. The first resulted from the widely distributed videotape of the beating of motorist Rodney King in March 1991 and the LA uprisings that followed after a verdict was handed down in the case of his beating in 1992. The second concerned the arrest of former football player O.J. Simpson for the murders of his ex-wife Nicole Brown Simpson and Ron Goldman on 12 June 1994.

Although on the surface, the beating of Rodney King appeared to have little to do with the time-honored theme of black men assaulting white women, his violent beating resulted at least in part from that volatile ideological mix of sex and race. On 3 March 1991, Tim and Melanie Singer, husband and wife members of the California Highway Patrol, noticed King's Hyundai driving behind them at a high speed. Turning around, they gave chase. When King pulled the car over, his two companions complied with the Singers' orders for the car's occupants to leave the vehicle and lie on the ground face down, but King initially refused to get out of the car. Finally exiting the car, according to Melanie Singer's testimony, he "grabbed his right buttock with his right hand and he shook it at me" (Linder 2001). Officer Stacey Koon also testified that King "grabbed his butt with both hands and began to shake and gyrate his fanny in a sexually suggestive fashion. . . As King sexually gyrated, a mixture of fear and offense overcame Melanie. The fear was of a Mandingo sexual encounter" (quoted in Mercer 1994). Whether the brutality of the beating (King was struck 56 times by arresting officers, while at least 23 police officers looked on) directly resulted from the threat King's "sexually suggestive" gyrations seemingly posed to Melanie Singer was really beside the point. Koon believed that King's actions were sexual in nature, and on the basis of that belief he attributed fear and offense to Melanie Singer. Taking it one step further, Koon asserted that her fear was of "a Mandingo sexual encounter," a phrase which hopelessly muddled a popular culture reference to the 1975 film *Mandingo* (in which a black slave burns down the plantation and escapes with a blonde southern bombshell) and the historical fear of black male sexuality that accompanied this narrative.[25] The arresting officers used this description to frame the incident as a whole, and in so doing the fear a white male police officer ascribed to a white female police officer became the pretext for their violent assault on King. Her fear, to their thinking, was sufficient legitimation for their use of force. The parallel between this and lynching narratives was lost on mainstream journalists.

On 29 April 1992, a suburban Simi Valley jury, made up of eleven whites and one person of Philippino descent, found three officers not guilty of official misconduct, filing false police reports, excessive force, and assault with a deadly weapon. Los Angeles immediately erupted in the worst violence the city had seen since the 1965 Watts uprising. It was later estimated that between 50 and 60 people lost their lives, more than 4000 were injured, 12,000 people were arrested, and property damage was estimated at $1 billion. For residents of color who lived in a city that had not only had to deal with the crack epidemic of the early 1990s, with intensified surveillance conducted by a highly militarized police force, with endemic poverty, and with appallingly low employment rates for its African American residents, the verdict in the trial of the four officers proved simply too much to bear.[26]

The immediate causes for the violence were well known—namely, that after decades of racist police violence, members of the Los Angeles Police Department had finally been caught in the act and then, unbelievably, cleared of all charges. Despite the fact that an investigation resulting from the King beating, and led by Warren Christopher (later Secretary of State in the Clinton Administration), found widespread racism and sexism in the LAPD, the image that prevailed after the riots was not of a criminal justice system that shared the racism of the LAPD, but of a white man being dragged from the cab of his truck and brutally beaten by black youths (that Reginald Denny was rescued and driven to the hospital by two black men and two black women was not part of the story the media told). Echoing the media response to the Watts uprising in 1965, and in a move that could have been professionally scripted in nearby Hollywood, the media and politicians reinforced a frame that focused on lawless black youth and the single mothers and pathological family structure that were to blame for them, with Vice President Dan Quayle weighing in on the deleterious effects of single motherhood. A case that had begun with police brutality, attempts on the part of police officers to legitimize their actions by invoking the figure of the sexually menacing black male, and African American frustration with a criminal justice system that had two different standards for punishing violence when it came to blacks and whites, was subsequently transformed into a punitive narrative about single motherhood and black pathology.

The arrest and trial of former football player O.J. Simpson in 1994 needs to be understood within this narrative context of betrayal and anger, following as it did only two years after the Los Angeles uprising. Billed as the trial of the century in a century that had begun with the similarly billed Henry Thaw trial, the crime had all the makings of a high-profile serialized case. Simpson was a wealthy, famous black man. His ex-wife, Nicole, was white and had made at least one previous 911 call to report having been beaten by Simpson (O.J., she sobbed to the operator, was going "to beat the shit out of me"). The crime itself was an especially vicious one: both victims had had their throats cut and had been stabbed repeatedly.

If the verdict in the trial of the four police officers in the Rodney King beating shocked and dismayed African Americans, the jury's decision in the O.J. Simpson trial was said to take whites by surprise, "exposing," as innumerable news reports and round-the-clock reporting at what journalists referred to as "Camp O.J." routinely reminded viewers, an interpretive polarization between blacks and whites—a deep rift between races in terms of attitudes toward the dismissal of charges against Simpson.[27] The media coverage pitted race (represented as solely the concern of African Americans) against gender (which apparently only white people cared about), thereby managing to gloss over, or in numerous cases ignore, the cultural, economic, and political context in which the trial took place. Whether Simpson was guilty or not, he was being tried by a criminal justice system with a long history of incarcerating and executing African Americans for crimes they had not committed; a criminal justice system that, as the example of police officer Mark Furman illustrated during the course of the trial (Simpson's defense introduced tapes of Furman repeatedly using the word "nigger" and making overtly racist comments), was structurally racist. For many, Simpson himself was no more than a symbol of a wider system that had always treated blacks and whites differently when it came to crime and crime victims. As one resident of South Central later put it, acknowledging a truism not addressed by the mainstream media, "If O.J. had killed his first wife, who was an African American woman, all this wouldn't have happened." And another man more cynically recalled that when the verdict came down, "We said, 'wow,' at least a black guy got away sometimes. Because there are a lot of people—a lot of black folks—there's a lot of dead black folks that nobody ever went to jail for" (Del Barco 2005).

The theme repeated in endless media coverage of the trial and the verdict focused on African American prosecuting attorney Johnnie Cochran's use of what the media described as the "race card" in his introduction of the evidence about Furman. Assuming that race played no role in the police's handling of the Simpson case, the discourse of the "race card" suggested that Cochran was using Simpson's race as a ploy to beat the charges against him. Other than Cochran's introduction of race, this logic held that race had nothing to do with either the media attention to the case or the criminal justice system's investigation of the crimes. The rhetoric of the "race card" flew in the face of all evidence, as Cochran well knew, having won a series of landmark decisions about racist police misconduct in the 1980s. *Time* magazine's now infamous darkening of the image of Simpson used on the cover of their magazine was only one of the more egregious—and obvious—examples of the racialized framework through which the Simpson case was understood ("An American Tragedy" 1994). Just as mainstream media had sought to explain the LA uprising through a framework that displaced issues of racism by blaming black communities, so the media in the Simpson case argued that race was not a fundamental part of how the case was investigated and understood, but was an issue artificially and manipulatively introduced by black people. The elite male privilege and the violence against women that were fundamental parts of this privilege were read through a prism that refracted only blackness.

Race and gender combined in these national crime stories to reinforce the historically over-determined ideologies governing white belief in black criminality. Although this white belief was temporarily challenged in the cases of Charles Stuart, Jesse Anderson, Robert Harris, and Susan Smith, it was never effectively confronted. In the case of the beating of Rodney King, the issue of gender—particularly as it was used by LAPD officers to "explain" their beating—was not scrutinized by the press and thus the brutality of the police officers themselves was widely attributed to King's violent behavior and not their interpretation of its sexualized dimensions. Gender only became a factor in later attempts to "analyze" the causes of the subsequent uprising, which in a system so entrenched in racialized androcentrism could not have possibly had to do with racism on the part of white society, but strictly involved pathologies and causes internal to a monolithic black culture. A similar myopia ran throughout the O.J. Simpson case, where an older narrative about black masculinity effectively erased references to elite male privilege and the violence against women that was a cornerstone of it.

Gender and the war on drugs

High-profile racial hoaxes and crime cases involving African Americans as both victims and perpetrators were only one strand of the racialized narratives about crime that abounded in the 1980s and 1990s. The credibility and sympathy extended to white crime victims and suspects also affected serialized coverage of the war on drugs, offering stark examples of racialized disparity not only in arrests and sentencing, but in the narrative frameworks used to explicate drug use and to depict users of illegal drugs. Representations of drug use were themselves both raced and gendered during this period, with coverage of the crack "epidemic" in the late 1980s and early 1990s a case in point.

Attention to crack, for example, focused squarely on black women, with the media consistently depicting female crack users as products of that now familiar culture of dependency, blaming their drug use on their shortcomings as individual human beings. In "On Streets Ruled by Crack, Families Die," reporter Gina Kolata described how crack cocaine was "rapidly accelerating the destruction of families in poor urban neighborhoods where mothers are becoming increasingly addicted and children are selling the drug in greater numbers than ever before" (1989: A1+). Kolata's article emphasized the behavioral problems associated with crack use, saying little or nothing about the effects of the drug itself or its production or distribution.[28] Scant sympathy was accorded to crack users; instead, journalists like Kolata concentrated on this culture of drug abuse, and "the unraveling family," in which ever younger children were enlisted in the trade. Invoking the image of the African American "crack mother" that became popular in the late 1980s, Kolata represented crack users as being predisposed to drug abuse, and thus as the agents of their own destruction.[29] In so doing, Kolata echoed the argument presented in an earlier *CBS News Special*—that "Drug abuse—not jobs, not the economy, not the issue of war and peace—drug abuse is the nation's leading overall concern right now" ("48 Hours on Crack Street," 2 September 1986).

Users of methamphetamine, increased use of which began in the early 1990s, were treated altogether differently by the media. In distinct contrast to black users of crack in urban settings, white users of crystal methamphetamine were featured as either victims of an all-powerful, addictive substance or an economic downturn. The social devastation caused by the introduction of crack into economically fragile areas remains undeniable, as those addicted to it lose sight of everything but their addiction. But methamphetamine is in many ways a more threatening drug, frequently used by those already predisposed to violence (particularly racist skinheads and other white supremacists). Unlike the euphoria of crack, methamphetamine causes paranoia and violence and induces symptoms similar to paranoid schizophrenia. Like alcohol, methamphetamine can cause users to become violent. In July 1995, a New Mexico man, high on methamphetamine and alcohol, beheaded his 14-year-old son and threw the severed head onto a crowded highway. Again in 1995, a San Diego man took a tank he had stolen from a National Guard armory for a joy ride on a freeway, threatening motorists and forcing the closure of the freeway. Since the mid-1990s, moreover, dozens of men, women, and children have died in the explosions common in improvised methamphetamine labs.

The utter contrast between coverage of black crack and white methamphetamine users appeared starkly in a 1996 *New York Times* front-page article entitled, "Good People Go Bad in Iowa, and a Drug Is Being Blamed" (Johnson 1996: A1+). In extensive and sympathetic detail, the article focused on the devastating social consequences of increasing availability of methamphetamine in the midwest. Methamphetamine users, the article stated, were "good people" victimized by a terrible drug. Methamphetamine, rather than a culture of poverty or pathological individuals, was to blame for the tragedies ensuing from its use, along with increasing unemployment, straitened economic circumstances, and even "an intense Midwestern work ethic" that encouraged reliance on this form of speed (Johnson 1996: A8). Reporting on methamphetamine linked individuals' use of it to their work ethic: one researcher consulted for an article described it as

> a drug of the times in that it's a drug for people who don't have enough time . . . You have the sense that it's moms trying to juggle jobs and three kids and day care, and women working as waitresses on their feet for 12 hours a day. And it's truck drivers, carpet layers, people who work long hours doing tedious, repetitive tasks.
>
> (Goldberg 1997: 16)

Where crack addicts were cast as people disposed to escape reality and responsibility—because of their essentially shiftless racialized natures, not because of the effects of racism, chronic poverty, and despair—white users were rural, hard-working members of the working class. Driven by circumstances to drug use, they found themselves hopeless captives to a powerful substance. The message was clear: white drug users were victims of their circumstances and therefore deserving of sympathy and rehabilitation; black drug addicts were social parasites, beyond redemption and worthy of nothing more than punishment.

Conclusion

By the late 1990s, the mainstream, national media rarely mentioned race without invoking the twinned themes of crime and black pathology. Far from encouraging white society to confront the legacy of racism, to understand the continued effects of racism and consequent economic exploitation on African American communities, these themes permitted white elites to wash their hands of the problems that continued to beset African Americans. Instead, these themes fully legitimized the mixture of fear and rage with which whites continued to regard African Americans. By the waning years of the century, US society had created a narrative of fear and denial that had entirely transformed the political challenges that the Civil Rights Movement had presented into a saga about African Americans' inherent criminality and racial shortcomings.

Typically, media scholars tend to think about the effects of media content on viewers in terms of "vulnerable" populations like children, but the extent to which the behavior of law enforcement officials and police officers was affected by the racialized war on crime and war on drug discourses in the media has yet to be studied. Judging by cases of police brutality in the 1990s, and the testimony of police officers, it would appear that widespread media representations of blacks as criminals encouraged a violence-prone, trigger-happy culture when it came to treatment of African Americans. Twelve-year-old Michael Ellerbee would not have been shot in the back and killed on Christmas Eve 2002 by two Pennsylvania State Police officers had he been white.

Although it is outside the scope of this book to provide an analysis of the effects of racialized crime coverage on police, it should be clear that the kind of media narratives discussed thus far had effects on the stories that victims, suspects, and police told about their actions—that, broadly speaking, the social construction of crime as blackness had all too material effects on a range of institutional practices. Skolnick and Fyfe have argued that "Evidence from historical sources, observational studies of police—our own and others—and legal materials shows that contemporary police brutality is both historically and sociologically related to lynching and related vigilante activites" (1993: 24). A century after the coverage of lynching discussed in chapter 4, journalists continue to draw from an inventory of discourses that seeks to explain rather than condemn such violent behaviors.

National coverage of high-profile crimes involving African Americans as either suspects or victims and serialized coverage of the war on drugs combined to firmly rearticulate race with crime during the 1980s and 1990s. But alongside these highly visible, national, and mostly serialized narratives about race and gender, against the backdrop of escalating incarceration rates for African American women and men, a revolution of sorts was taking place in local television news. Unlike national news stories, whose serialized nature and visibility elicited some criticism of their racism, as we will see in the next chapter, these local, episodic crime stories not only supported the broader themes pursued by national news stories, but in a more low-key, mundane fashion helped to represent crime as a key issue of political and cultural concern and as a constant source of white fear.

Conclusion

> I do know that it's true that if you wanted to reduce crime, you could, if that
> were your sole purpose, you could abort every black baby in this country and
> your crime rate would go down. That would be an impossible, ridiculous, and
> morally reprehensible thing to do, but your crime rate would go down.
>
> (William Bennett, *Morning in America*, 29 September 2005)

At the center of this book has been a single, simple, depressing argument: that
crime narratives have long understood black people as a group to be uniquely
criminal, that the producers of these narratives have historically refused to
acknowledge the victimization of black people, and that the perspective from
which these narratives have been produced has been one that views crime and
deviance through a prism that has reproduced the most harmful ideologies of
race and gender. On the few occasions when black voices have gotten a hearing over the past three decades, these either have been dismissed as the shrill
rantings of unreliable individuals or they have reproduced the perspective of a
privileged minority of African Americans, like Bill Cosby, Condoleezza Rice,
and Clarence Thomas who are then used as what civil rights activist Julian
Bond (2003) described as "human shields" for racist arguments and policies.

A concurrent theme has been that media narratives about crime have material effects, particularly insofar as they inform the practices and routines of
institutions like the media, as well as the everyday lives of ordinary people. News
narratives, moreover, are not just any narratives, but have a cultural legitimacy
and effectivity not ascribed to fiction or entertainment programming. From the
war on crime that began in the late 1960s to the passage of the Omnibus Crime
Bill in 1994—in the words of one congressional report, "the most sweeping federal anti-crime bill in US history" (Lusane 1994: 14)—to the war on terror,
politicians, policy-makers, and institutions put great faith in the news' constructions of reality. They also seek justification and legitimacy for their behavior in
the stories that the news media tell about crime, deviance, and social problems.

William Bennett's comment with which this section opened offers a sad and
compelling example of the common sense that news discourses about crime have
generated over the past thirty years. Bennett, Reagan's chairman of the National

Endowment for the Humanities 1981–85, Secretary of Education 1985–88, and "drug czar" under President George H.W. Bush, repeated the very sentiment that thirty years of media coverage of African Americans and crime had proposed all along: that black people alone are responsible for crime in the USA and that eliminating them would, presumably, eradicate crime. In the wake of criticism, Bennett responded by issuing a statement that left his main point— that eliminating blacks would lower crime rates—intact:

> I was putting forward a hypothetical proposition. Put that forward. Examined it. And then said about it that it's morally reprehensible. To recommend abortion of an entire group of people in order to lower your crime rate is morally reprehensible. But this is what happens when you argue that the ends can justify the means.
>
> ("Bennett under Fire for Remarks on Blacks, Crime" 2005)

In an era in which the most imminently deserving of victims, the fetus—that "pre-born" yet worthy subject of right-wing politics—has been the alibi for intensified surveillance and punishment of women of color in particular, a prominent conservative's reference to abortion as a "means" to reduce crime further emphasizes the premise of this study: in the racialized economy of victimization in the USA, the phrase "black victim" is strictly oxymoronic.

Bennett's underlying logic, that crime and, by extension, social violence are inextricably linked to blackness, returns us full circle to the openly genocidal discourse of an earlier epoch in US history. At the same time, it also underscores the preferential treatment still accorded to white men in political life. Had a black man uttered such hateful words about whites (and members of the Nation of Islam, to take one example, have been excoriated for much less inflammatory statements), one can only imagine the response of white media and pundits.

That in the first decade of the twenty-first century, a public figure could once again so openly espouse this form of thinking not only demonstrates the strength of the historical link between blacks and crime, it also demonstrates the ephemeral nature of 1960s counternarratives about race, gender, and crime (see Figure 8.1). While other ethnic and racial groups have been temporarily criminalized over the course of US history, only blacks have remained associated with crime for several hundred years, despite Reconstruction and Jim Crow, despite the demographic and cultural dislocations of the Great Migration, despite the heroic efforts of the Civil Rights Movement, with virtually no change in the assertions that underlie that association.[1] As Dennis Rome points out, only "whites have escaped being associated with crime" (2004: 5), not surprisingly, since whites have been responsible for producing cultural representations of crime.[2] In the 1980s and 1990s, alongside the raced and gendered high-profile serialized crime cases examined in the previous chapter, the link between race and crime was being quietly and very actively reproduced in the form of the episodic crime reporting that has long been a staple of local news production.

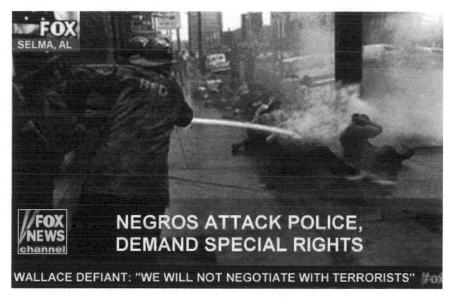

Figure 8.1 Fox News parody from http://mysite.verizon.net/vze1ldyn/id2.html

Crime comes home: local television news in the 1990s

Watching US television during the 1990s, it was difficult to avoid the sense that the USA was being swept by a crime wave the enormity of which had never been seen before. During the last decade of the twentieth century, prime-time police dramas—from *Hill Street Blues* to *Miami Vice* to the *Law and Order* and *CSI* franchises—all but replaced other genres of prime-time drama, and reality programs like *American's Most Wanted*, *Cops*, and *Rescue 911* proliferated.[3] One study financed by the cable industry discovered that, in 1997, 67 percent of programs analyzed contained violent content (Mifflin 1998: A14). Belligerent people of color even dominated the daytime talk show format, where they aired now predictable criminal behaviors before studio audiences (Rome 2004: 7).

As we have seen, crime news has been a central element of commercial news production since what historian Steven Jaffe described as the rise of the modern reporter in the 1830s, especially when foreign or domestic news themes are lacking. But in the 1980s and 1990s, crime news took over local television newscasts in historically unprecedented ways. One 1996 study of local evening newscasts, conducted by Joe Angotti, found that in local markets across the country, 29.3 percent of news time was devoted to crime and criminal justice. Government and politics garnered 15.3 percent, with calamities and natural disasters at 10 percent. Education was at the bottom of the chart with 2 percent, and race relations comprised 1.2 percent. In February 1997, a survey of 100 stations by Rocky Mountain Media Watch found that 72 news shows led with a crime story and one-third of all news stories were about crime. More recently, Media Watch's analyses of hundreds of local newscasts from 55 cities found that half of local nightly newscasts were devoted to violence and that almost 75 percent of lead stories dealt with crime or disaster (Lloyd 1998: 4). According to the Columbia School of Journalism's *Project for Excellence in Journalism*, in 1999 crime coverage consumed 22 percent of news time (Geisler 2000). Locally, crime coverage skyrocketed during a period that saw crime rates decreasing (Krauss 1994: 9). By the end of the 1990s, a researcher for WCNC (an NBC affiliate in Charlotte, North Carolina) repeated what had become industry common sense: "local doesn't mean 'regional'; local means 'crime'" (quoted in Freedman 2001: 26).[4]

Predictably, increases in local television news programming devoted to crime have been accompanied by an over-representation of African Americans in local crime stories during a period in which they have been under-represented in all other areas of news coverage, an increase that strengthened the ideological connection between race and crime. In one study of news coverage in the Chicago area, Robert Entman and Andrew Rojecki found not only that African Americans were represented far more often as criminals than whites, but that white victims outnumbered African Americans 241 to 160, despite the fact that African Americans were more likely to be victims of crime than whites (2001: 81). Similar studies in Los Angeles, Albuquerque, NM and Honolulu, HI confirm Entman's findings (Gilliam *et al.* 1996: 13; 2002; Gilliam and Iyengar 2000; Heider 2000; Lipschultz and Hilt 2002). News broadcasts further spent three times as much coverage on white victims as on African American victims (Entman and Rojecki 2001: 81). Steven Chermak's study of news portrayals of victims also found that "crime victims are generally presented in the news as male, white, fairly young (17–25 years old), and married" (1995: 59).

In addition to the disproportionate representation of blacks as criminals and whites as victims, representational practices specific to television reinforced the link between blacks and crime.[5] In the first place, where print media must either specifically refer to the racial identity of both criminals and victims (or refer to neighborhoods that are themselves racially coded), television images ensured that criminals and victims would be identifiably raced. In televisual representations, blacks were presented "in physical custody more than twice as much as Whites" and were less likely to be identified by name than whites (Entman and Rojecki 2001: 82). Even when suspects were clearly white, studies demonstrated that when white viewers were asked to identify the suspect later, they consistently misidentified the suspect as African American, a disturbing finding that suggests that white viewers have been primed through years of viewing African Americans almost exclusively as criminals to see *all* criminals as African American (Oliver 1999: 46–60; Oliver *et al.* 2004).

The industry's responses to criticisms about the abundance of crime news have been at once predictable and ideologically revealing. Generally, they blame audiences, arguing that audiences want crime news and, because the networks are so responsive to audience demands, they merely cater to consumer desires. But these often spurious arguments about catering to audiences' desires dodge questions about the multifaceted forms of racism that flourish within media industries not only in terms of who appears on-screen, but also in terms of whom the industry understands to be its audience.[6] Crime news is popular among producers not only because it is a cheap way to create dramatic news, but because it is seen as politically uncontroversial, at least from the quarters that count in the media industry: advertisers, other corporations, official sources, politicians, and an imagined white, middle-class audience made up of 18- to 49-year-olds, who are understood to have no interest in black people. As former network television producer Av Westin observed, "The conventional wisdom among many assignment editors is that white viewers will tune out if blacks . . . are featured in segments" (2000: 21). Where investigating corporate practices in a given community might get producers, editors, and reporters in hot water with their sources and corporate parents, where discussions of race continue to be too "controversial" in the eyes of conservatives, crime news is unlikely to anger elites, particularly when it focuses on individualized "street" crimes and African American youths. Outrage and dissatisfaction on the part of those consistently represented as criminal do not matter, since networks and advertisers do not consider African Americans a particularly valuable audience.

The historical continuity between nineteenth-century local crime news and late twentieth-century local broadcast news is instructive. Just as newspaper reporters' visits to the Five Points neighborhood of New York City in the 1830s and 1840s provided what Mike Davis has described as "a terrain of pseudo-knowledge and fantasy projection" for white audiences, so late twentieth-century "ghetto" conflicts and "gang wars" were considered to be "a voyeuristic titillation to white suburbanites devouring lurid imagery in their newspapers or on television" (Davis 1992a: 270). Although we know little about what white suburbanites crave when it comes to news coverage (most scholarly and industry studies suggest that the majority of viewers tune into local news for weather coverage), crime news about "deviants" in economically fragile neighborhoods has long been imagined by those who produce the news to be titillating and exotic fare for those more advantaged audiences remote from such locations and the problems faced by their inhabitants. What African American readers or viewers, as well as anti-racist whites, want is thus immaterial. Print and television news' closed circuit of producers and sources bound in the tight racialized embrace of advertisers gave these media the ability to reaffirm the racist beliefs and practices of media industries, political structures, and government institutions. Denying the very presence of African Americans, as victims of crime or as consumers of news, and as multidimensional human beings, the news media continue to encourage the white fear that local news representations of African Americans always underwrote.

Projecting fear

Well before the terrorist attacks of 11 September 2001, media and politicians alike had become accustomed to speaking for an ever more fearful entity known as the public. Increases in incarceration, harsher legislation governing crime like the reinstatement of the death penalty in 1977, the 1994 Omnibus Crime Bill, the notorious three strikes legislation—all these were passed in the name of a public that lived in perpetual fear of being victimized by black criminals. This public considered crime to be one of the most important social problems. According to Gallup Reports, the number of respondents who identified crime as the most important problem facing the USA peaked at 52 percent in August 1994 (Lowry *et al.* 2003: 62). So attached were the media to crime coverage that even as the FBI began to announce steep decreases in crime in the early 1990s, they were already conjuring a new threat, in the shape of what one reporter described as an imminent juvenile crime wave, or a coming generation of potential "superpredators" (Annin 1996; see also Butterfield 1995b, 1997: 16; Schiraldi 1997: 19).[7]

The fear projected by the media is at once homogeneous and notoriously difficult to analyze. According to Barrie Gunter, "Fear of crime is a distinct conceptual judgment from perceptions of likelihood of personal victimization" (1987: 3). Skogan adds, "It is important to distinguish between the fear of crime (as manifested by reduced activity or an unwillingness to venture onto the street) and concern over crime as a public issue" (1977: 15), although this is too fine a distinction for the media to make.[8] These and other researchers suggest that if people were actually fearful of crime, it would have observable effects on their behaviors and thus would be very different from the "fear of crime" invoked by politicians and pundits.[9] Instead, both politicians and the news media use "*fear*" of victimization and *concern* about crime interchangeably," despite the fact that, as sociologist Frank Furstenberg observed, "the two reactions to crime turn out to be completely unrelated to each other" (1971: 603–5).

To complicate things even more, Canadian researchers have pointed out that perceptions of fear and danger may themselves be caused by factors not easily attributable to a single cause such as perceptions of crime. One reanalysis of Baltimore public opinion data about fear of crime "found that perceived seriousness of the crime problem was related to measures of resentment of changing social conditions," (Sacco 1982: 489) primarily opposition to racial integration. Another study linked concern with crime to religiosity and political conservatism, while a third suggested "that public perceptions of crime are influenced by a dislike of leftist political positions and a resentment of social and political change" (Sacco 1982: 490). Conversely, those least likely to be concerned about crime are more likely to be victims of crime, but their concerns lie elsewhere (employment, education, and discrimination); where "As risk of victimization decreases, concern about crime goes up" (Furstenberg 1971: 605).

This research suggests that "fear of crime" is consistently racialized by informants and geographically projected onto predominantly African American neighborhoods.[10] In one audience study, for example, an informant told the researcher "she first encountered black Americans through television news, and those encounters formed an image that she found hard to shake." In a critical vein, she continued, "It's because you see so much of it on television, and that was so true for me. And that's the only way I ever saw them portrayed" (Alters 2002: 175).

The racial dimensions of fear and the effects of this are more distinctly observable in the language used by the radical right. From a reactionary political position, the sense made of these images is somewhat different. In a review of sociologist Kathleen Blee's *Inside Organized Racism* (2003), an account of white women's roles in white supremacist organizations, D.W. Miller observed:

> women are drawn to the [white supremacist] movement more by personal concerns than by ideology. They feel estranged from family and victimized by economic uncertainty, rising crime rates, and other social ills. Most spoke articulately about their fear of dark-skinned people destroying what white people had built up.
>
> (Miller 2002)

Here, what is typically not articulated in mainstream discussions of fear of crime gets made manifest: that it operates as a code language through which segments of the population express racial hostilities that can no longer be voiced in a directly antagonistic or racist language.

That the fear of crime expressed by the small percentage of people who respond to surveys is unreasonable—that it flies in the face of an empirical reality in which African Americans risk their lives when they venture into white neighborhoods—is a sentiment not expressed in the white world of news production. To take just one example of this, on 12 October 1995, police in the white Pittsburgh suburb of Brentwood pulled over Jonny E. Gammage, a 31-year-old African American man. He had been driving a Jaguar owned by his cousin, Ray Seals, who played football for the Pittsburgh Steelers, and he was stopped, according to testimony, because his "brake lights kept flashing on" (Connelly 1995). Gammage was beaten and suffocated by five Pittsburgh-area police officers. Certainly, Gammage had much to fear when he encountered white police officers at 1.30 a.m. that October morning and reason indeed to be fearful.[11] That "people of color have the most to fear from police institutions and other state agencies" (Stabile and Rentschler 2005: xv) is not the kind of fear invoked by media and politicians invested in their own identities as protectors.

The second era of Jim Crow

> My journey was done, and behind me lay hill and dale, and Life and Death. How shall man measure Progress there where the dark-faced Josie lies? How many heartfuls of sorrow shall balance a bushel of wheat?
>
> (DuBois 1903/1994: 45)

Historically, heightened attention to the criminal "nature" of African Americans has followed on the heels of increased black resistance to white supremacy. Just as the response to the challenges that the end of slavery posed to the structure of US society was the enforcement of segregation through Jim Crow laws in the south and less formal forms of apartheid in the north, so the response to the challenges made by the Civil Rights Movement has taken the shape of an increasingly punitive, carceral approach to problems stemming from racial disparities and racism.[12]

In place of acknowledging the historicity of racism, and its continued effects, media discourses about "cultural" pathology and black crime mistake the effects of racism for its primary cause, confirming the belief of conservatives like George Gilder that "racism explains next to nothing about black poverty and crime" (1995: A20). The problems besetting African American communities are well documented and include much higher rates of unemployment and poverty than whites; lower wages than whites; lower life expectancy; what Lane describes as "the raging frustration" (1979: 137) that results in higher homicide and suicide rates among young black men; and infant mortality rates in some cities greater than those in third world countries. In place of understanding the nature and causes of these complicated problems, US society has relied on racist narratives about crime, violence, and victims to explain why African Americans are to blame for everything from the slave trade to lynching to the forms of repression that followed the civil rights era. Blacks are, to repeat William Bennett's logic, the cause of crime and so the real and legitimate source of white fear.

Yet as we have seen, what constitutes a crime as well as the categories used to describe criminal behaviors change over time. While the media focus on homicides in particular, as Ray Surette reminds us, "Even with steady annual increases, murder remains a minute piece of all violent crime, comparing in 1990 for example to over 100,000 aggravated assaults, or about one-fourth of one percent of all violent crime" (1994: 139). Additionally, not all violent acts (including murder) or socially unacceptable behaviors get defined as crimes, depending on who is understood to have been victimized. While most would agree that the enslavement of Africans was at root morally wrong and unacceptable, there is no public discourse about its criminal nature or the criminal behavior of the white people who devised and maintained this system. And while arguments that the slaughter of Native Americans across the Americas was morally acceptable and justifiable are hard to sustain today (although some still do), no textbook would dare to claim that the founding of the USA lay in violent acts of genocide.

Rather than seeking to define crime as violent, socially unacceptable behavior, it would be more accurate and useful to follow Eric Monkkonen in asserting that insofar as it is the state which decides "which private wrongs should be elevated to offenses against the state," it is the state that causes crime (1981: 18). If we understand the state—and those institutions that provide defenses of the state—as "constructing" crime in the manner suggested by Richard Quinney (1970), then we can better understand why that same state has an interest in calling attention to particular types of crime, committed by specific groups of people. In the USA instance, rather than confronting the magnitude of the crimes committed against African Americans in particular, which might entail forms of restitution that would destabilize institutions and policies that, however, indirectly uphold ideologies and practices of white supremacy, rather than criminalizing and better still acting aggressively in the name of that criminalization when it came to punishing those who denied blacks access to voting, employment, housing, and human rights, US society has instead denied blacks victim status at all. Invested in reproducing the mandates of racialized androcentrism, this system of meaning and practices offers up explanations that effectively decriminalize its own actions. In this fashion, the historically most vulnerable are rendered as the most significant threat to the dominant social order.

In the forms of threat construction that follow from this, gender and race have combined in often improbable and inconsistent ways. Black people could not be construed as a direct threat to white masculinity. To do so would have been to undermine the very aggression, violence, and power ascribed to white men, as well as to call into question constructions of black masculinity as supremely inferior. For white men to be seen as vulnerable to the predations of black men, moreover, would have been to suggest that white men were neither as powerful nor superior as dominant ideologies maintained. The threat constructed by this system of belief, meaning, and practical action was thus an indirect one—one that threatened the moral or family values of white folk through attacks on the weakest link, those who were irrevocably linked to the private sphere: white women. Representations of slave revolts and other acts of insurrection against white supremacy were rendered as attacks on white femininity, from the myth of Mandingo, who wanted white women more than he wanted freedom, to the lynching narratives that prevailed during the height of the first age of Jim Crow, to the resurrection of the figure of the black rapist in the 1980s. All these narratives conveyed the belief so fundamental to racialized androcentrism that white violence against blacks could be justified by exaggerating black attacks on white women and that, in the end, white violence against blacks could also be disavowed by calling upon white fear of black violence.[13]

Crime stories in the mainstream news media have historically disseminated these modes of thought. From the very beginnings of the commercialized press in the USA, in an implicit acknowledgment of white fears about the effects of oppression on the oppressed, blacks were accorded a threat status not assigned to other ethnic or racial groups. Constructing African Americans as criminals, priming white audiences to understand race and racial issues solely through the prism of crime, these narratives denied African Americans the status of victim and thereby robbed them of one of the most powerful cultural avenues for sympathy and restitution. For crime news functions more powerfully than any other form of news reporting to provoke outrage, anger, and action. Civil Rights Movement activists understood that the distribution of images of nonviolent African Americans subjected to aggressive white violence would have an effect on readers and viewers. Victims are, they recognized, essential to the emotional work of crime reporting. They at once "humanize" stories and provide affective connections to audiences. Members of a culture learn to sympathize with those worthy victims presented through a range of narratives: they mourn the violence and injustice inflicted upon victims and honor white victims in what the *New York Times* called "portraits of grief." The invisibility of African Americans as victims of crimes committed by anyone but themselves, the suspicion and derision with which the words of African Americans are greeted by the media and criminal justice institutions, the inviolability of white testimony and white perspective, all these continue to guarantee the reproduction of the link between blackness and crime.[14]

Even coverage of the effects of Hurricane Katrina, in which the innocence of mainly poor, black victims was indisputable, succumbed to these now second-nature narrative frames. Rumors of looting, prowling armed gangs, rape, the brutal murder of a 2-year-old girl in a restroom abounded. News photographs further provided a vivid illustration of the double standard to which black and white victims are treated in the media. *Yahoo! News* published two photographs on 30 August 2005 (see Figures 8.2 and 8.3). In one, an AP photo showed a teenaged African American youth wading through waist-high flood waters, clutching a trash bag full of groceries and a refrigerator pack of soda. According to the caption, he had just "looted" a grocery store. Another photograph from the AFP depicted a young white man and woman, wading through similar flood waters and carrying groceries, who were braving the waters according to the caption, after "finding bread and soda from a local grocery store."

Forced as they were by the storm and its effects on black residents to confront the materiality of African American victims, the media and politicians drew from their time-honored toolkit of racialized stereotypes to narrate these events. During a segment on American Public Media's "Marketplace," regarding Texas' housing of homeless people from New Orleans in the Houston Astrodome, former first lady Barbara Bush picked up on the discourse of poor blacks as threatening yet also cunning victims of poverty. Observing that people were "overwhelmed" by Texan hospitality, she remarked,

> What I'm hearing which is sort of scary is they all want to stay in Texas. Everyone is so overwhelmed by the hospitality. And so many of the people in the arena here, you know, were underprivileged anyway, so this—this (she chuckles slightly) is working very well for them.
> ("Houston, We May Have a Problem" 2005)

Even when the events that had caused their suffering were so completely beyond their control—poor people did not choose to stay in the city of New Orleans, but had no way to evacuate—they were thrust into a frame that criminalized them and rendered them "scary." These narratives functioned as legitimation for racist fears and for the literal arming of white uptown New Orleanians, some of whom rented "old Soviet choppers, along with four-to-six man Israeli commando units," to protect themselves from the "Zulu nation" they feared "might be coming out of the woods" (Lewis 2005: 49).

The speed with which disaster victims were transformed into criminals further attests to the tenacity of these racialized news narratives. It would be the height of scholarly hubris to suggest that changing these media frames is

Figure 8.2 "A young man walks through chest deep flood water after looting a grocery store," Dave Martin. Reproduced by permission of AP Images.

the solution to addressing the criminalization of African Americans. As civil rights activists have long argued, and as numerous reports have recommended, addressing racism in the USA requires an effort and a commitment that are so profound as to be well beyond the scope of any number of books on the subject. As this book has demonstrated, as an institution, the media are inseparable from a broader institutional framework that legitimizes and reinforces racist social understandings at every step. Unwilling to address the continued presence of racism in US society, loathe to admit to differential treatment of blacks and whites, incapable of acknowledging the magnitude of US society's historical wrongs against African Americans, swift to mistake the effects of racism for its causes, it would take a wholesale revolution in the way that institutions, politicians, and policy-makers think about race, and act on those forms of thinking, in order to effect widespread change.

The pressures that converge to reproduce news frames of black criminality remain enormous. Chapter 6 showed how powerful social movements devoted to fighting racism forced reporters and news institutions to take notice of the victimization of African Americans. This example underscores the fact that commercial media institutions do not change or reform themselves strictly of their own volition or in response to criticisms made by policy-makers or academics. In the current absence of such a social movement, and given the intransigent division between anti-racist social movements and women's organizations, which, as authors as various as William Saletan (2003) and Rickie Solinger (2001) have pointed out, abandoned women on welfare in their struggle for abortion rights, it is difficult to imagine where the impetus for change might emerge.

Figure 8.3   "Two residents wade through chest-deep water after finding groceries," Chris Graythen, AFP/Getty Images. Reproduced by permission of Getty Images.

Ideologies of objectivity and the presumed neutrality of institutions and institutional sources, against which anti-racist activists are always depicted as biased, angry, and unreliable, further reinforce the tendencies built into the commercial news media. The news media's reliance on police sources in particular makes it unlikely that these narratives will change, although certainly more news accounts of African Americans in non-criminal roles (real news stories and not the vapid "hometown hellos" that were the industry's response to criticisms in the 1990s) and more news devoted to issues of race and racism might serve to pressure institutions to be more responsive. Of course, any such programming would be controversial and it is doubtful that industries as risk-averse as commercial media would take the lead in doing this.

To acknowledge the structural nature of these problems and the enormity of the obstacles blocking change does not mean that we should abandon struggles over what counts as crime news and who counts as victims. As we saw in chapter 6, media representations matter, particularly insofar as they assist in the mobilization of social movements, but also in the myriad ways they lend support to the status quo. In 1968, the National Advisory Commission on Civil Disorders published its *Report of the National Advisory Commission on Civil Disorders*, or what came to be known as the Kerner Commission Report, a report that recognized the central role media played in shaping cultural understandings of race. The media, the report concluded, "report and write from the standpoint of a white man's world. The ills of the ghetto, the difficulties of life there, the negro's burning sense of grievance, are seldom conveyed" (203).

The absence of perspectives that would challenge the intrinsic whiteness of perspective with which the majority of journalists approach their subjects pretty much guarantees that the problems confronting black Americans will continue to be cast as problems of their own making. Inclusion of perspectives that challenge "the standpoint of a white man's world" makes a difference—journalists can make a difference—an assertion borne out by a news story that originated in Tulia, Texas, and became national news only after the combined efforts of the American Civil Liberties Union, the NAACP, a *Texas Observer* writer named Nate Blakeslee who first broke the story, and a *New York Times* journalist named Bob Herbert, who over the course of months would write column after column about what he called "the Tulia madness."[15]

On 23 July 1999, police in the small panhandle town of Tulia, Texas, arrested 46 people in a pre-dawn drug sting operation. With the exception of one person, all of those arrested were black. The first trial was of a 60-year-old African American hog farmer, who received a 90-year sentence. Other defendants received similarly lengthy sentences. Joe Gardner, a white resident of Tulia, who had employed the hog farmer and who believed the charges to be false, began to write to local newspapers, attorneys, and officials, but to no effect. According to Gardner, the arrests in Tulia stemmed from the convergence of religious fundamentalism, economic turmoil, and racism. The economy in Tulia had once relied on farming, but when the aquifer that supplied irrigation waters dried up, according to Gardner, "the town's black families were no longer seen as the necessary farmhands they once had been." Instead, "Tulia's poor black community was viewed as a source of trouble, a source of drugs, a threat to the town's decent people." Some of the women who were arrested, Gardner observed, "were single mothers, never been married, maybe had two kids living in welfare housing" (Goodwyn 2003). In Gardner's words, "Tulia had set up a production line to send everybody they wanted out of town to the pen."

The cases against Tulia's black residents, based on the testimony of a single undercover police officer named Tom Coleman, were riddled with innumerable inconsistencies. The majority of arrests were for distribution of powder cocaine, hardly the favored drug of impoverished rural blacks. In addition, Coleman had been arrested, even as the sting was taking place, for theft. He was admittedly an open racist, known for being unreliable and mendacious. But Coleman was a white undercover police officer and that was enough to make his testimony both believable and irrefutable in the mind of the district attorney, Terry McEachern, who prosecuted the cases against Tulia's black residents.[16] Texas State Attorney General John Cornyn, now a US Senator, who named Coleman Lawman of the Year, shared these sentiments.

In Tulia, the work of journalists like Blakeslee and Herbert combined with the efforts of the NAACP in particular to challenge the literal and figurative framing of black citizens as criminals. Blakeslee's investigative reporting brought the story to the attention of national news media, while Herbert's privileged position at the *New York Times* allowed him to bring this case to a wider, national audience. Their perspectives on events in Tulia differed dramatically from those of state and federal officials, particularly since both writers were trenchant critics of the drug war and its catastrophic effects on the lives of poor people. As Herbert later put it, the case in Tulia involved "drug task forces which are financed by the federal government. It's set up in such a way that the more arrests you make, actually the more funding you will get." Thus, what mattered was not that the arrests were clean or "good," but that "federal funding continues to come in." Acknowledging the structural racism of the criminal justice system in the USA, Herbert concluded that while "it's acknowledged that—whites and blacks of this country use drugs. Whites and blacks in this country deal drugs," the arrest record of these task forces demonstrates that those arrested are overwhelmingly Latino and black ("Truth and Lies" 2003). Ultimately, Blakeslee and Herbert told stories otherwise unspoken in mainstream media about the cost exacted for blind acceptance of the words of official sources, about drug war policies that continue to fail, about what it feels like to watch a loved one imprisoned for life for a crime he did not commit, about lives irreparably damaged by institutional racism.

Nearly 40 years ago, one of Johnson's crime commissions produced a report entitled *The Challenge of Crime in a Free Society* that offered a very different understanding of what eradicating crime would entail:

> Warring on poverty, inadequate housing, and unemployment is warring on crime. A civil rights law is a law against crime. Money for schools is money against crime. Medical, psychiatric, and family-counseling services are services against crime. More broadly and most importantly every effort to improve life in America's "inner cities" is an effort against crime. A community's most enduring protection against crime is to right the wrongs and cure the illnesses that tempt men to harm their neighbors.
>
> (Ruth 1971: 16)

In place of the criticism and self-reflection such policy-makers called for, US politicians pursued neoliberal "muscular solutions" (Stabile and Rentschler 2005: xiv) to social problems, using police power, as vice presidential candidate Edmund Muskie once put it, "to keep the black man in his place." By the late 1970s, Philip Jenkins notes that ideas about crime "had changed considerably . . . In the new political agenda, criminals were less victims of society than ruthless predators upon it. Solutions to crime were to be found in the justice system, rather than in social or family policy" (1988: 5).

The enormous build-up of the prison-industrial complex over the past three decades has had huge pay-offs for some and awful effects for black people.

Some 65 percent of offenders are sentenced to prison for property, drug and public disorder crimes, the majority of them are poor, and close to half of them are black men: at the end of 2003, there were 3218 black male sentenced prison inmates per 100,000 black males in the United States compared to 463 white male sentenced prison inmates per 100,000 white males ("Prison Statistics" 2004).[17] In addition to the incarceration of African Americans in the USA, the now global racial economy of victimization that structures news reporting has made victims of civil wars and disease in Africa all but disappear from television screens and newspaper pages in the USA.

Here we have cause to recall the words of Ida Wells, W.E.B. Dubois (1903/1994), Angela Davis (1983, 1988, 2003, 2005), and a host of other anti-racist writers, educators, and activists. As rates of incarceration for African American women and men increase, as women are removed from their families and their communities, the threadbare lie that was conservative concern about the "vanishing black family" is exposed as such. US society did "turn away, in fear and hostility, from the problems that black America has pressed for equality," as Muskie put it. The build-up of the prison-industrial complex, or what Pierre Bourdieu has referred to as the right hand of the state (which has ben-efited large corporations), has occurred at the expense of the left hand of the state—all those social programs that once lay at the center of the war on poverty (Bourdieu 1998).

Still, in order for African Americans to make the news in ways that attest not to their criminality, but to the diversity and complexity of their own communities and the problems they confront, it is not enough to cover more African Americans as victims. Instead, journalists and other cultural producers need to break out of the crime news frame altogether, to seek the causes and solutions to such deeply entrenched social problems in places other than the criminal justice system, and to offer perspectives that do not merely reproduce the logic of racialized androcentrism.

Muscular solutions remain the province of a system that is fundamentally androcentric, that cares about its feminized and female victims only insofar as they further a wider agenda of punishment and a state oriented toward repression. Gender and race remain intertwined at the heart of constructions of crime and social violence. While decrying contemporary manifestations of the forms of black masculinity made most visible in the media—forms of masculinity that themselves are refractions of a masculinized white lens— the USA has pursued a politics of punishment that is proving far more devastating and fear inducing than any internal or external enemy it can construct. If we are to educate ourselves and our students about the history of the narratives that endorse solutions whose punishing effects are now felt around the world, we urgently need a new vocabulary for understanding the causes and effects of violence, and stories that are more true to the experiences of those who are its main casualties.

Notes

Introduction

1 Strohmeyer avoided the death penalty by pleading guilty, but David Cash was never charged.

2 See Wood (2005) on race and victimization in cases involving young girls.

3 A similarly deafening silence around the murders of black children is not new, of course. In addition to historical silences and unreported murders of black children, as recently as the 1980s the murders of 29 black children in the city of Atlanta received very little media coverage until a black suspect was identified. See also the 2001 killing of Erica Michelle Marie Green, known until 2005 as "Precious Doe," which was also given very little coverage (Sedensky 2005: A-9).

4 See Rentschler (2002) on the post-Vietnam era victims' rights movement for an example of this.

5 Although it is outside the scope of this study to consider the history of crime and crime waves in Britain, the scholarship that exists on this topic in the British context has greatly influenced the present volume: Hay *et al.* (1975), Chibnall 1977, Mayhew's (1861/1968) classic sociological study of poverty in nineteenth-century London, and Pearson (1984), as well as recent scholarship on the relationship between gin consumption and crime waves in eighteenth-century England (Dillon 2003; Warner 2003).

6 I refer here to two cases that took place in western Pennsylvania: the murder of Jonny Gammage by police officers in Pittsburgh in October 1996 and the shooting death of Michael Ellerbee in Uniontown on 24 December 2002.

7 Willard (2000) provides an analysis of how African Americans functioned as objects of nostalgia and as vanishing others in advertising at the end of the nineteenth century.

8 See Anderson (1995), Dixon (2003), Dixon and Linz (2000a, 2000b), Entman and Rojecki (2001), Hall *et al.* (1978), Oliver (1999), Oliver *et al.* (2004), Reeves and Campbell (1994), Rome (2004), Russell (1998) for a sample of this scholarship.

9 For analyses of these and other forms of popular criminal literature, see Biressi (2001), Black (1991), Cohen (1993), Davis (1957), Halttunen (1998), Knight (1980), Knox (1998), Mandel (1984), Most and Stowe (1983), Nord (1984), Rafter (1998, 2000), and Willett (1996). See Petrick (1969) on press use of police blotters.

10 See Goetting (2000), Raphael (2000, 2004), and Schneider (2002), and Moran (2003) on gender and family violence. See Williams (1991) on race and class.

11 Traces of such regional forms of demonization persist today in local television news broadcasts. In a city like Pittsburgh, Pennsylvania, for instance, crime is generally linked to African Americans (there being no other significant population of color), while in San Diego, crime is often linked to Hispanic and Latino populations, fused under the category of "illegal aliens."

1 Gender and race in the episodic crime news of the 1830s

1 For a description of the material geographies that also shaped these understandings, see Abbott (1974).

2 The following textual analysis was based on reading the crime news (both episodic and serialized) contained in issues of the *New York Sun* from its founding in 1833 until coverage of the disappearance of Mary Rogers in 1841, as well as crime news in the *New York Herald* from its founding in 1835 until the Rogers case in 1841.

3 See Nerone, "The Mythology of the Penny Press" (1987), for the definitive discussion of this.

4 See Stephen Jaffe, "The Rise of the Urban Newspaper Reporter in New York City, 1800–1850" (1985) for a thorough account of this process.

5 I hesitate to describe these papers as "tabloids" because, unlike twentieth-century tabloids, they also featured "hard" and respectable financial and political news.

6 According to Karen Halttunen, these forms also correspond to what she describes as the two narrative patterns into which popular criminal literature had developed by the late seventeenth century: "The first was the picaresque tale of criminality, a loosely structured, amoral, escapist kind of narrative . . . The second was the spiritual biography of the criminal-as-sinner" (1998: 10).

7 It was not until the late nineteenth century that statistics began to be used as the organizing principle for moral panics. See Lincoln Steffens' (1931) chapter entitled "I Make a Crime Wave" for a firsthand account of the making of one moral panic.

8 See Lee (1937: 184–205), Mott (1941: 223); and Pray (1970: 180) for accounts of crime coverage and the newspaper industry. See Garland (1993, 2002) and Lardner and Repetto (2001) for histories of the penal system and the New York Police Department respectively.

9 The *Sun* began its run on 3 September 1833 and the first Police Office appeared on 9 September, only six days later. According to Mott, Wisner approached Day one week after the first edition was published (1941: 222)—a physical impossibility. Pray's account, written in 1855, that Wisner was recommended to Day as he prepared to launch the paper, seems more credible (1962: 180).

10 As such, the characters presented in episodic crime reporting bear more than a passing resemblance to the heroes of the picaresque novels Davidson discusses (1986: 151 211). See Rosenberg (1971) for an analysis of the role that religion played in cultural production in the new city, and Williams (1993) for examples of more ephemeral forms of popular criminal literature.

11 On occasion, penny press papers printed excerpts from confessions of criminals published in other newspapers and magazines, as in "the confessions of Teller and Reynolds, the malefactors executed at Hartford" (*Sun*, 20 November 1833: 1). But even these accounts typically did not focus on the religious dimensions of the confession. In "The Execution of Samuel Ackley," for example, the accused claimed that the murder of his wife was caused by "bestial frenzy, excited by the demon of drink. When the horrid deed was done, he declares himself to have been in a state of infuriate intoxication, and that the unhappy woman was also in the last stage of inebriation" (*Herald*, 16 January 1837: 2). Accounts like this conspicuously avoided religious discourses of humiliation and redemption.

12 In our punitive era, as in the gallows genre that preceded the era of the Police Office, there is nothing considered comic or humorous about either police or criminals in the mainstream press.

13 The *Sun* was the first New York City newspaper to identify suspects by name, a practice that was rewarded by numerous libel suits. See Bradshaw (1979–80) for more on this.

14 Haller (1971) provides a historical overview of the development of scientific discourses of racial inferiority.

15 For historical accounts of family violence, see Gordon (1988/2002) and Pleck (2004).
16 See Cohen (1997), Cowan (1983), Rosenberg (1985), Srebnick (1995), Stansell (1987), and Walkowitz (1992) for excellent accounts of women's changing roles during different phases of industrialization.
17 See D'Emilio and Freedman (1997) for further accounts of violent encounters in the streets.
18 Lepore (2005) presents an incisive analysis of the construction of such worry and fear in New York City.
19 See John Nerone's chapter on abolitionism in *Violence against the Press* (1994) for a cogent discussion of newspapers and abolitionist movements.
20 The convention of identifying African Americans and, more inconsistently, immigrants by ethnic group was a trait shared by nineteenth-century newspapers. It was not until around World War I that this practice began to disappear. See McGucken (1987) for more about this disappearance.
21 See Allen (1994, 1997), Hale (1998), Roediger (1996), and Saxton (1996) for analyses of the construction of whiteness.
22 See Roediger's chapter 7 on the Irish, as well as Allen (1994) and Ignatiev (1995).
23 The discourse of miscegenation that appeared during the Civil War was a distinctly different one, whose even more inflammatory connotations suggested a more mature racist discourse on gender and race.
24 Richard Mentor Johnson, from Kentucky, was a member of the House and Senate for 20 years and served as Martin Van Buren's Vice President from 1837 to 1841. He never married, but had a long-term relationship with a slave, Julia Chinn, with whom he raised two daughters.
25 Not only did the penny press play a central role in producing and disseminating the figure of the sexually menacing black male, it also dismissed organizations and moral-reform crusades that attempted to formulate alternative threats to the social order. A case in point was the New York Magdalen Society, an organization devoted to eradicating prostitution. Founded in 1830, the society issued a report in 1831 that generated much controversy among New York's elite by claiming that there were some 10,000 prostitutes in New York City and that these prostitutes were patronized by some of the scions of the most respectable, bourgeois families. The city's bourgeoisie (who had significant investments in the business of brothels) along with newspapers like James Watson Webb's the *Morning Courier*, "fanned the flames against the Magdalen Society and Arthur Tappan," denouncing the society and its president, the prominent Arthur Tappan. Harris also observes that "a coalition of these wealthy and politically powerful men had already defeated several proposals before New York's Common Council to raze houses of prostitution in the Five Points" (2003: 191), where many of the brothels that people like George Lorillard and Robert R. Livingston profited from were located. Although the Magdalen Society collapsed under this assault, its members later founded the Female Moral Reform Society in 1834. This society published a weekly, *The Advocate of Moral Reform*, which understood emerging forms of hegemonic masculinity as the main threat to the spiritual, moral, and physical well-being of the city's women.
26 Both Lane (1997) and Monkkonen (2001) comment on the fact that historical increases in homicides can be linked to population increases among young, single, unemployed men.

2 The cult of dead womanhood

1 See also Hibbard and Parry (2006) for an incisive analysis of the narrative ferment that followed the trial of Amelia Norman for murdering the man who had seduced her.

2 What Jaffe describes as the rise of the urban reporter in the 1820s and 1830s coincided with the growing emphasis on evangelicalism in the USA. Early journalists borrowed quite liberally from the evangelical press, which had been using moral crusades around prostitution in the 1820s and 1830s to save souls and sell tracts. According to David Nord, "centralized, systematic mass publication had become part of the American way of doing things" and the origins of this success were "religious and evangelical" (1984: 24). Although the moral crusades produced by newspapers were secular, the traffic between evangelical and secular presses was advantageous to both, particularly insofar as the two could draw life and inspiration from one another.

3 Christopher Castiglia (1996) consistently uses the term "captivity narrative" to describe similar narratives well into the twentieth century. While I think that he is correct in pointing out the persistence of this cultural form in US history, as well as its contradictions, true captivity narratives appear only rarely in the nineteenth and twentieth centuries, save perhaps in the form of post-World War II alien abduction narratives.

4 The inversion of real social relations runs throughout the captivity narratives recounted by Linda Colley (2002) and Peter Linebaugh and Marcus Rediker (2000). White men, for example, were more likely to be "kidnapped" and forced into military service by the British government than they were to be captured by "natives" or pirates. The fact that captivity narratives never featured stories about the very real captives—African slaves—who were being transported to the colonies underscores the genre's inversion of reality.

5 Historian Linda Colley brilliantly illustrates the centrality of racist and ethnocentric captivity narratives to Britain's dreams of global supremacy from the early seventeenth century through the mid-nineteenth century. But according to Colley, gender only became vital to captivity narratives in the context of the USA. That is not to say that captivity narratives were not gendered. Masculine protection of feminized victims was, as Colley observes, definitive of the genre. While the taking of male captives was certainly a political concern in America before the mid-eighteenth century, it was the capture of women that set the imaginations of US cultural producers on fire.

6 For alternatives to this way of thinking, see Linebaugh and Rediker (2000) and Zinn (2003). These authors argue that Native American cultures might well have been preferable to the often-murderous labor regimes of the colonists, as well as the rigid social and cultural norms of colonial societies.

7 As Roger Lane (1979) points out, the vast majority of murders (with the notable exception of lynching) have been intraracial rather than interracial.

8 Although some attention was granted to Native American women in captivity narratives, this attention hinged on their relationships with white men (Pocahontas and Sacagawea, to take the best-known examples).

9 From the time that the *Sun* first began publishing in 1833 until 1841, no other cases were covered in such detail by the penny press. No other cases created a similarly large market for ephemera. In fact, between 1833 and 1836, the *Sun* covered only three murder cases for more than two days: the death of Mrs. Eleanor Bannen, mistakenly, as it turned out, attributed to poison in 1834; the trial of Richard Jackson, a sailor indicted for murder in 1835; and the trial of the Master of a brig for murdering his Maltese cook in 1836.

10 Penny press accounts inconsistently use both "Helen" and "Ellen" Jewett in referring to the victim. I follow Cohen (1998) in using the first name "Helen."

11 See Anthony (1997) for an account of masculinity and the press in what he describes as the moral panic about the Helen Jewett murder.

12 Although we may think that the dramatic increases in the population of New York City during the first half of the nineteenth century resulted from immigration,

two-thirds of the swell in New York City's population in the 1830s and 1840s resulted from the rural-to-urban shift.

13   Edgar Allen Poe, who wrote a short story about the death of Mary Rogers, writes of a similarly desirable corpse in "Ligeia" (1838).

14   Biressi (2001) has written an impressive account of the development of the true crime genre, observing that, in the USA and UK contexts, many nineteenth-century journalists wrote news narratives about crime as well as true crime stories. The *National Police Gazette*, which serialized the story of Helen Jewett under the editorial control of George Wilkes and which became more widely popular under the editorship of Richard Fox, was perhaps the most popular example of the true crime genre in the nineteenth century. See Smith and Smith (1972) for a sampling of *National Police Gazette* stories and style.

15   "The Fruits of Seduction" was reprinted in both the *Herald* and the *Transcript* in April 1836.

16   The *Sun*, in fact, did not conduct a moral crusade in the Jewett case, although it did weigh in with an opinion after the verdict was handed down. "At present," Day acerbically observed, "we shall only repeat the remark which was made throughout the city yesterday, that any good looking young man, possessing or being able to raise among his friends, the sum of fifteen hundred dollars to retain Messrs Maxwell, Price and Hoffman for his counsel, might murder any person he chose, with perfect impunity" (9 June 1836: 2).

17   References to Millwood and Barnwell run throughout popular literature of this era. Writers clearly expected their audiences to understand even the most cryptic references to these. See Charles Dickens' *The Pickwick Papers*, where Mr. Jingle refers Mr. Samuel Weller "to the well-known case in Barnwell" and Mr. Weller reiterates the androcentric logic of the tale: "it's always been my opinion, mind you, that the young 'ooman deserved scragging a precious sight more than he did" (1836/1986: 145).

18   Revolutionaries made much of this story in criticizing the British's inability to protect white women, going so far as to suggest that the British were no longer really white—"some Revolutionary writers linked them with blacks as well as Native Americans" (Colley 2002: 231).

19   Had Bennett been inclined, such an argument could have been extended to Robinson himself (as it was in George Wilkes' *The Lives of Helen Jewett and Richard P. Robinson*). Only a few short years earlier, Robinson probably would have lived not in a boarding-house, where he was completely unsupervised, but in the home and under the watchful eyes of the artisan to whom he had been apprenticed.

20   Phebe Mather Rogers would have been 42 when Mary Rogers was born. Amy Srebnick believes that Mary was really Phebe's granddaughter—the illegitimate daughter of Phebe's second child by her first husband (1995: 43).

21   See Roger Lane's discussion of drowning deaths (1979: 46–52).

22   Thomas McDade's *The Annals of Murder* (1961), a comprehensive listing of non-fiction literature concerning homicides before 1900, is replete with cases in which women (who vary in terms of age, class, and ethnicity, but do not include African American women) were murdered for refusing to have sex with men—a grim reminder of men's violently proprietary attitudes toward women's bodies.

23   Elma Sands had been murdered in 1799, her body thrown into a well in Manhattan. Levi Weeks, a carpenter who lived in the same boarding-house and who had by all accounts been courting Sands in the weeks before her death, was tried for her murder. Defended by the unlikely duo of Aaron Burr and Alexander Hamilton, Weeks was acquitted, Sands' death was judged a suicide, and the ensuing public outcry forced Weeks to leave the northeast forever. Bennett refers here to *Norman Leslie: A Tale of the Present Times*, by Theodore S. Fay. This fictionalized account of the Sands murder was published anonymously in 1835.

24   The identification of a racially ambiguous suspect was later to be echoed in Poe's

fiction, where he claimed that "An omnibus-driver, Valence, now also testified that he saw Marie Roget cross a ferry on the Seine, on the Sunday in question, in company with a young man of dark complexion" ("The Mystery of Marie Roget" 1850a).

25 At the time of Rogers' death and until 1845, when the city created a unified, full-time day-and-night police force of 800 men, the city's police force consisted of "100 marshals, 16 'police officers,' 108 Sunday officers (who enforced the laws of the Sabbath), and, at the ward level, 34 constables and roughly a thousand watchmen" (Lardner and Reppetto 2001: 23). Before 1845, magistrates stood at the top of the criminal justice system's food chain. Constables and marshals were paid by the piece: 37 cents for a warrant and 50 cents for a jury summoned. Victims, however, could offer their own rewards directly to the police, which exacerbated corruption and graft. As for the night watchmen, they were something of a joke among working people. Some were ill, some infirm, and even the able-bodied, who stood watch at night after having worked a ten-hour day, were not always lively in their pursuit of criminals (Lardner and Reppetto 2001: 15–16).

26 See Srebnick (1995: 97–107) for a thorough discussion of the link between Mary Rogers, Madame Restell, and abortion, as well as a fine reading of the case in all its historical and cultural complexity.

27 Solinger's *The Abortionist* (1994) provides a compelling account of the criminalization of abortion and abortionists.

28 On the newspaper industry in this era, see Cohen (1998), Crouthamel (1989), Lee (1937), Mott (1941), Schiller (1981), Schudson (1978), and Srebnick (1995).

29 Crouthamel claims that Bennett was also beaten by William Leggett, the abolitionist editor of the *New York Evening Post*, but other accounts suggest that Bennett was caned three times by Webb, as well as being whipped by an irate Wall Street broker (Stevens 1991: 40). It seems unlikely that Webb fought Leggett, since there is no mention of a physical fight with Leggett in the pages of the *Herald*.

30 See also coverage of Webb's trial on 25 February 1837: 2.

31 See King (1994) for an analysis of the religious and political background against which the moral wars occurred.

32 Colt killed Adams with a hatchet and then attempted to ship the body to New Orleans. Like the Rogers case, the Adams murder made its way into the literature of the time. T.H. Giddings (1974), among others, analyzed the case's influence on Melville's "Bartleby the Scrivener."

3 Black victims of the 1863 anti-draft riots

1 These accounts are drawn from archival materials located at the New York City Municipal Archives, Special Committee on Draft Riot Claims, 1863–1865, A-I, Box 1, 19105, Folder B.

2 In popular culture and some scholarly literature, terrorist violence against African Americans is seen to be a southern, and therefore regional, phenomenon. See Jacqueline Goldsby's *A Spectacular Secret* (2006), which argues that lynching was a fundamental part of the making of a national consciousness in the USA.

3 As both Bernstein (1990) and Cook (1974) observe, the number of African American casualties is difficult to estimate with any precision, since the bodies of men drowned in the Hudson River may never have been recovered and since so many African American men—some of them wounded—fled the city during that week, never to return.

4 Both the *New York Herald*'s and the *New York Times*' political positions closely resembled those, respectively, of the *World* and the *Tribune*.

5 Herbert Asbury's 1928 *Gangs of New York*, which drew almost exclusively from newspapers for its account of the anti-draft riots, offers a stunning example of the role

that newspapers played in erasing black victims from cultural memories of violence.

6 The *World*'s political perspective was an overtly white supremacist and genocidal one. During the anti-draft riots, the *World* made its support for the genocide against Native Americans perfectly clear in an article that approvingly commented on the bounty on Sioux scalps offered by the governor of Minnesota. The first scalp offered by bounty hunters came from a young Sioux man, shot while "engaged in picking berries." This, the *World* lamented, was the only "hostile one who has been killed since October" and "the race of barnacles [is] seemingly inexhaustible" (15 July 1863: 8).

7 The first class of draftees included all unmarried men between the ages of 20 and 45 and married men from 20 to 35, while the second class referred to married men between 35 and 45 (the second class was not to be called up until all those in the first class had been either drafted or exempted). Reasons for exemption were mental or physical disabilities or proof that a man was sole support of orphaned children or elderly parents.

8 According to the *Evening Post*, a "Copperhead" newspaper exhibited the following characteristics: (1) it overestimated confederate victories and downplayed those of the union; (2) it featured clippings and quotes from southern newspapers about the strength and prowess of the confederate army; (3) it continuously spoke of the need for the end to a hopeless war; (4) it ridiculed the north as an economic system; (5) it complained about "niggers" in the army and in the labor force; (6) it fomented resistance to the draft (*Evening Post*, 20 May 1863).

9 All testimony cited in this chapter is drawn from the microfilmed records of the New York County District Attorney Indictment Records housed in the New York City Municipal Archives and Records Center.

10 The use of the relatively innocuous "one or two instances" of blacks being "chased off the docks" concealed the fact that few of these urban dwellers could swim and throwing them off the docks was in fact attempted murder.

11 On Thursday, 23 July 1863, well over a week after the riots had begun, the *Evening Post* also carried an article on "Colored People in the Woods Near Harlem" (first edition, 23 July 1863: 1).

12 During the two-week period examined, the *World* referred to black victims a total of 25 times, while the *Evening Post* contained 18 references, and the *Tribune* 21.

13 The *New York Times* was among the first purchasers of a machine gun, which it used to protect its property during the anti-draft riots. See Ellis (1986).

14 It is worth adding that while the *World* consistently used the word "negro," as opposed to "colored," it alone used the word "nigger" to describe African Americans. Both the *Evening Post* and the *Tribune* used "colored" and "negro" interchangeably.

15 This understanding of the effects of suffering also held true for children in nineteenth-century popular culture, like the title character in Dickens' *Oliver Twist* (1838/2003) and Little Eva from *Uncle Tom's Cabin*. Although it could apply to white men (as in the "Calamus" poems from Whitman's 1860 *Leaves of Grass*), such representations were more rare, perhaps because the position of ennobled victimization was so clearly a feminized one.

16 This quotation comes from the testimony of Ellen Foose, who described the mob's preparations to lynch and burn an African American child ("Testimony of Ellen Foose" 1863).

17 See Tolnay and Beck's chapter 3 (1995) for a discussion of the causal link between economic recession and lynching.

18 See the *World*'s coverage for lurid examples of this, like the following: "The dead bodies of the killed were to be seen being borne away by their friends, the blood trickling on the pavement. Pools of blood would be met at frequent intervals" (15 July 1863: 1).

19 See Bernstein (1990: 29), Cook (1974: 143), and Harris (2003: 284) regarding the beating of Abraham Franklin.
20 Although the *Tribune* criticized the Irish for their participation in the anti-black violence, none of the papers blamed the Irish as a group. Indeed, both the *Evening Post* and the *World* took pains to distinguish between the majority of law-abiding Irish citizens of New York and those who participated in the violence.
21 Newspapers, as institutions, also had a stake in downplaying their role in fomenting violence. Anti-abolitionist papers like the *Herald* and the *World* helped to create a climate in which widespread acts of violence against blacks were seen as both reasonable and practical. Like hate radio in Rwanda over a century later, these newspapers inflamed racist sentiments against blacks, provided racists with an at once mendacious and ideologically effective logic for murder (in the case of the anti-draft riots, that blacks were directly competing with white workers for both employment and women), and continued to foment anti-black sentiment even after the horrible and violent events of July 1863. See "Hate Radio: Rwanda" (2003/4) for an analysis of the role that radio played in the Rwandan genocide.
22 Croly's wife, Jane Cunningham Croly, was one of the first female journalists in the USA. She wrote for the *New York Times* under the pseudonym Jennie June and ran the first women's department at the *New York World*.

4 Lynch narratives and criminalization

1 Frances Willard was the national president of the Women's Christian Temperance Union from 1879 until 1898. See Wells (1892/1997: 138–48) for her criticism of Willard and white women's organizations' attitudes toward lynching.
2 See Downey and Hyser (1991) for a book-length treatment of the case in Coatesville, Pennsylvania.
3 During the Homestead Steelworkers' Strike in 1892, the *World* supported the workers and their demands, even after anarchist Alexander Berkman stabbed capitalist Henry Clay Frick. The looming showdown at Homestead, according to the *World*, resulted from the injustice of the law: "Protection is for the rich to make them richer. It is hostile to the poor, and the poor are beginning to know it." The *World* also crusaded against what its editorial page described as "Pinkertonism," asking "Is it well that a body of armed mercenaries shall be held thus at the service of whomsoever has money with which to hire them?" (*World*, 7 July 1892: 4).
4 See Larson (2004) for an account of Holmes' crimes.
5 Only African American papers like the *Chicago Defender* and the *Pittsburgh Courier* covered lynching in a serialized, crusading fashion.
6 See Wasserman and Stack (1994) for a detailed analysis of *New York Times* coverage of lynching.
7 These included articles on impending lynchings, cases involving multiple lynchings, two references to clergy opposing lynching, and two articles referring to African American anti-lynching social movements.
8 As we will see in chapter 6, the northern news media did just this in their televised coverage of the struggle for civil rights in the 1960s, displacing structural racism onto the figure of the southern "redneck." See Graham (2001) for an analysis of this.
9 See Nerone (1994), especially chapter 6, as well as Tolnay and Beck (1995: 207–9) for accounts of this and other acts of violence against the African American press.
10 This was not the only time in which an African American was burned at the stake. One year later, Henry Smith was burned at the stake in Paris, Texas, for an alleged child murder (Wells 1892/1997: 91; *World*, 2 February 1893).
11 The use of "Jewett" rather than "Jewell" in the story's lead sentence is an interesting error, suggesting that the writer had an earlier worthy victim in mind as well.

12 As Rose (1988) observed in relation to Margaret Thatcher, violence proposed and enacted by a woman is seen to have enhanced legitimacy.

13 This lynching was also said to be the inspiration for Port Jervis native Stephen Crane's short story "The Monster" (Crane 1901/1940).

14 See Burrell (2002) for a thorough account of Port Jervis society and the lynching of Robert Lewis.

15 In writing about the Lewis case, Burrell notes Wells' hypothesis that Foley was blackmailing McMahon because he knew of a relationship between her and Robert Lewis (2002: 44). I concur with Burrell: it is impossible from this historical distance to know with any certainty what transpired on that June day. The testimony of all witnesses was too contradictory and too shot through with inconsistencies to support the allegation that Robert Lewis was a rapist and guilty beyond any reasonable doubt of the crime for which he was tortured and executed.

16 In this case, as well as in the murders of other black men, the *World* used nicknames or shortened versions of the men's names, consistently referring to Robert Lewis as "Bob" Lewis, Edward Coy as "Ed" Coy, Ephraim Wheeler as "Eph" Wheeler.

17 Conversely, white men were sometimes lynched for exceptionally brutal instances of family violence—as in the case of Joe Lytle of Findlay, Ohio, who assaulted his wife and two young daughters with a hatchet (*World*, 21 April 1892: 1)—but never on charges of sexual assault.

18 See Rammelkamp (1967) for an account of Pulitzer's formative years.

19 See Jones (1990), Salem (1990), and Wesley (1984) for more on African American women's crusades against lynching.

20 Beasley's "The Muckrakers and Lynching: A Case in Racism"s (1982) offers compelling evidence of this silence.

21 The increase in attention to lynching coverage overlaps with increased attention to kidnapping. What made these two crimes distinguishable, in terms of both legal and cultural categories? For although the extremes of these acts might be distinguishable—the hegemonic definition of lynching as a crime involved executing a suspect without due process, while kidnapping referred to seizing someone unlawfully and typically (but not always) for ransom—there was a great deal of fuzzy middle ground. In August 1955, when 14-year-old Emmett Till was abducted from his uncle's home in the Mississippi Delta by two white men, severely beaten, and then thrown into the Tallahatchie River to drown, why was this act of violence defined as a "lynching" rather than a "kidnapping/murder"?

22 Dorr correctly observes that "it is unreasonable to assume that black men as a group were able to refrain entirely from sexual violence," but given the tenacity of the black-on-white rape narratives that pervaded newspaper discourses in the era of miscegenation, to speak of exceptions to the rule of white supremacist logic can be problematic.

23 Because my focus in this chapter is on newspaper accounts of lynching, and the ideological perspective shared by news producers, I do not consider the production, distribution, and reception of the kind of "souvenir" photographs of lynching presented and analyzed by Allen (2000). Photography did not appear in New York City newspapers until the late nineteenth century, moreover, and during the period in question neither the *Times* nor the *World* featured any photographs of lynching.

24 See Hochschild (1999) for an account of the genocide of Congolese at the turn of the nineteenth century and Gourevitch (1999) and Powers (2003) on Rwanda.

5 The demise of sentimental crime reporting

 1 See Gordon (1988/2002) and Pleck (2004) for histories of family violence. Gordon observes the related disappearance of family violence from the radar of policy-making, a disappearance that was not reversed until the rise of the 1970s feminist

movement. She suggests that the disappearance corresponded to the absence of feminist movement and organizing from the US political scene.

2 Both Suellen Hoy (1996) and Naomi Schor (1987) offer pertinent dicussions of this feminized attention to detail and its social consequences.

3 According to Mott (1941), headlines were used as early as 1762, although these were seldom more than label headings. It was not until the 1840s that headlines in multiple decks began to appear.

4 See Haller (1971) for an account of the development of these ideologies.

5 Although there is a tendency to see the *World*'s coverage as singularly tabloidesque, the *New York Times* covered the Korn case in similarly elaborate detail, featuring interviews not only with police officers, but also with the building's janitor, and "gossips" as well (6 May 1893: 1).

6 Donna Haraway's *Primate Visions* (1989) remains one of the most important critiques of the forms of vision associated with scientific objectivity. See also Harding (1991), Keller (1984, 1985), and Longino (1990).

7 As we have seen, the mainstream press has never routinely included the perspectives of African Americans, Native Americans, and other similarly disenfranchised populations.

8 See Walker (1977) for an account of the history of police reform in the USA.

9 Ferguson (1994) also remarks upon the political struggles over policing and police forces that have long been characteristic of New York City. I am grateful to the author for sharing this unpublished paper with me.

10 Here again, the reform efforts of journalists would prove to be decisive. For example, Jacob Riis' well-publicized experience as a new immigrant in a police station-house was used to argue against using police stations in this way (Riis 1901; Lardner and Repetto 2001: 50–51).

11 See Idanna Pucci's *The Trials of Maria Barbella* (1996) for one such account.

12 These annual reports can be found today in the Police Department Museum located on Water Street.

13 See Robyn Muncy (1991) and Camilla Stivers (2000) for more on the relationships between gender, the settlement movement, and public administration during this period.

14 David Roediger (1996) talks about the emergence of the term "white slavery" in the 1830s, which served as a way of appropriating some of the affective force that abolitionists were using to mobilize around slavery and attaching it to the plight of laboring people. In its first incarnation in the 1830s, white slavery referred not to the sexual enslavement of women, but to a very problematic analogy between chattel slavery and wage labor. "White slavery" thus sought to sentimentalize (and to an extent feminize) the situation of working-class white men by suggesting that their plight was similar to that of slaves. In fact, until the late nineteenth century, "white slavery" exclusively referred to the predicament of white men. As Lawrence Glickman points out, this was "primarily a male discourse about the reproduction of masculinity in a wage-labor regime" (1999: 39). In the early part of the twentieth century, "white slavery" was redefined so as to lose its earlier association with waged labor.

15 Throughout his life, Thaw was repeatedly arrested on charges of beating prostitutes.

16 Ironically, elite heterosexual abusers of women like White were represented through some of the same codes used to represent "fairies" at the turn of the century. See George Chauncey (1994), chapter 2, for samples of progressive-era discourses about "fairies."

17 However skeptical newspapers may have been, the burgeoning film industry kept the panic alive in films like *The Fatal Hour* (1908), *Traffic in Souls* (1913), *The Inside of the White Slave Traffic* (1913), *House of Bondage* (1914), *The Little Girl Next Door* (1916), and *Is Any Girl Safe?* (1916).

18 Muncy (1991) and Stivers (2000) offer analyses of the promise and the limitations of this female professionalism.

19 Langum (1994: 35–37) describes the internal inconsistencies in the reports issued by various vice commissions between 1909 and 1911.

20 See Diffee (2005) for more on how the white slavery panic played out in popular culture of the time. Susan Courtney (2005) also offers a comprehensive reading of the filmic obsession with gender and race from 1903 to 1967.

21 See Jennifer Davis' "The London Garotting Panic of 1862: A Moral Panic and the Creation of a Criminal Class in mid-Victorian England" (1980) for an earlier example of the role that data and proof played in the institutional creation of a moral panic. As in most matters regarding policing, England was at least 50 years ahead of the USA when it came to institutional organization and data collection.

22 The Creel Commission, established during World War I to distribute pro-war propaganda, first points to the emergence of this, but it was not until the post-war period that government and law-enforcement officials began to recognize the importance of managing information.

23 According to Theoharis and Cox, Hoover's first job was at the Library of Congress, where his mastery of "the mammoth card catalogue" prepared him for "the gargantuan task of collating the information to be gathered on the country's estimated 10,000 Communists" (1988: 56).

24 Ultimately, these files would contain over 200,000 names (Ungar 1976: 43).

25 During the 1910s and 1920s, the term "alternative press" included a vibrant immigrant press. See Parks (1922).

26 Indeed, if we accept the mythology of the industry itself—that its origins lie in John D. Rockefeller's hiring of Ivy Lee in 1914 to handle the negative publicity that ensued from a massacre in Ludlow, Colorado, where 20 striking miners, their wives, and children were slaughtered by militia hired by the Rockefellers—then the need to manage victim narratives was a cornerstone of the industry's formation. Public outcry on behalf of victims understood to be distinctly undeserving of their fate caused Rockefeller to hire Ivy Lee in order, according to Stuart Ewen, to "secure publicity for their views" (1996: 78). In a now classic example of spin (one currently favored by George W. Bush advisor Karl Rove) through various forms of communication to opinion leaders and middle-class audiences, Lee sought to persuade the public that the union itself had been responsible for the massacre and that the victims were really perpetrators.

27 See Rashke (2000) and Churchill and Vander Wall (1990) for further information about the FBI's use of informants. Sometimes the line between sympathetic journalist and informant was non-existent, as in the case of Whitaker Chambers, who claimed to be a journalist when he first met Alger Hiss (Fariello 1995: 49).

28 This list included George Sokolsky, a prominent Hearst columnist; Drew Pearson, another syndicated columnist; Frederick Woltman, a conservative reporter; and the Washington bureau chiefs of the United Press and *Chicago Tribune* (Schrecker 1998: 216).

29 See Potter (1998), Powers (1983), Walker (1977), and Wilson (2000) for more on the FBI's exploitation of a wide range of genres and cultural forms.

30 The film industry, however, did not offer the kind of control that Hoover desired, especially since Hoover's narrowly moralistic idea of "good" film precluded sex, violence, or much action altogether. Indeed, by 1937, Hoover had convened a convention in Washington, DC for the International Association for Identification that explicitly called for mandatory fingerprinting of all employees in the film industry. Arguing that "Hollywood is over-run with criminals of every sort, particularly those specializing in blackmail, shakedowns, badger games, and kidnapping threats" ("Hollywood Finger-Printing Urged" 1937: 1), fingerprinting was held up as the solution to problems ranging from identifying runaway girls, to keeping out "floaters and other undesirables."

31 Radio provided a more hospitable environment for this project. In 1935, radio

producer, director, and star Phillip H. Lord approached Hoover with an idea for a program based on cases from the FBI's files. Hoover teamed Lord up with another friendly contact, Rex Collier, and was granted a contract that gave them complete control over the resultant "G-Men" (Powers 1983: 204). "Tour of the FBI," broadcast on 7 July 1935 on *NBC Red*, featured the dispassionate, scientific, and rational national police force that Hoover was presenting to the public. Opening and concluding with ringing telephones ("National 7117")—an audible reminder of the Bureau's use of new technologies, as well as a measure of how busy the agents were—the program was organized around kidnapping: not only did the program begin by giving "the kidnap number" ("the number which should be listed on the memorandum pad of every family in the United States"), during the course of the program four different kidnapping cases were mentioned. Most of the action took place in "Oscar's Room," or the crime laboratory, where narrator Ryley Cooper (a freelance reporter, speechwriter for Hoover, and author of a series of crime stories that glorified the FBI) showed "a few things that science is doing to solve crime these days," like using the fluoroscope. In the laboratory, listeners were further reminded, "Perception, ingenuity, and the ability to run down every possible clue forms the backbone of a special agent ("Tour of the FBI," *NBC Red*, 7 July 1935).

32 See the following articles, all appearing in less than one year in the *New York Times*: "Law Experts Score Our Crime Record; Committee Reports to American Institute Lawlessness Here Exceeds That in England" (10 May 1925: 21); "Enright Sees Peril in Bad Boy Gangs; Juvenile Crime Increases 60 Percent" (6 April: 3); and "Crime in Chicago Increased Heavily" (11 January 1925: 30).

33 According to Philip Jenkins, the FBI popularized "the terms serial crimes and serial murder" (quoted in Rhodes 1999: 212) in order to build support for its Behavioral Sciences Unit.

34 According to Potter, "It is no surprise that bandits who emerged in the United States during this period were overwhelmingly white and native-born, raised among working people whose migrations between rural and urban areas intensified with better transportation and a worsening economy" (1998: 84), but this was not a narrative that the FBI sought to tell.

35 African American migration to midwestern cities produced regional moral panics, but cities like New York, and the nationalizing media headquartered there, were largely unaffected by this. See Grossman (1989).

36 Hoover wrote to his superiors, saying "that while 'unfortunately' Garvey had not yet violated any federal laws that would permit his deportation, perhaps a fraud case involving Garvey's promotion of the steamship line might be a way of getting him out of the country" (Powers 1987: 128). Four years later, in 1923, Hoover's investigation triumphed: Garvey was convicted of fraud and, after serving his sentence, he was deported to Jamaica in 1927.

37 One letter sent to the Union League Club of New York City by an African American club stated that "negroes are disenfranchised . . . lynched . . . in peonage and on convict farms in the South . . . Jim-Crowed" (Lowenthal 1950: 125). The FBI submitted this letter to Congress as evidence of the seditious nature of the African American press.

38 Robin D.G. Kelley's *Hammer and Hoe: Alabama Communists during the Great Depression* (1990) offers abundant evidence of law enforcement agencies' attitudes toward interracial organizing.

39 See Cook (1964: 21–24) for more on the FBI's hiring practices.

40 Of course, Hoover's racism was evident to those white journalists who were not too racist or too fearful to look. One radio narrative depicted "a local NAACP leader opening a chapter meeting with a person-by-person loyalty oath to unmask communist infiltrators. 'All entered denials until he got to the back of the room where the state organizer for the Communist party was sitting with a white woman.'" As

Powers goes on to point out, "The phrase 'white woman' was pointless unless the bureau assumed that this detail would trigger a response in the reader of emotional revulsion against miscegenation" (1987: 234).

6 From the war on poverty to the war on crime

1 See Musto (1987) for a definitive history of narcotics control efforts in the USA.
2 In her content analysis of the *New York Times*, McGucken (1987) notes a decline in crime stories identifying the race and ethnicity of the suspect in the years between 1900 and 1940. Where 8 percent of crime stories published during the first decade of the twentieth century mentioned the race of the offender, the number of stories identifying race subsequently decreased by more than half in the following four decades.
3 Cohen (2003) offers an astute analysis of these contradictions. See in particular chapter 4.
4 As William Boddy puts it, "The history of commercial television is the story of the deliberate shepherding of a technological apparatus by powerful established interests in electronic manufacturing and broadcasting" (1993: 16).
5 That the intellectual vacuity of much television broadcasting might offend large segments of the population was of no concern, because advertisers were the primary audience for television programming and the gatekeepers for content.
6 Lynn Spigel (1992) comments on a similar dynamic with regard to a marketing emphasis on the putative educational content of entertainment programming during the 1950s.
7 The enormous profitability of news across the media was not as apparent in the late 1950s as it was a few short years later. Until the 1960s, families had privately owned most of the leading newspapers. These family-owned corporations had avoided paying inheritance taxes for three generations. As owners neared the end of this grace period, they began to seek ways to avoid enormous taxes, either by "trading shares on the stock market and [thereby] relieving family members of inheritance taxes on the entire property" or by selling "the paper outright to an outside corporation" (Bagdikian 2000: 12). When major papers began offering their stock publicly in the early 1960s, as Bagdikian puts it, "the investing world discovered that the newspaper industry, like the legendary Hetty Green, had assiduously presented itself to the public in mendicant rags, but was now exposed, as Mrs. Green had been, as fabulously rich" (13). At the same time, Wall Street began to exert pressure on broadcasting. According to Halberstam, "CBS had been public and listed on the New York Stock Exchange as far back as 1937, but it was only in the late fifties, with the soaring new revenues from television profits, that Wall Street really discovered the industry" (1979: 417). As they recognized this profit-making potential, large corporations began to buy newspapers and other media companies. The radio industry underwent a similarly massive shift with the expansion of FM stations.
8 Both CBS and NBC had been experimenting with longer formats from as early as 1956. The first 30-minute news program (which had been two years in the making) aired after the March on Washington in spring 1963, before Kennedy's assassination. ABC was the first to begin regular 30-minute news programs in late 1963.
9 See Gray (1995), MacDonald (1992), and Means-Coleman (1998) for analyses of sitcoms and representations of African Americans.
10 The movement's most significant loss in the south resulted from the media-savvy tactics of police chief Laurie Pritchett in Albany Georgia: a man who understood "the need to make ends and means cohere in a political strategy to win the hearts and minds of the public" (Chappell 1994: 130). Pritchett effectively turned the Southern Christian Leadership Council's (SCLC) strategies against the protesters. His forces were ordered to behave nonviolently for as long as the cameras were

trained on them. In 1962, after the national press corps had departed, the police reverted to "more orthodox methods of police work" (Chappell 1994: 220), but Pritchett, unlike Sheriff Jim Clark in Selma and Eugene "Bull" Connor in Birmingham, "realized that there are limits to what the public—now with ringside seats, owing to recent changes in the technology and organization of news reporting—will accept as reasonable, fair, proportional, necessary" (Chappell 1994: 130).

11 An all-white jury acquitted both men who went on to sell their story to *Look* magazine for $4,000. In response to evidence uncovered by documentary maker Keith Beauchamp, in 2004, the US Department of Justice reopened an investigation of the case and in November 2005 the FBI concluded its investigation. It remains to be seen whether indictments will be handed down, over 50 years after Till's murder. See Beauchamp's documentary, *The Untold Story of Emmett Louis Till* (2005) and Whitfield (1988) on the murder and its aftermath.

12 *Jet* magazine published photographs of Till's battered corpse on 22 September 1955, just three days after his murderers went on trial in Mississippi, which also brought pressure on northern news media to cover the story. See Feldstein (1994) for a provocative analysis of how codes of normative motherhood were used by, and against, Mamie Bradley during her struggle for justice.

13 There were casualties in this war. Of the two deaths that occurred in Oxford, Mississippi, the first was Paul Guihard, a reporter from *Agence France-Presse*, who was shot at close range in the back by an assassin's bullet "because he was a reporter, or foreign, or both" (Rather 1977: 74–75). According to Charles Dunagin (1987), who worked for the *Jackson State Times* and other Mississippi papers, in 1964 alone, during Freedom Summer, 20 incidents of violence against the press were reported in McComb, Mississippi.

14 In 1964, the United Church of Christ petitioned the FCC to block WLBT's license renewal on the grounds "that the hostile, systematic exclusion by WLBT of nearly half the viewing audience (negroes) violated legal obligation to broadcast in the public interest" (Branch 1998: 265). See Barnouw (1970: 241), Classen (2004), and Donovan and Scherer (1992: 10).

15 Stuart Hall's distinction between overt and inferential racism in "The Whites of Their Eyes" (1990) is an instructive one here. Where overt racism, like the use of racist language or epithets, is direct and makes no attempt to conceal its meaning, inferential racism proceeds more euphemistically, deriving its meaning from more subtle, symbolic associations. Broadcasters' avoidance of "controversy" was inferentially racist when it came to prohibiting African Americans from appearing on televised entertainment programming. Similarly, charges that the media were too "liberal" were inferentially racist insofar as these meant that the media were critical of white supremacy. It should be noted, however, that the effects of both overt and inferential racism are indistinguishable.

16 There was further fall-out from the documentary. CBS's Birmingham affiliate disaffiliated from CBS, and the City Commissioner of Birmingham sued CBS for libel. More chillingly, and as a result of the lawsuit, CBS pulled its reporters from Birmingham

17 A little more than two weeks after the March on Washington, NBC aired a 3-hour special on race, *American Revolution '63*. As was the case with CBS' earlier program, *American Revolution '63* was "aired without commercial interruption, as regular sponsors declined to be associated with controversy" (Branch 1998: 134).

18 The coverage of Rustin in particular was remarkable: the FBI had long been fomenting discord between Rustin and Roy Wilkins and the NAACP, based on Rustin's "defects as a vagabond ex-Communist homosexual" (Branch 1989: 133). In fact, Wilkins had not wanted to have Rustin as the march's principal organizer at all—"Wilkins was wary because of Rustin's left-wing associations when he was young and because he was gay, something, because it had showed up on the occasional police blotter, that the white conservative world might seize on, and

something which in particular would offend J. Edgar Hoover" (Halberstam 1998: 450). Also see D'Emilio (2004) for an excellent biography of Rustin.

19 Bill Alatney worked for *Who's Who in Black America, Michigan Chronicle, Detroit News,* and NBC News.

20 See Goode and Ben-Yehuda (1994) and Jenkins (1998) for analyses of the complexities of moral panics.

21 These emerging divisions were only barely concealed at the March on Washington: Roy Wilkins insisted that John Lewis delete the following line from his speech, which Wilkins considered inflammatory: "We will march through the South, through the heart of Dixie, the way Sherman did. We shall pursue our own 'scorched earth' policy and burn Jim Crow to the ground, nonviolently. We shall crack the South into a thousand pieces and put them back together in the image of a democracy" (Halberstam 1998: 451).

22 By the middle of the decade, critics of the emerging crime war had also begun to speak out. See Cipes (1967) for just one example of this.

23 See Donovan and Scherer (1992: 75) for an elaboration of this point.

24 Indeed, the National Advisory Commission on Civil Disorders, or Kerner Commission, established by President Johnson to investigate the causes of civil disorders concluded that although the news media did not cause these riots, "news organizations have failed to communicate to both their black and white audiences a sense of the problems America faces and the sources of potential solutions" (1968: 366), a failure that could only have exacerbated the frustration that African American activists already felt.

25 This is not to deny the fractures that were dividing the Civil Rights Movement by the mid-1960s, not to mention the destructive nature of urban uprisings that destroyed African American neighborhoods and whose casualties were overwhelmingly black. But television's romance with violence, its visual feeding frenzy around images of armed black youths and exclusion of coverage of peaceful protests, breakfast programs, free clinics, and literacy programs, cannot be explained by assigning blame on the movement. To do so—to hold the movement responsible for the very social problems it sought to address—is to reproduce the logic that gave birth to the twentieth century's second war on crime.

26 This comment made headlines throughout the country. See "FBI's Hoover Scores Ramsey Clark, RFK," *Washington Post,* 17 November 1970; "Hoover Reported Describing Clark as Jellyfish," *New York Times,* 17 November 1970; Donner 1980: 107; Ungar 1976: 62.

27 The institutional legacy of this hatred was to endure after both their deaths. Theoharis and Cox write that "when the director learned that Senate Republican minority leader Hugh Scott proposed to introduce a bill to strike a commemorative medal in honor of King," he had the senator briefed about King's "background" (1988: 360). Later, Hoover briefed the House Appropriations Committee about the information contained in the FBI's King dossier in an effort "to defeat a proposed congressional resolution to make a national holiday of King's Birthday" (Theoharis and Cox 1988: 410–11). FBI charges that King had plagiarized his speeches continued to resurface into the 1990s.

28 The FBI's folder on Martin Luther King eventually ran to some 500 to 600 pages in length, although an unspecified number of pages were withheld under a court order of 31 January 1977 (Theoharis and Cox 1988: 358).

29 Hoover's misogyny was to get him into trouble in this case, since he clearly did not believe that newspaperwomen actually reported any news. See Theoharis and Cox (1988: 355–6).

30 Since the FBI did not hire African American agents until 1973, FBI agents attending political meetings stuck out like sore thumbs.

31 In response to Republican calls for security from "domestic violence" (quoted in

Cipes 1967: 67), as Barry Goldwater termed it in 1964, President Johnson began to focus more attention on crime. Nevertheless, the Democratic Platform for 1968 had not yet abandoned an at least discursive commitment to eradicating poverty.

32 After Hoover's death, the *UCR* became the subject of intense criticism. The US Law Enforcement Assistance Administration and the federal Census Bureau conducted a study in 1974 that suggested that most categories of serious crime went unreported, that some police forces kept "their crime incidence rate down in order to claim a higher solution rate," and that dramatic increases and decreases could be fudged in many different ways. As Eric Monkkonen observes, the resulting crime rate is a better indicator of police behavior than criminal activity: "When arrest rates soar or decline, one must make only the most qualified observations on the relationship of arrests to actual bad behavior—precisely speaking, 1863, the 1870s, and 1890s had arrest waves, not crime waves" (1981: 71). The 1974 study also raised questions about a sudden, nationwide drop in crime reported by the FBI before the 1972 election. As Ungar points out, "The suspicion was that someplace along the line— perhaps in some local police departments—the figures had been tampered with to help the law-and-order reputation of the Nixon administration" (1976: 389). A more recent example of the doctoring of statistics occurred in 1998 in New York City, when mid-level transit officials began to complain about record-keeping problems. A subsequent investigation revealed that the Police Department had been intentionally underreporting subway crime "for nearly 20 years" (Kocieniewski 1998: A11). These examples cast further doubt on the validity of the figures Hoover used in 1968 to support his contentions about social disorder. See also Biderman and Lynch (1991) for a discussion of why statistics in the FBI's *Uniform Crime Reports* diverge from the *National Crime Victim Survey* administered by the Department of Justice.

33 In one of those ironies less obvious in the era of real-time-only television viewing, this clip ran immediately after Agnew had publicly apologized for previous references to "Pollacks and fat Japs."

7 Criminalizing black culture

1 Before Stuart's suicide, suspect William Bennett was identified as "Willie" Bennett in a move that—consciously or unconsciously—linked him to Willie Horton. After Stuart's suicide, news reports identified him by his proper name, "William."
2 See Rome (2004: 64), Russell (1998: 70), and Theoharis and Woznica (1990) for more detailed analyses of the Stuart case.
3 Russell provides summary data on racial hoaxes between 1987 and 1996 (1998: 72–75).
4 Numerous biographies, autobiographies, and historical accounts provide rich source material for a study of the female leaders of the Civil Rights Movement. See Evers-Williams (1999), Fleming (1998) for a biography of Ruby Doris Smith Robinson, Lee (2000) on Fannie Lou Hamer, Ransby (2005) on Ella Baker, as well as Branch (1989, 1998), Garrow (1988), and Halberstam (1998) for just a few examples.
5 Abramowitz (1996), Gordon (1995), Katz (1993), Kessler-Harris (2003), Mink (1996), Quadagno (1994), Roberts (1998), and Solinger (2001) offer excellent analyses of poverty, women, race, and the welfare state. See Kelley (1997) on the demonization of black urban poor people.
6 See Ortner's "Is Female to Male as Nature is to Culture?" (1974) for an expansion of this point.
7 Kunzel's "White Neurosis, Black Pathology: Constructing Out-of-Wedlock Pregnancy in the Wartime and Postwar United States" (1994) provides an excellent analysis of the pathologization of black families by twentieth-century experts. Also, see Solinger (1992) on the racialization of single white motherhood in the post-war era.

8 This example abundantly illustrates how the misogyny of psychoanalysis became the alibi for racism. Thus does racialized androcentrism reproduce itself both in theory and practice.

9 Anthropologist Eleanor Leacock (1981) argued that this is the way that the imposition of patriarchy proceeds. In the case of the First Nation people she was studying, Jesuits first had to win the Montagnais to patriarchy—to a belief system in which women were the property of husbands and one that insisted that masculinity depended on men's ability to dominate women—before they could be effectively colonized. Some tactics of racialized androcentrism never go out of fashion.

10 When the National Advisory Commission on Civil Disorders (established by Lyndon Johnson in 1967) published the Kerner Commission Report, the report concluded that the causes for such urban uprisings lay in "deepening racial division," and that in place of "blind repression" the US needed "a compassionate, massive, and sustained" commitment to action (1968: 1–2) in order to reverse this movement. The Kerner Commission's analysis and recommendations—which included a scathing indictment of the role that the news media had played in framing events—proved popular to neither journalists nor politicians, both of whom favored the explanatory framework put forth in the Moynihan Report.

11 According to the US Bureau of the Census, 22.7 percent of African Americans were poor in 2001 (http://www.census.gov/Press-Release/www/2002/cb02-124.html, accessed 20 May 2003).

12 The first references to the term welfare queen appeared in broadcast and print coverage of Taylor (*CBS Evening News*, 18 March 1977; *New York Times*, 19 March 1977: 8). The welfare queen and the crack mother are part of a broader fabric of racist discourses about African American mothers. See Quadagno (1994), Roberts (1998), and Humphries (1999) for further analyses. Humphries, in particular, is concerned with moral panics and processes of criminalization.

13 The effects of these resilient racist stereotypes should not be underestimated. According to Martin Gilens, "the dimension of racial attitudes with the strongest effect on welfare views is the extent to which blacks are perceived as lazy, and this perception is a better predictor of welfare attitudes than such alternatives as economic self-interest, egalitarianism, and attributions of blame for poverty" (1996: 594).

14 Slightly over half of all registered voters voted in the 1980 presidential election. Of these, 50.75 percent of the popular vote went to Reagan, while 49.24 percent went to Jimmy Carter and all "others." See Schudson and King (1995: 124–41) on the construction of Reagan's popularity by beltway journalists, as well as Michael Rogin's 1987 classic, *Ronald Reagan, The Movie.*

15 Culverson (2002) analyzes the twinned use of Horton and the welfare queen in the 1988 presidential campaign, arguing that the two worked hand-in-hand to appeal to racist fears.

16 Annin (1996) offers a vivid illustration of the emerging discourse about "super-predators."

17 J. Edgar Hoover, who had strenuously lobbied to prevent King's birthday from becoming a holiday, would have been pleased with this sort of coverage.

18 Charges against four of the youths were dropped in 2003. Imprisoned rapist Matias Reyes testified that he had committed the crime alone. See Alluh (2002), Little (2002a), and Schanberg (2002). See Best (1999) on the emergence of new vocabularies for understanding crime, like "wilding" and "carjacking."

19 A violent serial rapist, Reyes (who was known for gouging out the eyes of his victims) was convicted in 1991 of four rapes and the murder of a pregnant woman and was linked to eight rapes in the seven-month period that included the night of 19 April 1989.

20 Journalists who did cover the story did not invest much effort in doing so. McFadden's 1990 article contains paragraphs lifted verbatim from his 1989 article.

21 In the 18 months following the rape, the Central Park Jogger case appeared in eleven national network news segments. The Brooklyn rape case did not make national network news.

22 One wonders what "noted" meant in this context, particularly during an era when investment bankers typically came to the attention of the mass media for their criminal behavior.

23 See Carter (1969) for a vivid historical example of the disparity attributed to racialized testimony in the case of the Scottsboro suspects.

24 Although in these cases white victims were revealed to be perpetrators, there is no way of determining how many white perpetrators' racial hoaxes have never been revealed.

25 As Kevin Alexander Gray notes, "Mandingo" also conjured an earlier meaning of the word: "Mandinkas were the fiercest warriors of Africa. After a Caribbean slave revolt in the 1800s, John C. Calhoun of South Carolina, the leading intellectual of the Southern gentry, invoked the specter of Mandingo slaughtering white masters as justification for their enslavement" (2004).

26 Two of the officers acquitted, Officer Laurence Powell and Sergeant Staccy Koon, were later tried and convicted on federal civil rights charges. See Davis (1992b) for an account of the events that led to the uprising.

27 Revealingly, there was no similar discussion of an interpretive rift in the case of the dismissal of charges against the police officers in the King beating case.

28 See journalist Gary Webb's *Dark Alliance: The CIA, the Contras, and the Crack Cocaine Explosion*. According to him, "it is undeniable that a wildly successful conspiracy to import cocaine existed for many years . . . innumerable American citizens—most of them poor and black—paid an enormous price as a result" (1999: xiii).

29 See Reeves and Campbell (1994) and Humphries (1999) for detailed analyses of these media representations. See Bourgois (2003) for a rich ethnographic study of Puerto Rican crack users in East Harlem.

Conclusion

1 According to Rome, "The public picture of Latinos and crime most closely resembles that of blacks . . They, however, are not perceived as posing the same kind of criminal threat as blacks" (2004: 5).

2 The two exceptions to Rome's claim are the Tramp Acts passed in the last third of the nineteenth century and the serial killer panic of the 1980s. The Tramp Acts explicitly criminalized itinerant white men, although this criminalization was temporary (see Donner 1990). See Jenkins (1988) on the serial killer panic. Although the serial killer panic clearly involved white men, whiteness was of course never an issue.

3 See Biressi (2001), Fishman and Cavender (1998), and Hill (2005) for more on reality programming and true crime shows.

4 The increase in crime news had direct economic causes. First, although fewer and fewer cities and towns had more than one daily newspaper by the late 1990s, the number of local television stations increased. By 2000, New York City had seven major stations, Miami six, Sacramento five, Orlando four, and many smaller cities like Pittsburgh gained a fourth in the early part of the twenty-first century with the introduction of Fox News. In addition to the proliferation of stations, the amount of time devoted to local news increased dramatically. Until about 1980, most stations carried one and a half hours of local news daily: half-hour programs at noon, 6 p.m., and 11 p.m. In many markets, local news broadcasts tripled to five hours daily, forcing producers to rely more and more on that traditional staple of local news—crime stories. The increases in both the number of stations and the amount of time local stations devote to news—what media historian Michael Schudson describes as the "newsification" (1995: 180) of popular culture—are in part an effect of the

deregulation of the cable industry in the 1980s and the resulting erosion of the network system, as well as the sheer profitability of TV news itself. For TV news is one big fat cash cow. Cheap to produce, particularly when sustained by a steady diet of crime coverage, it commands high advertising rates, since it is said to attract an upscale demographic. Indeed, the most profitable part of a station's operation is news programming, with crime news being the cheapest news to produce, since it requires little more than a police radio, friendly police sources, a reporter, a camera crew, and a van. According to Winerip, "the operating profit margin at a typical station is between 40 and 50 percent, two to three times more than newspapers own. The Pulitzer Company, owner of the *St. Louis Post-Dispatch*, has a 15 percent operating margin on its newspapers, while its nine stations . . . have a 37 percent margin. *The Washington Post Company* . . . makes a 15 percent margin on its newspapers, while its six television stations have an operating margin of 46 percent" (Winerip 1998: 40). See "The State of the News Media 2005" for a remarkably comprehensive analysis of contemporary news production on television and radio, as well as in newspapers, magazines, and online.

5 See also Dixon and Linz's (2000a, 2000b) research on representations of African Americans on local television news, as well as Dixon (2003).

6 Such criticisms also need to be extended to newsrooms themselves. See Pritchard and Brzezinski (2004) for a discussion of "racial profiling" in newsrooms, both in terms of hiring practices and assignments.

7 See Grossberg (2005) and Males (1996a, 1996b) for criticisms of what amounts to a war on kids.

8 Sparks and Ogle (1990) also make what they see as a necessary analytic distinction between fear and victimization on one hand and the probability of being victimized on the other.

9 There is considerable dissent among sociologists (particularly criminologists) about the accuracy of this and other categories. See Farrall *et al.* (1997) and Ditton and Farrall (2000).

10 See Frankenberg (1993: 43–47) for more on the social geography of race, as well as Monmonier (1997: 239–62) on "crimescapes."

11 Pittsburgh was the site of a string of police murders of black suspects at the turn of the last century, a list that includes 12-year-old Michael Ellerbee, shot in the back on Christmas Eve 2002 as he fled from two police officers, as well as Dion Hall, Charles Dixon, Bernard Rogers, Michael Hunter, Damian Jordan and Andrea Umphrey. High-profile cases in New York City included the rape and torture of Haitian immigrant Abner Louima in 1999 and the shooting death of Amadou Diallo in 1999. Both men were unarmed.

12 Lichtenstein (1996) provides a comprehensive analysis of how just this kind of approach emerged during the Jim Crow era.

13 Jill Lepore's *New York Burning* (2005) describes a 1741 "witch hunt" in Manhattan, in which 30 slaves were executed, that ably details how shame and fear on the part of whites about slavery was translated into the construction of a threatening black population.

14 The contrast between plagiarism cases involving black and white journalists is also illustrative of these points. Steven Glass, a writer for the *New Republic*, which had a small but highly influential audience, was found to have completely fabricated at least 27 stories that had been published under his byline. Jayson Blair, a reporter for the *New York Times*, was accused of plagiarism in 2003. The treatment of these two journalists—one white, the other African American—by the media underscores the differential treatment along the lines of race of even white-collar criminals.

15 It is important to keep in mind that perspectives are not fixed or unchanging. In fact, when Bob Herbert covered the Central Park Jogger case in 1989 for the *Daily News* his descriptions of the suspects mirrored the wider racist coverage of the case.

Although Herbert later described coverage of the Central Park Jogger case as "racist," as Lynnell Hancock (2003) points out, he never acknowledged his own contribution to what she describes as the "wolf pack" mentality.

16 See Blakeslee (2005) for an account of the case and its context.

17 Since 1850, the prison population has been on the rise, with three steep periods of increase: the first from 1850 to 1870, the second between 1920 and 1940, and the most recent from 1970 to the present (Christie 1996: 85). In 1991, the USA incarcerated 504 out of 100,000 inhabitants. The closest figure from a European country was Northern Ireland with 106 out of 100,000 (Christie 1996: 30). See Reiman (1996) for an unsettling economic analysis of the boom in prisons.

Bibliography

Abbott, C. (1974) "The Neighborhoods of New York, 1760–1775," *New York History*, 55(1): 47–52.

Abernathy, R.D. (1989) *And the Walls Came Tumbling Down*, New York: Harper and Row.

Abramowitz, M. (1996) *Regulating the Lives of Women: Social Welfare Policy from Colonial Times to the Present*, revised edition, Boston, MA: South End Press.

Addams, J. and I. Wells (1977) *Lynching and Rape: An Exchange of Views*, New York: The American Institute for Marxist Studies.

Alatney, B. (1987) "Panel 6: Aftermath—1968 to the Present," *Covering the South: A National Symposium on the Media and the Civil Rights Movement*, videorecording of Conference Proceedings, Oxford, MI: University of Mississippi, Center for the Study of Southern Culture.

Allen, J. (2000) *Without Sanctuary: Lynching Photography in America*, Santa Fe, NM: Twin Palms Publisher.

Allen, T.W. (1994) *The Invention of the White Race*, vol. I: *Racial Oppression and Social Control*, New York: Verso.

—— (1997) *The Invention of the White Race*, vol. II: *The Origin of Racial Oppression in Anglo-America*, New York: Verso.

Alluh, D. (2002) "Marked as the Enemy: Central Park Five Members Speak," *Village Voice*, 6–12 November. Online. Available: http://www.villagevoice.com/news/0245,allah,39685,1.html (accessed 26 September 2005).

Alters, D. (2002) "The Family Audience: Class, Taste, and Cultural Production in Late Modernity," PhD dissertation, School of Journalism and Mass Communication, University of Colorado.

"An American Tragedy" (1994) *Time* magazine, 143(26), 27 June: 28–35.

Anbinder, T. (2001) *Five Points*, New York: The Free Press.

Anderson, D.C. (1995) *Crime and the Politics of Hysteria: How the Willie Horton Story Changed American Justice*, New York: Random House.

Annin, P. (1996) "'Superpredators' Arrive: Should We Cage the New Breed of Vicious Kids?" *Newsweek*, 22 January: 57.

Anthony, D. (1997) "The Helen Jewett Panic: Tabloids, Men, and the Sensational Public Sphere in Antebellum New York," *American Literature* 69(3): 486–514.

Aptheker, B. (1977) "Introduction," in J. Addams and I. Wells, *Lynching and Rape: An Exchange of Views*, New York: The American Institute for Marxist Studies.

Asbury, H. (1928/1998) *The Gangs of New York*, New York: Thunder's Mouth Press.

Athens, L.H. (1992) *The Creation of Dangerous Violent Criminals*, Urbana, IL: University of Illinois Press.

Bagdikian, B. (2000) *The Media Monopoly*, 5th edition, Boston, MA: Beacon Press.

Barnes, D.M. (1863) *The Metropolitan Police: Their Services During Riot Week. Their Honorable Record*, New York: Baker and Godwin.

Barnouw, E. (1968) *A Tower of Babel: A History of Broadcasting in the United States*, vol. II: *To 1933*, New York: Oxford University Press.

—— (1970) *The Image Empire: A History of Broadcasting in the United States*, vol. III: *From 1953*, New York: Oxford University Press.

Beasley, M. (1982) "The Muckrakers and Lynching: A Case Study in Racism," *Journalism History* 9: 3–4 (Autumn–Winter): 86–91.

"Bennett under Fire for Remarks on Blacks, Crime" (2005) *CNN.com*, 30 September. Online. Available: http://www.cnn.com/2005/POLITICS/09/30/bennett.comments/ (accessed 10 October 2005).

Bermanzohn, S.A. (2001) "Violence, Nonviolence, and the U.S. Civil Rights Movement," in K. Worcester, S.A. Bermanzohn, and M. Ungar (eds) *Violence and Politics: Globalization's Paradox*, New York: Routledge, 146–64.

Bernstein, I. (1990) *The New York City Draft Riots: Their Significance for American Society and Politics in the Age of the Civil War*, New York: Oxford University Press.

Best, J. (1999) *Random Violence: How We Talk About New Crimes and New Victims*, Berkeley, CA: University of California Press.

Biderman, A.D. and J.P. Lynch (1991) *Understanding Crime Incidence Statistics: Why the UCR Diverges from the NCS*, New York: Springer-Verlag.

Biressi, A. (2001) *Crime, Fear and the Law in True Crime Stories*, New York: Palgrave.

Black, J. (1991) *The Aesthetics of Murder: A Study in Romantic Literature and Contemporary Culture*, Baltimore, MD: Johns Hopkins University Press.

Blakeslee, N. (2005) *Tulia: Race, Cocaine, and Corruption in a Small Texas Town*, New York: Public Affairs Books.

Blee, K.M. (1992) *Women of the Klan: Racism and Gender in the 1920s*, Berkeley, CA: University of California Press.

—— (2003) *Inside Organized Racism: Women in the Hate Movement*, Berkeley, CA: University of California Press.

Blumin, S.M. (1989) *The Emergence of the Middle Class: Social Experience in the American City, 1760–1900*, New York: Cambridge University Press.

Boddy, W. (1993) *Fifties Television: The Industry and Its Critics*, Urbana, IL: University of Illinois Press.

Bond, J. (2003) unpublished public lecture, "Center for Race and Social Problems,", Pittsburgh: University of Pittsburgh, 26 March.

Bourdieu, P. (1998) *Acts of Resistance: Against the Tyranny of the Market*, trans. R. Nice, New York: The New Press.

—— (2001) *Masculine Domination*, trans. R. Nice, Stanford: Stanford University Press.

Bourgois, P. (2003) *In Search of Respect: Selling Crack in El Barrio*, New York: Cambridge University Press.

Bradshaw, J.S. (1979–80) "George W. Wisner and the New York *Sun*," *Journalism History* 6(4), (Winter): 112–21.

Branch, T. (1989) *Parting the Waters: America in the King Years, 1954–1963*, New York: Simon and Schuster.

—— (1998) *Pillar of Fire: America in the King Years, 1963–65*, New York: Simon and Schuster.

Burrell, K. (2002) "Bob Lewis' Encounter with the 'Great Death,'" unpublished paper, New York: City University of New York.

Butterfield, F. (1995a) *All God's Children: The Bosket Family and the American Tradition of Violence*, New York: Alfred A. Knopf.

—— (1995b) "Grim Forecast Is Offered on Rising Juvenile Crime," *New York Times*, 8 September: A6.

—— (1997) "F.B.I. Report Finds that Crime Is Down for 5th Straight Year," *New York Times*, 5 October: 16.

Caputi, J. (1989) "The Sexual Politics of Murder," *Gender and Society* 3(4) (December): 437–56.

Carby, H. (1985) "'On the Threshold of Woman's Era': Lynching, Empire, and Sexuality in Black Feminist Theory," *Critical Inquiry* 12(1) (Autumn): 262–77.

Carter, D.T. (1969) *Scottsboro: A Tragedy of the American South*, Baton Rouge, LA: Louisiana State University.

—— (1995) *The Politics of Rage: George Wallace, the Origins of the New Conservatism, and the Transformation of American Politics*, Baton Rouge, LA: Louisiana State University.

Castiglia, C. (1996) *Bound and Determined: Captivity, Culture-Crossing, and White Womanhood from Mary Rowlandson to Patty Hearst*, Chicago, IL: University of Chicago Press.

CBS News Special Report (1963), 11 June.

Chappell, D. (1994) *Inside Agitators: White Southerners in the Civil Rights Movement*, Baltimore, MD: Johns Hopkins University Press.

Chauncey, G. (1994) *Gay New York: Gender, Urban Culture and the Making of the Gay Male World, 1890–1940*, New York: Basic Books.

Chermak, S.M. (1995) *Victims in the News: Crime and the American News Media*, Boulder, CO: Westview Press.

Chibnall, S. (1977) *Law-and-Order News: An Analysis of Crime Reporting in the British Press*, London: Tavistock Publications.

Christie, N. (1996) *Crime Control as Industry*, 2nd edition, New York: Routledge.

Churchill, W. and J. Vander Wall (1990) *Agents of Repression: The FBI's Secret Wars against the Black Panther Party and the American Indian Movement*, Boston, MA: South End Press.

Cipes, R.M. (1967) *The Crime War: The Manufactured Crusade*, New York: The New American Library.

"Claim filed on behalf of Alfred Nicholson" (1863) *Special Committee on Draft Riot Claims, 1863–1865*, New York: New York City Municipal Archives, A–I, Box 1, 19105, Folder B.

"Claim filed by Ann Garvey" (1863) *Special Committee on Draft Riot Claims, 1863–1865*, New York: New York City Municipal Archives, A–I, Box 1, 19105, Folder B.

"Claim filed by Charles Guihard" (1863) *Special Committee on Draft Riot Claims, 1863–1865*, New York: New York City Municipal Archives, A–I, Box 1, 19105, Folder B.

"Claim Filed by Elizabeth Dewitt" (1863) *Special Committee on Draft Riot Claims, 1863–1865*, New York: New York City Municipal Archives, A–I, Box 1, 19105, Folder B.

"Claim filed by Eugenia Brown" (1863) *Special Committee on Draft Riot Claims, 1863–1865*, New York: New York City Municipal Archives, A–I, Box 1, 19105, Folder B.

"Claim filed by George Spriggs" (1863) *Special Committee on Draft Riot Claims, 1863–1865*, New York: New York City Municipal Archives, A–I, Box 1, 19105, Folder B.

"Claim filed by Gilbert Mapes" (1863) *Special Committee on Draft Riot Claims, 1863–1865*, New York: New York City Municipal Archives, A–I, Box 1, 19105, Folder B.

"Claim filed by James P. Black" (1863) *Special Committee on Draft Riot Claims, 1863–1865*, New York: New York City Municipal Archives, A–I, Box 1, 19105, Folder B.

"Claim filed by Mary Cisco" (1863) *Special Committee on Draft Riot Claims, 1863–1865*, New York: New York City Municipal Archives, A–I, Box 1, 19105, Folder B.

"Claim filed by Mary Frazer" (1863) *Special Committee on Draft Riot Claims, 1863–1865*, New York: New York City Municipal Archives, A–I, Box 1, 19105, Folder B.

"Claim filed by Robert N. Van Dyne" (1863) *Special Committee on Draft Riot Claims, 1863–1865*, New York: New York City Municipal Archives, A–I, Box 1, 19105, Folder B.

Clark, R. (1970) *Crime in America: Observations on Its Nature, Causes, Prevention and Control*, New York: Simon and Schuster.

Classen, S.D. (2004) *Watching Jim Crow: The Struggles over Mississippi TV, 1955–1969*, Chapel Hill, NC: Duke University Press.

Cohen, D.A. (1993) *Pillars of Salt, Monuments of Grace: New England Crime Literature and the Origins of American Popular Culture, 1674–1860*, Cambridge, MA: Oxford University Press.

—— (1997) "The Beautiful Female Murder Victim: Literary Genres and Courtship Practices in the Origins of a Cultural Motif, 1590–1850," *Journal of Social History* 31(2) (Winter): 277–306.

Cohen, L. (2003) *A Consumers' Republic: The Politics of Mass Consumption in Postwar America*, New York: Alfred A. Knopf.

Cohen, P.C. (1998) *The Murder of Helen Jewett: The Life and Death of a Prostitute in Nineteenth-Century New York*, New York: Alfred A. Knopf.

Colley, L. (2002) *Captives*, New York: Pantheon Books.

Collins, P.H. (1990/2000) *Black Feminist Thought: Knowledge, Consciousness, and the Politics of Empowerment*, New York: Routledge.

—— (2004) *Black Sexual Politics: African Americans, Gender, and the New Racism*, New York: Routledge.

Connelly, B. (1995) "His Last Words Were 'Keith, Keith, I'm only 31,'" *FOCUS* magazine, Pittsburgh: Carnegie Mellon University. Online. Available: http://www.cs.cmu.edu/~pshell/gammage/interview.html (accessed 17 October 2005).

Cook, A. (1974) *The Armies of the Streets: The New York City Draft Riots of 1863*, Lexington, KY: The University Press of Kentucky.

Cook, F.J. (1964) *The FBI Nobody Knows*, New York: Macmillan.

Cooper, J.F. (1826/2001) *The Last of the Mohicans*, New York: Modern Library.

Courtney, S. (2005) *Hollywood Fantasies of Miscegenation*, Princeton, NJ: Princeton University Press.

Cowan, R.S. (1983) *More Work for Mother: The Ironies of Household Technology from the Open Hearth to the Microwave*, New York: Basic Books.

Crane, S. (1901/1940) *Twenty Stories by Stephen Crane*, New York: Alfred A. Knopf.

Crenshaw, K. (1991) "Mapping the Margins: Intersectionality, Identity Politics, and Violence Against Women of Color," *Stanford Law Review* 43(6) (July): 1241–99.

Croly, D.G. and G. Wakeman (1863) *Miscegenation: The Theory of the Blending of the Races: Applied to the American White Man and Negro*, New York: H. Dexter, Hamilton and Co.

Crouthamel, J.L. (1989) *Bennett's New York Herald and the Rise of the Popular Press*, Syracuse, NY: Syracuse University Press.

Culverson, D. (2002) "The Welfare Queen and Willie Horton," in C.R. Mann and M.S. Zatz (eds) *Images of Color, Images of Crime*, 2nd edition, Los Angeles: Roxbury Publishing Company: 126–36.

Davidson, C.N. (1986) *Revolution and the Word: The Rise of the Novel in America*, New York: Oxford University Press.

Davis, A.Y. (1983) *Women, Race, and Class*, New York: Vintage Books.

—— (1988) *An Autobiography*, New York: International Publishers.

—— (2003) *Are Prisons Obsolete?* New York: Open Media.

—— (2005) *Abolition Democracy: Beyond Prisons, Torture, and Empire: Interviews with Angela Y. Davis*, New York: Open Media.

Davis, D.B. (1957) *Homicide in American Fiction, 1798–1860: A Study in Social Values*, Ithaca, NY: Cornell University Press.

Davis, J. (1980) "The London Garotting Panic of 1862: A Moral Panic and the Creation of a Criminal Class in Mid-Victorian England," in V.A.C. Gatrell, B. Lenman, and G. Parker (eds) *Crime and the Law: The Social History of Crime in Western Europe since 1500*, London: Europa: 190–213.

Davis, M. (1992a) *City of Quartz: Excavating the Future in Los Angeles*, New York: Vintage Books.

—— (1992b) "LA: The Fire This Time," *CovertAction* 41 (Summer): 12–21.

DeJonge, Jodie (1992) "Victim's Husband May be Charged," *Capitol Times*, 27 April 1992: 3A.

Del Barco, M. (2005) "O.J. Simpson Verdict Leaves Lasting Legacy," *All Things Considered*, National Public Radio, 3 October. Online. Available: http://www.npr.org/templates/story/story.php?storyId=4934510 (accessed 5 October 2005).

D'Emilio, J. (2004) *Lost Prophet: The Life and Times of Bayard Rustin*, Chicago, IL: University of Chicago Press.

D'Emilio, J. and E.B. Freedman (1997) *Intimate Matters: A History of Sexuality in America*, Chicago, IL: University of Chicago Press.

Dickens, C. (1836/1986) *The Pickwick Papers*, Oxford: Clarendon Press.

—— (1838/2003) *Oliver Twist*, New York: Penguin Books.

—— (1842/1934) *American Notes*, New York: E.P. Dutton.

Diffee, C. (2005) "Sex and the City: The White Slavery Scare and Social Governance in the Progressive Era," *American Quarterly* (June): 411–38.

Dillon, P. (2003) *Gin: The Much-Lamented Death of Madam Geneva*, Boston, MA: Justin, Charles and Company.

Ditton, J. and S. Farrall (2000) "Introduction," in *The Fear of Crime*, Aldershot: Ashgate.

Dixon, T.L. (2003) "Racialized Portrayals of Reporters and Criminals on Local Television News," in R.A. Lind (ed.) *Race/Gender/Media: Considering Diversity across Audiences, Content, and Producers*, Boston, MA: Pearson Education: 132–39.

Dixon, T.L. and D. Linz (2000a) "Overrepresentation and Underrepresentation of African Americans and Latinos as Lawbreakers on Television News," *Journal of Communication* 50(2): 131–54.

—— (2000b) "Race and the Misrepresentation of Victimization on Local Television News," *Communication Research* 27: 547–73.

Donner, F. (1980) *The Age of Surveillance: The Aims and Methods of America's Political Intelligence System*, New York: Alfred A. Knopf.

—— (1990) *Protectors of Privilege: Red Squads and Police Repression in Urban America*, Berkeley, CA: University of California Press.

Donovan, R.J. and R. Scherer (1992) *Unsilent Revolution: Television News and American Public Life*, New York: Cambridge University Press.

Doob, A.N. and G.E. Macdonald (1979) "Television Viewing and Fear of Victimization: Is the Relationship Causal?" *Journal of Personality and Social Psychology* 37(2): 170–79.

Dorr, L.L. (2004) *White Women, Rape, and the Power of Race in Virginia, 1900–1960*, Chapel Hill, NC: University of North Carolina Press.

Dorsey, B. (2002) *Reforming Men and Women: Gender in the Antebellum City*, Ithaca, NY: Cornell University Press.

Douglas, A. (1977) *The Feminization of American Culture*, New York: Alfred A. Knopf.

Downey, D.B. and R.M. Hyser (1991) *No Crooked Death: Coatesville, Pennsylvania, and the Lynching of Zachariah Walker*, Urbana, IL: University of Illinois Press.

DuBois, W.E.B. (1903/1994) *The Souls of Black Folk*, New York: Dover Publications

Dunagin, C. (1987) "Panel 2: The Mass Movement, 1960–64 (Part 1)," *Covering the South: A National Symposium on the Media and Civil Rights Movement*, videorecording of Conference Proceedings, Oxford, MI: University of Mississippi, Center for the Study of Southern Culture.

Ellis, J. (1986) *The Social History of the Machine Gun*, Baltimore: Johns Hopkins University Press.

Entman, R.M. and A. Rojecki (2001) *The Black Image in the White Mind: Media and Race in America*, Chicago, IL: University of Chicago Press.

Evers-Williams, M. (1999) *Watch Me Fly: What I Learned on the Way to Becoming the Woman I Was Meant to Be*, New York: Little, Brown and Company.

Ewen, S. (1996) *PR! A Social History of Spin*, New York: Basic Books.

Fariello, G. (1995) *Red Scare: Memories of the American Inquisition*, New York: W.W. Norton and Company.

Farrall, S., J. Bannister, J. Ditton, and E. Gilchrist (1997) "Open and Closed Question," *Social Research Update* 17, Summer. Online. Available: http://www.soc.surrey.ac.uk/sru/SRU17.html (accessed 17 June 2003).

Fay, T.S. (1835) *Norman Leslie: A Tale of the Present Times*, New York: Harper.

Feldstein, R. (1994) "'I Wanted the Whole World to See': Race, Gender, and Constructions of Motherhood in the Death of Emmett Till," in J. Meyerowitz (ed.), *Not June Cleaver: Women and Gender in Postwar America, 1945–1960*, Philadelphia: Temple University Press: 263–303.

Ferguson, R.B. (1994) "The Evolution of the New York City Police," paper presented to the American Anthropological Association, Atlanta, GA, November–December.

Fermer, D. (1986) *James Gordon Bennett and the New York Herald: A Study of Editorial Opinion in the Civil War Era, 1854–1867*, New York: St. Martin's Press.

Fielding, R. (1972) *The American Newsreel, 1911–1967*, Norman, OK: University of Oklahoma Press.

Fields, B.J. (1990) "Slavery, Race and Ideology in the United States of America," *New Left Review* 181 (May/June): 95–118.

Fishman, M. and G. Cavender (1998) *Entertaining Crime: Television Reality Programs*, New York: Aldine de Gruyter.

Fleming, C.G. (1998) *Soon We Will Not Cry: The Liberation of Ruby Doris Smith Robinson*, New York: Rowman and Littlefield Publishers, Inc.

Fleming, K. (1987) "Panel 2: The Mass Movement: 1960–64 (Part 1)," *Covering the South: A National Symposium on the Media and the Civil Rights Movement*, videorecording of Conference Proceedings, Oxford, MI: University of Mississippi, Center for the Study of Southern Culture.

"Forty-Eight Hours on Crack Street" (1986) *CBS News Special*, 2 September.

Foster, G. (1850/1990) *New York by Gas-Light and Other Urban Sketches*, Berkeley, CA: University of California Press.

Frankenberg, R. (1993) *White Women, Race Matters: The Social Construction of Whiteness*, Minneapolis, MN: University of Minnesota Press.

Frazier, E.F. (1939) *The Negro Family in the United States*, Chicago, IL: University of Chicago Press.

Freedman, S.G. (2001) "Fighting to Balance Honor and Profit on the Local News," *New York Times*, Section II, 30 September: 26.

Friedman, B.J. (1955) "The Day of the Lynching," *Saga* magazine (April): 47+.

Friendly, F. (1976) *The Good Guys, The Bad Guys, and the First Amendment: Free Speech vs. Fairness in Broadcasting*, New York: Random House.

Furstenberg, F.F., Jr. (1971) "Public Reaction to Crime in the Streets," *The American Scholar* 40 (1971): 603, 605.

Garland, D. (1993) *Punishment and Modern Society: A Study in Social Theory*, Chicago, IL: University of Chicago Press.

—— (2002) *The Culture of Control: Crime and Social Order in Contemporary Society*, Chicago, IL: University of Chicago Press.

Garrow, D.J. (1988) *Bearing the Cross: Martin Luther King, Jr., and the Southern Christian Leadership Conference*, New York: Vintage.

Geisler, J. (2000) "Blacked Out," *American Journalism Review*, May. Online. Available: http://www.ajr.org/Article.asp?id=360 (accessed 5 October 2005).

Giddings, T.H. (1974) "Melville, the Colt-Adams Murder, and 'Bartleby,'" *Studies in American Fiction* 2: 123–32.

Gilder, G. (1995) "The Roots of Black Poverty," *The Wall Street Journal*, 30 October: A20.

Gilens, M. (1996) "'Race Coding' and White Opposition to Welfare," *The American Political Science Review* 90(3) (September): 593–604.

Gilje, P. (1996) *Rioting in America*, Bloomington, IN: Indiana University Press.

Gilliam, F.D. and S. Iyengar (2000) "Prime Suspects: The Influence of Local Television News on the Viewing Public," *American Journal of Political Science*, 44(3), July: 560–73.

Gilliam, F.D., S. Iyengar, A. Simon, and O. Wright (1996) "Crime in Black and White: The Scary World of Local News," *Harvard International Journal of Press/Politics* 1(3): 6–23.

Gilliam, F.D., N.A. Valentino, and M.N. Beckman (2002) "Where You Live and What You Watch: The Impact of Racial Proximity and Local Television News on Attitudes about Race and Crime," *Center for Communications and Community: Research on Media Coverage*, 1 January 2002: Paper 004. Online. Available: http://repositories.cdlib.org/ccc/media/004 (accessed 23 September 2005).

Glenn, E.N. (2004) *Unequal Freedom: How Race and Gender Shaped American Citizenship and Labor*, Cambridge, MA: Harvard University Press.

Glickman, L.B. (1999) *A Living Wage: American Workers and the Making of Consumer Society*, Ithaca, NY: Cornell University Press.

Goetting, A. (2000) *Getting Out: Life Stories of Women Who Left Abusive Men*, New York: Columbia University Press.

Goldberg, C. (1997) "Way Out West and Under the Influence," *New York Times*, 16 March, Section 4: 16.

Goldman, A.L. (1989) "Minister's Job is Advocacy for Blacks," *New York Times*, 17 July: B1.

Goldsby, J. (2006) *A Spectacular Secret: Lynching in American Life and Literature*, Chicago, IL: University of Chicago Press.

Goode, E. and N. Ben-Yehuda (1994) *Moral Panics: The Social Construction of Deviance*, New York: Basic Books.

Goodwyn, W. (2003) "12 Texas Prisoners Released on Drug Conviction Appeal," *All Things Considered*, National Public Radio, 16 June.

Gordon, L. (1988/2002) *Heroes of Their Own Lives: The Politics and History of Family Violence*, Urbana, IL: University of Illinois Press.

—— (1995) *Pitied but Not Entitled: Single Mothers and the History of Welfare*, Cambridge, MA: Harvard University Press.

Gourevitch, P. (1999) *We Wish to Inform You That Tomorrow We Will Be Killed with Our Families: Stories from Rwanda*, New York: Picador.

Graham, A. (2001) *Framing the South: Hollywood, Television, and Race during the Civil Rights Struggle*, Baltimore, MD: Johns Hopkins University Press.

Gray, H. (1995) *Watching Race: Television and the Struggle for "Blackness,"* Minneapolis, MN: University of Minnesota Press.

Gray, K.A. (2004) "Segregation and Hypocrisy Forever: The Legacy of Strom Thurmond," *CounterPunch*, 8 March. Online. Available: http://www.counterpunch.org/gray03082004. html (accessed 7 October 2005).

Gresham, J.H. (1989) "The Politics of Family in America," *The Nation* 249(4) (24/31 July): 116–22.

Grossberg, L. (2005) *Caught in the Crossfire: Kids, Politics, and America's Future*, New York: Paradigm.

Grossman, J.R. (1989) *Land of Hope: Chicago, Black Southerners, and the Great Migration*, Chicago, IL: University of Chicago Press.

Guglielmo, T.A. (2003) *White on Arrival: Italians, Race, Color, and Power in Chicago, 1890–1945*, New York: Oxford University Press.

Gunter, B. (1987) *Television and the Fear of Crime*, London: Libbey.

Gutman, H. (1977) *Work, Culture and Society in Industrializing America*, New York: Vintage Books.

Hale, G.E. (1998) *Making Whiteness: The Culture of Segregation in the South, 1890–1940*, New York: Vintage Books.

Halberstam, D. (1979) *The Powers That Be*, New York: Alfred A. Knopf.

—— (1998) *The Children*, New York: Random House.

Hall, S. (1984) "The Narrative Construction of Reality: An Interview with Stuart Hall," *Southern Review*, 17 (March) Online. Available: http://www.centerforbookculture.org/ context/no10/hall.html (accessed 13 November 2005).

Hall, S. (1990) "The Whites of Their Eyes: Racist Ideologies and the Media," M. Alvarado and J.O. Thompson (eds), *The Media Reader*, London: BFI.

Hall, S., C. Critcher, T. Jefferson, J. Clarke, and B. Roberts (1978) *Policing the Crisis: Mugging, the State, and Law and Order*, New York: Holmes and Meier.

Haller, J.S., Jr. (1971) *Outcasts from Evolution: Scientific Attitudes of Racial Inferiority, 1859–1900*, Carbondale, IL: Southern Illinois University Press.

Halttunen, K. (1998) *Murder Most Foul: The Killer and the American Gothic Imagination*, Cambridge, MA: Harvard University Press.

Hancock, L. (2003) "Wolf Pack: The Press and the Central Park Jogger," *Columbia Journalism Review*. 1 (January/February) Online. Available: http://www.cjr.org/issues/2003/1/ rapist-hancock.asp (accessed 7 October 2005).

Haraway, D. (1989) *Primate Visions: Gender, Race and Nature in the World of Modern Science*, New York: Routledge.

Harding, S. (1991) *Whose Science? Whose Knowledge? Thinking from Women's Lives*, Ithaca, NY: Cornell University Press.

"The Harlem Temper" (1963) *CBS Reports*, 11 December.

Harris, L.M. (2003) *In the Shadow of Slavery: African Americans in New York City, 1626–1863*, Chicago, IL: University of Chicago Press.

"Hate Radio: Rwanda" (2003–4) *Peace News*, December 2003–February 2004: 13–15.

Hay, D., P. Linebaugh, J.G. Rule, E.P. Thompson, and C. Winslow (eds) (1975) *Albion's Fatal Tree: Crime and Society in Eighteenth Century England*, New York: Pantheon Books.

Heider, D. (2000) *White News: Why Local News Programs Don't Cover People of Color*, Mahwah, NJ: Lawrence Erlbaum Associates.

Herman, E.S. and N. Chomsky (1988) *Manufacturing Consent: The Political Economy of the Mass Media*, New York: Pantheon.

Hermann, W. (1996) "The Practice Homicides," in L.B. Pulitzer (ed.) *Crime on Deadline*, New York: Boulevard Books: 87–112.

Hibbard, A. and J.T. Parry (2006) "Law, Seduction, and the Sentimental Heroine: The Case of Amelia Norman," *American Literature*, 78 (June): 325–55.

Hill, A. (2005) *Reality TV: Audiences and Popular Factual Televi*sion, London: Routledge.

Hochschild, A. (1999) *King Leopold's Ghost*, New York: Mariner Books.

"Hollywood Finger-Printing Urged by U.S. Police to Curb Crime" (1937) *Variety*, 6 October: 1+.

"Houston, We May Have a Problem" (2005) "Marketplace," *American Public Media*, 5 September. Online. Available: http://marketplace.publicradio.org/shows/2005/09/05/PM200509051.html (accessed 13 October 2005).

Hoy, S. (1996) *Chasing Dirt: The American Pursuit of Cleanliness*, New York: Oxford University Press.

Hughes, H.M. (1968) *News and the Human Interest Story*, New York: Greenwood Press.

Humphries, D. (1999) *Crack Mothers: Pregnancy, Drugs, and the Media*, Columbus, OH: Ohio State University Press.

Ignatiev, N. (1995) *How the Irish Became White*, New York: Routledge.

"Indictment of Patrick Butler" (1863) *Case of Patrick Butler*, New York County District Attorney Indictment Records, 26 July.

Iyengar, S. (1987) *Is Anyone Responsible? How Television Frames Political Issues*, Chicago, IL: University of Chicago Press.

Iyengar, S. and R. Reeves (eds) (1997) *Do the Media Govern? Politicians, Voters, and Reporters in America*, Thousand Oaks, CA: Sage.

Jaffe, S. (1985) "The Rise of the Urban Newspaper Reporter in New York City, 1800–1850," PhD dissertation: Harvard University.

Jeffords, S. (1989) *The Remasculinization of America: Gender and the Vietnam War*, Bloomington: Indiana University Press.

—— (1991) "Rape and the New World Order," *Cultural Critique* (Fall): 203–15.

Jenkins, P. (1988) "Myth and Murder: The Serial Killer Panic of 1983–5," *Criminal Justice Research Bulletin* 3(11): 1–7.

—— (1998) *Moral Panic: Changing Concepts of the Child Molester in Modern America*, New Haven: Yale University Press.

Johnson, D. (1996) "Good People Go Bad in Iowa, and a Drug Is Being Blamed," *New York Times*, 22 February: A1+.

Johnson, H. (1987) "Panel 4: The Political Movement: 1965–67," *Covering the South: A National Symposium on the Media and the Civil Rights Movement*, videorecording of Conference Proceedings, Oxford, MI: University of Mississippi, Center for the Study of Southern Culture.

Johnson, L.B. (1966) "To Fulfill These Rights: Commencement Address at Howard University, 4 June 1965," *Public Papers of the Presidents of the United States: Lyndon B. Johnson, 1965*, vol. II, entry 301, Washington, DC: Government Printing Office: 635–40. Online. Available: http://www.lbjlib.utexas.edu/johnson/archives.hom/speeches.hom/650604.asp (accessed 6 October 2005).

Jones, B.W. (1990) *Quest for Equality: The Life and Writings of Mary Eliza Church Terrell, 1863–1954*, New York: Carlson Publishing.

Juergens, G. (1966) *Joseph Pulitzer and the New York World*, Princeton, NJ: Princeton University Press.

Kaniss, P. (1991) *Making Local News*, Chicago, IL: University of Chicago Press.

Kaplan, S. (1949) "The Miscegenation Issue in the Election of 1864," *The Journal of Negro History* 34(3) (July): 274–343.

Katz, M.B. (ed.) (1993) *The "Underclass" Debate: Views from History*, Princeton, NJ: Princeton University Press.

Keller, E.V.F. (1983) *A Feeling for the Organism: The Life and Work of Barbara McClintock*, San Francisco, CA: W.H. Freeman.

—— (1985) *Reflections on Gender and Science*, New Haven, CT: Yale University Press.

Kelley, R.D.G. (1990) *Hammer and Hoe: Alabama Communists during the Great Depression*, Chapel Hill, NC: University of North Carolina Press.

—— (1997) *Yo' Mama's Disfunktional!: Fighting the Culture Wars in Urban America*, Boston, MA: Beacon Press.

Kessler-Harris, A. (2003) *In Pursuit of Equity: Women, Men, and the Quest for Economic Citizenship in 20th-Century America*, New York: Oxford University Press.

King, E. (1994) "James Gordon Bennett and His Critics: The Robinson–Jewett Murder Case of 1836, the Newspaper Moral War of 1840 and the 'Myth of Origin' Debate in Journalism History," Paper presented to the History Division of the Association for Education in Journalism and Mass Communication, Atlanta, GA: August.

King, M.L. (1963) "Letter from Birmingham Jail," Online. Available http//www.nobelprizes.com/nobel/peace/MLK-jail.html (accessed 22 March 2006).

Knight, S. (1980) *Form and Ideology in Crime Fiction*, Bloomington, IN: Indiana University Press.

Knox, S.L. (1998) *Murder: A Tale of Modern American Life*, Durham, NC: Duke University Press.

Kocieniewski, D. (1998) "Police Official's Ouster Sought in Case of Doctored Statistics," *New York Times*, 28 February: A11.

Kolata, G. (1989) "On Streets Ruled by Crack, Families Die," *New York Times*, 11 August: A1+.

Korobkin, L.H. (1998) *Criminal Conversations: Sentimentality and Nineteenth-Century Legal Stories of Adultery*, New York: Columbia University Press.

Kotz, N. (1987) "Panel 6: Aftermath: 1968 to the Present," *Covering the South: A National Symposium on the Media and the Civil Rights Movement*, videorecording of Conference Proceedings, Oxford, MI: University of Mississippi, Center for the Study of Southern Culture.

Krauss, C. (1994) "Urban Crime Rates Falling This Year," *New York Times*, 8 November: 9.

Kunzel, R.G. (1994) "White Neurosis, Black Pathology: Constructing Out-of-Wedlock Pregnancy in the Wartime and Postwar United States," in J. Meyerowitz (ed.) *Not June Cleaver: Women and Gender in Postwar America, 1945–1960*, Philadelphia, PA: Temple University Press: 304–34.

Lane, R. (1979) *Violent Death in the City: Suicide, Accident, and Murder in Nineteenth-Century Philadelphia*, Cambridge, MA: Harvard University Press.

—— (1997) *Murder in America: A History*, Columbus, OH: Ohio State University.

Langum, D.L. (1994) *Crossing over the Line: Legislating Morality and the Mann Act*, Chicago, IL: University of Chicago Press.

Lardner, J. and T. Reppetto (2001) *NYPD: A City and Its Police*, New York: Henry Holt.

Larson, E. (2004) *The Devil in the White City: Murder, Magic, and Madness at the Fair that Changed America*, New York: Vintage Books.

Leacock, E. (1981) *Myths of Male Dominance: Collected Papers on Women Cross Culturally*, New York: Monthly Review Press.

Lee, A.M. (1937) *The Daily Newspaper in America: The Evolution of a Social Instrument,* New York: Macmillan.

Lee, C.K. (2000) *For Freedom's Sake: The Life of Fannie Lou Hamer,* Urbana, IL: University of Illinois Press.

Lepore, J. (2005) *New York Burning: Liberty, Slavery, and Conspiracy in Eighteenth-Century Manhattan,* New York: Alfred A. Knopf.

Lewis, J. (1987) "Panel 2: The Mass Movement: 1960–64," *Covering the South: A National Symposium on the Media and the Civil Rights Movement,* videorecording of Conference Proceedings, Oxford, MI: University of Mississippi, Center for the Study of Southern Culture.

Lewis, M. (2005) "Wading toward Home," *New York Times* magazine, 9 October: 44+.

Lichtenstein, A. (1996) *Twice the Work of Free Labor: The Political Economy of Convict Labor in the New South,* New York: Verso.

Lillo, G. (1776) *The London Merchant, or the History of George Barnwell,* London: John Bell and C. Etherington at York

Linder, D. (2001) "The Trials of Los Angeles Police Officers in Connection with the Beating of Rodney King," Online. Available: http://www.law.umkc.edu/faculty/projects/ftrials/lapd/lapdaccount.html (accessed 4 October 2005).

Linebaugh, P. and M. Rediker (2000) *The Many-Headed Hydra: Sailors, Slaves, Commoners, and the Hidden History of the Revolutionary Atlantic,* Boston, MA: Beacon Press.

Lippard, G. (1844/1995) *The Quaker City or, the Monks of Monk Hall,* Amherst, MA: University of Massachusetts Press.

Lipschultz, J.H. and M.L. Hilt (2002) *Crime and Local Television News: Dramatic, Breaking, and Live from the Scene,* New York: Lawrence Erlbaum Associates.

Little, R.G. (2002a) "Across 110th Street: Changed Lives Among Central Park Five Family Members," *Village Voice,* 6–12 November. Online. Available: http://www.villagevoice.com/news/0245,little,39686,1.html (accessed 26 September 2005).

—— (2002b) "Rage before Race: How Feminists Faltered on the Central Park Jogger Case," *Village Voice,* 16–22 October. Online. Available: http://www.villagevoice.com/news/0242,little,39205,1.html (accessed 26 September 2005).

Lloyd, J. (1998) "Film at 10: Whose News Judgment?" *Christian Science Monitor,* 3 April: 1.

Longino, H.E. (1990) *Science as Social Knowledge,* Princeton, NJ: Princeton University Press.

Loory, S.H. (2003) "Reporter Tails 'Freedom' Bus, Caught in Riot," in *Reporting Civil Rights: Part One: American Journalism 1941–1963,* New York: The American Library: 573–79.

Lowenthal, M. (1950) *The Federal Bureau of Investigation,* New York: William Sloane Associates.

Lowry, D.T., T.J.C. Nio, and D.W. Leitner (2003) "Setting the Public Fear Agenda: A Longitudinal Analysis of Network TV Crime Reporting, Public Perceptions of Crime, and FBI Crime Statistics," *Journal of Communication* 53(1) (March): 61–73.

Lusane, C. (1994) "Congratulations, It's a Crime, Bill," *CovertAction* 50 (Fall): 14–22.

McDade, T. (1961) *The Annals of Murder: A Bibliography of Books and Pamphlets on American Murders from Colonial Times to 1900,* Norman, OK: University of Oklahoma Press.

MacDonald, F. (1992) *Blacks and White TV: African Americans in Television since 1948,* New York: Wadsworth.

McFadden, R.D. (1989) "2 Brooklyn Rape Suspects Charged in 2nd Case," *New York Times,* 6 May 1989: 31.

—— (1990) "2 Men Get 6 to 18 Years for Rape in Brooklyn," *New York Times,* 2 October 1990: B1.

McGucken, E.N. (1987) "Crime News Reporting in the *New York Times*, 1900 to 1950: A Content Analysis," PhD dissertation, University of Akron.

Males, M. (1996a) *Scapegoat Generation: America's War on Adolescents*, Monroe, ME: Common Courage Press.

—— (1996b) "Wild in Deceit: Why 'Teen Violence' Is Poverty Violence in Disguise," *Extra!* 9(2), March/April: 6–9.

Mandel, E. (1984) *Delightful Murder: A Social History of the Crime Story*, Minneapolis: University of Minnesota Press.

Marable, M. (2003) *The Great Wells of Democracy: The Meaning of Race in American Life*, New York: Basic Books.

Mayhew, H. (1861/1968) *London Labour and the London Poor*, vol. IV, New York: Dover Publications, Inc.

Means-Coleman, R. (1998) *African American Viewers and the Black Situation Comedy: Situating Racial Humor*, London: Garland.

Meili, T. (2004) *I Am the Central Park Jogger*, New York, Scribner.

Mercer, K. (1994) "Fear of a Black Penis – White Males' Perceptions of Black Males – Man Trouble," *ArtForum*, April. Online. Available: http://www.findarticles.com/p/articles/mi_m0268/is_n8_v32/ai_16109614 (accessed 4 October 2005).

Mifflin, L. (1998) "Increase Seen in Number of Violent TV Programs," *New York Times*, 17 April: A14.

Miller, D.W. (2002) "Are Racist Women the Weakest Link?" *The Chronicle of Higher Education*, 11 January. Online. Available: http://chronicle.com/weekly/v48/i19/18a01401.htm (accessed 29 January 2002).

Mindich, D.T.Z. (1998) *Just the Facts: How "Objectivity" Came to Define American Journalism*, New York: New York University Press.

Mink, G. (1996) *The Wages of Motherhood: Inequality in the Welfare State, 1917–1942*, Ithaca, NY: Cornell University Press.

Monkkonen, E.H. (1981) *Police in Urban America, 1860–1920*, New York: Cambridge University Press.

—— (1990) "The American State from the Bottom Up: Of Homicides and Courts," *Law and Society Review* 24(2): 521–31.

—— (2001) *Murder in New York City*, Berkeley, CA: University of California Press.

Monmonier, M. (1997) *Cartographies of Danger: Mapping Hazards in America*, Chicago, IL: University of Chicago Press.

Moran, M.H. (2003) *Finding Susan*, Carbondale, IL: Southern Illinois University Press.

Morgan, C. (1987) "Panel 3: The Mass Movement: 1960–64 (Part 2)," *Covering the South: A National Symposium on the Media and the Civil Rights Movement*, videorecording of Conference Proceedings, Oxford, MI: University of Mississippi, Center for the Study of Southern Culture.

Most, G.W. and W.W. Stowe (1983) *The Poetics of Murder: Detective Fiction and Literary Theory*, New York: Harcourt Brace Jovanovich.

Mott, F.L. (1941) *American Journalism: A History of Newspapers in the United States through 250 Years, 1690–1940*, New York: Macmillan.

Muncy, R. (1991) *Creating a Female Dominion in American Reform, 1890–1935*, New York: Oxford University Press.

Murrow, E. (1958) "A Broadcaster Talks to His Colleagues," *The Reporter*, 13 November: 32–36.

Musto, D.F. (1987) *The American Disease: Origins of Narcotics Control*, New York: Oxford University Press.

Myrdal, G. (1944) *An American Dilemma: The Negro Problem and Modern Democracy*, New York: Harper.

National Association for the Advancement of Colored People [NAACP] (1969) *Thirty Years of Lynching in the United States, 1889–1918*, New York: Arno Press.

National Advisory Commission on Civil Disorders (1968) *Report of the National Advisory Commission on Civil Disorders (Kerner Commission Report)*, Washington, DC: US Government Printing Office.

The Negro Family: The Case for National Action (1965) Washington, DC: Office of Policy Planning and Research, United States Department of Labor, Online. Available: http://www.dol.gov/asp/programs/history/webid-meynihan.htm (accessed 21 September 2005).

"The Negro in America: What Must Be Done: A Program for Action" (1967) *Newsweek*, 20 November.

Nerone, J. (1987) "The Mythology of the Penny Press," *Critical Studies in Mass Communication* 4: 376–404.

—— (1994) *Violence against the Press: Policing the Public Sphere in U.S. History*, New York: Oxford University Press.

"Nineteen Sixty-Three: A TV Album" (1963) *CBS News*, 22 December.

Nord, D.P. (1984) "The Evangelical Origins of Mass Media in America," *Journalism Monographs*, 88 (May): 1–30.

Novick, P. (2000) *The Holocaust in American Life*, New York: Mariner Books.

O'Brien, F. (1928) *The Story of the Sun*, New York: D. Appleton and Company.

O'Connor, T. (2003) "Lynch Law in Georgia: 4 Murdered," in *Reporting Civil Rights, Part One: American Journalism 1941–1963*, New York: The Library of America, 78–81.

Oliver, M.B. (1999) "Caucasian Viewers' Memory of Black and White Criminal Suspects in the News," *Journal of Communication*, 49(3), Summer: 46–60.

Oliver, M.B., R.L. Jackson II, N.N. Moses, and C.L. Dangerfield (2004) "The Face of Crime: Viewers' Memory of Race-Related Facial Features of Individuals Pictured in the News," *Journal of Communication* 54(1) March: 88–104.

Ortner, S. (1974) "Is Female to Male as Nature is to Culture?" in M.Z. Rosaldo and L. Lamphere (eds) *Woman, Culture, and Society*, Stanford, CA: Stanford University Press.

Parks, R.E. (1922) *The Immigrant Press and Its Control*, New York: Harper and Brothers.

Pearson, G. (1984) *Hooligan: A History of Respectable Fears*, New York: Schocken Books.

Petrick, M.J. (1969) "The Press, the Police Blotter and Public Policy," *Journalism Quarterly* 46(3): 475–81.

Pleck, E. (2004) *Domestic Tyranny: The Making of Social Policy against Family Violence from Colonial Times to the Present*, New York: Oxford University Press.

Poe, E.A. (1838) "Ligeia," *American Museum*, September.

—— (1850a) "The Mystery of Marie Roget," Online. Available: http://eserver.org/books/poe/mystery_of_marie_roget.html (accessed 1 November 2005).

—— (1850b) "The Philosophy of Composition," *The Works of the Late Edgar Allan Poe*, vol. II, New York: J.S. Redfield: 259–70.

Porter, J. (1810/1921) *The Scottish Chiefs*, New York: A.L. Burt Company.

Potter, C.B. (1998) *War on Crime: Bandits, G-Men, and the Politics of Mass Culture*, New Brunswick, NJ: Rutgers University Press.

Powers, R.G. (1983) *G-Men: Hoover's FBI in American Popular Culture*, Carbondale, IL: Southern University Press.

—— (1987) *Secrecy and Power: The Life of J. Edgar Hoover*, New York: Free Press.

Powers, S. (2003) *A Problem from Hell: America and the Age of Genocide*, New York: Harper Perennial.

Powledge, F. (1987) "Panel 3: The Mass Movement: 1960–64," *Covering the South: A National Symposium on the Media and the Civil Rights Movement*, videorecording of Conference Proceedings, Oxford, MI: University of Mississippi, Center for the Study of Southern Culture.

Pray, I.C. (1970) *Memoirs of James Gordon Bennett and His Times*, New York: Arno Press.

"The Press" (1852) *Democratic Review* (April): 359–66.

"Prison Statistics" (2004) *Bureau of Justice Statistics*, Washington, DC: Department of Justice. Online. Available: http://www.ojp.usdoj.gov/bjs/prisons.htm (accessed 29 November 2005).

Pritchard, D. and S. Brzezinski (2004) "Racial Profiling in the Newroom: A Case Study," paper presented at the annual meeting of the Association for Education in Journalism and Mass Communication, Toronto, Canada, August.

Pucci, I. (1996) *The Trials of Maria Barbella: The True Story of a 19th Century Crime of Passion*, New York: Four Walls Eight Windows.

Quadagno, J. (1994) *The Color of Welfare: How Racism Undermined the War on Poverty*, New York: Oxford University Press.

Quinney, R. (1970) *The Social Reality of Crime*, New York: Little, Brown, and Company.

Rafter, N.H. (1998) *Creating Born Criminals*, Urbana, IL: University of Illinois Press.

—— (2000) *Shots in the Dark: Crime Films and Society*, New York: Oxford University Press.

Rammelkamp, J.S. (1967) *Pulitzer's Post-Dispatch, 1878–1883*, Princeton, NJ: Princeton University Press.

Rand, M.R. (1994) "Carjacking: National Crime Victimization Survey," *Bureau of Justice Statistics Crime Data Brief*, NCJ-147002, March, Washington, DC: Office of Justice Programs.

Ransby, B. (2005) *Ella Baker and the Black Freedom Movement: A Radical Democratic Vision*, Chapel Hill, NC: University of North Carolina Press.

Raphael, J. (2000) *Saving Bernice: Battered Women, Welfare, and Poverty*, Boston, MA: Northeastern University Press.

—— (2004) *Listening to Olivia: Violence, Poverty, and Prostitution*, Boston, MA: Northeastern University Press.

Rashke, R. (2000) *The Killing of Karen Silkwood: The Story behind the Kerr-McGee Plutonium Case*, Ithaca, NY: Cornell University Press.

Rather, D. with M. Herskowitz (1977) *The Camera Never Blinks: Adventures of a TV Journalist*, New York: William Morrow and Company.

Reed, R. (1987) "Panel 4: The Political Movement, 1965–67," *Covering the South: A National Symposium on the Media and Civil Rights Movement*, videorecording of Conference Proceedings, Oxford, MI: University of Mississippi, Center for the Study of Southern Culture.

Reeves, J.L. and R. Campbell (1994) *Cracked Coverage: Television News, the Anti-Cocaine Crusade, and the Reagan Legacy*, Durham, NC: Duke University Press.

Reiman, J. (1996) *. . . And the Poor Get Prison: Economic Bias in American Criminal Justice*, Boston, MA: Allyn and Bacon.

Rentschler, C. (2002) "The Crime Victim Movement in US Public Culture," PhD dissertation, University of Illinois at Urbana-Champaign.

Reppetto, T. (2004) *American Mafia: A History of Its Rise to Power*, New York: Owl Books.

Republican National Platform 1968 (1968) Harrisburg, PA: Republican State Committee of Pennsylvania.

Rhodes, R. (1999) *Why They Kill: The Discoveries of a Maverick Criminologist*, New York: Alfred A. Knopf.

Richardson, S. (1740/1914) *Pamela, or Virtue Rewarded*, New York: E.P. Dutton.

—— (1748/1930) *Clarissa; Or, The History of a Young Lady, Comprehending the Most Important Concerns of Private Life*, Oxford: Basil Blackwell.

Riis, J. (1890/1996) *How the Other Half Lives: Studies among the Tenements of New York*, New York: Bedford Books.

—— (1901) *The Making of an American*, New York: Macmillan.

Roberts, D. (1998) *Killing the Black Body: Race, Reproduction, and the Meaning of Liberty*, New York: Vintage.

Robinson, C.J. (1997) *Black Movements in America*, New York: Routledge.

Roediger, D. (1996) *The Wages of Whiteness: Race and the Making of the American Working Class*, New York: Verso.

Rogin, M.P. (1987) *Ronald Reagan, the Movie and Other Episodes in Political Demonology*, Berkeley, CA: University of California Press.

Rome, D. (2004) *Black Demons: The Media's Depiction of the African American Male Criminal Stereotype*, Westport, CT: Praeger.

Rose, J. (1988) "Margaret Thatcher and Ruth Ellis," *New Formations* 6: 3–29.

Rosenberg, C.S. (1971) *Religion and the Rise of the American City: New York City Mission Movement, 1812–1870*, Ithaca, NY: Cornell University Press.

—— (1985) *Disorderly Conduct: Visions of Gender in Victorian America*, New York: Alfred A. Knopf.

Rowlandson, M. (1682/1998) *The Narrative of the Captivity and Restoration of Mrs. Mary Rowlandson*, London: Chapman Billies.

Russell, K.K. (1998) *The Color of Crime: Racial Hoaxes, White Fear, Black Protectionism, Police Harassment, and Other Macroaggressions*, New York: New York University Press.

Ruth, H.S. (ed.) (1971) *The Challenge of Crime in a Free Society*, New York: De Capo.

Sacco, V.F. (1982) "The Effects of Mass Media on Perceptions of Crime: A Reanalysis of the Issues," *Pacific Sociological Review* 25(4) October: 475–93.

Salem, D. (1990) *To Better Our World: Black Women in Organized Reform, 1890–1920*, New York: Carlson Books.

Saletan, W. (2003) *Bearing Right: How Conservatives Won the Abortion War*, Berkeley, CA: University of California Press.

Saxton, A. (1996) *The Rise and Fall of the White Republic: Class Politics and Mass Culture in Nineteenth-Century America*, New York: Verso.

Schadt, A. (1987) "Panel 4: The Political Movement, 1965–67," *Covering the South: A National Symposium on the Media and the Civil Rights Movement*, videorecording of Conference Proceedings, Oxford, MI: University of Mississippi, Center for the Study of Southern Culture.

Schakne, R. (1987) "Panel 1: Birth of the Movement: World War II through the 1950s," *Covering the South: A National Symposium on the Media and the Civil Rights Movement*, videorecording of Conference Proceedings, Oxford, MI: University of Mississippi, Center for the Study of Southern Culture.

Schanberg, S. (2002) "A Journey through the Tangled Case of the Central Park Jogger," *Village Voice*, 20–26 November. Online. Available: http://www.villagevoice.com/news/0247,schanberg,39999,1.html (accessed 26 September 2005).

Schiller, D. (1981) *Objectivity and the News: The Public and the Rise of Commercial Journalism*, Philadelphia, PA: University of Pennsylvania Press.

Schiraldi, V. (1997) "Hyping Juvenile Crime: A Media Staple," *The Christian Science Monitor*, 9 November: 19.

Schneider, E. (2002) *Battered Women and Feminist Lawmaking*, New Haven, CT: Yale University Press.

Schor, N. (1987) *Reading in Detail: Aesthetics and the Feminine*, New York: Routledge.

Schrecker, E. (1998) *Many Are the Crimes: McCarthyism in America*, Boston, MA: Little, Brown, and Company.

Schudson, M. (1978) *Discovering the News*, New York: Basic Books.

—— (1995) *The Power of News*, Cambridge, MA: Harvard University Press.

—— (2001) "The Objectivity Norm in American Journalism," *Journalism* 2(2): 149–70.

—— with E. King (1995) "The Illusion of Ronald Reagan's Popularity," *The Power of News*, Cambridge, MA: Harvard University Press: 124–41.

Sedensky, M. (2005) "Mother, Stepfather Charged in '01 Killing of Precious Doe," *Pittsburgh Post-Gazette*, 6 May: A-9.

Simon, D. and E. Burns (1997) *The Corner: A Year in the Life of an Inner-City Neighborhood*, New York: Broadway Books.

Sitton, C. (1987) "Panel 2: The Mass Movement: 1960–64 (Part 1)," *Covering the South: A National Symposium on the Media and the Civil Rights Movement*, videorecording of Conference Proceedings, Oxford, MI: University of Mississippi, Center for the Study of Southern Culture.

Skogan, W.G. (1977) "Public Policy and the Fear of Crime in Large American Cities," in J.A. Gardiner (ed.) *Public Law and Public Policy*, New York: Praeger Publishers: 1–18.

Skolnick, J.H. and J.J. Fyfe (1993) *Above the Law: Police and the Excessive Use of Force*, New York: The Free Press.

Slotkin, R. (1973) *Regeneration through Violence: The Mythology of the American Frontier*, Middletown, CT: Wesleyan University Press

Smith, G. and J.B. Smith (1972) *The Police Gazette*, New York: Simon and Schuster.

Smith, H.K. (1996) *Events Leading up to My Death*, New York: St. Martin's Press.

Soderlund, G. (2002) "Covering Urban Vice: the *New York Times*, 'White Slavery,' and the Construction of Journalistic Knowledge," *Critical Studies in Media Communication* 19(4) (December): 438–60.

Solinger, R. (1992) *Wake Up Little Susie: Single Pregnancy and Race before Roe v. Wade*, New York: Routledge.

—— (1994) *The Abortionist*, New York: The Free Press.

—— (2001) *Beggars and Choosers: How the Politics of Choice Shapes Adoption, Abortion, and Welfare in the United States*, New York: Farrar, Straus, and Giroux.

Sparks, G.G. and R.M. Ogle (1990) "The Difference between Fear of Victimization and the Probability of Being Victimized: Implications for Cultivation," *Journal of Broadcasting and Electronic Media* 34(3) (Spring): 351–58.

Spigel, L. (1992) *Make Room for TV: Television and the Family Ideal in Postwar America*, Chicago, IL: University of Chicago Press.

Spivak, G. (1988) "Can the Subaltern Speak?" in C. Nelson and L. Grossberg (eds) *Marxism and the Interpretation of Culture*, Urbana, IL: University of Illinois Press: 271–313.

Srebnick, A.G. (1995) *The Mysterious Death of Mary Rogers: Sex and Culture in Nineteenth-Century New York*, New York: Oxford University Press.

Stabile, C. and C. Rentschler (2005) "Introduction: States of Insecurity and the Gendered Politics of Fear," *NWSA Journal* 17(3) (Fall): vii–xxv.

Stansell, C. (1987) *City of Women: Sex and Class in New York, 1789–1860*, Urbana, IL: University of Illinois Press.

"The State of the News Media 2005" (2005) *The Project for Excellence in Journalism*. Online,

New York: Columbia University. Available: http://www.stateofthemedia.org/2005/index.asp (accessed 18 October 2005).

Steffens, J.L. (1931) *The Autobiography of Lincoln Steffens*, New York: Harcourt Brace.

Stevens, J.D. (1991) *Sensationalism and the New York Press*, New York: Columbia University Press.

Stiehm, J.H. (1982) "The Protected, the Protector, the Defender," *Women's Studies International Forum* 5(3/4): 367–77.

Stivers, C. (2000) *Bureau Men, Settlement Women: Constructing Public Administration in the Progressive Era*, Lawrence, KS: University of Kansas Press.

Stolley, R. (1987) "Panel 5: The Bottom Line: The Decision Makers," *Covering the South: A National Symposium on the Media and the Civil Rights Movement*, videorecording of Conference Proceedings, Oxford, MI: University of Mississippi, Center for the Study of Southern Culture.

Stowe, H.B. (1852/1966) *Uncle Tom's Cabin*, New York: Signet Classics.

Sullivan, W.C. with B. Brown (1979) *The Bureau: My Thirty Years in Hoover's FBI*, New York: W.W. Norton and Company.

Summers, A. (1993) *Official and Confidential: The Secret Life of J. Edgar Hoover*, New York: G.P. Putnam's Sons.

Surette, R. (1994) "Predator Criminals as Media Icons," in G. Barak (ed.) *Media, Process, and the Social Construction of Crime: Studies in Newsmaking Criminology*, New York: Garland Publishing.

"Testimony of Edward Ray" (1863) *The People vs. John McAllister*, New York County District Attorney Indictment Records, 8 October.

"Testimony of Ellen Foose" (1863) *The People vs. William Cruise*, New York County District Attorney Indictment Records, 21 December.

"Testimony of Mary Keirny" (1863) *The People vs. John Nicholson*, New York County District Attorney Indictment Records, 17 October.

Theoharis, A. (1978) *Spying on Americans: Political Surveillance from Hoover to the Huston Plan*, Philadelphia, PA: Temple University Press.

—— (1995) *J. Edgar Hoover, Sex, and Crime*, Chicago, IL: Ivan R. Dee.

Theoharis, A. and J.S. Cox (1988) *The Boss: J. Edgar Hoover and the Great American Inquisition*, Philadelphia, PA: Temple University Press.

Theoharis, J. and L. Woznica (1990) "The Forgotten Victim: The Collision of Race, Gender, and Murder," *Was It Worth It?* February. Online. Available: http://www.digitas.harvard.edu/~perspy/old/issues/2000/retro/forgotten_victim.html (accessed 3 October 2005)

Tice, K.W. (1998) *Tales of Wayward Girls and Immoral Women: Case Records and the Professionalization of Social Work*, Urbana, IL: University of Illinois Press.

Tolnay, S.E. and E.M. Beck (1995) *Festival of Violence: An Analysis of Southern Lynchings, 1882–1930*, Urbana, IL: University of Illinois Press.

Tompkins, J. (1985) *Sensational Designs: The Cultural Work of American Fiction, 1790–1860*, New York: Oxford University Press.

"Tour of the FBI," *NBC Red*, 7 July 1935, New York: Museum of Radio and Television.

"Truth and Lies" (2003) *Now with Bill Moyers*, PBS, 22 August. Online. Available. http://www.pbs.org/now/transcript/transcript_tulia.html (accessed 13 October 2005).

Tucher, A. (1994) *Froth and Scum: Truth, Beauty, Goodness, and the Axe Murder in America's First Mass Medium*, Chapel Hill, NC: University of North Carolina Press.

Turner, G.K. (1909) "The Daughters of the Poor," *McClure's* magazine 34 (December): 45–61.

Ungar, S. (1976) *FBI*, Boston, MA: Little, Brown and Company.

Valeriani, D. (1987) "Panel 4: The Political Movement: 1965–67," *Covering the South: A National Symposium on the Media and the Civil Rights Movement*, videorecording of Conference Proceedings, Oxford, MI: University of Mississippi, Center for the Study of Southern Culture.

Vanderlyn, J. (1803–4) *The Murder of Jane McCrea*, Hartford, CT: Wadsworth Atheneum Museum of Art.

"The Vanishing Black Family: Crisis in Black America" (1986) *CBS Special Report*, 25 January.

Walker, S. (1977) *A Critical History of Police Reform: The Emergence of Professionalism*, Lexington, MA: Lexington Books.

Walkowitz, J.R. (1992) *City of Dreadful Delight: Narratives of Sexual Danger in Late-Victorian London*, Chicago, IL: University of Chicago Press.

Warner, J. (2003) *Craze: Gin and Debauchery in an Age of Reason*, New York: Four Walls Eight Windows.

Wasserman, I.M. and S. Stack (1994) "Communal Violence and the Media: Lynchings and Their News Coverage by the *New York Times* between 1882 and 1930," in G. Barak (ed.) *Media, Process, and the Social Construction of Crime: Studies in Newsmaking Criminology*, New York: Garland: 49–68.

"We Are All Policemen: A Look at Crime and the Community" (1968) *WNBC-TV*, 19 April.

Webb, G. (1999) *Dark Alliance: The CIA, the Contras, and the Crack Cocaine Explosion*, New York: Seven Stories Press.

"Weight-Gain Angle Cited in Slaying" (1992) *Capital Times*, 6 August: 1B.

Wells, I.B. (1892/1997) *Southern Horrors and Other Writings: The Anti-Lynching Campaign of Ida B. Wells, 1892–1900*, Boston, MA: Bedford Press.

—— (1970) *Crusade for Justice: The Autobiography of Ida B. Wells*, A.M. Duster (ed) Chicago, IL: University of Chicago Press.

Welter, B. (1966) "The Cult of True Womanhood: 1820–1860," *American Quarterly* 18: 151–74.

Wertheim, S. and P. Sorrentino (1994) *The Crane Log: A Documentary Life of Stephen Crane, 1871–1900*, New York: G.K. Hall and Co.

Wesley, C.H. (1984) *The History of the National Association of Colored Women's Clubs: A Legacy of Service*, Washington, DC: National Association of Colored Women's Clubs.

Westin, A. (2000) *Practices for Television Journalism*, Arlington, VA: The Freedom Forum.

Whitfield, S.J. (1988) *A Death in the Delta: The Story of Emmett Till*, Baltimore, MD: Johns Hopkins University Press.

Whitman, W. (1973) *The Portable Whitman*, New York: Viking

"Who Will Speak for Birmingham?" (1961) *CBS Reports*, 18 May.

Wilentz, S. (1984) *Chants Democratic: New York City and the Rise of the American Working Class, 1788–1850*, New York: Oxford University Press.

Wilkes, G. (1849) *The Lives of Helen Jewett and Richard P. Robinson*, Philadelphia, PA: W.B. Zelber.

Willard, C. (2000) "Conspicuous Whiteness: The New Woman, the Old Negro, and the Vanishing Past of Early Brand Advertising," in C. Stabile (ed.) *Turning the Century: Essays in Media and Cultural Studies*, Boulder, CO: Westview Press: 187–216.

Willett, R. (1996) *The Naked City: Urban Crime Fiction in the U.S.A*, New York: Manchester University Press.

Williams, D.E. (1993) *Pillars of Salt: An Anthology of Early American Criminal Narratives*, Madison, WI: Madison House.

Williams, L. (2004) "Skin Flicks on the Racial Border: Pornography, Exploitation, and Interracial Lust," *Porn Studies*, in L. Williams (ed.) Durham, NC: Duke University Press: 271–308.

Williams, P. (1991) *The Alchemy of Race and Rights*, Cambridge, MA: Harvard University Press.

Wilson, C. (2000) *Cop Knowledge: Police Power and Cultural Narrative in Twentieth-Century America*, Chicago, IL: University of Chicago Press.

Winerip, M. (1998) "Looking for an 11 O'Clock Fix?" *New York Times* magazine, 1 November: 30+.

Wisner, G.F. (1918) *The Wisners in America and Their Kindred: A Genealogical and Biographical History*, Baltimore, MD: on microfilm.

Wood, J.M. (2005) "In Whose Name? Crime Victim Policy and the Punishing Power of Protection," *NWSA Journal* 17(3) (Fall): 1–17.

Younge, G. (2005) "Trial That Split America," *Guardian Weekly*, 14–20 October: 17+.

Zangrando, R.L. (1980) *The NAACP Crusade against Lynching: 1909–1950*, Philadelphia, PA: Temple University Press.

Zelizer, B. (1993) "Journalists as Interpretive Communities," *Critical Studies in Mass Communication* 10: 219–37.

Zinn, H. (2003) *A People's History of the United States*, New York: Perennial Classics.

Zucchino, D. (1997) *Myth of the Welfare Queen: A Pulitzer Prize-Winning Journalist's Portrait of Women on the Line*, New York: Scribner.

Index

Related titles from Routledge

After Empire
Melancholia or Convivial Culture?
Paul Gilroy

'This is a work of startling range, insight and originality.'

Stephen Howe, The Independent

'[A] perceptive book.'

Andy Beckett, The Guardian

Paul Gilroy's *After Empire* – in many ways a sequel to his classic study of race and nation, *There Ain't No Black in the Union Jack* – explores Britain's failure to come to terms with the loss of its empire and pre-eminent global standing.

Drawing on texts from the writings of Fanon and Orwell to Ali G and *The Office*, *After Empire* shows that what we make of the country's postcolonial opportunity will influence the future of Europe and the viability of race as a political category.

Taking the political language of the post 9/11 world as a new point of departure, he defends beleaguered multiculturalism against accusations of failure. He then takes the liberal discourse of human rights to task, finding it wanting in terms of both racism and imperialism.

Gilroy examines how this imperial dissolution has resulted not only in hostility directed at blacks, immigrants and strangers, but also in the country's inability to value the ordinary, unruly multi-culturalism that has evolved organically and unnoticed in its urban centres.

A must-read for students of cultural studies, and Britain in the post 9/11 era.

ISBN 10: 0–415–343070 (hbk)
ISBN 10: 0–415–343089 (pbk)

ISBN 13: 9–78–0–415–343077 (hbk)
ISBN 13: 9–78–0–415–343084 (pbk)

Available at all good bookshops
For ordering and further information please visit:
www.routledge.com

New Black Man
Mark Anthony Neal

'One of the most brilliant cultural critics of his generation . . . Neal writes grace-fully, thinks sharply, speaks cogently and is old school and new school at once. He's my favourite cultural critic and one hip brother.'

Michael Eric Dyson, Chicago Sun-Times

'Mark Anthony Neal has always been a daring scholar, but in this work he does pirouettes on a razor's edge, deliberately and deftly defying the keepers of the weary worn "race man" trope and all its essentialist trappings.'

E. Patrick Johnson

From headlines to street corners, the message resounds: Black men are in crisis.

Politicians, preachers, and pundits routinely cast blame on those already ostracized within African American communities. But the crisis of black mascu-linity does not rest with 'at-risk' youth of the hip-hop generation or men "on the down low' alone.

In this provocative new book, acclaimed cultural critic Mark Anthony Neal argues that the 'Strong Black Man' – an ideal championed by generations of African American civic leaders – may be at the heart of problems facing black men today.

Read Mark Anthony Neal's blog to accompany his latest book *New Black Man*: http://newblackman.blogspot.com/

ISBN 10: 0–415–971098 (hbk)
ISBN 10: 0–415–979919 (pbk)

ISBN 13: 9–78–0–415–971096 (hbk)
ISBN 13: 9 78–0–415–979917 (pbk)

Available at all good bookshops
For ordering and further information please visit:
www.routledge.com

Look, A Negro!

Robert Gooding-Williams

In *Look, a Negro!*, political theorist Robert Gooding-Williams imaginatively and impressively unpacks fundamental questions around issues of race and racism. Inspired by Frantz Fanon's famous description of the profound effect of being singled out by a white child with the words 'Look, a Negro!', his book is an insightful, rich and unusually wide ranging work of social criticism.

These essays engage the themes that have centrally occupied recent discussion of race and racial identity, among them, the workings of racial ideology (including the interplay of gender and sexuality in the articulation of racial ideology); the viability of social constructionist theories of race; the significance of Afrocentrism and multiculturalism for democracy; the place of black identity in the imagination and articulation of America's inheritance of philosophy; and the conceptualization of African American politics in post-segregation America.

Look, a Negro! will be of interest to philosophers, political theorists, and critical race theorists, students of cultural studies and film, and readers concerned with the continuing importance of race-consciousness to democratic culture in the United States.

ISBN 10: 0–415–974151 (hbk)
ISBN 10: 0–415–97416X (pbk)

ISBN 13: 9–78–0–415–974158 (hbk)
ISBN 13: 9–78–0–415–974165 (pbk)

Available at all good bookshops
For ordering and further information please visit:
www.routledge.com

Media and Power

James Curran

Media and Power addresses three key questions about the relationship between media and society.

- How much power do the media have?
- Who really controls the media?
- What is the relationship between media and power in society?

In this major new book, James Curran reviews the different answers which have been given, before advancing original interpretations in a series of ground-breaking essays.

Media and Power also provides a guided tour of the major debates in media studies. What part did the media play in the making of modern society? How did 'new media' change society in the past? Will radical media research recover from its mid-life crisis? What are the limitations of the US-based model of 'communications' research? Is globalization disempowering national electorates or bringing into being a new, progressive global politics? Is public service television the dying product of the nation in an age of globalization? What can be learned from the 'third way' tradition of European media policy?

Curran's response to these questions provides both a clear introduction to media research and an innovative analysis of media power, written by one of the field's leading scholars.

ISBN 0–415–07739–7 (hbk)
ISBN 0–415–07740–0 (pbk)

Available at all good bookshops
For ordering and further information please visit:
www.routledge.com

News Around the World
Content, Practitioners and the Public
Pamela J. Shoemaker and Akiba A. Cohen

What's news? A front-page news story in the United States might not appear in a newspaper in China. Or a minor story on German television may be all over the airwaves in India. But *News Around the World* shows that the underlying nature of news is much the same the world over and that people – no matter what their jobs or their status in society – tend to hold similar notions of newsworthiness.

In this richly detailed study of international news, news makers and the audience, the authors have undertaken exhaustive original research within two cities – one major and one peripheral – in each of ten countries: Australia, Chile, China, Germany, India, Israel, Jordan, Russia, South Africa, and the United States. The nations were selected for study based on a central principle of maximizing variation in geographic locations, economic and political systems, languages, sizes, and cultures. The remarkable scope of the research makes this the most comprehensive analysis of newsworthiness around the globe:

- 10 countries studied, each with a university country director
- 2 cities in each country examined, one major and one peripheral
- 60 news media studied (newspapers, television, and radio news programmes), resulting in 32,000+ news items analyzed
- 80 focus groups with journalists, public relations practitioners, and audience members
- 2,400 newspaper stories ranked according to newsworthiness and compared with how prominently they were published.

News Around the World provides remarkable insight into how and why news stories are reported, testing and improving a theory of cross-cultural newsworthiness. It is essential reading for anyone seeking to understand international media and journalism.

ISBN 0–415–97505–0 (hbk)
ISBN 0–415–97506–9 (pbk)

Available at all good bookshops
For ordering and further information please visit:
www.routledge.com

Power without Responsibility

Sixth edition
James Curran and Jean Seaton

'This is a useful and timely book.'

Richard Hoggart, Times Educational Supplement

'In a fast-changing media scene this book is nothing less than indispensable.'

Julian Petley, Brunel University

'*Power without Responsibility*, the best guide to the British media.'

Nick Cohen, The New Statesman

Power without Responsibility is a classic, authoritative and engaged introduction to the history, sociology, theory and politics of media and communication studies. Written in a lively and accessible style, it is regarded as the standard book on the British media. This new edition has been substantially revised to bring it up-to-date with new developments in the media industry. Its three new chapters describe the battle for the soul of the internet, the impact of the internet on society and the rise of new media in Britain. In addition, it examines the recuperation of the BBC, how international and European regulation is changing the British media and why Britain has the least trusted press in Europe.

ISBN 0–415–24389–0 (hbk)
ISBN 0–415–24390–4 (pbk)

Available at all good bookshops
For ordering and further information please visit:
www.routledge.com

True Crime

Mark Seltzer

Browse a bookstore and you will find a healthy shelf labelled 'Crime'. Beside it may be a smaller, seedier shelf labelled 'True Crime'. The first is popular crime fiction, the second crime fact. Fictional crime has taken over, writes Mark Seltzer, and the confusion of reality and event has saturated – and even defined – contemporary American culture.

In his widely read *Serial Killers*, American studies scholar Mark Seltzer analysed the American obsession with violent accident – vehicular homicide, serial murders, and other spectacularly awful events. *True Crime* carries the argument of *Serial Killers* into a broader arena. Using crime as his canvas, Mark Seltzer offers a dazzling analysis of how our cultural fantasies, fears, and desires have blurred the distinction between fiction and real event.

True Crime is a serious, readable examination of how a violence-wracked (and violence-addicted) society confuses fact and fiction.

ISBN 0–415–97793–2 (hbk)
ISBN 0–415–97794–0 (pbk)

Available at all good bookshops
For ordering and further information please visit:
www.routledge.com

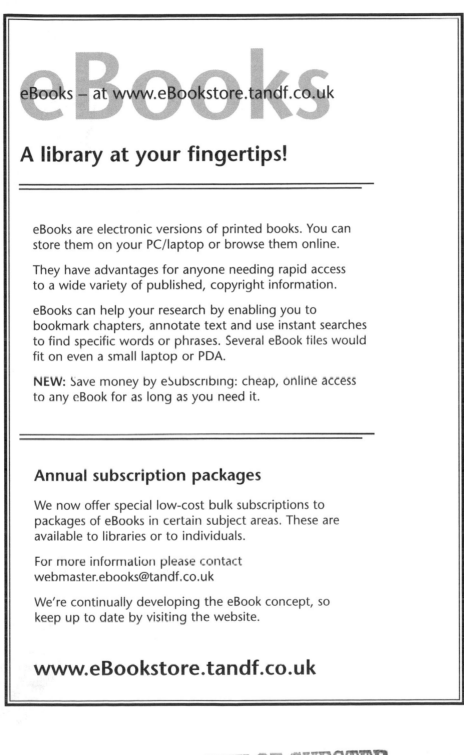

eBooks

eBooks – at www.eBookstore.tandf.co.uk

A library at your fingertips!

eBooks are electronic versions of printed books. You can store them on your PC/laptop or browse them online.

They have advantages for anyone needing rapid access to a wide variety of published, copyright information.

eBooks can help your research by enabling you to bookmark chapters, annotate text and use instant searches to find specific words or phrases. Several eBook files would fit on even a small laptop or PDA.

NEW: Save money by eSubscribing: cheap, online access to any eBook for as long as you need it.

Annual subscription packages

We now offer special low-cost bulk subscriptions to packages of eBooks in certain subject areas. These are available to libraries or to individuals.

For more information please contact webmaster.ebooks@tandf.co.uk

We're continually developing the eBook concept, so keep up to date by visiting the website.

www.eBookstore.tandf.co.uk

LIBRARY, UNIVERSITY OF CHESTER